De-Centering Cold War History

Cold War histories are often told as stories of national leaders, state policies, and the global confrontation that pitted a Communist Eastern Bloc against a Capitalist West. *De-Centering Cold War History* takes a new analytical approach to reveal unexpected complexities in the historical trajectory of the Cold War.

This book challenges the Cold War master narratives that focus on superpower politics by shifting our analytical perspective to include local-level experiences and regional initiatives that were crucial to the making of a Cold War world. Contributions from an international group of scholars take a fresh look at historical agency in different places across the world, including Africa, Asia, Europe, and the Americas. This collaborative effort shapes a street-level history of the global Cold War era, one that uses the analysis of the "local" to rethink and reframe the wider picture of the "global", connecting the political negotiations of individuals and communities at the intersection of places, and of meeting points between "ordinary" people and political elites to the Cold War at large.

Jadwiga E. Pieper Mooney is Associate Professor of History at the University of Arizona, USA. Her publications include *The Politics of Motherhood: Maternity and Women's Rights in Twentieth-Century Chile* (2009).

Fabio Lanza is Associate Professor of History and East Asian Studies at the University of Arizona, USA. His publications include *Behind the Gate: Inventing Students in Beijing* (2010).

De-Centering Cold War History
Local and Global Change

Edited by
Jadwiga E. Pieper Mooney
and Fabio Lanza

LONDON AND NEW YORK

First published 2013
by Routledge
2 Park Square, Milton Park, Abingdon, Oxon OX14 4RN

Simultaneously published in the USA and Canada
by Routledge
711 Third Avenue, New York, NY 10017

Routledge is an imprint of the Taylor & Francis Group, an informa business

© 2013 Jadwiga E. Pieper Mooney and Fabio Lanza for selection and editorial matter; individual extracts, the contributors

The right of Jadwiga E. Pieper Mooney and Fabio Lanza to be identified as authors of this work has been asserted by them in accordance with sections 77 and 78 of the Copyright, Designs and Patents Act 1988.

All rights reserved. No part of this book may be reprinted or reproduced or utilised in any form or by any electronic, mechanical, or other means, now known or hereafter invented, including photocopying and recording, or in any information storage or retrieval system, without permission in writing from the publishers.

Trademark notice: Product or corporate names may be trademarks or registered trademarks, and are used only for identification and explanation without intent to infringe.

British Library Cataloguing in Publication Data
A catalogue record for this book is available from the British Library

Library of Congress Cataloging in Publication Data
De-centering cold war history : local and global change / edited by Jadwiga E. Pieper Mooney and Fabio Lanza.
p. cm.
1. Cold War--Political aspects. 2. Cold War--Social aspects.
3. Cold War--Economic aspects. 4. History, Modern--1945-1989.
5. World politics--1945-1989. I. Mooney, Jadwiga E. Pieper.
II. Lanza, Fabio, 1967-
D843.D32 2012
909.82'5--dc23
2012017479

ISBN: 978-0-415-63639-1 (hbk)
ISBN: 978-0-415-63640-7 (pbk)
ISBN: 978-0-203-08327-7 (ebk)

Typeset in Times New Roman
by Taylor & Francis Books

Printed and bound in Great Britain by the MPG Books Group

Contents

List of figures vii
Notes on contributors viii
Acknowledgments xi

Introduction: de-centering Cold War history 1
JADWIGA E. PIEPER MOONEY AND FABIO LANZA

PART I
Cold War activisms: crossing borders and building bridges 13

1 Thermonuclear weapons and tuna: testing, protest, and knowledge in Japan 15
ANN SHERIF

2 The Cold War, Indonesian women and the global anti-imperialist movement, 1946–65 31
KATHARINE E. MCGREGOR

3 Fighting fascism and forging new political activism: the Women's International Democratic Federation (WIDF) in the Cold War 52
JADWIGA E. PIEPER MOONEY

PART II
Separating enemies from friends: communism, anti-communism, and the construction of Cold War realities 73

4 Cold War happiness: singing pioneers, internal enemies and Hungarian life under Stalinism 75
LÁSZLÓ KÜRTI

5 New men of power: Jack Tenney, Ronald Reagan, and postwar labor anticommunism 99
JENNIFER LUFF

6 Female terrorists and vigilant citizens: gender, citizenship and Cold War direct-democracy 123
DOMINIQUE GRISARD

PART III
Rethinking opposition and conformity **145**

7 Making sense of "China" during the Cold War: global Maoism and Asian studies 147
FABIO LANZA

8 Anti-Communist entrepreneurs and the origins of the cultural Cold War in Latin America 167
PATRICK IBER

9 A "new man" for Africa?: some particularities of the Marxist *Homem Novo* within Angolan cultural policy 187
DELINDA COLLIER

10 The Cold War and Orange County 207
DIMITRI PAPANDREU

Index 227

Figures

3.1 Fanny Edelman in Vietnam, 1973 — 64
8.1 A poster advertising the *Congresso Paulista pela Paz* — 172
8.2 An anti-Communist poster depicting Joseph Stalin as angel and devil — 173
9.1 Viteix, *Construção Civil* — 202

Contributors

Delinda Collier researches and writes on the art history of southern Africa, with a special interest in the history of media objects within colonial conquest. She is currently Assistant Professor at the School of the Art Institute of Chicago and teaches courses on contemporary art in Africa, the history of old and new media, and constellations of Cold War-era art.

Dominique Grisard is a Swiss National Science Foundation fellow at the New School for Social Research, where she is working on her second book, a history of femininity and sexuality through and around the color pink. Grisard teaches Gender Studies and History at the University of Basel, Switzerland. She has published on legal, political and media aspects of left wing terrorism, on the imprisonment of women in 1970s Switzerland and on gender theory more generally. Grisard is the author of *Gendering Terror*, a history of leftist terrorist groups in 1970s Switzerland and Germany (Frankfurt/New York: Campus, 2011) and the editor of two anthologies on gender theory.

Patrick Iber is currently an Andrew W. Mellon Fellow in the Humanities at Stanford University, where he teaches modern Latin American history. He completed his dissertation, "The Imperialism of Liberty: Intellectuals and the Politics of Culture in Cold War Latin America," at the University of Chicago in 2011. He publishes in both academic and popular journals, with work appearing in *Nexos*, *Letras Libres*, and the *Chicago Review*, and forthcoming contributions in *Diplomatic History*, *istor*, and multiple edited volumes. His current research interests include the politics of culture and intellectuals, the history of social democracy, and the history of poverty.

László Kürti teaches and researches at the Institute of Political Science at the University of Miskolc in Hungary. His expertise includes the Culture of Socialism and Post-Socialist States, Gender, Popular Culture, Media and Visual Anthropology, Communication and Body Language, Inter-Ethnic Relations and Identities, and Political Anthropology.

Fabio Lanza is a Modern Chinese historian and holds a joint appointment in History and East Asian Studies at the University of Arizona. His research has focused on the cultural and intellectual history of modern China, particularly on the history of modern student activism in the twentieth century. Currently, he is working on two new research projects. The first is an analysis of the role of Maoist China in inspiring and defining political and intellectual activism in the US and France between the late 1960s and the late 1970s. The second is a street-level history of a district of Beijing between 1953 and 1983, tracing how communism (and capitalism) redefined and transformed the practices and rhythms of the everyday.

Jennifer Luff is the research director of the Kalmanovitz Initiative for Labor and the Working Poor at Georgetown University, where she also teaches history. She is the author of *Commonsense Anticommunism: Labor and Civil Liberties between the World Wars* (University of North Carolina Press, 2012).

Katharine E. McGregor is a Senior Lecturer in Southeast History in the School of Historical and Philosophical Studies at the University of Melbourne, Australia. She is author of *History in Uniform: Military Ideology and the Construction of Indonesia's Past* (South East Asia Series, National University of Singapore Press, 2007) and co-editor with Douglas Kammen of *The Contours of Mass Violence in Indonesia, 1965–1968* (South East Asia Series, National University of Singapore Press, 2012). Her key research interests are Indonesian historiography, history and memory, and violence and the Cold War. This paper is part of a larger project entitled "Indonesians on the World Stage from 1945–65" and was supported by a research grant from the Faculty of Arts at the University of Melbourne.

Dimitri Papandreu is a Lecturer in the Department of History at California State University, Fullerton. He studied at the University of California, Santa Cruz.

Jadwiga E. Pieper Mooney is an Associate Professor of History at the University of Arizona, teaching and researching Latin America, gender, and global/comparative history. Her research has focused on the politics of motherhood and women's rights, in Chile and other Latin American countries. Pieper Mooney has also written about forced sterilization campaigns and human rights violations in Peru and North Carolina, about political participation in rural Chile, and about Latin American feminisms. Her ongoing projects include a book on (global) leftist politics in the Cold War through the lens of histories of Chilean exile, as well as studies of transnational women's activism, and the forging of global feminisms in the post-World War II era.

Ann Sherif is Professor of Japanese in the East Asian Studies Program at Oberlin College, near Cleveland Ohio, USA. Her current research focuses on independent and regional publishers, and literary production in twentieth-century Japan. Her publications include *Japan's Cold War: Media, Literature, and the Law* (Columbia University Press, 2009), and translations of modern Japanese literature and criticism.

Acknowledgments

This edited volume is the outcome of an international conference Jadwiga E. Pieper Mooney, Fabio Lanza, and Elizabeth Oglesby organized at the University of Arizona in November 2010. We set out to gather a group of scholars willing to contribute new perspectives on Cold War histories (and histories about the Cold War), and interested in sharing our efforts to tie the overarching global conflict to the national, the regional, and the local, down to the daily lives of people in Africa, Asia, Europe, and the Americas. We would like to thank all those who responded to our initial call for papers. The number of potentially great contributions far exceeded our expectations, and we apologize to all those we could not invite. We also extend our special thanks to the terrific scholars who were conference participants but did not contribute to this volume: Tarah Brookfield, Benjamin Cowan, Charles Kim, Hai Ren, Elizabeth Oglesby, and Megan Strom. We are particularly grateful for the conference participation of Malcolm Byrne of the National Security Archive at George Washington University, who delivered a fantastic keynote address that was both truly informative and wonderfully engaging. Our Department Chair, Kevin Gosner, kindly welcomed participants, and our colleague Martha Few generously agreed to chair a panel. Many thanks also to two of our history graduate students, Kathryn Gallien and Tyler Ralston, who provided sharp and stimulating comments in their roles as discussants.

Moreover, we owe the success of our conference to generous funding from the University of Arizona in the form of an Arts, Humanities, and Social Sciences (AHSS) grant. We greatly appreciate the support by Leslie P. Tolbert (Vice President for Research, Graduate Studies, and Economic Development), and extend our gratitude to the University of Arizona's Confluence Center, founded shortly after the AHSS grant initiative. At the University of Arizona, the Graduate College, the College of Social and Behavioral Sciences and the Department of History all made priceless contributions to our endeavors. Robin Zenger and Sarah Howard provided invaluable support in many months of preparation that preceded the conference, and were essential in making sure that everything worked. We could not have done it without them. And special thanks to the History Department's (former) business manager Cynthia Malbrough (still painfully missed in the History

Department after she accepted a position in the Dean's Office). Without her dedication, attention to detail, and admirable patience, the administrative processes would have been impossible to handle. Our publication was much enhanced by the generous editing support of Cathy Lyders. Finally, thanks to Laura Mothersole and Eve Setch at Routledge for setting up the project, and to production editor Ruth Berry and copy editor Judith Oppenheimer for moving it along.

Introduction
De-centering Cold War history

Jadwiga E. Pieper Mooney and Fabio Lanza

In December 1964, the Special Operations Research Office (SORO) of American University in Washington, D.C., invited a group of carefully selected scholars, most of them university professors and researchers, to attend a four-week conference planned for August 1965.[1] The invitation included the description of a new "Project Camelot," defined as a study " ... which would make it possible to predict and influence politically significant aspects of social change in the developing nations of the world."[2] More specifically, its objectives included devising "procedures for assessing the potential for internal war within national societies" and identifying "those actions which a government might take to relieve conditions which are assessed as giving rise to a potential for internal war."[3]

Project Camelot was, in actuality, a social science research project, aimed at identifying the causes of violent protests or revolutions (referred to as "internal wars" in the document) as well as the major actors who could initiate such disruptions. As threats of revolutions gained new meanings with the rise of the Cold War, and as political leaders in the United States feared Soviet-inspired revolutionaries who could threaten unsuspecting governments in the so-called Third World, Project Camelot also sought to identify the actions a government could take to prevent its own overthrow. At a cost of one and a half million dollars a year, Project Camelot was intended to last three to four years; the United States Army and the Department of Defense were its chief sponsors. "Camelot's" purpose was also to collect primary data to prevent revolutions around the globe. The Department of the Army's Office of Research and Development envisioned a process in which one study would lead to further comparative studies. And under the code names "Project Revolt" (concerning French Canada) and "Project Simpático" (relating to rural politics in Colombia) for example, additional projects were planned by the Department of Defense.[4]

Camelot's first geographic target was Latin America, more specifically Chile, but Camelot was never put into practice as planned, due to a number of unsolicited long-distance phone calls, personal conversations, and the angry reaction of Chilean Senate members who saw the project as an attempt at espionage in scholarly guise. Chilean journalists and intellectuals grew furious—as more details about Project Camelot were disclosed by one of the prospective research participants when he discussed the project with fellow social scientists in Chile and the United States. He set in motion the first wave of criticism, claiming social scientists should not be involved in research to provide the tools to control, dominate, and change the undesirable political processes of specific nations.[5] Other academics and politicians followed, arguing that the project represented a misuse of social science research. Indeed, some political leaders in Latin America read Camelot's official goal of "assessing the potential for internal war within national societies" as an act of imperialism, aimed at crushing revolutionary movements in far-off lands.[6] Soon, scholars all over the Americas, including the United States, angrily rejected military patronage of academic social research. International complaints about Camelot's imperialistic implications led to its official cancellation by Defense Secretary Robert McNamara's office—which held veto power over the military budget. The debates over Project Camelot never disappeared completely. Some scholars even claim that, in reality, Project Camelot just went underground and that potential revolutionaries became the subject of study—and the target of espionage to control revolutions—through new channels.[7]

Camelot's life, and public death, inspire careful consideration of the centrality of political developments and political concerns in the production of knowledge during and about the Cold War. In the 1960s, it incited a wide-ranging debate about the relations between "the Academy" and the White House, between Cold War politics and military patronage for the social sciences in the United States, and about the realities of a politics–patronage–social science nexus.[8] The Camelot affair inspired immediate soul searching among researchers on the ethical implications of their involvement in government-sponsored research. Today, scholars still examine the ways in which "social science in the late twentieth century was—and was not—a creature of the Cold War," and often distinguish between "Social Science in the Cold War," on the one hand, and "Cold War Social Science," on the other. The latter term emphasizes the supposed inherent bias in work scholars produced when they conducted research supported by government monies, or when institutions like the ACLS (American Council of Learned Societies) or the SSRC (Social Science Research Council) recruited scholars for projects serving the national interest.[9] In the contributions to this volume, authors present evidence to show that scholarship produced in the long Cold War was influenced by the political climate of the time and that research priorities, as well as gaps in scholarly production worldwide, were sometimes related to the same rigid political binaries that some sought to overcome.[10] While some scholars, like Frances Stonor Saunders, seek to condemn the bias produced by monies government agencies funneled into universities, or set out to expose "who paid the piper" in the Cold War, others encourage a focus on "what the piper actually bought."[11] In the spirit of the latter, we argue that the master discourse of the Cold War was always contested (as Camelot was) and never fully dominant.[12]

Street-level histories and state policies: questioning the master discourse

The contributions in this volume seek to engage the knowledge produced by the Cold War and to explore the multilayered complexities of its history by emphasizing the power individual acts, personal decisions, or local-level actions acquired in the midst of superpower politics. The rise and fall of Project Camelot, for example, reveal different levels of political influences that mattered, including "street-level" politics. Camelot was planned by US Army officials who relied on support from established institutions such as the military, the government, and research institutions. Yet, when individuals questioned their motives, took action, and incited a new collectivity that opposed the project, they contributed to Camelot's decline. If we apply this dynamic to other historical trajectories, or to chronologies of a familiar master discourse of the Cold War, we gain insights into complex, unexplored histories that were often subsumed under the maneuvers of the "big players."

We acknowledge the difficulty of assessing the specific impact of individuals' actions or street-level politics on the course of the global Cold War, but argue that simple cause-and-effect relationships are as misleading as the exclusive focus on superpower politics itself. In 1982, a ten-year-old girl from the United States, Samantha Smith, wrote a letter to Soviet leader Yuri Andropov, sharing her fear about the possibility of nuclear war and pleading for peace. Her individual effort to stop the arms race gained global attention because she provoked a Soviet reaction from the highest level. In a response that was both personal and public, Andropov sought to acknowledge the legitimacy of Samantha's fears and claimed to recognize that the question she asked about the imminence of nuclear war was "the most important of those that every thinking man can pose." He depicted his fellow Soviets as human beings by emphasizing that they shared Samantha's desire for peace. And he convinced her to accept his invitation to travel from her native Maine to Moscow. While Samantha did not meet Andropov personally during the two weeks she spent in the Soviet Union with her parents, her itinerary brought her into contact with children of her age and was meant to convey that Soviets were not warmongers but were, instead, just as human as Samantha's fellow citizens at home.[13]

The individual actions of a peace-minded girl from the United States did not stop the arms race, but her story illustrates the insights we gain by focusing on state policies *and* on the roles of individuals or organized actors, on people and groups whose activities were related to but not directly dependent on Cold War state policies at the highest levels. Samantha Smith found a way to "globalize" her personal fears and link those to peace initiatives she engaged in for the rest of her life (she died in a plane crash in 1985). Others took advantage of the Cold War binary that pitted communists against capitalists by using the fear of communism in the capitalist world to their own (independent) advantage. A case in point is the activity of anti-communist entrepreneurs in Latin America that Patrick Iber presents in this volume. United States' interests in the region allowed some entrepreneurs to use the fear of communism for their own personal benefit, thereby increasing the influence and visibility of existing political and economic projects by presenting them in a new anti-communist guise. Independent actors, working in an anti-communist marketplace, used the threat of communism to develop a language of legitimacy that was, in reality, a new form of agency quite independent from state interests.

Other examples of the appropriation of Cold War discourse for alternative projects include the conflation of fear of radical left-wing (communist) activism with fear of feminist (now reframed as communist) activism. Dominique Grisard's chapter draws on evidence from Switzerland, where citizens equated supposed threats by armed left-wing terrorists with the fear of un-feminine feminist women who would interrupt the public peace of the Swiss nation. But the rhetoric and practice of superpower confrontation also opened up new spaces for political and intellectual experimentation. In two related chapters, Katharine McGregor and Jadwiga Pieper Mooney illustrate that individual women and women's organizations found ways to strengthen the political effectiveness of their campaigns for rights by enlisting the support of the Eastern Bloc. Fabio Lanza's chapter depicts the Cold War-inspired intellectual experimentation of concerned Asian Scholars in the United States, who, by taking Maoist China as a paradigm of alternative politics, were able to produce scholarship that was both politically engaged and intellectually innovative.

These examples also show how, in the Cold War framework, the notion of a stark division between individual, private acts, and public politics is misleading at best. First, because, in the orbits of Soviet and US influence, Cold War politics permeated everyday life; in the words of historian Susan Buck-Morss, these global competitions were not limited to the political realm, but Cold War "imaginaries were fostered in the popular imagination through mass culture."[14] Teenagers in the United States learned not only to "duck and cover" in response to a possible nuclear attack, but to distinguish between "good" and "evil" as they followed the heroic achievements of such characters as James Bond in popular culture. Buck-Morss herself testifies to the effect the images of Soviet evil had in the United States. Prior to her extensive work with Soviets, in the Soviet Union, and on Soviet culture, she confessed her surprise that a Soviet bureaucrat who came to Vassar College, where she was a student in the 1960s, "looked like any bureaucrat; there was nothing devilish about him."[15] Children in the United States were trained to fear the "red empire," and learned to equate peace and happiness with the capitalist world. Similarly, the Hungarian children that László Kürti describes in his contribution to this volume were trained, through the repetition of cheerful songs, to be happy; so much so that being happy (with the regime, its policies, its ideology) became a defining character of the patriotic citizen. And individual children sang the songs they learned as a confirmation of their belonging to a "happy" collective order.

The pervasiveness of the political in individual actions—even when those were framed explicitly in cultural terms—raises new questions about the political implications of cultural cold wars. Scholars have provided multiple definitions of the "cultural Cold War" and, according to Gordon Johnston, a recent renewed interest in the subject reflects four general themes: the impact propaganda and psychological warfare had on international politics; studies of culture as a way to illustrate what ordinary people "really think"; culture and ideas as evidence to explain the supposed "crisis of legitimacy across the Soviet bloc," as well as the supposed end of the Cold War; and finally, the theme of cultural conflict as the "real" source of conflict, following Samuel Huntington's assessment that "the great divisions among humankind and the domination source of conflict will be cultural."[16] Indeed, some scholars, such as Frances Stonor Saunders, cite evidence to depict the Cold War as a war among cultures, a "psychological contest, of the manufacturing of consent by 'peaceful' methods, of the use of propaganda to erode hostile positions."[17] In this volume, Patrick Iber reminds us that the Soviet-inspired "Peace" Movement and subsequent anti-communist counter-mobilization are generally taken to mark the beginning of the "cultural Cold War." Iber suggests thinking of it in terms of an "ideological Cold War," shaped by a specific type of artist and writer. Many of the supposed "cultural" figures were, in fact, professional ideologists. In Brazil, Chile, Mexico, and Uruguay, the "cultural" activism of the so-called Partisans of Peace engendered "cultural" anti-communist counter-organizing.

A more complex and nuanced understanding of the relationship between politics, culture, and ideology in the Cold War era also allows us to rethink and reframe the meaning and scope of activism in this period. Activism was not necessarily addressed against the state or even against the status quo; much Cold War activism was collaborative, without being necessarily directed from above, as the chapters by Iber and Jennifer Luff (on US labor anti-communism) illustrate. Moreover, street-level activism did not always arise in a direct causal relationship with national or international politics. To portray the emergence of mass movements as well as the actions of organized groups and individuals mainly as consequences of the shifts in global diplomacy and state policies has the effect of denying any political autonomy and meaning to these actions, which then end up being just a blurred reflection of the more serious game at the top.[18] Finally and more importantly, as the Cold War pushed politics down to the level of the quotidian and the intimate realms of the private, political activism came to be similarly displaced in "cultural" activities, in everyday actions, in seemingly mundane facets of daily life. In this perspective, the discovery of everyday life that took place in theoretical debates[19] and political practice in the 1960s developed in the same environment that gave us both Project Camelot and the Hungarian fostering of "happy children." To state that "the private is political," as protestors did in the 1960s and 1970s, meant also to reclaim activism for a different kind of politics in the private sphere that Cold War propaganda had for years tried to invade and appropriate.

Complexities of space and time

The dominant Eurocentric perspective that describes the Cold War as a conflict between East and West presents one obvious aspect of misconstrued Cold War geography, but through examining street-level histories and local perspectives, we can also re-think old notions of center and periphery. In Grisard's chapter, some "peripheral" Swiss citizens, theoretically on neutral political grounds outside the Cold War (Switzerland), become vigilantes over other "peripheral" Swiss citizens, the latter supposedly located on the "wrong" political side of the Cold War—and made even more peripheral by their gender. In Iber's chapter, we learn that some of the most dedicated (and influential) Cold War ideologues, Spaniards exiled from Franco's Spain, lived in the so-called Latin American "periphery." Authors, theorists, and revolutionaries from supposed peripheries could also acquire important roles in the formation of politics and cultures across the globe. Delinda Collier's contribution to this volume, for example, provides evidence to show that the writings of the Argentine Ernesto "Che" Guevara and the Brazilian Paulo Freire inspired Angolan artists to shape a post-colonial and nationalistic theory of art.

The geographical limits to the logic of Cold War "centers" and "peripheries," as well as the supposed rigid binary opposition that the global rivalry depended on, are undermined by the individual street-level actors whose place in Cold War histories we seek to find: travelers who moved across the blocs, and whose movements were not confined by the solid walls or iron curtains that purportedly divided Cold War worlds. Studies of transnational political activists, such as the delegates of the Women's International Democratic Federation (WIDF) presented in the chapters by McGregor and Pieper Mooney, show that the "centers" of ideas and political projects were not geographically bound. WIDF activists built their headquarters in East Berlin, but in their campaigns for world peace they moved between the East and the West and negotiated their relationship with political leaders both globally and locally. The nature of their campaigns, and the wide variety of agendas women brought to the WIDF, also makes us rethink the relationship between communist and feminist mobilization. Although some communists have condemned feminist activism as a product of bourgeois politics, we find rich evidence of communist women's activism in support of women's rights.

Examples from the realms of politics and culture also compel us to reconsider notions of the beginnings and endings of what we think of as Cold War competitions. Soviet fiction writers, for example, had juxtaposed "utopian communist heaven" with "capitalist hell" at least since the 1920s. Authors described happy citizens who lived free of conflict and who experienced "comradely cooperation" and "egoless friendships." In this environment, people had reason to be content with everyday life; they were living happy lives because of the absence of competition, struggle, and violence.[20] Without the threat of exploitation or alienation from the product of their labor, workers would just want to work. Yakov Okunev's *The Coming World* (1923), for example, depicted labor as pleasant and rotational, a work experience that bears no resemblance to Upton Sinclair's 1906 portrayal of the Chicago stockyards as a dirty, horrific "jungle."[21] Several contributions to this volume provide alternative evidence to illustrate that the perceived threats or promises of communism were hardly new phenomena and existed long before the Cold War allegedly began. In her chapter on labor activism, Jennifer Luff shows that "red scares" in the United States were neither exclusive to the Cold War nor solely linked to the McCarthy era immediately following World War II. Luff explores the strategies of labor organizers in the decades preceding the Cold War, and shows that they employed anti-communism as a political tool to increase their control over workers' organizations.

As we consider the Cold War in public, private, political, *and* cultural terms, we also need to re-think the supposed end of the Cold War. Lasting evidence of the "cultural Cold War," as well as lingering practices that originated as weapons of superpower politics, still shape contemporary political discourse, evident, for example, in opponents' references to US President Barack Obama as a dangerous "socialist."[22] Although the nuclear arms race between the US and the Soviet Union ended after political negotiations at the highest level, and although the Soviet Union no longer exists as an empire that competes with US power, citizens from countries of the former Eastern and Western blocs are still working out the terms of their relationships. In a united Germany, for example, contemporary politics are still negotiated through the lens of the political and cultural practices of the former East and West that are not always easy to reconcile. It is difficult to set a precise end to the Cold War (or to firmly conclude that it is over), and it is just as hard to celebrate one side's victory or lament the other side's defeat. Contributions to this volume confirm that historical change consists of ruptures and continuities and illustrate that we cannot ignore that many Cold War practices linger on. The Huntingtonian model of a culturally bipolar world ready to clash still serves as a model to frame fear of this or that emerging power (only the names of emerging powers have changed repeatedly). And the Cold War is with us also in more subtle and unforeseen ways: it lingers on, for example, in the Lucky Dragon museum in Tokyo described in Ann Sherif's chapter, where the memory of the Bikini nuclear incident of 1954 merges with the Fukushima disaster of 2011 and where anti-nuclear activism of yesterday joins the renewed skepticism about nuclear plants in today's Japan. We can find evidence even in the cultural, political, and spatial structure of Orange County, which, as Dimitri Papandreu illustrates in the final essay in this collection, was both a Cold War invention and the embodiment of the successes and disasters of victorious capitalism.

Organization of the volume

The chapters in this volume are organized in three thematic parts, widely defined, to introduce diverse types of political activisms, to illustrate the limitations of dominant Cold War categories and the framing of the world in binary oppositions, and, finally, to raise questions about the positioning of individuals and collectives in opposition to or in conformity with Cold War structures.

The three essays in Part I, "Cold War activisms: crossing borders and building bridges," emphasize activists' mobilizational and organizational strategies that spurred local movements and forged global ties beyond and across the Cold War divide. Ann Sherif follows the formation and evolution of the anti-nuclear grass-roots movement following the Bikini incident (test Bravo) and traces the complex evolution of the anti-atomic weapon and pro-nuclear energy discourses that have dominated Japan up until the recent Fukushima tragedy. She outlines the difficult route that activists had to navigate in Japan, where the US alliance framed foreign policy so that Japanese "peace" initiatives could potentially be labeled as "pro-communist." The history of the anti-nuclear mobilization is interesting also from a gendered perspective: the "ordinary homemakers" of Suginami Ward, for example, became non-threatening symbols of the maternal worries about contamination.

Two related essays in Part I explore histories of activists who organized specifically as women (and mothers) in the Women's International Democratic Federation (WIDF). Katharine McGregor contributes new evidence to show that developments of the Cold War united diverse peoples from across the globe in opposition to the lingering effects of colonialism, economic imperialism, and militarism as well as to ongoing nuclear testing and the escalating arms race. Exploring the relationships, shared rhetoric, and joint activism between women in the transnational WIDF and the Indonesian Women's Movement (Gerakan Wanita Indonesia-Gerwani), McGregor argues that the WIDF lent (temporary) strength to Gerwani's domestic campaigns. Indonesian women could use the WIDF to draw attention to their anti-imperialist mobilization. When the bureau meeting of the WIDF was held in Jakarta in 1960, this signaled both the growing prominence of Indonesia in the anti-imperialist movement and the impressive achievements of the Indonesian Women's Movement. Yet, McGregor makes clear that we cannot see Gerwani's success as just one step on a timeline of linear progress of women's activism. In 1965, the Indonesian government violently attacked Gerwani women in a wide-scale campaign to repress the Indonesian left. Half a million people were murdered by the army and by civilian anti-communists; hundreds of thousands were imprisoned without trial. Pieper Mooney's study links women's activism in the WIDF to the political discourses and competitions of the Cold War. In her exploration of the history of the federation, particularly its anti-fascist roots and its relation to the Eastern bloc, she illustrates that Cold War political affiliations and actions cannot be reduced to competitions between the communist East and the capitalist West. Anti-fascist campaigns and WIDF activities in defense of women's rights provide evidence of alternative mobilizational strategies and multiple languages of women's activism, too easily conflated with communism in light of the dominant paradigms at the time.

In Part II, "Separating enemies from friends: communism, anti-communism, and the construction of Cold War realities," authors explore how individual actors or groups deployed the dualities that framed Cold War ideology in everyday life; Cold War ideology, based on the binary oppositions of capitalism/communism, East/West, warmongering/peaceful, etc., shaped pervasive political practices. Yet, individuals, groups, and governments also appropriated and re-used these binaries for alternative political purposes. László Kürti examines popular media, children's songs, and public discourse to analyze how Hungarian daily life was remodeled through a transfer of Soviet cultural models evident in the cult of personality of Stalinist leader Mátyás Rákosi. In the 1950s, Hungarian political leaders deployed specific models of masculinity and femininity, of production and reproduction, as well as of happiness and patriotism. Through these models, they also waged a war against internal enemies, and purges became a less public yet utterly cruel side of a more profound division that affected the daily lives of Hungarian citizens. Jennifer Luff's essay complicates our understanding of Cold War binaries by demonstrating that anti-communism had deep roots in US labor organizations well before the McCarthy era. In addition, she illustrates that anti-communism itself is a complex category: the camp of labor anti-communism was divided, and competing factions were driven by competitions for power and control. Examining the iconic figures of Jack Tenney and Ronald Reagan, Luff illustrates how the split between conservative and liberal anti-communist labor organizers had less to do with ideology than with their respective experiences in labor struggles. The Cold War, she argues, "was a project that began on factory shop floors and picket lines as well as Washington offices and corporate suites." Political leaders and citizens constructed "alternative" Cold War projects not only in the United States, but also in other, less familiar sites of the Cold War. Dominique Grisard analyzes citizen watch groups in supposedly neutral Switzerland, where concerned citizens set out on their own to fight the ideological infiltration of communism and the dangers of terrorism. In the 1970s, these activists responded to anti-communist and anti-feminist sentiments. They linked the widespread fears of communism to the uneasiness with women's liberation, thereby contributing to the making of a gendered embodiment of the Soviet threat in the form of the female terrorist. By showing how these actors both were empowered by prevalent Cold War fears and contributed to the Cold War discourse in Switzerland, Grisard alerts us to the pitfalls of seeing ideology as an exclusively top-down mechanism.

The essays in Part III, "Rethinking opposition and conformity," invite us to re-evaluate how individuals and groups articulated both opposition and conformity to the official Cold War ideologies. Fabio Lanza's chapter investigates the role of China, more specifically of the Maoist experiments of the Cultural Revolution, in shaping activism in US academia. By analyzing the founding, development, and dissolution of the Committee of Concerned Asian Scholars, Lanza shows how this group of young professors and graduate students used the Chinese case as a starting point from which to challenge not only US state policies, but also the paradigms of their own academic fields. Next, as discussed above, Patrick Iber's chapter focuses on anti-communist entrepreneurs in Latin America, whose ideological position predates the official Cold War but whose economic success and political relevance increased as a result of United States' interest in their services. Delinda Collier leads us to Africa, where she examines a group of young artists and writers who began to envision a cultural policy for the newly independent Angola. Through the language of New Man (*Homem Novo*), these cultural innovators attempted a synthesis of Marxist ideas of collectivism and developmentalism with a pragmatic awareness of the specificities of Africa and Angola. The same artists and writers were also part of international networks that spanned from Cuba to Brazil, and from Portugal to East Germany. Some of them held academic degrees obtained in European capitals. Their national affiliation and international ties allowed them to borrow from both sides of the global ideological divide, while they remained fiercely connected to their national and regional specificities. Through their cultural and political practices, these artists illustrate the limits of a binary understanding of Cold War cultural politics.

In the last chapter of this collection, Dimitri Papandreu explores Orange County, California, as the contradictory embodiment of the long history of Cold War ideology in the United States. Papandreu highlights how this place, which still epitomizes the most extreme neoliberal and conservative trends in the country, was actually built and came to prosper because of government programs connected with the Cold War expansion of the military-industrial complex. Tracing the long history of Orange County, he shows how the agricultural pre-Cold War past is connected to its post-industrial present in large part through the continuing exclusion of Mexican-American workers, who, during the Cold War, came to constitute the feared Other of anti-communism. In this sharply polemical essay, Papandreu reminds us how the Cold War is still very much part of contemporary everyday life.

Notes

1 According to Irving Louis Horowitz, the project was first planned in 1963 by a group of high-ranking Army officers with connections to the Army Research Office of the Department of Defense. See Irving Louis Horowitz, "The Life and Death of Project Camelot," *Society* 3, no. 1 (1965): 4.
2 Irving Louis Horowitz, ed., *The Rise and Fall of Project Camelot: Studies in the Relationship between Social Science and Practical Politics* (Cambridge, Mass.: M.I.T. Press, 1974), 4–5.
3 Horowitz, *The Rise and Fall of Project Camelot*, 4–5.
4 Horowitz, *The Rise and Fall of Project Camelot*, 16.
5 Stanley R. Ross reminds us that "the academic community in general and Latin Americanists in particular are indebted to Professor Irving Louis Horowitz for the most systematic and penetrating examination of the rise and fall of Project Camelot." See Stanley R. Ross, ed., *Latin America in Transition: Problems in Training and Research* (Albany: State University of New York Press, 1970), xiv

Introduction 11

    for quote and xiii–xix for additional comments on Camelot; Horowitz's edited volume, *The Rise and Fall of Project Camelot*, was first published in 1967, and contributors not only discussed the history of the project itself, but also addressed the academic and political responses to Camelot, as well as what they saw as Camelot's general implications. See also Horowitz's chapter "The Rise and Fall of Project Camelot," in Irving Louis Horowitz, *Ideology and Utopia in the United States, 1956–1976* (New York: Oxford University Press, 1977), 225–57.
6 For quote see Horowitz, *The Rise and Fall of Project Camelot*, 5.
7 See, for example, the American Anthropological Association's publication, *AAA Newsletter* (January 1967), 506; and Donald Freed and Fred Simon Landis, *Death in Washington: The Murder of Orlando Letelier* (Westport, Conn: Lawrence Hill, 1980), 33.
8 See, for example, the insightful discussion by Mark Solovey, "Project Camelot and the 1960s Epistemological Revolution: Rethinking the Politics–Patronage–Social Science Nexus," *Social Studies of Science* 31/2 (April 2001): 171–206. For earlier reactions, see John Walsh, "Social Sciences: Cancellation of Camelot after Row in Chile Brings Research under Scrutiny," *Science* 49/3689 (Sep. 10, 1965): 1211–13; John Walsh, "Foreign Affairs Research: Review Process Rises on Ruins of Camelot," *Science* 150/3702 (Dec. 10, 1965): 1429–31.
9 David C. Engerman, "Social Science in the Cold War," *Isis* 101/2 (June 2010): 393–400.
10 See, for example, the silence on the history of the Women's International Democratic Federation discussed in the chapter by Jadwiga E. Pieper Mooney. The Committee of Concerned Asian Scholars (examined in Fabio Lanza's chapter) was extremely critical of the influence that government funding and direction had on the field of Asian Studies.
11 Frances Stonor Saunders, *The Cultural Cold War: The CIA and the World of Arts and Letters* (New York: New Press, 2000), originally published as Frances Stonor Saunders, *Who Paid the Piper?: The CIA and the Cultural Cold War* (London: Granta Books, 1999). For reference to these positions, see Engerman, "Social Science in the Cold War," 398.
12 David Engerman reminds us that even scholars who were commissioned and paid for their research often produced research results that contradicted the dominant view. Political scientist Merle Fainsod, for example, challenged dominant understandings of the Soviet Union early on. See Merle Fainsod, *Smolensk under Soviet Rule* (Cambridge, Mass.: Harvard University Press, 1958), as discussed by Engerman, "Social Science in the Cold War," 399.
13 For a copy of Samantha's letter and a translation of Andropov's response, see Elizabeth Sirimarco, *The Cold War* (New York: Benchmark Books, 2005), 100–02; see also Gail Underwood Parker, *It Happened in Maine* (Guilford, Conn: Globe Pequot Press, 2004), 109–14.
14 Susan Buck-Morss, *Dreamworld and Catastrophe: The Passing of Mass Utopia in East and West* (Cambridge, Mass.: MIT Press, 2000), 9.
15 Buck-Morss, *Dreamworld and Catastrophe*, 285, fn 75.
16 Gordon Johnston, "Revisiting the Cultural Cold War," *Social History* 35/3 (Aug. 2010): 291.
17 Saunders, *The Cultural Cold War*, 17.
18 Even Jeremi Suri's study of mass movements of the 1960s fosters a similar reduction; mass movements appear as non-political elements in a larger political game of international relations. Jeremi Suri, *Power and Protest: Global Revolution and the Rise of Détente* (Cambridge, MA: Harvard University Press, 2003).
19 On the theoretical side, see Roland Barthes, *Mythologies* (New York: The Noonday Press, 1972), originally published in 1957; Henri Lefebvre, *Critique of Everyday Life* (New York: Verso, 1992), originally published in 1961; Michel de

Certeau, *The Practice of Everyday Life* (Berkeley: University of California Press, 2011), originally published in 1980. On the political side, "the personal is political" was one of the slogans of the feminist movement in the very early 1970s.
20 Richard Stites and David Goldfrank, *Passion and Perception: Essays on Russian Culture* (Washington, DC: New Academia Pub, 2010), 242–43.
21 For reference to Okunev see Stites and Goldfrank, *Passion and Perception*, 241; Upton Sinclair, *The Jungle* (Cambridge, Mass.: R. Bentley, 1971).
22 References to US President Obama's "socialism" first appeared during the 2008 presidential campaign (http://www.salon.com/2011/03/29/bill_sammon_socialism/) and are continuing through the 2012 presidential race. See, for example http://nation.foxnews.com/mitt-romney/2012/01/09/perry-calls-obama-socialist-nh-debate.

Part I
Cold War activisms
Crossing borders and building bridges

1 Thermonuclear weapons and tuna
Testing, protest, and knowledge in Japan[1]

Ann Sherif

Nowhere in the vast city of Tokyo can one find a monumental structure that dramatically embodies the divisions and tensions of the Cold War, as Berlin's Wall once did. Neither does Tokyo's central city reveal any tangible reminders of Japan's status as a satellite state and ally of a Cold War superpower, as does Seoul, where United States Army Garrison Youngsan occupies prime space in the heart of the city. Tokyo's most striking monument to the Cold War past is quite modest by comparison: an uncarved rock with a single bold inscription: *maguro zuka* (burial mound for tuna). The rock and its setting—a grove of trees in Island of Dreams Park near Tokyo Bay—bring to mind benign and rather conventional attitudes toward the natural world, rather than political strife or global geopolitical rancor.

Yet the Tokyo residents who conceived of the ritual site intended the rock monument to bear witness to acts of the most unnatural violence and environmental pollution resulting from the atmospheric testing of thermonuclear weapons that was integral to the U.S.–Soviet Cold War arms race. The tuna monument planners were fully cognizant of the complex politics that defined that rivalry. The location of the tuna burial mound confirms this, for the rock is situated next to a small museum that houses the Lucky Dragon Number 5 (*Daigo fukuryū maru*), a tuna fishing boat that made headlines after it was exposed, in the course of a routine deep-sea expedition, to radioactive fallout from a hydrogen-bomb test. This chapter looks at the ways the tuna mound, the museum, the boat, and many people connected to them represent points of intersection of local culture with the global Cold War, sometimes in broadly public interactions, but also in intimate and mundane events.

The historical event that led to the Tuna Mound was the 1 March 1954 hydrogen-bomb test called Bravo, part of the U.S. military's Operation Castle in the Bikini Atoll, South Pacific. Test Bravo was one of the 215 above ground U.S. tests of thermonuclear devices executed during the 1950s, when the Cold War nuclear arms race between America and the Soviet Union was at its height. With a fireball more than four miles in diameter, Bravo turned out to be the largest American nuclear device ever detonated—in fact, more than three times larger than the planners anticipated, and a thousand times more powerful than the primitive atomic bombs at Hiroshima and Nagasaki. The unintended consequence of this huge release of destructive power was the spread of radioactive fallout, or powdered debris, across a wide swath of the South Pacific, far beyond the danger zone originally described by the U.S. government. As a result, tuna and other living creatures on land and in the ocean were exposed to unacceptably high dosages of radiation.

Not only did Bravo irradiate fish, but fishing boats as well, and most notably the *Daigo fukuryū maru* (Lucky Dragon), which was 85 miles from the shot. Radioactive ash (partly pulverized coral from the reef at Bikini Atoll) rained down on the boat's crew and catch. "Bikini Incident" (or "Lucky Dragon Incident" in English) is the term used to refer to the crew's encounter with the so-called "ashes of death" (*shi no hai* or fallout), the media coverage of the crew's radiation sickness and the death of one crew member, and the widespread protest and diplomatic negotiations that ensued.

The Cold War evolved partly out of the concept of deterrence, or mutual intimidation predicated on possession of bombs with unfathomably destructive power. Willingly, the U.S. and U.S.S.R. pursued the bizarre goal of creating arsenals of weapons that could destroy the earth many times over. Far from guaranteeing the safety of citizens, nuclear strategists turned their focus to the protection of the warheads and delivery systems from attack and destruction.[2] While the age of above ground nuclear testing ended decades ago, the burial mound and the Lucky Dragon museum serve as reminders of the Cold War nuclear regime, and its legacies in the post-Cold War world. This chapter, by examining local manifestations of the Cold War in Japan, seeks to highlight cultural and social expressions of this decades-long global conflict that is frequently understood primarily in diplomatic or strategic terms.

Historical contexts of the "Bikini Incident"

Although there is no scholarly consensus about the start date of the Cold War, the U.S. atomic bombings of Hiroshima and Nagasaki in August 1945, at the end stages of World War II and the Asia-Pacific War, have often been understood as significant early events. This is because nuclear weaponry would become a defining characteristic of the Cold War, giving rise to the concept of deterrence, contributing to the strategy of containment, and shaping the rivalry between the superpowers as a "war of nerves" accompanied by multiple "hot" proxy wars fought with conventional weapons in client nations (Korea, Vietnam, Afghanistan).

From the late 1940s and into the 1950s, the U.S. and the Soviet Union carried out their competition to develop new and more powerful nuclear weapons in public by testing thermonuclear devices above ground. Other possessor states joined in with these public displays. Even after the practice of atmospheric testing ceased as a result of the 1963 Limited Test Ban Treaty (LTBT), the image of mushroom clouds of thermonuclear devices, which dwarfed those of Hiroshima and Nagasaki, and talk of the destruction of humankind and the Earth by such weapons, continued to strike fear and wonder in the hearts of all who saw them. These iconic images also seized the imagination of the media, and artists around the world, giving rise to multiple cultural expressions of anxiety and alarm, but also admiration for the might of technology. Finally, the nuclear arms race during the Cold War raised ethical questions about the possession of apocalyptic weapons by civilized nations, and led to widespread protest on a grassroots level. The parallel development of nuclear technologies for use in power generation, moreover, was the flip side of the atomic coin, offering an apparently positive and desirable atomic energy. In Japan, local citizens and groups were exceptionally articulate about their critique of the nuclear arms race, as well as of Japan's status as a client state under its ally the United States' nuclear umbrella. Although pro-nuclear weapon constituencies exist in Japan, the anti-nuclear viewpoint emanating from Hiroshima and Nagasaki eventually became acceptable in the media, education, and even the government, as Prime Minister Satō Eisaku's advocacy of the Three Non-Nuclear Principles from 1967 demonstrates.[3]

Meanings of the *Maguro zuka*

In what ways is the Tuna Mound on Tokyo Bay related to Cold War power struggles as well as to local communities? Mr. Ōishi Matashichi, one of the former Lucky Dragon crew members who spearheaded the fundraising effort for the mound in 1999, describes the functions of the tuna mound.[4] Ōishi first regards the mound as a proper (though symbolic and belated) burial for the thousands of tuna whose bodies were contaminated with high levels of radiation from hydrogen-bomb testing. In the aftermath of Test Bravo, these "A-Bomb tuna" (*genbaku maguro*) were dumped into deep pits near the Tsukiji Wholesale Fish Market in Tokyo and then unceremoniously covered with dirt as a means of making sure that they did not circulate in the marketplace. The hurried mass burial ensured that no human would consume the toxic flesh, and also that the poisonous corpses would be quickly hidden from public view. By functioning as a memorial, the tuna mound seeks to undo this undignified end. The grassroots group that spearheaded the memorial describes the dedication of the mound as a rite of separation or farewell (*kuyō*) to the creatures so closely bound to human populations, who normally would fish them for a living, and who prepare and eat them daily.

Mr. Ōishi further explains that he regards the tuna mound also as a milestone on the road to a more peaceful society, pointing the way to future generations. A "simple stone," he notes, is ideal for this purpose, as the material will last for a thousand years.[5] The unyielding stone also symbolizes resistance to the apocalyptic lure of nuclear weapons. He further elaborates on his reason for choosing such hard rock for the tuna mound: it will survive centuries of fires and earthquakes.[6] As an enduring reminder of the dangers of radiation released by nuclear weapons and their destructive force, the solid rock contrasts with the coral reefs that Test Bravo fractured into millions of bits of radioactive ash and swept up thousands of meters into the atmosphere, before the ash rained down over the Lucky Dragon boat, the Pacific, and far beyond. The green of the stone refers to the waters of the South Pacific where the tuna dwell, and where they, along with other sea creatures, were exposed to radioactive fallout from testing. Through their words and deeds, Mr. Ōishi and his grassroots group champion this modest object as a critique of the sacrifice demanded of humans and the environment during the Cold War.

Test Bravo and the Bikini Incident

Given that Japan experienced the atomic bombings of Hiroshima and Nagasaki, why did the Bikini Incident have such a galvanizing effect on citizens and government? This partly has to do with the complex historical and cultural processes in the decades after the war's end that resulted in the bombs simultaneously being naturalized and made strange. Thanks to the bomb, the threat of apocalypse became part of daily life. On the other hand, the manifold cultural, social, and political meanings attached to the bomb, depending on history and culture, led to the realization that this bomb is not mere machine, not a conventional weapon as the generals had once assumed. In the early years after the war, many Americans celebrated the bomb as contributing to the final Allied victory over fascism and the last of the Axis powers.

For the bombed nation, in contrast, the atom bombs symbolized conflicting feelings of relief over the end of a long and costly war, shame at defeat, and also a long-delayed public debate. During much of the Occupation of Japan (1945–52), the American occupiers used censorship of text and image in order to curtail public engagement with "the nature and meaning of this new world," the new atomic age.[7] This enforced silence in the media and publishing about what had happened in Hiroshima and Nagasaki, as well as the ethical and political issues raised by the bomb, was due to two factors: first, America's "general policy of secrecy concerning nuclear matters" during the Cold War and, second, the Occupation authorities' concern that full revelation of the A-bomb's short-term and lasting destructive force might provoke accusations of atrocities.[8] The Bikini Incident occurred only several years after the end of this enforced period of silence and restraint about nuclear attack, and at a time when the newly independent Japanese state was affirming its alliance with the "Free World" led by its great ally, the U.S.

Though the bomb had ushered in the Allied triumph, the Soviet test of weapons quickly made clear that Americans could also be victims of the bomb one day. A-bombs became abstract objects of fear and black humor in popular culture and in the propaganda about and performance of civil defense. The superpowers aggressively promoted the peaceful uses of nuclear technologies (in President Eisenhower's Atoms for Peace program from 1953, for example, and Soviet boasting about its peaceful uses for atomic energy), partly inspired by the long-anticipated utopian potential of the atom, but also as a means of distracting an anxious public from their other project: the development of thermonuclear weapons as part of Cold War security. In Japan, however, the legacies and meanings of Hiroshima and Nagasaki remained perplexing and only partly explored because of the strategic value of the new weapons as one defining aspect of a Cold War that kept "both sides in a state of nervous apprehension."[9] For many decades, people in those cities lived with the medical, psychological, and social burdens of the radiation poisoning (*genbaku byō*, literally, A-bomb disease), cancer and other long-term health effects of the August 1945 bombings.

In the aftermath of Test Bravo, the intrusion on daily life of hydrogen-bomb testing thousands of miles away had a drastic psychological effect on huge populations around the world, but the anxiety was especially acute in Japan. The arms race, which had up until then seemed material for newspaper headlines, begin to manifest itself in the most mundane places. During the 1950s, tuna and other seafood made up the most significant source of protein in the Japanese diet. The discovery of the Lucky Dragon's contaminated catch, and the news that radioactive tuna had been shipped to markets in 14 prefectures, led to immediate suspicion about the safety of that staple. Sliced tuna sashimi and tuna roll were favorite dishes at the sushi shop; tuna simmered in soy broth was a familiar dish with rice at the evening meal. Every newspaper featured photographs of doctors in white lab coats holding the wand of the Geiger counter over what had, until that moment, been nourishment, safety, and home. Part of ordinary domesticity was rendered toxic; eating "A-bomb tuna" could lead to internal exposure to harmful levels of radiation (*naibu hibaku*). Beyond the disruption of the family's daily diet, many communities suffered a huge economic blow because of the banning of sales of the catch and the reticence of consumers to buy fish at markets and in restaurants. By May of 1954, furthermore, the public learned that fallout also contaminated spinach and other vegetables and fruit.[10]

The possibility of internal exposure through familiar foods was not the only warning that H-bomb tests presented a danger to all. Daily newspapers displayed photographs of the darkened and peeling skin of Lucky Dragon crew members, and explained the various symptoms of the radiation disease (loss of hair, burns, diarrhea) that resulted after the "ashes of death" settled on their skin and burrowed into their clothing (external exposure, *gaibu hibaku*). The Marshall Islanders, the other population that was exposed to "local fallout" (particles of 0.1–0.2 millimeter in size that fall within hundreds of miles of a nuclear event within the same day or so) after Test Bravo, called it "powder" and asked why it felt hot on the skin. Within days after news of the crew's exposure, evidence came that the radioactive fallout knew no borders. The H-bomb explosion sent "particles into the upper air" that then "sink and reach the surface" of the Earth "in the form of deadly dust or rain."[11] The radioactive debris moved around the Earth.

Two months after Test Bravo, and during the months following the Lucky Dragon's return to Yaizu port, it became clear that this now famous boat was not the only vessel that had been exposed to high levels of radiation. Higher than normal levels were detected in more than 850 other Japanese boats. Some fishing boats, such as the *Daihachi Junko-maru*, showed even higher levels of contamination than did the Lucky Dragon, even though it was over 3,000 kilometers from the Bikini Atoll when it was exposed more than two months after Bravo.[12] And it was not only ocean-going vessels that were exposed to tropospheric fallout (smaller particles of "radioactive weapon debris" that are swept up into the troposphere and then carried around the globe by strong winds for a month or so, before falling to the Earth in the form of wet or dry precipitation).[13] Scientists throughout Japan started detecting higher than usual levels of radiation and radioactive substances in the rain.[14]

Newspapers throughout the country alerted their readers to the potential danger of exposure to rain. Scientists immediately went about investigating the effects of fallout on soil, fruits, vegetables, and milk. Understandably, public anxiety increased tremendously when it was learned that the safety of basic foodstuffs could be compromised months after an H-bomb test, and that every place on earth was vulnerable to fallout. The widely publicized death of Lucky Dragon crew member Kuboyama Ai in September 1954, served as the most vivid evidence that nuclear weapons waste was not safe. In Japan, the media coverage of the hazards of fallout was much more detailed and extensive than in the U.S. and other allies. The Bikini Incident, nonetheless, sparked global awareness of the dangers of nuclear testing. Eventually, the controversy contributed to diplomatic agreements to end atmospheric testing.

In the parlance of the time, the toxicity that literally rained down onto fields, forests, and cities was not construed of as environmental pollution, damaging ecosystems, but rather was described primarily in social terms, as *kōgai* (public nuisance), much as industrial waste that caused illness. But, even so, production of poisonous nuclear waste contradicts what we would now call sustainable practice.[15] During the 1950s, anti-nuclear activism was framed primarily as antiwar protest or advocacy for peace, rather than as an environmental activism.

Political engagement in a new democratic society: the free world and the Bikini Incident

The story of the widespread anti-nuclear protest that arose after the Bikini Incident often paints a picture of an apolitical citizenry that was prompted to anti-nuclear awareness because the Cold War had intruded on their daily lives. In such accounts, the "Ban the Bomb" protest is described as being entirely separate from the ideological rivalry that characterized the Cold War.

During the late 1950s, the Japanese media was full of iconic images of the "ordinary homemakers" in Suginami Ward, Tokyo. After extensive coverage of the Lucky Dragon's exposure to fallout, these women, we are told, spontaneously organized to learn more; they carried out petition drives that would collect millions of signatures. The political awareness of these homemakers arose from the intrusion of nuclear weapons into their daily lives; radioactive fallout contaminated the rain, the crops, and fish, which was an essential part of the diet (like Strontium-90, milk, and baby teeth in the U.S.). The Suginami Ward activists devoted tremendous energy for what for most of them was the first engagement with a newly democratic civil society in post-defeat, post-Occupation Japan. It is worth noting that, although the Suginami groups were important in the anti-nuclear movement, they were only one part of a much larger movement, one that can be traced back to the early postwar period. The popular image of women as the main cohort that made up the anti-nuclear protesters comes from the media and many historians who, consciously or not, fashioned a gendered image of the anti-nuclear movement as a whole after Lucky Dragon. The bomb mattered to women, such critics wrote, because women were mothers. This maternalist explanation defines the anti-bomb movement after Bikini as spontaneous, and apparently apolitical protest, but also excludes mention of a preexisting anti-nuclear movement that was tremendously complex, diverse, and rancorous. Such an approach makes the movement broadly acceptable, by detaching it from specific political or ethical points of view. While it is true that the Lucky Dragon incident motivated a movement on a scale unknown before, it is also the case that a feminized and domesticated movement was more politically palatable to newspaper readers than were the leftist activists who had been protesting in Hiroshima and Nagasaki since 1946. In this way, an apparently non-threatening group of homemakers from Suginami Ward, Tokyo, is repeatedly credited with creating the anti-nuclear movement in reaction to the news about the Lucky Dragon, even though it is well known that peace movements existed long before. More than anything, the voices of these women represented the momentary unity of a divided movement given temporary mass appeal at that historical moment.

If it was poisoned tuna and spinach that initially mobilized such previously non-activist women, they could also claim common cause with Nobel Prize scientists who warned of apocalypse. Indeed, Bertrand Russell and Albert Einstein credit the Bikini test, and by extension the Japanese protesters, with promoting global awareness of the apocalyptic dangers presented by the new bombs: ("all are equally in peril" under the threat of hydrogen bombs: "we now know, especially since the Bikini test, that nuclear bombs can gradually spread destruction over a much wider area than had been supposed.")[16]

From the end of World War II until the time of the Bikini Incident, many, though by no means all, of the leaders of the peace and anti-nuclear movements were affiliated with the Japan Communist or Socialist Party, or Leftist labor unions. Although the long-term conflict between conservative, socialist, and communist constituencies is portrayed clearly in Nobel Prize-winner Ōe Kenzaburō's reportage *Hiroshima Notes*, many scholars have emphasized the pathologies of a fractured Left, rather than take seriously the ideological terms of this debate. It is worth remembering that the public held diverse views of communism then. On the one hand, the Japanese media and political scene felt the influence of the virulently anti-communist atmosphere promoted by McCarthyism in the United States. But at the same time the Chinese Revolution of 1949, with which the People's Republic of China was founded, gave the "socialist camp tremendous prestige" around the world.[17]

Such ideological complexity reflected the ideological tensions of a highly unstable stage of the Cold War. Indeed, a wide spectrum of anti-nuke, anti-war groups had been gathering in Hiroshima and Nagasaki for years, from Christians to Stalinists, from Socialists to surrealist poets. In the years of the Allied Occupation from 1945–52 these groups marched, voicing opinions that the U.S. especially sought to silence. The Soviet Union, some claimed, would bring peace, not the warmongering capitalists. After Japan was granted sovereignty, the Japanese government increasingly threw in its lot with America, which meant some in the government would toe the pro-nuclear line. With the Red Purge under the increasing anti-communism of the U.S. ally provoked by the perceived threat of the new People's Republic of China, the Korean War, and McCarthyism, "peace" became a dirty word. People who marched with peace and anti-nuke signs—were they communists? Certainly some of them were, but were they Soviet spies? Many people shunned the word "peace," fearing they might be labeled "Red."

During the Cold War, Japan "served as the outpost of the U.S. global strategy to counter communist expansionism."[18] Extensive American military bases on Japanese soil, and strong economic, political, and cultural ties were key components of this alliance. Although the U.S. relationships with its client states in Asia were characterized by more "power and dominance" than in Europe, Japan's growing stature as an economic and political presence meant that Japan had greater latitude than some other allies. For most of the Cold War era, furthermore, Japan was the sole American ally in East Asia that was not an authoritarian regime.[19] Whether compliant or resistant, Japanese citizens had to adjust to the new reality of the U.S. nuclear umbrella that the alliance guaranteed.

Pictures of the Lucky Dragon crew members' darkened and peeling skin and hair loss led not only to their hospitalization in leading Tokyo hospitals, but also to complex diplomatic negotiations between the Japanese and U.S. governments. On the Tokyo side, Japan made demands for compensation. Washington, however, not wanting to confirm the Bikini tests as the cause of their illness, settled eventually by paying to the Lucky Dragon crew members a one-time monetary payment as a show of "concern" (*mimaikin*). The crew, in turn, agreed the matter was thereby settled, and they could pursue no further legal claims. Even though many other fishing boats and seafood-related businesses had suffered devastating financial and other consequences, no other monetary claims were recognized. The Japanese government's inability to negotiate for anything even remotely resembling compensation beyond the single, highly publicized case of the Lucky Dragon brought widespread criticism from the public as yet another sign of Japan's willing subservience to the superpower as part of its Cold War global strategy.

The Allied Occupation had brought a version of liberal democracy to defeated Japan, and it was precisely within this framework of a free press and freedom of speech that citizens expressed their political views about the evolving Cold War world order. Japan's subordinate position was not the only issue: the alliance's ideological basis in free-market capitalism and rabid anti-communism was also a matter of contention among citizens and the media in Japan. The tone of the U.S. stance on the incident, furthermore, showed evidence of the hubris with which America conducted nuclear matters. Rather than taking seriously the injuries that the crew had sustained or calling into question the possible toxicity of fallout, members of the U.S. Congress publicly accused the Lucky Dragon crew of being Soviet spies. The context of McCarthyism in the U.S. provides context for such thoughtless denunciation.

American authorities in Japan initially denied that the H-bomb test was in any way connected to the Lucky Dragon crew's ailments. After the media showed vivid images and published stories about Bravo and the ashes, the connection was undeniable. Even so, the U.S. refused to acknowledge the true extent of the danger of above-ground testing. In the arms race, faith in the new weapons, at any cost, had become a basis of Cold War strategy.

Considering Japan's strong military, political, and economic alliance with the Western Bloc, the Japanese scientists and physicians who chose to do research on the effects of fallout on humans and the environment were taking a risk. Although H-bombs were truly dirty bombs, the U.S. and other possessor nations sought to play down the potential dangers not only in the media and national discourses, but also by demonizing scientists who sought to study the effects (without official sanction), as well as those who challenged the development of thermonuclear weapons (as the case of Robert Oppenheimer demonstrates). This denial came from the very top: Atomic Energy Commission chief Lewis Strauss initially denied that the crew members' peeling skin and other symptoms had anything to do with U.S. testing. When Japanese doctors asked the U.S. government about the make-up of the Bravo bomb so they could better treat the ailing crew members, the U.S. rebuffed them and doubted their motives.

Significantly, less than a decade earlier, scientists and doctors in Hiroshima and Nagasaki had found themselves facing an ethical dilemma related to the U.S. Atomic Bomb Casualty Commission (ABCC), formed to study the effects of the Hiroshima and Nagasaki bombs. The U.S. government authorized the ABCC to gather data about the *hibakusha* (or A-bomb survivors), but not to treat them. In other words, the doctors and scientists who examined *hibakusha* were conducting research for nuclear-weapon development. From the mid-1940s, then, Japanese scientists took the lead in conducting research independent of the ABCC for humanitarian reasons, so they could develop methods of treating radiation disease.

Not surprisingly, at the time of the Bikini Incident in 1954, newspapers featured many letters to the editor expressing resentment that the U.S. seemed willing to use Japanese people as test subjects or guinea pigs not once, not twice (in Hiroshima and Nagasaki), but now, with the Bikini Incident, three times. A 1959 feature film about the Bikini Incident directed by Shindō Kaneto shows the Lucky Dragon crew members in their hospital ward refusing to be examined by U.S. doctors because they do not want to be sources of data that might contribute to H-bomb development. Similarly, crew member Mr. Ōishi reported that he stopped going to annual physicals in the early 1980s, when he learned more about the planned uses of the data "for future H-bomb and nuclear energy plant accident survivors."[20]

In the aftermath of the Bikini Incident, the anti-nuclear movement had extraordinary breadth. A huge number of ordinary citizens who gladly added their names to the Stockholm Appeal, the anti-nuclear petition campaign that had many ties to communist groups in Europe. Iconic images that came out of this protest include the large-scale paintings by the well-known painters Maruki Iri and Toshi (1955), who emphasized social issues in their post-1945 art.[21]

Restoring the Lucky Dragon

At the time of the Bikini Incident, media focus on the intrusion of nuclear weapons on daily life not only broadened the movement hugely by mobilizing literally millions of people who had not been involved in oppositional movements before, but also helped to forge a unified voice in the movement. For a while in the mid-1950s, at least, the divisions between socialist and communist, progressive and apolitical seemed to vanish. However, during the 1960s and 1970s, the continuing Cold War ideological contest once again exposed real ideological differences. How to find a common cause at a time when Vietnam had so illuminated the critique of U.S. "Imperialism?" What is more, the arms race had not come to an end with the test ban treaty in the early 1960s, it had only gone underground.

Domestically, the Japan Socialist Party especially, but also the Japan Communist Party, had grown in influence, at a time when the state and ruling Liberal Democratic Party (LDP) had repeatedly committed itself forcefully (and against pubic opinion) to renewals of the U.S.–Japan Security Treaty (AMPO). From the 1960s, high economic growth was in full swing. In such an atmosphere, the Lucky Dragon boat itself, after it cooled down, was abandoned and destined to be sold as scrap.

Even as the nation was increasingly swept up in the abundance that the economic miracle brought, the news of this plan to scuttle the Lucky Dragon led to meetings of a group of activists and former crew members, who expressed their determination to save the ship. Initially, one impetus behind the preservation movement was the idea that the ship would help to reunify the various constituencies that shared anti-nuclear sentiment, and reinvigorate the movement. A member of the planning committee recalls, "Given the long-standing divisions in the anti-nuclear movement, we saw the project of restoring the boat as central to uniting forces, bringing people with a common cause together again. We also recognized the noteworthy efforts of a network of scientists such as Miyake Yasuo, who have long devoted themselves to researching and speaking out about nuclear issues ... These were people of conscience, notable for their opposition to issues such as nuclear submarines in Japanese ports and the radiological pollution at Sasebo U.S. naval base."[22]

The goal of restoring and exhibiting the Lucky Dragon would be expensive and controversial. The Lucky Dragon advocates needed to build a coalition of groups that had been engaged in ideological battle for decades. The support of then Governor (Mayor) of Tokyo, Minobe Ryokichi, was also key to the success of the project. It was under the administration of this socialist mayor that the boat was saved; the municipal government allocated funds for the "eternal preservation" of the Lucky Dragon.

It took until 1976 and the efforts of many people to restore the Lucky Dragon and build a museum (*tenjikan*, or exhibit hall). A modest place, the museum nonetheless became a important focal point for the anti-nuclear movement for the remaining decade and a half of the Cold War, and, since nuclear weapons are still with us, remains so today. Conservative Tokyo governors, such as the long-lived Ishihara Shintarō, have maintained the exhibit hall, but with a budget that allows for a paid staff of one, and just enough to keep the lights on and the water in the restrooms running. A dedicated group of volunteers contribute generously of their time and energy.

Carpenters and scientists stabilized the decaying wood and loosening joints of the Lucky Dragon. The architect charged with protecting the boat forever took his assignment seriously, designing a maintenance-free glass-and-steel structure that enclosed the ship much like a clamshell. The space inside creates an intimate sense of contact with the boat, as one walks around the hull, touch the flaking paint and the wood. The Lucky Dragon Exhibition Hall is situated only a short walk from Tokyo Bay. A visitor finds two memorials in the grounds. One is for Mr. Kuboyama, the crew member who died, inscribed with the words "May I be the last person to die by an H-bomb." The other is the tuna mound or *maguro-zuka*.

Creating local knowledge

Remarkably, this small museum has stayed alive.[23] The hall itself functions as an educational and historical museum, and as a focal point for anti-nuclear activism both domestically and transnationally. In this sense, the Lucky Dragon museum has much in common with the numerous "peace museums" in Japan (not war museums or history museums, as are common in the U.S.). This genre of peace museum conventionally displays texts, artifacts, and images, and does programming related to some significant local history (such as Hiroshima or Nagasaki bombing, the Osaka fire bombing). The aim is to educate visitors about history, but also to inspire a desire for "peace" (now divorced from the 1950s anti-communist negative connotations). Some museums, such as the Ritsumeikan Peace Museum in Kyoto, define peace not as the "absence of conflict" or nuclear abolition alone, but also address issues of social justice and the environment.[24]

The Lucky Dragon museum presents the history of the boat and the nuclear arms race with the stated aim of providing "lessons for humanity" (nuclear weapons should be abolished). On one level, then, it delivers a similar message to those which peace museums in Hiroshima and Nagasaki emphasize in their effort to avoid political strife. But perhaps because it is out of the limelight, so close to the streets, and waterways, and not in a "City of Peace," the Lucky Dragon museum succeeds in its mission of constructing knowledge about nuclear weapons. Whether visitors experience ethical transformation as a result of visiting is not within the scope of this article. From its inception, though, despite its modest budget and staff, the hall has created ways to educate many publics about nukes, which is challenging, considering how unfathomably lethal, yet simultaneously abstract, how remote from daily lives, the bombs are. Nukes have, since their inception in the Cold War, been normally the business of nuclear strategists, heads of state, ministers of war, the military-industrial complex, infinitely complex computers, rocket scientists, propagandists. The remoteness of nuclear weapons encourages amnesia about the problems common to peaceful nuclear technologies such as radioactive waste.

This small hall with its wooden fishing boats and historical exhibits makes the bomb more accessible on a human level, for the Japanese and visitors from abroad. From the museum's inception, the people involved in this project conceived of it in dynamic interaction with its community of visitors. As soon as the boat had been pulled up onto land, the committee sponsored events such as a "renaming ceremony" (the Government of Japan had changed the boat's name to hide the shame), and Lucky Dragon Clean-Up Day. The volunteers sought ways to attract the public. School groups frequently visit so they can see the boat and look at the exhibit. As John Dower notes, artifacts don't speak for themselves, so the volunteer storytellers who bring the history alive are particularly important. Among the volunteers is Ōishi Matashichi, who speaks to groups in the space next to the boat, but also goes out to classrooms all over the Tokyo area. In addition, school children can participate in hands-on projects, musical concerts, and films, all in this small space around the boat.

Among the many dedicated volunteers, Mr. Ōishi is the sole surviving crew member of the Lucky Dragon who will talk about his experiences in public. He regards himself not as a political activist but as a "witness," as someone who must tell his story. He uses the authority derived from his experience of witnessing Bravo. The Lucky Dragon experience radicalized him—the complex power dynamic between the Japanese government and the U.S., widespread denial about the dangers of radiation, resentment by others in the fishing industry because only the Lucky Dragon was compensated. From the point of view of many in Hiroshima, the Lucky Dragon museum and Mr. Ōishi have a clear political agenda, linked with the Left. It took twenty years after the Cold War, but the port of Yaizu, where the boat sailed from in 1954, finally recognized the value and accomplishments of the Lucky Dragon museum and its most dedicated volunteers.[25]

The museum also mounts exhibits around the hull of the boat, aimed at capturing diverse audiences: exhibits of contemporary international artists on the theme of war, illustrations of a children's book about the Battle of Okinawa by one of the best-known anime filmmakers. An unexpectedly successful exhibit showed traditional carpentry methods and tools, since the Lucky Dragon is the last remaining example of early postwar wooden fishing boats that were made with the same techniques used in temples and shrines. This exhibit was conceived as a means of bringing in visitors who normally may not be interested in the political and historical content of the museum.

A powerful means of protest and engagement took the form of creating local knowledge through the preservation of the boat, the museum, scientific research, and dissemination, despite the political efforts to marginalize and silence. Such programming would later be described as *jimotogaku* (community study, field work), as advanced by Yoshimoto Tetsuro in Minamata. Throughout Japan, the goal of community development or revitalization through local awareness and study, and building a "sustainable lifestyle" in local communities, is based on local study, knowledge, decision making about lifestyle, and local development.

The museum has invited *hibakusha* from the Marshall Islands, and has visited them. Part of the exhibit shows *hibakusha* from Nevada, Central Asia, Chernobyl, people exposed to radioactive fallout not by an enemy but by their own state. The bomb was an integral part of the Cold War, and its status in our age remains up in the air.

The tuna mound after Fukushima

After the 11 March 2011 Fukushima nuclear disaster caused by the giant earthquake and tsunami, the Lucky Dragon museum attracted great interest. The spring exhibit around the base of the boat featured newspaper clippings from the time of the Bikini Incident, showing the extremely high level of media attention to radioactivity and nuclear testing at the time. The museum itself was a reminder of the existence of extensive research about massive radiation releases, and the dangers of nuclear technologies that had gone unheeded since the mid-1950s, and during the decades when nuclear reactors became one of the main prongs of Japanese energy policy.

The Fukushima disaster prompted much soul searching on the part of citizens throughout Japan about why the country had accepted nuclear energy so easily, given the lessons presented by the 1945 atomic bombings and the mid-1950s Bikini Incident, and subsequent nuclear energy-plant accidents that were reported in the media. From the 1953 Eisenhower Atoms for Peace talk, the U.S. and Japanese governments collaborated in generating an "atoms for peace"-based propaganda campaign in Japan in order to promote acceptance of nuclear energy. As in America and other parts of the world, this re-education campaign sought to disconnect nuclear technologies that generate power from those that are part of military weapons. This extremely effective media and educational campaign resulted in widespread acceptance of nuclear energy, but for decades, protest against construction of nuclear plants by local communities continued, partly out of fears of safety on the part of neighbors. In addition, Cold War ideological tensions were in evidence in the involvement of leftist labor unions and leftist protest groups in the anti-nuclear power protest. The 1982 book *Anti-Nuclear Energy Movement: Our Struggle Against The Chûgoku Power Electric Power Company*, written by labor union members in the Hiroshima region, is but one piece of evidence of this struggle. The unions objected not only to the dangers of nuclear power and the impossibility of solving the issue of nuclear waste, but also to the structures of monopoly capitalism that enabled the suppression of workers' safety and welfare.[26]

From summer, 2011, the Lucky Dragon museum planned a series of programs about nuclear energy that included a well-attended film series of pro- and anti-nuclear energy documentaries from the 1960s and 1970s. It also brought in speakers such as physicist and anti-nuclear activist and educator Anzai Ikuro. One of the most widely publicized events was a conversation between Mr. Ôishi and Nobel Prize-winning novelist Ôe Kenzaburô on the deck of the Lucky Dragon, which was also featured on NHK television.

In this way, dynamics of the Cold War ideological struggles, as well as the nuclear arms race, were very much alive on the local level in Japan. The legacies of the arms race and Cold War notions of progress are still in evidence decades after the superpower rivalry ended.

Notes

1 The author thanks the staff and volunteers at the Museun, Kozawa Setsuko, Steven Leeper, and Tashiro Akira.
2 Carol Cohn, "Slick 'ems, Click 'ems, Christmas Trees, and Cookie Cutters: Nuclear Language," *Bulletin of the Atomic Scientists* (June 1987): 17–24.
3 The Three Non-Nuclear Principles, adopted by the Japanese Diet in 1971, articulate Japan's "policy of not possessing, not producing and not permitting the introduction of nuclear weapons into Japan." http://www.mofa.go.jp/policy/un/disarmament/nnp/index.html.
In his 1974 Nobel Prize for Peace speech, Satō highlighted the link between these principles and Article 9 of the postwar Japanese Constitution, by which Japan renounced the right to wage offensive war. http://www.nobelprize.org/nobel_prizes/peace/laureates/1974/sato-lecture.html.

4 In this chapter, Japanese names are given in Japanese name order, with the family name first, followed by the given name.
5 Ōishi, Matashichi, *Bikini jiken no shinjitsu* (Tokyo: Misuzu Shobō, 2003), 136–37.
6 Ōishi, *Bikini jiken no shinjitsu*, 137.
7 Dower, "The Bombed," *Diplomatic History* 19 (1995): 275–95.
8 Dower, 275.
9 "The Russell-Einstein Manifesto," 9 July 1955. http://www.pugwash.org/about/manifesto.htm. Accessed on August 16, 2011.
10 Kawasaki, *Daigo fukuryū maru: Present-day Meaning of the Bikini Incident* (Tokyo: Daigo Fukuryu Maru Foundation, 2008), 24.
11 "Russell-Einstein Manifesto."
12 Kawasaki, *Daigo fukuryū maru*, 21.
13 L.D. Hamilton. "Fallout and Countermeasures," in *Bulletin of Atomic Scientists* 19, No. 7 (September, 1963): 36–40. P. 38: "It is confusing that there is today no clear idea of the point at which countermeasures should actually be taken (rather than merely considered)."
14 Kawasaki, *Daigo fukuryū maru*, 22.
15 Kada Yukiko, et al. "From *Kogai* to *Kankyo Mondai*: Nature, Development, and Social Conflict in Japan," in *Forging Environmentalism: Justice, Livelihood, and Contested Environments*, ed. Joanne R. Bauer (Armonk NY: M.E. Sharpe, 2006): 109–82.
16 "The Russell-Einstein Manifesto."
17 Hasegawa, Tsuyoshi, ed. *The Cold War in East Asia 1945–1991* (Washington DC: Woodrow Wilson Center Press, 2011), 3.
18 Hasegawa, 1.
19 Hasegawa, 3.
20 Kozawa, S. *Daigo fukuryū maru kara "3–11" go e: Hibakusha Ōishi Matashichi no tabiji* (Tokyo: Iwanami Shoten, 2011), 20–21.
21 See John Dower and John Junkerman, *The Hiroshima Murals: The Art of Iri Maruki and Toshi Maruki* (New York: Kodansha International, 1985) and Charlotte Eubanks, "The Mirror of Memory: Constructions of Hell in the Marukis' Nuclear Murals," *PMLA* 124, No. 5 (2009): 614–31.
22 Kawasaki, *Daigo fukuryu maru*, 39.
23 Lucky Dragon Exhibition Hall website: http://d5f.org/top.htm.
24 Ritsumeikan Peace Museum, http://www.ritsumei.ac.jp/mng/er/wp-museum/english/index.html. Akiko Takenaka and Laura Hein compare peace museums and war museums in their "Exhibiting World War II in Japan and the United States," *The Asia-Pacific Journal*, http://www.japanfocus.org/-Laura-Hein/2477.
25 An English translation of Mr. Ōishi's book about the Bikini Incident was published by the University of Hawaii Press. The translation was done by Richard Minear, Emeritus Professor of History at University of Massachusetts Amherst.
26 Gogatsusha Editorial Board, ed., *Hangenpatsu rōdō; undō: densan Chūgoku no tatakai* (Tokyo: Gogatsusha, 1982).

Selected bibliography

Barker, H. *Bravo for the Marshallese: Regaining Control in a Post-Nuclear, Post-Colonial World.* Belmont, CA: Wadsworth Publishing, 2003.
Cohn, Carol. "Slick 'ems, Click 'ems, Christmas Trees, and Cookie Cutters: Nuclear Language and How We Learned to Pat the Bomb." *Bulletin of the Atomic Scientists* (1987): 17–24.
Daigo fukuryû maru. DVD. Directed by S. Kaneto. Tokyo: Asmik, 1959.

Hasegawa, Tsuyoshi, ed. *The Cold War in East Asia 1945–1991*. Washington DC: Woodrow Wilson Center Press, 2011.

Kada, Yukiko, Tanaka Shigeru, Aoyagi-Usui Midori, Arakaki Tazusa, Watanabe Shinichi and Steven Hoffman. "From *Kogai* to *Kankyo Mondai:* Nature, Development, and Social Conflict in Japan." In *Forging Environmentalism: Justice, Livelihood, and Contested Environments*, edited by Joanne R. Bauer, 109–39. Armonk NY: M.E. Sharpe, 2006.

Kawasaki, S. *Daigo fukuryū maru: Present-day Meaning of the Bikini Incident*. Tokyo: Daigo Fukuryū Maru Foundation, 2008.

Kozawa, S. *Daigo fukuryū maru kara "3–11" go e: Hibakusha Ōishi Matashichi no tabiji*. Tokyo: Iwanami Shoten, 2011.

Lapp, Ralph E. *The Voyage of the* Lucky Dragon. New York: Harper & Brothers, 1958.

Ōishi, Matashichi. *Bikini jiken no shinjitsu*. Tokyo: Misuzu Shobô, 2003.

——*Kore dake wa tsutaete okitai: Bikini jiken no omote to ura*. Kyoto: Kamogawa shoten, 2007.

——*Shi no hai o seotte*. Tokyo: Shinchōsha, 1991.

——*The Day the Sun Rose in the West: Bikini, the* Lucky Dragon*, and I*. Trans. Richard H. Minear. Honolulu: University of Hawai'i Press, 2011.

Toyosaki, H. *Suibaku buraboo: 3gatsu tsuitachi Bikini kansho-Daigo fukuryûmaru*. Tokyo: Kusanone Shuppankai, 2004.

Yoshimoto, T. *Jimotogaku o hajimeyō*. Iwanami Junia shinsho. Tokyo: Iwanami Shoten, 2008.

——*Watashi no jimotogaku: Minamata kara no husshin*. Tokyo: NEC Kurietibu, 1995.

2 The Cold War, Indonesian women and the global anti-imperialist movement, 1946–65[1]

Katharine E. McGregor

In 1960 the world's largest women's organization, the Women's International Democratic Federation (WIDF), held a bureau meeting in Jakarta, the capital city of Indonesia. In a rather gushing account a journalist for the women's newspaper *Api Kartini* (Kartini's Flame), named after Indonesia's first feminist, wrote:

> Women of different skin colours declared in several languages, feelings of love and affection towards one another and towards children, feelings of respect and value as well as the support for the struggle of people in general and for the struggle of Indonesian women; this was in brief the atmosphere of the WIDF bureau meeting.[2]

The meeting, like other WIDF meetings and congresses, brought women of diverse national backgrounds together to discuss global issues affecting both women and children. It resulted in a resolution to further support the struggle of the women of Asia and Africa, recognizing the many achievements of women in these continents, but also the many challenges wrought by the remnants of both colonialism and feudalism, as well as the dangers the Cold War posed to the achievement of independence. That this WIDF meeting was held in Jakarta signaled both the growing prominence of Indonesia in the anti-imperialist movement by the early 1960s and the impressive achievements of the WIDF member organization, the Indonesian Women's Movement (Gerakan Wanita Indonesia–Gerwani).

Gerwani experienced a rapid growth in membership from the late 1950s until 1965 as a result of the organization's proactive efforts to improve the lives of female peasants and workers. Women in the organization focused specifically on issues important to poorer women, such as raising literacy, campaigning for equal wages on the plantations, offering practical assistance in the form of credit co-operatives and childcare. They also continued to protest against imperialism in Indonesia in the form of continuing foreign intervention, foreign dominance of the economy and the failure of the Dutch to relinquish the territory of Western New Guinea. Due largely to its efforts to help Indonesian women, Gerwani experienced rapid growth, from 100,000 members in 1957, to 700,000 in 1960, to 1.5 million only three years later, with branches in every province of Indonesia and auxiliary branches in 40 percent of the villages.[3] From 1965 onward Gerwani women were violently attacked in a wide-scale repression of the Indonesian left. Half a million people were murdered by the army and civilian anti-communists and hundreds of thousands were imprisoned without trial.

Since the pioneering work of Dutch scholar Saskia Wieringa, which examined the history of Gerwani and its violent demise,[4] there have been an increasing number of studies on Gerwani women focusing mostly on the military repression these women suffered.[5] Apart from these works there are passing references to the organization in studies of the broader Indonesian women's movement,[6] but the connection between Gerwani and the WIDF has not yet been explored in detail. This is in part attributable to the tendency to focus only on national histories, but also to the destruction of the Indonesian left and the emphasis on survivors of the political violence as victims without political histories.[7] In fact the WIDF and Gerwani were closely linked and shared many agendas in addition to Gerwani's devotion to nationalist causes.

In this chapter I consider how the developments of the Cold War united diverse peoples from across the globe in opposition to the following: continuing interference in the affairs of sovereign nations, the persistence of colonialism, economic imperialism, the rise of militarism, an escalating arms race and nuclear testing. I focus in particular on the developing relationship, shared rhetoric and activism of women in the transnational organization, the WIDF, and in Gerwani. I argue that the WIDF assisted Gerwani in its domestic campaigns and provided an important compass for the organization. Furthermore, Gerwani made political use of its link to the WIDF as an international organization and increased its domestic legitimacy as a result. Gerwani used the WIDF to draw attention to the ongoing impact of anti-imperialism and the Cold War in Indonesia, but by the mid-1960s tensions developed over how much priority should be placed on peace in the context of ongoing imperialist struggles.

Gerwani and the WIDF: building the relationship, 1946–55

The WIDF was established in Paris in late November 1945 at the first World Congress of Women. The congress was attended by over 800 women from 41 different countries, including a large contingent from Eastern Europe, and also from England, China, India, the United States, the Soviet Union, Spain, Finland, Poland, Greece, Yugoslavia, Hungary and Czechoslovakia. The horrors of World War II had united many people in the belief that the postwar period offered an important opportunity for establishing a new set of core human values. In this context the women who founded the WIDF espoused four key principles: anti-fascism, lasting peace, women's rights and better conditions for children.[8] The founders of the

WIDF were passionate supporters of these causes as a result of their involvement in armed resistance against Nazism and fascism in Europe and Asia. Some had survived prison camps or lost husbands and children in the war.[9] In contrast to earlier transnational women's organizations that had perpetuated colonialism,[10] the WIDF emphasized national self-determination and a commitment to ending racism worldwide.

The Indonesian Women's Congress (Kowani), a nationalist organization which represented all Indonesian women's organizations, requested to become a member of the WIDF in the year of its creation, 1946, largely because of the federation's support for ending colonialism.[11] Beginning in 1945, Indonesians were forced to engage in a struggle for independence from Dutch rule. In 1947, after receiving a report from Kowani on renewed Dutch aggression against the Republic, the WIDF called on all member organizations to protest against this "violation to the peace of Indonesia."[12]

Despite this support, after only three years as a member organization, Kowani withdrew its membership from the WIDF in 1949 and chose instead to be only a contact organization. The decision was due to the objections of Muslim women organizations in Kowani to the WIDF's socialist orientation.[13] By 1949 the United States government had categorized the WIDF, with its headquarters in East Berlin, as a Soviet front.[14]

The Movement for Politically Aware Women (Gerakan Wanita Sadar, Gerwis), which was socialist in orientation, took over membership of the WIDF beginning in 1949.[15] It is likely that the greatest appeal that the WIDF offered to Gerwis (later Gerwani) was its inclusive attitude, its opposition to imperialism and its continuing commitment to women's rights and the independence of nations. The WIDF had strong representation from socialist countries, but its leadership was quite diverse. In 1952 the Executive Committee of the WIDF, for example, included one representative each from Brazil, Bulgaria, Chile, China, Denmark, Spain, Finland, India, Indonesia, Mongolia, Sweden, Switzerland and Turkey, and multiple representatives from Denmark, the United States, France, Great Britain, Greece, Hungary, Iran, Italy, Norway, Poland, Romania, Czechoslovakia and the U.S.S.R.[16] The WIDF also projected an image of inclusion in its major publication, *Women of the Whole World*, which was published in English, German, French, Russian, Japanese and Spanish.[17] The WIDF supported the decolonization of Asian, African and South American countries and espoused a commitment to "left feminism," meaning it critiqued the sources of women's oppression, but also wider structures of power that underpinned repression.[18] This matched the vision of the women of Gerwis, many of whom had fought in or supported the independence struggle at the same time that they had fought for women's rights.[19]

At the time Gerwis took over Kowani's affiliation with the WIDF, the membership was under severe pressure. Following the 1948 Madiun Uprising, which the Republic accused the Indonesian Communist Party (Partai Komunis Indonesia, PKI) of master minding, the Republic led a major crackdown on all leftists. Gerwis was never formally affiliated with the Communist Party, but it followed the party line on many issues. It took the Indonesian left several years to re-establish itself as a legitimate political force. In 1950 the WIDF published an anonymous update on the situation in Indonesia in its regular bulletin. The author, who possibly avoided using her real name for fear of repression, was most likely Darmini, who was serving as the first Gerwis representative on the WIDF Secretariat. The article claims that, following the Dutch and Japanese, the Americans were now also exploiting Indonesia: "The Rockefeller Corporation owns hundreds of oil wells here. More than a million acres of rubber plantations belong to American monopolists."[20] Her critique focuses on what she sees as excessive foreign investment in Indonesia and U.S. efforts to use Indonesia to support its involvement in the Korean War. From the 1920s the Dutch had granted American companies oil concessions, which were preserved following Indonesian independence.[21] In March 1950 the Republic signed an agreement to take over remaining Marshal Plan aid and to fulfil U.S. stockpiling demands, thereby cementing economic cooperation with the United States.[22] With the outbreak of the Korean War, Americans turned to Indonesia to fill the increased demand for oil and rubber.

Further critiquing the Republic's "American policies," the author noted that Indonesian policemen were being sent to the United States to learn repressive techniques. In August 1950 the Republic had signed an agreement with the United States for the provision of police training for Indonesians to improve law and order.[23] The article ended with the admonition that, despite this "period of reaction," Indonesians were resisting these moves and women were fighting for their rights, for peace and to prevent Indonesia from "becoming a base for foreign aggression."[24]

In 1951 and 1952 the Indonesian Communist Party and other left-oriented organizations like Gerwis were subject to further political repression under a government that leaned towards the United States. Prime Minister Sukiman Wirjosandjojo (April 1951–February 1952) from the conservative Islamic party Masyumi authorized anti-communist raids following strikes and small-scale disturbances throughout Indonesia. Around 15,000 people, including many PKI and labor union leaders were arrested.[25] Gerwis's first congress was held in Surabaya in 1951 under conditions of uncertainty and fear. Many branches of Gerwis were unable to send delegates to the congress because their members were in prison or feared further repression.[26]

In the context of continuing repression, Gerwis members were able to reach out to a sympathetic audience in the WIDF to convey the ongoing challenges they faced in their fight for women's rights and against imperialism. In 1952 *Women of the Whole World* printed an update, again most likely written by Darmini, in which she noted that the 1945 Constitution guaranteed equal rights for men and women; yet, since the signing of the 1949 Round Table Agreement and the increasing intervention of the United States in Indonesia, "equality exists only on paper."[27] The author described the Round Table

Agreements as "legaliz[ing] the exploitation of the country's wealth by foreign capital," claiming that a flood of foreign imports and capital had forced local businesses to close down. The terms of the transfer of Indonesian sovereignty in 1949, the Round Table Agreements, were extremely harsh for the Republic, including the responsibility to pay for most of the debts of the Netherlands Indies and the provision for the continuation of Dutch businesses in Indonesia.[28] Dutch dominance of the economy was overwhelming, with 60 percent of exports in 1950 produced by eight Dutch firms, of which 50 percent were controlled by four firms.[29] Both the PKI and Gerwani focused on the Round Table Agreements as a case of treachery by republican leaders, which had left the country in a "semi colonial and semi-feudal state."[30] Referencing the recent crackdowns on the Indonesian left, the author reported that the women of Gerwis had launched an appeal to all Indonesian women to reject anti-democratic legislation and war preparations.

In the years 1950 to 1953 the WIDF focused on achieving peace and curtailing militarism in the world. The outbreak of the Korean War in 1950 and the ongoing anti-colonial war in Vietnam received a lot of attention.[31] In 1951 the WIDF sponsored a women's commission to go to Korea to investigate war atrocities. In the resulting document, entitled *We Accuse*, the committee accused South Korean, American and United Nations allies of atrocities including the use of weapons such as napalm bombs, incendiaries, petrol bombs and time bombs banned by international conventions and called for those responsible to be tried for war crimes.[32] The rapid outbreak of the Korean War also prompted increased attention to peace. The WIDF vigorously supported the World Peace Council Congress held in Vienna in December of 1952. Following the WIDF's lead Gerwis sent three representatives, Umi Sardjono (Vice-Chair of Gerwis), Tam and Warsini, to attend this congress and delivered 17,711 Indonesian signatures in support of peace.[33]

Gerwis publicized the forthcoming 1953 WIDF World Congress of Women widely in Indonesia and sent five representatives to the congress in Copenhagen to join Darmini. During the congress, delegates from many countries emphasized the state of women's rights in each country, including those suffering imperial repression. In her address Dr. Andrea Andreen, a Swedish member of the International Scientists Commission who had recently returned from Korea, sent a special welcome to "our sisters from Korea, Vietnam and Malaya who are fighting alongside their peoples to expel the aggressors, to defend their right to life, national independence and peace," and encouraged all women to unite together and defend their rights "as mothers, workers and citizens" and for a world at peace.[34]

In her report to the congress Indonesian delegate Sumampouw-Lapian, president of the Women's Union of Minahasa, continued Gerwis's critique of the Round Table Agreement of 1949 and its ongoing consequences. She referred especially to the U.S. role in negotiating this agreement and persistent pressure to join the American side of the Cold War by means of the San

Francisco Agreement, negotiations concerning the Mutual Security Aid, the Technical Cooperation Act and the embargo against the People's Republic of China.[35] The San Francisco Agreement of September 1951, signed by Japan and 48 other nations, brought the U.S. occupation of Japan to an end, but at the same the United States used the agreement to attempt to co-opt new security partners to counter communism.[36] When the Sukiman cabinet signed this agreement the United States read this as a signal of a move toward an American alliance and hence escalated discussions about a potential security pact. The government had almost concluded an agreement under the Mutual Security Act to formalize U.S. technical, financial and military aid in return for fighting communism. In February 1952, when these negotiations were exposed, however, the Sukiman cabinet in its entirety stepped down, after being accused of compromising Indonesian sovereignty and neutrality.[37] The next Indonesian government, the Wilopo cabinet, reached an agreement in 1953 providing for only technical and economic aid, with military aid being on the basis of reimbursement, not a grant. The United States thus gave Indonesia a loan under the Technical Cooperation Administration (usually reserved for neutralist countries like Burma and India) and not under the Mutual Security Act.[38] The Sukiman government had also, to the pleasure of the United States, agreed to an embargo on trade with communist China. Gerwis representatives sought to expose these ongoing efforts to co-opt Indonesia at the congress.

By 1953, with the end of the Korean War, Indonesia experienced an economic downturn, owing to the cessation of American stockpiling of Indonesian raw materials and continuing high debt repayments to the Netherlands. Sumampouw-Lapian spoke of rising unemployment for women in factories, plantations and other sites of work. She believed many national enterprises were forced to close down "because they could not compete with imported goods, especially textiles, 75% of the textile industries in Indonesia are closed down, and 80% of these workers are women. They are still the first victims of dismissal."[39] She tied Indonesian poverty to liberal trade regulations. Further to this she reported that women's wages were only 80 percent of men's, regulations regarding maternity leave were not observed, there was chronic illness amongst workers and the state budget for health was only 3.5 percent whereas the military budget was 39 percent. She concludes her remarks by noting that "war preparations bring poverty and unemployment. High budgets for military expenditure take away health and education for children."[40] Sumampouw-Lapian mostly sought explanations outside of Indonesia for why it was still a poor country with inadequate rights for women, yet she also critiqued the Indonesian army. The army's budget was large because it remained a significant political force as a result of its role in the struggle against the Dutch and officers had resisted an attempt at army rationalization in 1952.[41] The themes in her report of economic exploitation, the developing Cold War and the detriments of high defense spending mirrored those of the broader Copenhagen congress.

The congress resulted in two documents entitled "Appeal to Women of the Whole World" and "Declaration of the Rights of Women," both of which also connected the Cold War to a curtailment of women's rights. The appeal demanded "an armistice be signed on a just basis and that the cessation of hostilities in Korea be followed by a just and lasting peace"; an end to the wars in progress in Vietnam and Malaya; a peaceful settlement of the German, Austrian and Japanese questions (a reference to the occupation and re-militarization of Japan and West Germany and the joint allied occupation of Austria); an end to colonial and foreign domination; support for people struggling for independence; and the equality of all races. The appeal called for a peace pact between the five great powers and tied this to the prosperity of people in a direct way: "such a pact will make possible a reduction of the enormous military expenditure which today is lowering the standard of living of peoples of many countries and seriously affecting the future of our children." It urged all women to call on their governments to ban "all weapons of mass destruction."[42] The appeal contained generalized messages, but also some very specific references to struggles evolving in the context of the Cold War and competition for spheres of influence, with an emphasis on critiquing the United States and European powers such as France and Britain and their attempts to resume colonization in the formerly occupied territories of Indochina and Malaya.

The second major document of the congress was the Declaration of the Rights of Women, which included a demand from the women of the 70 countries who participated for a radical change and improvement in the political and legal position of women in these countries, including equal pay for equal work; women's right to work; access to childcare; and rights to political representation.[43] The declaration stated: "In the midst of war preparations, when the economic conditions of the workers are deteriorating and the offensive against democratic rights and liberties is being intensified, women's lives are becoming still more difficult."[44] The WIDF continually linked war with the curtailment of women's and children's rights.

The declaration and the appeal provided a validation of many of the causes Gerwis had already begun to struggle for and assisted the organization in its efforts to lobby the government as well as Indonesian women to support both women's rights and peace. In her contribution to the 1954 WIDF executive meeting Gerwis representative Darmini detailed how Gerwis had spread news of the declaration in public meetings and provincial congresses held on the different islands of Indonesia and via special publications for Gerwis branches. Continuing the theme of the fight against American imperialism in Indonesia, she noted the Republic had lifted the embargo on rubber trade with China endorsed by the United States. She reported that Indonesian women had held a meeting to express solidarity with Vietnam and not only were preparing to participate in the January 1954 Peace Congress but were campaigning "to oppose the military treaties with America, and the remilitarization of Japan."[45] Gerwis women were thus connecting Indonesian struggles with those of women around the world and at the same time supporting those struggles. In the early 1950s they were united with the WIDF on the need to oppose imperialism and "war preparations."

In 1954 Gerwis hosted its second national congress in more favourable conditions following the rise of a new coalition government including both Masyumi and the Indonesian National party, with which the Indonesian Communist party had begun a rapprochement. In the 1954 congress Gerwis changed its name to Gerwani (Gerakan Wanita Indonesia) to reflect a broadening of the organization's reach.[46] The WIDF sent its vice-president, Monica Felton, from Britain to the congress. She reported to WIDF members on the challenges Indonesian women faced in providing sufficient food for their children, achieving peace, security, democratic rights and marriage rights.[47] Reflecting on her visit, she stated that she felt "accepted not as a stranger from the other side of the world, but as a sister, as a member of the great family of women, who are striving to build a better life for all women everywhere."[48] She expressed admiration for the courage and achievements of Gerwani members.

Bandung and continuing opposition to Dutch colonialism and American intervention, 1955–60

In 1955 Indonesia received a major boost in prestige when President Sukarno hosted the Asia–Africa Conference in Bandung. Sukarno championed the idea that Indonesia was at the helm of a global struggle against all forms of colonialism and imperialism. The conference resulted in an agreement to respect human rights, to continue to challenge colonialism, to work toward disarmament, including a ban of the manufacture and use of atomic and thermonuclear weapons, to oppose tests of these weapons and to adopt a neutral position in the Cold War in the interests of peaceful co-existence.[49] *Women of the Whole World* published the speech of Gerwani Vice-President Suharti on Bandung, which she delivered to the fifth council meeting of the WIDF in Geneva.[50] Suharti highlighted the commitment to peace outlined at Bandung and the role of Indonesian women in strengthening Indonesian independence and peace efforts. She praised the government's rejection of SEATO (the Southeast Asian Treaty Organization), a regional anti-communist security treaty initiated by the United States and signed by Thailand, Pakistan, the Philippines, Australia and New Zealand in the context of the escalating war in Vietnam. She lamented the high mortality rate of Indonesian children and the lack of opportunities they had, due to poverty. Suharti tied their poverty to the inadequate wages received by parents as a result of the continuing foreign ownership of plantations and efforts by these owners to avoid observing the labor laws, owing to the contractual nature of plantation work.[51] Indonesia had in fact passed progressive labor laws in 1951, but there were difficulties enforcing them.[52] Building on a key theme at the Bandung conference Suharti drew attention to ongoing colonialism in Indonesia, with the continuing Dutch occupation of Western New Guinea.

The Netherlands had agreed in the Round Table Agreement to resolve the future of the territory together with the Republic by the end of 1950. When the Dutch incorporated Western New Guinea into the Netherlands in 1952, the Republic took the dispute to the United Nations. After three years and no progress Indonesia abrogated the Round Table agreements in 1956 and ceased further payment of debts to the Netherlands. A year later Indonesia withdrew the case from the United Nations and nationalized all Dutch assets in Indonesia. Suwarti Bintang Suradi, who served on the WIDF secretariat in Berlin, explained in *Women of the Whole World* that Western New Guinea made up about 20 percent of the territory of the former possession and that Indonesians were struggling to reunite their country.[53] She reasoned that Indonesia had tried to settle the issue peacefully, but with no success, due to a lack of Dutch cooperation.

In many submissions to the WIDF Indonesian women tried to connect the causes of Indonesian women with developments worldwide. Mudigdo, Vice-President of Gerwani, provided an update on Indonesia at the fourth WIDF Congress in Vienna in June 1958. She began by sending warm greetings from the 633,740 Gerwani members and acknowledged the vital role of the WIDF for the last 12 years and, in particular, the significance of the declaration of the rights of women. She noted that the timing of the 1958 congress was critical because of the "dangerous moment in international affairs when peace is threatened."[54] She welcomed the steps of the Soviet Union, which had resolved to terminate atomic and hydrogen-bomb testing unilaterally, and she urged the United States and Britain to follow this move. She wrote:

> The majority of men and women in the world, including those of Asia and Africa, desire peaceful coexistence, as laid down in the principles of the Bandung conference. But the instigators of war are still indulging in aggressive acts, as they did in Egypt during the Suez Canal conflict, and in Algeria, where the people are fighting for their liberation and where the heroine, Djamila Bouhired, has become the symbol of their fight. The same pattern has been followed in other African countries and also in Indonesia too, where they are interfering in our internal affairs.[55]

Mudigdo demonstrated an acute awareness of world affairs and how the Cold War and imperialism were continuing to affect the countries of Asia and Africa. Following Egypt's nationalization of the Suez Canal in 1956, British, French and Israeli troops attempted unsuccessfully to invade Egypt. The Algerian struggle for independence from the French was also intensifying in the same period. Mudigdo referenced the discovery of foreign support for the PRRI (Pemerintah Revolusioner Republik Indonesia, Revolutionary Government of the Republic of Indonesia), noting that "the intervention of the USA, the Philippines and Taiwan cannot be covered up."[56] The rebellion, led by local Sumatran commanders, proclaimed a counter-government in Bukitinggi Sumatra in February 1958. The CIA provided weapons, bomber planes, 15 pilots and air drops of supplies to the rebels and, as Mudigdo noted, Taiwan and the Philippines also assisted. A month before the Vienna Congress the Indonesian government had exposed the CIA's role in the rebellion following the capture of an American bomber pilot, Allen Pope.[57]

Gerwani also reported to the WIDF on how women had worked "shoulder to shoulder with men" to directly oppose foreign intervention in Indonesia. Throughout the operation to suppress the PRRI they had collected and delivered supplies and set up public kitchens to feed the armed forces and others who were fighting the rebels. In West Sumatra they had demonstrated against rebel groups and some women had been shot, burnt alive or abused by the rebels in carrying out this work.[58] In this report Gerwani highlighted their bravery and heroism, projecting an image of what Wieringa has described as "militant motherhood."[59]

In 1959, in light of regional rebellions and ongoing disputes in the government, President Sukarno introduced a new political system of "Guided Democracy" to replace parliamentary democracy. In the new political system there would be no elections and the 1945 Constitution, which emphasized presidential power, was reintroduced. Sukarno moved to center stage in national politics and declared that Indonesia was now returning to "the rails of the revolution."[60] During this period anti-imperialist sentiment became even more pronounced and Gerwani continued to thrive with the support of Sukarno.

In recognition of Gerwani's growing membership the WIDF hosted its 1960 council meeting in Jakarta. Opening the meeting, Marie Pritt, Vice-President of the WIDF and head of the British Women's Council, stated: "Where there is friendship there is understanding and tolerance. And with this the danger of war will be lost."[61] The meeting was attended by women from 13 countries and resulted in three resolutions: a letter to the four powers that were meeting, requesting an end to the testing of all nuclear weapons and steps toward total disarmament; a statement of protest against the French tests in the Sahara; and a resolution recognizing the struggles of the women of Asia and Africa.[62] Mrs. Tambunan also attended the meeting as the representative of Kowani's 28 member organizations and wished the meeting success. With the leftward shift in Indonesian politics from 1959 onward the causes for which the WIDF stood were increasingly relevant for all Indonesian women.

Anti-imperialism, militarism and peace, 1960–65

In 1960 the crisis over Western New Guinea escalated when the Dutch sent a warship (the *Karel Doorman*) to the disputed territory. In this context Gerwani drew on its links with the WIDF to try to internationalize the Indonesian protest and praised the women of several countries who had protested in support of Indonesia.[63] The WIDF issued a formal statement of protest:

We condemn these maneuvers which constitute an aggressive provocation towards the people of Indonesia and which threaten peace in Southeast Asia. We are certain that the continuous struggle of the people of Indonesia will result in respect for their territorial integrity and create greater possibilities for progress and development in their homeland and for better lives for their children. We hope this statement will be forwarded by Indonesian women, who actively support women around the world.[64]

Replicating their transnational support for Indonesia in the 1940s,[65] the Dutch Women's Movement (Nederlands Vrouwen Beweging) also sent a letter of protest to the Dutch parliament and cabinet, reminding them of the Dutch police actions in the 1940s in which many young Dutch men died. They organized petitions in the Netherlands amongst hundreds of workers.[66] The WIDF thus firmly supported the Western New Guinea campaign and through its links with the WIDF Gerwani was able to rally increased support from member-country organizations.

Gerwani members continued to frame the issue of Western New Guinea (referred to also as West Irian and Irian Jaya) as an anti-imperialist struggle and to speak out against foreign aggression and the negative impacts of war and aggression, but there were increasing contradictions in their position. In 1961 it became clear that the Dutch were trying to prepare the territory for self-rule. In response, Sukarno formed the Supreme Command for the Liberation of West Irian (Trikora) and began small-scale military incursions into the territory. The campaign also resulted in a dramatic increase in military spending, reaching 75 percent of the state budget.[67] Despite earlier condemnation of high defense spending in Indonesia in the 1950s, Gerwani continued to fully back the campaign and by 1962 it was encouraging women to engage in military training to assist the campaign.[68] They did so at Sukarno's request, but also because they believed they would be granted more rights if they participated equally with men in this struggle.[69]

Meanwhile the WIDF continued to emphasize the message of peace in the context of continuing tests of weapons of mass destruction. In 1954 the United States tested a hydrogen bomb in the Bikini Atoll off the coast of Japan, which killed a Japanese fisherman and damaged marine life. Amidst ongoing fears in Japan about continuing contamination of food and the environment, Japanese women led a petition to ban the bomb. There were further French, Soviet and British tests in the late 1950s, which led the WIDF and member organizations to hold disarmament protests and write petitions stressing the choice the world faced concerning the preservation or destruction of life.[70] In 1961 the Soviet Union and the United States both broke the nuclear weapons testing ban. Despite this development the WIDF, which was accused by the United States of being a Soviet front organization, continued to protest against nuclear testing.

In 1962 the WIDF held the World Gathering of Women for Disarmament in Vienna. In her speech to the gathering, President of the WIDF Eugenie Cotton stressed how "the arms race had disastrous consequences in all aspects of social, economic, cultural and political life."[71] Connecting war with poverty, General Secretary of the Argentine Women's Union Fanny Edelman argued that disarmament would: "favour the national sovereignty and economic development of every people and would allow the defeat of the scourges of hunger, disease and ignorance."[72] Indonesian delegates Sunardi Surachman and S. Hanafi attended this meeting. They closely followed the discussions on the relationship between disarmament and struggles for national independence. *Api Kartini* reported that the Indonesian delegation's position was that all Indonesian women who love peace support disarmament, yet they were aware that

> imperialists with modern weapons are holding up the people's struggle for independence. In several of Indonesia's neighbouring countries like South Vietnam and Laos they are interfering and aggressive. Because of this we must be aware that alongside the struggle for disarmament for people already facing the aggressive actions of the imperialists there is no other way than to attack the imperialists. This is why also in this stage of the struggle to free Irian Jaya the people of Indonesia, in carrying about President Sukarno's Trikora, have already firmly ordered the Dutch to get out of Irian Jaya, with confrontation in all fields.[73]

This was a careful statement of Indonesia's position on how and why it was necessary to deal firmly with continuing imperialist threats. Sunardi noted that the Gerwani representative's speech to the WIDF was spirited by President Sukarno's words: "we love peace but we love independence more".[74] The Indonesian delegates gained support from the women of 18 countries for the struggle to free Western New Guinea in the form of a resolution signed by representatives of the women of Japan, India, Australia, the Netherlands, Vietnam, England, the Soviet Union, Mexico, El Salvador, Colombia, Ecuador, West Germany, Argentina, France, Cuba and China. The resolution stated that Western New Guinea was a part of Indonesia "such that the Dutch effort to hold on to that area with the help of other imperialists is a threat to peace in Southeast Asia and in the world." It encouraged all women to "conduct solidarity actions in support of the people of Indonesia in their struggle which is right and fair."[75] By October 1962, following pressure from the United States and then the United Nations, the Dutch handed Western New Guinea over to UN supervision for a year. The territory was transferred to Indonesia in May 1963. By this stage Indonesia had already commenced another anti-imperialist campaign.

From 1961 onward President Sukarno began to critique the formation of the new nation of Malaysia on the basis that this was a neo-imperialist project. The proposed nation of Malaysia comprised the Malay peninsula,

Singapore, Sabah and Sarawak. Sukarno objected to this formulation because he believed the people of Sabah and Sarawak were hostile to the proposal, as it favored the Malay sultans and allowed the continuation of extensive British economic interests in Malaysia and the retention of a naval base in Singapore.[76] Indonesia's campaign to oppose Malaysia escalated from 1962 onward and included largely unsuccessful armed incursions into Malaysia, attacks on British companies and the British embassy in Indonesia as well as attacks on American interests.

Confrontation was a campaign largely driven by Sukarno, but firmly backed by both the Indonesian Communist Party and Gerwani. The campaign gained the backing of several countries, including the Philippines, China and the Soviet Union.[77] Bradley Simpson notes that the Soviet Union backed Confrontation, at least publicly, because it was trying to enforce its continuing commitment to anti-imperialist struggles following Chinese criticism of the Soviet Union's stance on this issue.[78] Yet the WIDF took a different position on Confrontation, consistent with its prioritization of peace.

A major conflict related to Indonesia's aggressive approach to Confrontation erupted between the WIDF and Gerwani at the fourth WIDF congress in Moscow, held in June 1963. Gerwani women were involved in planning this congress and a large delegation of 30 women from a range of women's mass organizations attended. Umi Sardjono, who by this stage was a member of the WIDF secretariat, reported that at this congress the WIDF for the first time passed a resolution without unanimous support. In her view the resolution concerning women and peace "did not fulfill the aspirations of women who wanted to be free from the shackles of imperialism and feudalism."[79] The resolution for peace and universal disarmament advocated, amongst other factors, for the defense of world peace; an end to war preparations; withdrawal of troops stationed on foreign soil; respect for sovereignty and territorial integrity; and a peaceful solution to international differences by discussion and negotiation.[80] Because they disagreed with the resolution, Gerwani women abstained from voting, yet out of respect for the unity with the world struggle of women, Gerwani did not withdraw from the WIDF. They agreed to the congress resolution on national independence, but did not approve the congress's future programs. Gerwani representatives proposed that the leadership of the WIDF, including the Secretariat, should reflect the rise and development of the struggles of "revolutionary women from Asia and Africa by giving them positions to reflect the national organizations they represented which had real influence and militance in their countries."[81] This was a direct slight towards the WIDF for not having done enough to award more senior positions in the WIDF to Gerwani. By this stage only one Gerwani woman was on the executive as an ordinary member. Meanwhile ten vice-presidential positions and two honorary vice-presidential positions in the executive were held by women from Sweden, Spain, Argentina, France, Great Britain, India, Italy, Japan, Nigeria, the People's Republic of China, Czechoslovakia and the Soviet Union.[82]

In a Gerwani publication Umi Sardjono claimed that Gerwani's work was being compromised by "a revisionist attitude in the WIDF which was more feminist and passive than revolutionary democratic, anti-fascist and anti-imperialist."[83] She argued that the WIDF's position of neutrality was opposed to the principles according to which it was founded:

> They offer 1001 excuses not to talk about the anti-imperialist struggle and only emphasize the struggle of women for peace as an abstract principle, "peace for peace." It is not possible, however, to achieve peace as long as there is still imperialism, when it still results in the death of patriots of independence and when it is a source of the danger of war.[84]

This was a strong rebuke and it reflected the disappointment of Gerwani leaders that they had not been able to draw more support for Confrontation. In her notes on her life experiences Gerwani member Sulami, who served on the WIDF Secretariat, comments that there was increasing friction in the years 1963 and 1964 over how much priority should be placed on peace in contexts where imperialism was also a major concern.[85] As Saskia Wieringa has noted, the dispute reflected a larger split in the communist world between the Chinese and Soviet communists on the question of the use of armed force.[86] In this division Indonesia increasingly leaned toward China and its endorsement of the use of violence when necessary.

In 1964 Gerwani held a plenary meeting in Bandung establishing a work program, strengthening the united front to crush Malaysia and implementing land reform as a solution to the crisis of supplying basic necessities. In her report on the meeting Gerwani Chair Umi Sardjono declared, "We are proud because we are a mass organization of revolutionary women that is already large and which has an important role both inside Indonesia and overseas."[87] A section of her report is dedicated to "upholding the banner of emancipatory revolutionism" in the international women's movement. She claimed that the international anti-imperialist front was growing broader, as evidenced by the rise of the struggles of the people of Asia, Africa and Latin America to oppose imperialism:

> Southeast Asia is at the centre of contradictions in the world with the people there fighting to oppose several forms of imperialist, colonial and neo-colonial power and terror. As a women's movement located in Southeast Asia, Gerwani has a duty to escalate their activities in winning the people's revolution in Southeast Asia. All Gerwani members should make a rapid effort to understand these forward developments.[88]

She claimed that American aggression and terror were increasingly being exposed in countries such as Korea, Japan and South Vietnam and those in Latin America. She also reported on the Moscow conflict. There was a clear departure here from the previous praise the WIDF received from Gerwani.

In 1964 the WIDF was congratulating itself for the role women had played in pressuring the superpowers to sign the Moscow Limited Nuclear Test Ban Treaty and continuing to promote a strong anti-weapons and anti-military message. A feature article by Helga Dickel in *Women of the Whole World* profiled recent anti-nuclear marches around the world on International Women's Day and the continuing threat of nuclear weapons.[89] The article featured poster-like pages with anti-war messages featuring an image of a mushroom cloud alongside lists of those who had perished in the two world wars, including Hiroshima, and then those who had died in the Spanish Civil War (1936–39), the Korean War (1950–53), in Algeria (1954–62), Angola (1961) and South Vietnam (1954–63). Dickel replicates a quote from Victor Hugo from the first Peace Congress in Paris of 1844: "We must devote to peace the billions spent on war."[90] The article provides facts on the then current spending worldwide on military preparations and compares this to what could alternatively be bought with this money to improve or build schools, hospitals or the conversion of nuclear energy to electricity. Simple diagrams juxtapose, for example, an atomic submarine alongside a modern hospital. These comparisons conclude with reflections on continuing inequities in the world, such as 50 percent illiteracy worldwide, 60 percent of people being undernourished, that could be alleviated by an alternative allocation of resources and an appeal to continue the campaign for disarmament.[91] In defiance of the WIDF's position on the Moscow treaty, the Chair of Gerwani, Umi Sardjono, expressed reservations about the treaty in her 1964 report to Gerwani, noting that America had become increasingly aggressive and had conducted more than 21 nuclear tests underground after signing the treaty. It would have been better, in her view, if there had been a total ban on weapons and on all efforts to make, use and trial weapons, whereas the treaty had in fact permitted underground testing, such that it would be better if there was never any treaty.[92] Again reflecting contradictions in Gerwani's position and the PKI's move toward China, in the same year a Gerwani-sponsored conference for housewives congratulated the Chinese government on its first nuclear test and expressed support for a future Chinese-sponsored conference on disarmament.[93]

Although Gerwani had continued to consistently attack American militarism and aggression, it fell silent on the issue of Indonesia's own move toward a more militarized society and the dramatically increased military expenditure, which was in part responsible for the shortfalls in food supplies and increased hardships for Indonesian women and children. Gerwani women were protesting against price hikes, yet they blamed these solely on the May 26 International Monetary Fund regulations which Indonesia had agreed to before the escalation of Confrontation.[94] The May 26 regulations included an end to price controls and subsidies, an end to export duties, exchange rate revision, budget cuts, increased imports and some compensatory salary and pension increases in return for U.S. aid. Commodity, transport and utility costs had risen between 200 and 500 percent.[95] The May 26 regulations were a key cause of inflation, yet Confrontation had also led to an increased military budget, an end to U.S. aid and the end of trade with Malaysia, thus further restricting the Indonesian economy.

In the years 1964 and 1965 there was very limited reporting in WIDF publications on the activities of Gerwani. This stood in contrast to the increasing attention they had received from the late 1950s to early 1960s. By September 1964 the UN Security Council had condemned Indonesian aggression against Malaysia, and when Malaysia became a new member of the UN, Indonesia withdrew its membership, resulting in further international isolation.[96] The Soviet Union increasingly distanced itself from Indonesia as Indonesia grew closer to China.

Some conclusions on the anti-imperialist WIDF–Gerwani alliance

So how are we to interpret the relationship between Gerwani and the WIDF? Joining the chorus of other feminist historians, Helen Laville suggests that "women's internationalism has too often been written about in heroic terms. Asserting a sisterhood with women across the globe, women have frequently invoked an idealized vision of women as internationalists."[97] Her critique is couched in terms of American women's international organizations; Koikari follows a similar line of critique in her study of the role of American women's organizations in Japan.[98] Both writers assert that American women's organizations were instead guises for American ascendancy, with American women dominating so-called international organizations. But it appears that there were not the same patterns of domination of women from only one country in the WIDF, despite some critiques from Gerwani that its members did not hold the highest positions in the organization. The reports filed by Gerwani to the WIDF, its submissions to the congresses, its actions at home and WIDF responses to its calls for help convey the impression of shared struggles. Gerwani was primarily concerned with the interests of Indonesian women, yet its members felt connected to women around the world as a result of the Cold War and the continuing impact of imperialism.

In Indonesia women were sometimes guided by the WIDF in the international causes they followed or supported, but does this make them Soviet dupes? Such an assumption might follow from the conceptualization of the WIDF as a Soviet front, an idea that Francisca de Haan challenges and suggests has carried over into scholarship,[99] but there is evidence that, even though the WIDF clearly favored socialist countries, it was prepared to continue opposition to the testing and use of bombs despite the Soviet violation of a weapons ban. Furthermore, in the context of the Cold War, the WIDF continued to prioritize national independence, which all Indonesians valued dearly. On the question of anti-imperialism, however, the WIDF was not as united with Gerwani in taking the struggle so far as to oppose the decolonization plan in Malaysia. Alongside its emphasis on peace and disarmament, the WIDF hesitated to back Confrontation.

Gerwani as an organization met a tragic end in 1965 when the Indonesian Communist Party and all associated organizations such as Gerwani were targeted in a campaign of terror including murder, imprisonment, forced labor and ongoing stigmatization. Gerwani members were singled out for brutal treatment following the widespread circulation of propagandistic rumors that it had tortured the seven army victims of the September 30 Movement which precipitated the attack on revolutionary forces.[100] In this context, with ties to the WIDF strained, I have found no reports on the persecution of Indonesian women in WIDF bulletins or other publications in late 1965 and 1966, including the specific publication of the WIDF entitled "For the Defence of Human Rights." This publication monitored human rights abuses against women around the world, with regular condemnations of the imprisonment and torture of women. The absence of coverage of Indonesia is striking, given that the bulletin provided ongoing critiques of imperialist aggression in Vietnam and many other cases of military repression. This suggests either that the WIDF was not receiving information about the Indonesian repression or that it was censoring its coverage. It is quite possible that it did not receive complete information on the repression. Gerwani women were either quickly killed, arrested or fled into hiding. Those in prison, including most WIDF representatives, had limited contact with the outside world. They themselves were also not fully aware of the scale of the repression.

The case of Gerwani and the WIDF demonstrates how, in the context of the Cold War, anti-imperialism served to unite women from diverse backgrounds for more than a decade. They were readily able to connect the local causes of Indonesian women, including women's rights, but also the struggle against economic exploitation and foreign intervention, with similar struggles in the Cold War. In doing so they drew sympathy and support from a wide range of women. Inside Indonesia they also used these international links to enhance the prestige and legitimacy of Gerwani in both hostile and more conducive political contexts.

Notes

1 The research for this paper was supported by a grant from the Faculty of Arts at the University of Melbourne. I would like to thank Jadwiga Pieper Mooney, Francisca de Haan and Saskia Wieringa for their useful critiques and feedback on earlier versions of this paper.
2 *Api Kartini* 2 (1960): 12.
3 Donald Hindley, *Communist Party of Indonesia 1951–1963* (Berkeley: University of California Press, 1964): 201–8.
4 Saksia Wieringa, *Sexual Politics in Indonesia* (Houndsmill: Palgrave Macmillan, 2002).
5 Diniah Hikmah, *Gerwani Bukan PKI: Sebuah Gerakan Feminisme Terbesar di Indonesia* (Yogyakarta: Carasvati Books, 2007); Amuwarni Dwi Lestariningsih, *Gerwani: Kisah Tapol Wanita di Kamp Plantungan* (Jakarta: Kompas, 2011).

6 Susan Blackburn, *Women and the State in Modern Indonesia* (Cambridge: Cambridge University Press, 2003); Elizabeth Martyn, *The Women's Movement in Post-Colonial Indonesia: Gender and Nation in a New Democracy* (London and New York: Routledge and Curzon, 2005).
7 Katharine E. McGregor, "Confronting the Past in Contemporary Indonesia: The Anti-communist Killings of 1965–66 and the Role of the Nahdlatul Ulama," *Critical Asian Studies* 41 (2) (2009): 195–224.
8 Fransisca de Haan, "Continuing Cold War Paradigms in Western Historiography of Transnational Women's Organizations: the Case of the Women's International Democratic Federation," *Women's History Review* 19 (4), September (2010): 548.
9 de Haan, "Continuing Cold War Paradigms," 550.
10 Fiona Paisley, *Glamour in the Pacific: Cultural Internationalism and Race Politics in the Women's Pan-Pacific* (Honolulu: University of Hawaii Press, 2009).
11 WIDF, *Information Bulletin* (12) (1947): n.p.
12 WIDF, *Information Bulletin* (22) (1947): 5–6.
13 Martyn, *Women's Movement in Post-Colonial Indonesia*, 157.
14 Harriet Hyman Alonso, *Peace as a Woman's Issue: A History of the U.S. Movement for World Peace and Women's Rights* (New York: Syracuse University Press, 1993), 189.
15 Martyn, *Women's Movement in Post-Colonial Indonesia*, 157.
16 *Women of the Whole World* 6 (1952): 2–3.
17 *Api Kartini* 4 (1961): 20–21.
18 de Haan, "Continuing Cold War Paradigms," 557.
19 Wieringa, *Sexual Politics*, 141–42.
20 WIDF *Information Bulletin* 10 (1950): 19.
21 Bradley R. Simpson, *Economists with Guns: Authoritarian Development and US–Indonesian Relations, 1960–1968* (Stanford: Stanford University Press, 2008), 199–200.
22 "Perjanjian Kerja Sama Ekonomi 24 Maret 1950," *Dokumen-Dokumen Pilihan tentang Politik Luar Negeri Amerika Serikat dan Asia*, ed. William Bradley and Mochtar Lubis (Jakarta: Yayasan Obor Indonesia, 1991), 153–55.
23 "Perjanjian Bantuan Militer, 15 Agustus 1950," *Dokumen-Dokumen Pilihan tentang Politik Luar Negeri Amerika Serikat dan Asia*, ed. William Bradley and Mochtar Lubis (Jakarta: Yayasan Obor Indonesia, 1991), 156–57.
24 WIDF, *Information Bulletin* 10 (1950): 19.
25 Herbert Feith, *The Decline of Constitutional Democracy in Indonesia* (Ithaca: Cornell University Press, 1962), 187–89.
26 DPP Gerwani, *Kenang Kenangan Kongres Wanita Gerwis Ke-2, 25–31 Maret 1954* (Jakarta: DPP Gerwani, 1954), 1–2.
27 *Women of the Whole World* 5 (1952): 23.
28 Alistair M. Taylor, *Indonesian Independence and the United Nations* (Westport: Greenwood Press Publishers, 2007), 240–63.
29 Meek 1956 as quoted in Bruce Glassburner, "Economic Policy Making in Indonesia, 1950–57," *Economic Development and Cultural Change* 10 (2) (1962): 19.
30 Rex Mortimer, *Indonesian Communism Under Sukarno: Ideology and Politics, 1959–1965* (Ithaca and London: Cornell University Press, 1974), 44.
31 Andrea Andreen, "With Our Sisters in Pyongyang," *Women of the Whole World* 7 (1952): 4; *Women of the Whole World* 1 (1953): 23–24; *Women of the Whole World* 3 (1953): 16.
32 WIDF, *We Accuse! Report of the Commission of the Women's International Democratic Federation in Korea, May 16 to 27, 1951* (Berlin: Women's International Democratic Federation, 1951).
33 DPP Gerwani, *Kenang Kenangan Kongres Wanita*, 27.

34 WIDF, *World Congress of Women (Copenhagen June 5–10, 1953): Reports, Speeches (Extracts), Documents* (Berlin: Women's International Democratic Federation, 1953), 35–36.
35 Sumampouw-Lapian, President of the Women's Union of Minahasa, *World Congress of Women (Copenhagen June 5–10, 1953): Reports, Speeches, Documents* (Berlin: Women's International Democratic Federation, 1953), 223.
36 Kimie Hara, "Rethinking the 'Cold War' in the Asia-Pacific," *Pacific Review* 12 (4) November (1999): 519.
37 Andrew Roadnight, *United States Policy towards Indonesia in the Truman and Eisenhower Years* (New York: Palgrave Macmillan, 2002), 92–97.
38 Roadnight, *United States Policy towards Indonesia*, 98.
39 Sumampouw-Lapian, *World Congress of Women*, 223.
40 Sumampouw-Lapian, *World Congress of Women*, 224.
41 Harold Crouch, *The Army and Politics in Indonesia* (Ithaca: Cornell University Press, 1988), 29.
42 WIDF, "Appeal to Women of the Whole World," in *World Congress of Women (Copenhagen June 5–10, 1953): Reports, Speeches (Extracts), Documents* (Berlin: Women's International Democratic Federation, 1953), 252–53.
43 WIDF, "Declaration on the Rights of Women," in *World Congress of Women (Copenhagen June 5–10, 1953): Reports, Speeches (Extracts), Documents* (Berlin: Women's International Democratic Federation, 1953), 254–55.
44 WIDF, "Declaration on the Rights of Women," 254.
45 Darmini, "XIVth Executive Session Executive Committee WIDF, Geneva 16–19th January 1954" (Berlin: WIDF, 1954), 34.
46 DPP Gerwani, *Kenang Kenangan Kongres Wanita*, 14–16.
47 Monica Felton, "Dawn Over the Equator," *Women of the Whole World* 7/8, July/August (1954): 10–11.
48 Felton, "Dawn Over the Equator," 11.
49 Ministry of Foreign Affairs, *Asia–Africa Speaks from Bandung* (Jakarta: Ministry of Foreign Affairs, Republic of Indonesia, 1955), 161–69.
50 Suharti, "Working for Peace in Asia," *Women of the Whole World* 6 (1955): 18–19.
51 Suharti, "Working for Peace in Asia," 19.
52 Blackburn, *Women and the State*, 176.
53 Suwarti Bintang Suradi, "The Struggle is Just and a Just Struggle will Surely be Victorious," *Women of the Whole World* 2 (1958): 8.
54 Mudigdo, *Plenary Session IV Congress of the WIDF, 1–5 June 1958 Vienna, WIDF Secretariat* (Berlin: WIDF, 1958), 89–90.
55 Mudigdo, *Plenary Session*, 90.
56 Mudigdo, *Plenary Session*, 91.
57 Baskara T. Wardaya, *Indonesia Melawan Amerika: Konflik Perang Dingin 1953–1963* (Yogyakarta: Galang Press, 2008), 175–95.
58 WIDF, *Information Bulletin* 10 (1958): 7–8.
59 Wieringa, *Sexual Politics*, 232–75.
60 Sukarno, "Returning to the Rails of the Revolution," in Herbert Feith and Lance Castles (eds.), *Indonesian Political Thinking 1945–1965* (Ithaca and London: Cornell University Press, 1970), 99–108.
61 *Api Kartini* 2 (1960): 12.
62 *Api Kartini* 2 (1960): 13.
63 *Api Kartini* 8 (1960): 12.
64 *Api Kartini* 8 (1960): 12.
65 WIDF, *Information Bulletin* 12 (1947): n.p.
66 *Api Kartini* 8 (1960): 12.
67 Hindley 1964, as quoted in Wieringa, *Sexual Politics*, 281.

68 *Api Kartini* 2 (1962): 1.
69 Wieringa, *Sexual Politics*, 173.
70 Anasuya Gyanchand and Beatrice Johnson "Ten Million March for Peace," *Women of the Whole World* 11 (1959): 6–7; Linsu Paulgin, "Our Choice Atomic Death or World War," *Women of the Whole World* 11 (1959): 8–10; *Women of the Whole World* 11 (1959): 11–14.
71 Yvonne Quilles, "Reflecting the World's Needs," *Women of the Whole World* 5 (1962): 17.
72 Quilles, "Reflecting the World's Needs," 17.
73 *Api Kartini* 5–6 (1962) 7.
74 Sukarno, "Pidato Presiden Sukarno pada Tanggal 17 Augustus 1946," (Lampiran 10) in Koesalah Soebagyo Toer and Ediati Kamil (eds.) *Kronik Revolusi Indonesia*, Vol. 1 (Jakarta: Kepustakaan Populer Gramedia, 1999), 642.
75 Quilles, "Reflecting the World's Needs," 17.
76 Robert Cribb and Colin Brown, *Modern Indonesia: A History since 1945* (London and New York: Longman, 1995), 86.
77 Baskara T. Wardaya, *Indonesia Melawan Amerika: Konflik Perang Dingin 1953–1963* (Yogyakarta: Galang Press, 2008), 327.
78 Simpson, *Economists with Guns*, 93.
79 Umi Sardjono, *Madju Terus untuk Integrasi Total Gerwani dengan Wanita Buruhtanimiskin (Laporan Umum Ketua DPP Gerwani Nj Umi Sardjono Kepada Sidang Pleno Ke-III DPP Gerwani)* (Djakarta: DPP Gerwani, 1964), 17.
80 WIDF, *World Congress of Women (1963, Moscow)*, n.p., n.d., 98.
81 Sardjono, *Madju Terus untuk Integrasi Total*, 17.
82 WIDF, *World Congress of Women (1963, Moscow)*, 101.
83 Sardjono, *Madju Terus untuk Integrasi Total*, 18.
84 Sardjono, *Madju Terus untuk Integrasi Total*, 18.
85 Sulami, Riwayat Hidup (1984), kindly provided by Saskia Wieringa.
86 Wieringa, *Sexual Politics*, 200–1.
87 Sardjono, *Madju Terus untuk Integrasi Total*, 3.
88 Sardjono, *Madju Terus untuk Integrasi Total*, 15.
89 Helga Dickel, "Never Again," *Women of the Whole World* 5 (1963): 16–21.
90 Dickel, "Never Again," 18.
91 Dickel, "Never Again," 18–21.
92 Sardjono, *Madju Terus untuk Integrasi Total*, 19.
93 *Api Kartini* 26 (1964): 29.
94 Sardjono, *Madju Terus untuk Integrasi Total*, 27.
95 Simpson, *Economists with Guns*, 109–10.
96 Wieringa, *Sexual Politics*, 105.
97 Helen Laville, *Cold War Women: The International Activities of American Women's Organizations* (Manchester and New York: Manchester University Press, 2002), 8.
98 Mire Koikari, *Pedagogy of Democracy: Feminism and the Cold War in the US Occupation of Japan* (Philadelphia: Temple University Press, 2008).
99 de Haan, "Continuing Cold War Paradigms," 552.
100 Wieringa, *Sexual Politics*, 280–89.

Selected bibliography

Alonso, Harriet Hyman. *Peace as a Woman's Issue: A History of the U.S. Movement for World Peace and Women's Rights*. New York: Syracuse University Press, 1993.
Blackburn, Susan. *Women and the State in Modern Indonesia*. Cambridge: Cambridge University Press, 2003.

Cribb, Robert and Colin Brown. *Modern Indonesia: A History since 1945*. London and New York: Longman, 1995.
Crouch, Harold. *The Army and Politics in Indonesia*. Ithaca: Cornell University Press, 1988.
Hikmah, Diniah. *Gerwani Bukan PKI: Sebuah Gerakan Feminisme Terbesar di Indonesia*. Yogyakarta: Carasvati Books, 2007.
Feith, Herbert. *The Decline of Constitutional Democracy in Indonesia*. Ithaca: Cornell University Press, 1962.
Glassburner, Bruce. "Economic Policy Making in Indonesia, 1950–57," *Economic Development and Cultural Change* 10 (2) (1962): 113–33.
de Haan, Francisca. "Continuing Cold War Paradigms in Western Historiography of Transnational Women's Organizations: the Case of the Women's International Democratic Federation," *Women's History Review* 19 (4), September (2010): 547–73.
Hara, Kimie. "Rethinking the 'Cold War' in the Asia-Pacific," *Pacific Review* 12 (4) November (1999): 515–36.
Hindley, Donald. *The Communist Party of Indonesia 1951–1963*. Berkeley: University of California Press, 1964.
Koikari, Mire. *Pedagogy of Democracy: Feminism and the Cold War in the US Occupation of Japan*. Philadelphia: Temple University Press, 2008.
Laville, Helen. *Cold War Women: The International Activities of American Women's Organizations*. Manchester and New York: Manchester University Press, 2002.
Lestariningsih, Amuwarni Dwi. *Gerwani: Kisah Tapol Wanita di Kamp Plantungan*. Jakarta: Kompas, 2011.
McGregor, Katharine E. "Confronting the Past in Contemporary Indonesia: The Anti-Communist Killings of 1965–66 and the Role of the Nahdlatul Ulama," *Critical Asian Studies*, 41 (2) (2009): 95–224.
Martyn, Elizabeth. *The Women's Movement in Post-Colonial Indonesia: Gender and Nation in a New Democracy*. London and New York: Routledge and Curzon, 2005.
Mortimer, Rex. *Indonesian Communism under Sukarno: Ideology and Politics, 1959–1965*. Ithaca and London: Cornell University Press, 1974.
Paisley, Fiona. *Glamour in the Pacific: Cultural Internationalism and Race Politics in the Women's Pan-Pacific*. Honolulu: University of Hawaii Press, 2009.
Roadnight, Andrew. *United States Policy towards Indonesia in the Truman and Eisenhower Years*. New York: Palgrave Mcmillan, 2002.
Simpson, Bradley R. *Economists with Guns: Authoritarian Development and US–Indonesian Relations, 1960–1968*. Stanford: Stanford University Press, 2008.
Sukarno, "Pidato Presiden Sukarno pada Tanggal 17 Augustus 1946" (Lampiran 10), in Koesalah Soebagyo Toer and Ediati Kamil, *Kronik Revolusi Indonesia*, Vol. 1, Jakarta: Kepustakaan Populer Gramedia, (1999): 628–44.
———, "Returning to the Rails of the Revolution," in Herbert Feith and Lance Castles (eds.), *Indonesian Political Thinking 1945–1965*. Ithaca and London: Cornell University Press, 1970: 99–108.
Taylor, Alistair M. *Indonesian Independence and the United Nations*. Westport: Greenwood Press Publishers, 2007.
Wardaya, Baskara T. *Indonesia Melawan Amerika: Konflik Perang Dingin 1953–1963*. Yogyakarta: Galang Press, 2008.
Wieringa, Saskia. *Sexual Politics in Indonesia*. Houndmills: Palgrave Macmillan, 2002.

3 Fighting fascism and forging new political activism

The Women's International Democratic Federation (WIDF) in the Cold War

Jadwiga E. Pieper Mooney

> Imagine a room full of women from all over the world, most of them in formal, native dress, and all leftists to varying degrees. ... I feel that there is much we do not understand about international politics. By our standard, WIDF is a liberal organization. Their political line is that men will make wars and that women, because of their roles as mothers, etc., must try to end them. I'm not sure what the group does, but it seems to benefit people, otherwise, why would so many third world women be here and take it so seriously?[1]
>
> Alice J. Wolfson, US feminist at the Women's International Democratic Federation (WIDF) Council Meeting in Budapest, 1970

In 1945, Thelma Dale, a member of the United States' Southern Negro Youth Congress (SNYC) and engaged political activist, attended the foundational meeting of the Women's International Democratic Federation (WIDF) in Paris, France. She described the gathering as an "exhilarating experience," and gave a glowing account of its civility and spirit of solidarity in stark contrast to everyday life under segregation back home. Dale cherished the opportunity to internationalize the struggle of Black women in the United States, and hoped for fruitful learning experiences and rewarding interactions "with women from the colonial countries, the Soviet Union and many other lands."[2] Indeed, about 850 women from 40 countries had accepted the invitation to the meeting from the *Union des Femmes Françaises*, women who had been active in the French Resistance movement in World War II and had close links to the Communist Party.[3] Unlike the international women's gatherings before World War II, the Paris gathering was far from exclusive, and participants' backgrounds ranged from housewives to trade unionists, doctors, artists, and women in government.[4] Most attendees represented organizations or parties in their home countries, predominantly affiliated with parties of the political left or with anti-fascist organizations.

From November 26 to December 1, 1945, the delegates at the Paris meeting debated strategies to prevent future wars and to thwart the resurgence of fascism, all for the sake of women and children. In response to the horror of World War II, they were dedicated to the cause of peace. Delegates agreed that the future of a democratic, peaceful world depended on equal rights of women and men. In the foundational resolution at the Paris conference, they insisted that "there can be no democracy nor full freedom in countries where women ... do not enjoy equality of rights in public life, and are kept out of the political and cultural life of the community." The Federation therefore set out to defend women's rights as "equal to those of men in all aspects of political, economic, legal, cultural and social life," so that women could "carry out their responsibilities as citizens, as mothers and as workers."[5] Struggles for peace, and for the welfare of mothers and children, required cooperation, and the delegates pledged to advocate for a peaceful coexistence between communism and capitalism; many of the founding members were affiliated with communist parties, but emphasized the need to leave political rivalry behind for the sake of peace. The meeting ended with the formal founding of the WIDF and with a pledge to strengthen women's solidarity across racial, national, religious, and socioeconomic boundaries. Participants long remembered the sense of sisterhood, the spirit of unity, and the remarkable harmony of the meeting in 1945, a cherished memory also because the global politics of the Cold War would often make cooperation across the Iron Curtain a difficult task.[6]

Even as, in 1949, a group of feminist observers from the United States reported that the WIDF had "grown to be the most tremendous women's organization that the world has ever seen,"[7] we find few historical accounts of its development, its international campaigns, and its role in the politics of the Cold War. Historian Francisca de Haan convincingly demonstrates that this silence is, in itself, a product of the Cold War.[8] Since the women of the *Union des Femmes Françaises* who hosted the conference had a known affiliation with the French Communist Party and women from, for example, the Soviet Union took on prominent roles in the WIDF, many scholars of the English-speaking or western world located the Federation behind the Iron Curtain and out of reach in terms of research and interest. In Europe, some women's organizations with a long history of activism, among them the International Alliance of Women (IAW), believed that the WIDF's reference to democracy and anti-fascism represented, in reality, coded language for communism – and thereby contributed to the self-imposed silence on the WIDF.[9] Neither scholars nor women activists were prepared to see that WIDF delegates, in reality, fostered multiple links to other international organizations, to women's groups all over the world, to anti-colonial activists in Africa and Asia, and, over the course of several decades, to a wide range of organizations that worked for peace, nuclear disarmament, and the rights of women and children across the blocs.

Indeed, the rigid, binary oppositions of East and West that the Cold War depended on were also present in the literature on women's activism: Western historians located women's groups such as the IAW in the capitalist West and considered them, as good, western organizations, to be "politically neutral"— dedicated to the cause of women's emancipation and women's rights. In this binary, some scholars constructed the WIDF as the political "other," a women's organization they considered deeply politicized in a wrong, possibly dangerous, way. Scholars, as well as feminists on the "right" side of the Curtain, assumed that communist members of the Federation could not possibly be feminists. Misleading Cold War categorizations, thereby, accounted for the fact that the Federation was given scarce notice by English-language scholars, and, in the words of de Haan, an "overwhelming silence" about the Federation prevailed in most English-language histories of transnational and international women's movements.[10] Yet, it is by looking at the history of the WIDF, the nature of its activism, and its contributions to women's rights that we can challenge the layered assumptions that the Cold War placed on such categories as "communist," "feminist," and "anti-feminist."

I argue that the history of the WIDF is remarkable not only because it exposes the silences mandated by the rigid binaries of the Cold War, but also because the stories of federation delegates and their political campaigns offer valuable insights into complexities well beyond the familiar (and far too simple) Cold War divide. A closer look at individual members and at selected WIDF campaigns from 1945 to 1975 (from its foundation in 1945 to its contributions to the United Nations' International Women's Year in 1975) illustrates that they broke new ground, even though they could not always overcome the confines of larger political paradigms. As we begin our inquiry into the Federation, we are met with the undeniable impact of top-down influences, the very influences that we (as social, political, gender, and feminist historians) have reservations about. We have to acknowledge that superpower politicos dealt heavy blows to some WIDF campaigns when they branded delegates as agents of Soviet plots or as dupes of the political interests of those in power. But the Federation's political campaigns were not just a replica of Soviet orthodoxies, even when outspoken communist women took over leadership positions in the organization. Instead, we find rich evidence of WIDF members negotiating the left/right, communism/capitalism dichotomies of the Cold War order and re-applying themes such as anti-imperialism, anti-colonialism and anti-racism as they linked those to their fight for women's rights and gender equity across the globe.

New interests in women's activism in the Cold War: campaigns for world peace and "communist fronts"

The tense political climate after World War II, growing antagonism over occupied Germany, and the "suspicious" presence of a large number of Soviet delegates at the Paris meeting provoked close observation by concerned politicians in the United States and contributed to a facile condemnation by the US media. Members of the Committee on Un-American Activities of the US House of Representatives, i.e., the House Un-American Activities Committee (HUAC), closely followed WIDF campaigns, called the participation rates at the first gathering "truly astounding," and claimed to have detected an overwhelming Soviet leadership.[11] HUAC warned that Nina Popova, the head of the Russian delegation and one of WIDF's vice presidents, controlled the course of the Federation as its most powerful member.[12] Although initial media reports by, for example, the *New York Times* praised women's international campaigns for peace, reporters soon changed their position on WIDF activists.[13] US feminist Gerda Lerner, who represented the Congress of American Women (CAW) at the 1948 WIDF Conference in Budapest, remembers the biased reporting of the conference by the media back in the US. Newspaper articles described US delegates in Budapest as "pathetic women who, in their desire to work for peace, had been duped into participating in the Kremlin's attack on America."[14] In 1948, the US Justice Department added CAW, the Federation's affiliate in the United States, to the government's list of subversive organizations, also citing its members' frequent trips to WIDF meetings in communist countries.[15]

Ironically, the very emphasis WIDF members placed on campaigns for world peace, a mission *all* humans should agree on, only increased their reputation as a Soviet front. The WIDF's major publications, the *Information Bulletin* and the magazine *Women of the Whole World*, wrote about the responsibility of mothers to create a peaceful world for their children, just when the Soviet Union claimed to be the true agent of peace in the changing international climate. In well-publicized worldwide campaigns, the Soviets began to label the US a warmongering nation, in stark contrast to the supposed communist devotion to the cause of peace.[16] A new, communist-led international peace movement, in line with Soviet policy, reminded the world of US aggression at the end of World War II, especially its use of nuclear weapons against Japan, acts of aggression that justify concerted action "against the warmongers."[17] Historian Lawrence Wittner effectively documents that, in 1948, this Soviet-led campaign took a leap forward at the "World Congress of Intellectuals for Peace" in Wroclaw, Poland, where communist leaders conflated the use of nuclear weapons with fascist ideology, and inaugurated peace campaigns led by communist, peace-loving nations.[18] Soviet officials exploited the Wroclaw meeting as evidence that communist parties and communist intellectuals were at the forefront of much-needed campaigns in "defense of peace and culture."[19] Non-communist participants at the conference reported that "there was no discussion in the ordinary sense of the word" and that presentations divided the world between "the heroes of the Soviet Union" and "fascists, who were plotting war."[20]

The message of Soviet officials' "peace offensive" had multiple and complex implications for WIDF campaigns for peace: on the one hand, it made the Federation's campaigns ever more suspicious in the eyes of the United States and the non-communist western world; on the other hand, it allowed WIDF organizers to use the resources and political networks of communist countries for peace campaigns under WIDF auspices.[21] The WIDF's reputation as a Soviet front grew because of the nature of Soviet propaganda, but also because the WIDF used resources communist countries offered to support its campaigns. Soviet-sponsored conferences, publications, and festivals, helped fund WIDF activities; in 1949, for example, when the WIDF began to prepare for its own World Peace Conference in Paris, organizers could count on reinforcement from the "International Liaison Committee of Intellectuals," just founded at the Wroclaw Congress. The Federation thereby enlisted the support of the powerful world communist apparatus in an effort to make its Peace Congress "an historic landmark."[22] WIDF members kept close ties to communist-led peace groups, greatly profited from these ties, but, nonetheless, continued to engage in a wide range of political and social activism. Political leaders in the US claimed that Soviet international campaigns systematically and deliberately targeted women. WIDF affiliates, however, were hardly passive victims of a changing world order. Instead, they gained international attention and found new spaces for political action in the course of the Cold War.

In 1951, when the WIDF relocated from Paris to East Berlin, it became clear just how prominently women activists and women's issues featured in new global political contests. Women's international movements were hardly a new phenomenon at the time, but political leaders now feared that women could fall prey to manipulation and therefore needed to be both protected and controlled. For example, the US Office of Military Government (OMGUS), since the end of the war in charge of supervising German developments, paid special attention to what it considered "vulnerable groups" easily influenced by propaganda. The Women's Affairs Section of the OMGUS insisted that, "in this formative period of the new Germany, women's organizations merit careful consideration as they are of important political potential. They may be developed as a democratic force or used as an effective instrument for propaganda. There is evidence of systematic efforts from the Eastern Zone to undermine the Western German state by appealing to certain women's organizations through slogans of peace and unity and condemning the division of Western Germany."[23] When WIDF delegates in East Berlin prepared for the International Women's Day celebrations on March 8, 1951, OMGUS concerns intensified, as the activities that targeted women seemed to fit the label of "concerted, deliberate, and well-planned propaganda."[24]

In 1951, the Federation's relocation to East Berlin also placed it in one of the foremost geographical centers where the political competitions of the Cold War took shape. WIDF activists gained attention because political leaders in both the eastern and western blocs thought of women as susceptible targets of propaganda campaigns, easily moved to either side of a divided Berlin or a divided world. From this perspective, women could become either prey of political opponents or invaluable political allies.[25] A closer look at the nature of WIDF campaigns and at the wide range of political projects that women delegates pursued in the organization illustrates that the image of women as victims is misleading at best. Campaigns by WIDF-affiliated women's groups covered a broad spectrum of issues from anti-fascist and anti-colonial mobilizations to struggles for women's suffrage. As an international organization, WIDF affiliation often increased the weight women's groups could have at the nation-state level. The WIDF also empowered individual women.

Anti-fascist, communist, and feminist activists: WIDF delegates and political campaigns

By the time the WIDF settled in East Berlin, US and Western European officials had firmly linked the Federation's campaigns to the Soviets' "peace offensive." French politicians no longer welcomed the Federation after delegates had protested French aggression in Vietnam and had urged mothers not to send their sons to war.[26] The WIDF's subsequent campaign for peace in Korea further contributed to its unfavorable reputation in the eyes of the West. In 1951, a delegation of 20 federation delegates from 17 countries traveled to Korea to learn the truth about the war. Upon their return, the women prepared a detailed and devastating report, accusing US occupiers in Korea of "a merciless and methodological campaign of extermination which is in contradiction not only with the principles of humanity, but also with the rules of warfare as laid down, for instance, in the Hague and the Geneva Convention."[27] Published in five languages, the official WIDF report, *We Accuse*, presented evidence of crimes committed against a peace-loving people, including innocent women and children. Its detailed accounts of American soldiers' bombings of civilians and of brutal killings, rape, and torture also became the source of information for the United Nations Security Council.[28]

The WIDF report about the United States' "campaign of extermination" in Korea caused immediate concern within the US government, provoking communication between the chief of the International Division of the Women's Bureau of the Department of Labor and the State Department, and, once again, raised fears of women being manipulated by the Soviet Union.[29] The head of the Women Bureau voiced concerns that a "distorted picture of America's character" would go global, tarnishing the country's reputation worldwide. She judged the WIDF campaign as propaganda that could become "an effective weapon in gaining support among women for the communist 'peace offensive.'"[30] Historian Helen Laville shows that neither the Women's Bureau nor the State Department issued an official response to the WIDF's Korea report, but a coalition of over 30 women's associations, coordinated by the *Women United for United Nations* (WUUN), drafted a document that assumed the status of a position paper. Information services of the US State Department assured its wide distribution, and even broadcast the contents of the document on Radio Free Asia and Radio Free Europe.[31] The WUUN authors, predominantly white middle-class women who promoted an idealized feminine patriotism, countered the WIDF accusations, and also helped separate "proper" from "improper" peace initiatives.[32] They encouraged US citizens, and audiences around the world, to identify those propaganda campaigns that used the issue of peace for the benefit of the Soviet Union, and warned that the Soviet peace offensive was dangerous, especially to those women who had a genuine commitment to the cause of peace "but whose enthusiasm might be directed and manipulated by the Soviets."[33]

With growing fears of communist expansion, even the Federation's ongoing campaigns against fascism did little to save its reputation in the eyes of US officials. Right after its inception, the WIDF began to voice its opposition to Franco's Spain, and effectively linked its verbal critique to campaigns against Francoist terror. Spanish anti-fascists, some of them exiled in France, had been active members of the Federation early on.[34] Together with the Spanish Anti-Fascist Women's Union (*Unión de Mujeres Antifascistas Españolas*, UME), the WIDF denounced the death sentences of Spanish activists back in Spain, worked closely with Spanish women on amnesty petitions for the victims of fascism, and, again, connected these campaigns to its quest for peace and the welfare of mothers and children. In 1947, the Federation also collaborated with international legal experts from different countries to organize a visit to Spanish jails, in an effort to prevent torture and mistreatment of political prisoners. As historian Mercedes Yusta Rodrigo puts it, "the WIDF, ... thanks to the prestige of its leaders and its good political relations, was able to go further than the women of the UME."[35] With the support of the WIDF, the Spanish Anti-Fascist Women's Union scored some successes, but in the Cold War, even anti-fascism gained its share of negative connotations. By 1950, global political reassessments transformed fascist dictators into potential allies against the threat of communism.

After US foreign policy changed from President Roosevelt's ambivalent position between isolationism and internationalism, to rapprochement under President Truman, to overt support of Franco's Spain by President Eisenhower, the WIDF's active opposition to Francoism made it an enemy to the US.[36] Although US leaders and public opinion in the United States had long negotiated between sympathy with the Loyalists who fought fascism, on the one hand, and fear of a Bolshevik Spain, on the other hand, foreign-policy decisions came to be increasingly influenced by the latter. After 1949, US fear of the influence of the global communist/capitalist divide replaced its fear of fascist threats, and, consequently, justified support of right-wing dictators as potential allies in the struggle against communism. In the words of historian Walter LaFeber, key political decision makers in the United States were convinced that "communists had to be fought, not fed."[37] By the 1950s, the Eisenhower administration not only sought to normalize relations with Franco, but became an active ally of the regime. Moved by the urgency of the communist threat, the United States and Spain signed a pact in 1953, allowing the US to set up air bases in Spain in exchange for military and economic aid to help stabilize Spanish development.[38]

The macro-level of the Cold War, the competition between the United States and the Soviet Union, contributed to the politicization of the

Federation's campaigns both for world peace and against fascism. Linked to the larger order of the global political contest, of the binary discourse that pitted communists against anti-communists, the meanings of WIDF peace campaigns and anti-fascist mobilization were shaped by the simple yet powerful dichotomies of the time. The transcendental character of superpower competitions fostered the politicization of WIDF campaigns and increased its ill-reputation in the capitalist West. Historians have shown that the Cold War contributed to the "politicization and internationalization of everyday life," and produced "imaginaries [that] were fostered in the popular imagination through mass culture."[39] Yet, even though specific and diverse meanings of political campaigns were subsumed in the larger order at first sight, we cannot conclude that Cold War binaries prohibited women's individual and collective empowerment. Paquita Merchán, for example, a seamstress by profession in her native Spain, experienced her work with the WIDF as a liberating alternative to "the moral, intellectual and political asphyxiation" of her life under Franco. When she attended the WIDF's 1961 World Congress in Budapest, she testified to the liberating potential that the Federation's activism had right from the moment of its inception: "I could not believe it. There I was with my sewing machine in Paris [1945], and suddenly I was in the middle of these great people, all these women, Africans, Asians, Poles, Russians ... " Merchán reminds us of the many meanings the Federation's gatherings could have: they encouraged individual contacts among women, opened up new channels of communication, and also enhanced alternative activist networks in the midst of the Cold War.[40]

"Anti-feminist communists," and activists in defense of women's rights

At first sight, even the WIDF delegates' approaches to women's rights were subsumed in the deeply polarizing global struggle of the Cold War. Some outspoken orthodox communists, often in leadership roles, rejected any affiliation with feminism and insisted that countries like the Soviet Union had already resolved the "woman question." In her 1949 book *Women in the Land of Socialism*, Soviet delegate and WIDF vice president Nina Popova insisted that there was no discrimination against women in the Soviet Union and concluded that the struggle for women's emancipation was a struggle confined to the capitalist West.[41] Some communist delegates held on to the "Soviet line" for decades, and attributed women's exploitation and the inadequate rights of women workers to capitalism. From their perspective, feminism and struggles that prioritized women's rights over those of men were bourgeois and divisive. Cuban communist and head of the Cuban Women's Federation (Federación de Mujeres Cubanas, FMC) Vilma Espín, for example, often claimed to share the outspoken anti-feminist position of fellow communists, but was especially critical of feminists of the "US variety." In 1977, she asserted that "We never had a feminist movement. We hate that. We hate the feminist movement in the United States. We consider what we are doing is part of the struggle. We see these movements in the USA which have conceived struggles for equality of women against men! That is absurd!"[42] Yet, outspoken orthodox communists still mixed and mingled with a wide range of women who set out to mobilize for women's citizenship rights, often blurring the supposed dividing line between communism and feminism. Evidence of some of the multiple agendas of delegates and insights into selected campaigns in defense of women's rights illustrate that both "feminists" and "anti-feminists" contributed new tools and brought new successes to women activists.[43]

Although Espín rejected feminist labels early on, she nonetheless sought to increase the political power of women in Cuba and other Latin American nations through the WIDF. In 1959, she joined the 1st Latin American Congress for the Rights of Women and Children in Santiago, Chile, organized under the auspices of the WIDF.[44] She described the Santiago Conference as "an effort to bring the voice of our women—revolutionary women from the first free territory in America—to our sisters throughout the continent."[45] She then went on to use her connections with fellow activist women, cemented at the Santiago Conference, to accelerate the foundation of the FMC back home. She reported that "at first our grouping was called the Congress of Cuban Women for the Liberation of Latin America. By August 23, 1960, with nearly 70,000 women integrated into revolutionary tasks, the single, all-encompassing women's organization was founded."[46] Named and sanctioned by Fidel Castro, the FMC mobilized women in support of the Cuban Revolution, but also linked its members to international networks and promoted new understandings of women's rights. These networks, the learning experience they provided, and the power they could lend affiliated organizations and women delegates, shaped the WIDF right from the start.

WIDF activists' references to feminism, in fact, challenged the categories of "feminism" and "anti-feminism"; furthermore, the Federation's initiatives, right from the start, illustrate the ambiguity of other binary oppositions of the Cold War.

At first sight, the women who helped create the WIDF aimed at building a "coalition of women of the anti-Fascist, pro-Communist left," but a closer look at the range of members' anti-fascist and "communist" positions reveals that easy Cold War classifications of political camps are misleading at best.[47] At the 1945 foundational meeting in Paris, attendees represented a wide variety of positions on women's rights. The delegation from the United States, for example, was headed by Elizabeth Gurley Flynn, first-generation Irish American, active labor organizer, and well known for her defense of women's rights since the first decades of the twentieth century. Self-declared feminist and communist, she mobilized for women's suffrage, supported birth control, and became an active member of and, in 1941, the first female chair of the Communist Party.[48] Among the 12 US delegates in Paris were Thelma Dale of the US Southern Negro Youth Congress (SNYC) as well as other African American women who believed that new international ties could strengthen their struggle for equal rights back in the US. Vivian Carter Mason, of the National Council of Negro Women (NCNW), shared her enthusiasm and learning experiences at the Paris meeting in a letter to Eleanor Roosevelt, asking the First Lady to encourage women in the United States "to participate in socially progressive movements in this country and to cooperate with women of other countries in the task of establishing a better world and enduring peace."[49] Many fellow attendees firmly believed in the strength of an international movement for women's rights to empower delegates' political agendas back home.

Women from different African countries who came to Paris linked anti-imperialist, anti-colonial, and nationalist struggles to quests for women's rights. Egyptian delegate Inji Aflatun, for example, arrived from Cairo to share experiences of the colonial dimension of gender inequalities. As leader of a young socialist feminist movement in her home country at the time, she argued that the liberation of the masses and the end of imperialism had to be linked to women's liberation. Even if her feminist organization was short-lived in Egypt, she rejected the incompatibility of feminism and communism that some women of the Left emphasized at the time.[50] Other evidence from African women's groups illustrates that WIDF affiliates successfully connected quests for women's rights to anti-colonial struggles. In Nigeria, for instance, the Federation supported pro-independence, pro-suffrage, nationalist women's organizations and helped them to put pressure on colonial governments to extend new political rights to women.[51]

Examples from Nigeria illustrate that women had ample space to choose the terms of their association with the Federation, that they found ways to overcome the "threat" of stigmatization that equated WIDF affiliation with communism, and that they stretched the boundaries set by Cold War binaries. The history of WIDF affiliations with women's movements in Nigeria is intimately tied to Funmilayo Ransome-Kuti, feminist and anti-colonial activist with an international reputation.[52] Ransome-Kuti's success lay in her ability to combine regional self-help initiatives and political campaigns that linked anti-colonialism with suffrage. Cheryl Johnson-Odim and Nina Emma Mba's account of her life portrays the remarkable, radical feminist components of her campaigns as well as her ability to negotiate Cold War constraints: Ransome-Kuti initially mistrusted the Federation's communist reputation, and carefully selected among the many international conferences she was invited to attend. In 1949 she responded to an invitation to a WIDF Congress in China by seeking advice from a trusted political counselor: "Now some people here say that we must not attend the congress because it is a communist organization and some say it is not. I really don't know what it really is ... "[53] Although she decided not to go to China in 1949, she did participate in the 1952 Vienna Conference on "The Defense of Children," and the 1953 World Congress of Women in Copenhagen, where she was elected as one of the WIDF vice presidents.[54] That same year she organized a conference of women's organizations in Nigeria, helped establish the Federation of Nigerian Women's Societies, and campaigned for women's suffrage.

We can find evidence of Ransome-Kuti's use of international ties to the WIDF as she organized protests against British policies such as the water rate, long a major source of discontent, as it disproportionally affected Nigeria's poor. When British officials confronted protestors with gas attacks and other violent measures, Ransome-Kuti contacted WIDF Secretary Marie Claude Vaillant-Couturier. Vaillant-Couturier set in motion a WIDF response, sending telegrams condemning the use of violence by British authorities. Demanding the abolition of the water rate in its newsletter, the Federation helped create international awareness of and support for the campaign. Ransome-Kuti continued to share the specifics of African women's struggles at international conferences organized by the WIDF, braving Cold War categorization of the Federation as a "communist front." In 1956, she attended a WIDF Council meeting in China, where she spent three weeks speaking to its citizens "about Nigerian women and children. I sang Yoruba songs and showed them various customs and traditions of my country ... I wonder if attending independence celebrations of other countries means social communism to our Prime Minister who cries wolf when there is none to come."[55] Her trip to China inspired the British press to write articles on "the indoctrination of Africans," citing her as a victim of indoctrination by the WIDF "international communist front."[56] Although these accusations made life for Ransome-Kuti more difficult in her own home country, they did not stop her from using her international connections to strengthen her local campaigns. Along with her affiliation with the WIDF, she also worked with another international group, the Women's International League for Peace and Freedom (WILPF). In the 1960s, she brought new life to a branch of the WILPF that was set up in Nigeria, continued to protest colonialism at home and in other African regions, and mobilized in support of women's rights.[57] Importantly, the combined forces of the WIDF and the Nigerian women had not only helped to organize women in the Christian south, but had pressured the British colonial government to also support women's suffrage in the Muslim north.[58] WIDF publications and international conferences aided in the creation of new networks among women of former colonies, provided new tools in struggles for women's rights, and helped place women's suffrage on the agenda of anti-colonial activism.

Maternalist mobilization and women's access to global political networks

The WIDF's effective use of maternalist strategies best accounts for its ability to unite different groups of women: federation delegates won the support of a wide range of political constituencies by emphasizing the need to fight for the rights of mothers and children.[59] Upholding their commitment to the 1945 charter and their pledge to prevent the recurrence of war and the resurgence of fascism for the sake of women and children, delegates worked for "the cause of achieving a lasting peace between nations, of creating everywhere the essential conditions for guaranteeing the real equality of women, [and] for the protection of the future of children."[60] In the 1950s, for example, the Federation denounced nuclear testing, nuclear weapons, and the arms race as threats to the inseparable mother–child unit. International WIDF publications evoked the horrors of Hiroshima through vivid images of Japanese children praying for their lost parents, of "women without children," of maimed young girls who "have lost their women's birthright, and will never be able to marry." One of its publications, a booklet titled "I Want to Live," had on its cover the picture of a young child, smiling at a distant future that she could have only if the Federation's call to "ban atomic weapons" would be heard.[61]

WIDF discourse appealed to the universality of motherhood, and could unite women across race, class, political, and national divisions. The Federation used gendered traditions, the responsibilities of mothers, as the backdrop for a wide range of activities, such as the need to end wars, control the arms race, and ban nuclear weapons. In the process, it also broke old boundaries: the Federation challenged those understandings of maternalism that linked women's responsibilities to an exclusive "female sphere," to the home, or to domestic activities. Women, as mothers, were now involved in international relations, global network building, and the construction of a new language and practice of women's rights.

The peace initiatives of the Federation to end the Vietnam War (or the American War, as the Vietnamese called it), illustrate the political weight maternalist activism had gained, and that federation delegates were successful in accessing political networks at the center of Cold War politics. The Vietnam Women's Union had been a WIDF affiliate since 1946, and soon after the war began, the WIDF helped distribute messages from Vietnamese women to women in the United States. Both sides realized that women played an important role in opposing the war. The Vietnam Women's Union, as well as other Vietnamese women's groups, claimed to know that American women were "on their side," and shared their thoughts in a letter to "Women Strike for Peace" member Ruth Gage-Colby in the United States: "From the radio, newspapers, and the message of the Women's International Democratic Federation, we are very elated to learn that American women are engaged in a campaign to safeguard world peace and to end the danger of nuclear war. With the same aspiration for peace—and to protect women's interests and children's happiness—Vietnam women always side with American women."[62]

In October 1970, the WIDF organized a meeting on the "Countries of Indochina and Solidarity with Their Peoples" in Budapest, encouraging individual encounters among women to build personal connections for the sake of peace. Women from the United States, such as Alice J. Wolfson, traveled to Budapest with the explicit goal to meet Vietnamese delegates and were inspired by their example to re-examine their understanding of global politics, of regional diversities, and of the different priorities women might set in their personal and local struggles. Wolfson, who was selected as a delegate to represent a loosely knit coalition of American women's liberation groups, had come to the conference to plan a women's liberation conference in Canada and to win Vietnamese women to join and support the project. She describes the difficulty of creating ties based on the various priorities of women's liberation, but remembers the common ground that was found to unite the women: "Out came everyone's pictures of children, grandchildren, husbands, friends, and also the stories. Almost all of them have at least one child who is missing ... "[63] Women, as mothers and family members, had similar interests that transcended political and national lines.

In 1973, five WIDF delegates, women from Argentina, India, the Soviet Union, France, and the Congo, traveled to Hanoi to attend the signing of the peace accord that ended United States involvement in Vietnam. The event, and the presence of WIDF delegates, confirmed not only the important influence women's internationalism had on political contests, but also the significant role the Federation had come to play in furthering the cause of peace. Historian Judy Wu documents that the Vietnamese valued and fostered global female networks as part of their campaign for national liberation. Women from the WIDF had come to Vietnam because the Vietnamese had requested their presence at the signing of the Peace Accord—an indication that this organization, in defense of mothers and children, had built connections to international networks central to the politics of the Cold War.[64] In Vietnam, WIDF representatives confirmed that they had been true to their mission in defense of peace. The Federation continued to support the Vietnamese Women's Union long after the end of the war, and WIDF Secretary Fanny Edelman traveled to Hanoi (Figure 3.1), collected testimonial accounts, and

Figure 3.1 Fanny Edelman in Vietnam, 1973

solidified the relationship among women that, in the words of one Vietnamese official, "made women invincible ... and was appreciated not only by women, but by all Vietnamese people."[65] Federation members pursued international missions to support women and children around the world, but they also attempted to improve women's lives through more formal channels.

"Women of the whole world" for women's rights as human rights

Activists, politicians, and scholars have referred to the year 1975 as "an engine for change," calling it a landmark in the history of women's rights, and crediting the United Nations for declaring 1975 International Women's Year (IWY); yet, IWY was also the product of WIDF initiatives. Hilkka Pietilä, one of the IWY organizers, remembers that the Federation, under the leadership of Finnish President Hertta Kuusinen, utilized its consultative status in the UN Commission on the Status of Women (CSW) and that Kuusinen represented the Federation as an observer at the CSW. In that capacity, she submitted a proposal for an "International Women's Year" in March 1972.[66] The drafting of the proposal itself was the outcome of negotiations about specific definitions of gender equality, and offers additional evidence of the involvement of women from East and West. Comparative gender expert Raluca Maria Popa notes that, for example, WIDF-affiliated women's organizations in Hungary and Romania stood out for their commitment to gender equality, and, at times, used the term "feminist" to characterize their activism, in spite of the ideological stigma it carried in the Cold War "East."[67] Romanian and Finnish representatives played a crucial role in supporting IWY and in securing its central place on the agenda of the UN Commission. Clearly, IWY was a product of cooperation among women from different organizations and from different parts of the world—and representatives from both sides of the "Iron Curtain" were interested in bringing the needs and views of women to the attention of the UN and the world.

Ongoing preparations for IWY and the related conference in Mexico City in July 1975 confirmed that women across the blocs not only shared a common interest in women's rights, but also jointly debated strategies for change. In 1974, WIDF President Freda Brown, also president of the International Preparatory Committee Meetings for the World Congress, set up conferences in East Berlin and in Tihany, Hungary. The meetings invited participants who believed "that all forms of discrimination against women constitute a violation of human rights," and who recognized "the equal responsibility of men and women in economic, political, social, and cultural life, in the family and in the rearing of children";[68] it counted on the attendance of members of a wide range of women's and youth organizations, including those from Africa, Asia, and the Americas, as well as UN representatives such as Helvi Sipilä, assistant UN secretary general.[69] When, finally, over 5,000 participants from all over the world came to Mexico City to attend the first IWY Conference, or the Non-Governmental

Organizations (NGO) Tribune that convened simultaneously, WIDF Secretary Fanny Edelman was one of the distinguished speakers defending gender equity.[70] Indeed, women on both sides of the Cold War divide helped to bring about a new stage in global networking initiatives and mobilization for women's rights. In Mexico, conference participants drafted *The World Plan of Action*, which defined the agenda for eliminating discrimination against women. It also extended International Women's Year to a Decade for Women (1975–85).[71]

International political orders and gendered relationships: new questions

WIDF delegates, "confined" to the communist side of a world divided by the so-called Cold War, encourage us to question that particular ideological construct. Women from many political and national backgrounds helped push for International Women's Year, fought for gender equity and human rights across the bloc, and, after 1975, continued to work for women's rights as human rights. Scholars have begun to present evidence to illustrate that women on both sides of the Iron Curtain made substantial contributions to a new global discourse on women's rights and to a new practice of gender equity that some of us might consider to be "feminist."[72]

In this study, selected examples of women's activism in the Women's International Democratic Federation (WIDF) demonstrate the complex nature of the politics of the Cold War. WIDF campaigns ranged from anti-fascist activism and anti-colonial struggles to mobilization for women's suffrage and the defense of women's citizenship rights equal to those of men. They provide evidence of multiple languages of women's activism, too easily conflated with communism (or anti-communism) and the dominant paradigms at the time. WIDF campaigns took place in the midst of the Cold War, and women carved out new spaces for political influence as they negotiated their affiliation with communism and their relationships with countries outside the Eastern bloc. From the site of their headquarters in East Berlin, women led campaigns for world peace and for the rights of women and children. The novelty of their defense of women's rights lay in their ability to negotiate between continuity and change: a maternalist, at times anti-feminist, discourse eased the legitimacy of their campaigns, united women with different political agendas, and, simultaneously, contributed new, liberating spaces for women's activism. In the process, WIDF members negotiated the left/right, communism/capitalism dichotomies of the Cold War order, and reapplied themes such as anti-imperialism, anti-colonialism, and anti-racism as they linked those to their fight for women's rights and gender equity across the globe.

Scholars have also begun to explore the specific types of relationships between the WIDF and its member organizations, and more detailed case studies will enhance our understanding of the gendered politics of the Cold

War. In this volume, Katharine McGregor illustrates how women in Indonesia used international ties to strengthen political struggles at home. McGregor documents that a WIDF meeting, held in Jakarta in 1960, signaled both the growing prominence of Indonesia in the anti-imperialist movement and the impressive achievements of Gerwani, the Indonesian Women's Movement. Like many of the women in this study, Gerwani activists used their affiliation with the WIDF and, temporarily, increased their influence on nation-state politics. Indeed, the relations between the WIDF and their affiliates pose new questions: How can we best understand the power women gained as they worked with a communist-connected international organization in the Cold War? To what extent did support from the Soviet Union increase or limit the decisions they were allowed to make? And do we find evidence of political practices that distinguished women's campaigns within the WIDF, an all-female international organization, from campaigns within male-dominated organizations in their home countries?

New studies on the WIDF may also contribute fresh insights into gender relations and the multiple ways women could employ their international ties to challenge patriarchal structures at home. Historian Cynthia Enloe affirms that the Cold War was "not simply a contest between two superpowers, each trying to absorb as many countries as possible into its own orbit, but also a series of contests within each of those societies over the definitions of masculinity and femininity that would sustain or dilute that rivalry."[73] When Enloe refers to the Cold War as a "thicket of gendered relationships that had to be either reshaped or entrenched," she reminds us that the Cold War might not have lasted without the reproduction of gender roles and gendered expectations that men and women negotiated on a daily basis. What she calls mutually constitutive relationships between sexual and international orders are relationships that are central to the history of the Cold War and deserve attention, even if simple Cold War dichotomies are, at best, misleading as we examine women's activism and changing gender relations in a Cold War world.[74]

Notes

1 Alice Wolfson, "Budapest journal," *Off Our Backs* (Dec. 14, 1970): 1. http://ezproxy.library.arizona.edu/login?url=http://search.proquest.com/docview/197136671?accountid=8360. The quote is from a "running journal" the author kept while in Budapest at a meeting of the WIDF. Wolfson "had been sent there as a representative of Women's Liberation to meet with Vietnamese and Cambodian women to help plan a spring conference in Montreal, Toronto, and Vancouver, Canada to be held March 24–April 7 between Indochinese, American and Canadian women." The journal was meant to be "an account of my feelings as I experienced them."
2 Erik S. McDuffie, *Sojourning for Freedom: Black Women, American Communism, and the Making of Black Left Feminism* (Durham, NC: Duke University Press, 2011), 155.
3 For reference to the number of participants, see Women's International Democratic Federation, *Congrès international des femmes; Compte rendu de travaux du*

Congrès qui s'est tenu à Paris du 26 novembre au 1er décembre 1945 (Paris: Fédération démocratique internationale des femmes, 1946), ix. Some scholars quote the important initiative of the Communist Party of Great Britain that inspired not only the first gathering in Paris, but also decided to have progressive women from around the world replace an earlier organization, the World Committee of Women against War and Fascism. See Mercedes Yusta Rodrigo, "The Mobilization of Women in Exile: The Case of the *unión de mujeres antifascistas españolas* in France (1944–50)," *Journal of Spanish Cultural Studies* 6/1 (March 2005): 53.

4 Joanne J. Meyerowitz, *Not June Cleaver: Women and Gender in Postwar America, 1945–1960* (Philadelphia: Temple University Press, 1994), 143.

5 Women's International Democratic Federation, *Original Resolutions of the Women's International Democratic Federation at the International Congress of Women, Paris, November–December 1945* (Paris, France: WIDF 1969), 1.

6 For a reference to the spirit of the meeting see also Francisca de Haan, "Hoffnungen auf eine bessere Welt: Die frühen Jahre der Internationalen Demokratischen Frauenföderation (IDFF/WIDF) (1945–50)," *Feministische Studien* 27/2 (November 2009): 243–46.

7 As cited in Amy Swerdlow, "The Congress of American Women," in *U.S. History as Women's History: New Feminist Essays*, ed. Linda K. Kerber, Alice Kessler-Harris and Kathryn Kish Sklar (Chapel Hill: University of North Carolina Press, 1995), 429, n. 2.

8 Francisca de Haan, "Continuing Cold War Paradigms in the Western Historiography of Transnational Women's Organizations: The Case of the Women's International Democratic Federation (WIDF)," *Women's History Review* 19/4 (September 2010): 547–73; see also de Haan, "Hoffnungen auf eine bessere Welt," 241–57.

9 Leila J. Rupp, *Worlds of Women: The Making of an International Women's Movement* (Princeton, NJ: Princeton University Press, 1997), 47.

10 de Haan, "Continuing Cold War Paradigms," 548. For new contributions to the scholarship on the WIDF, see Katharine McGregor, "The Cold War, Indonesian Women and the Global Anti-Imperialist Movement, 1946–65," in this volume; see also Mercedes Yusta Rodrigo, "The Mobilization of Women in Exile"; Wendy Pojmann, "For Mothers, Peace and Family: International (Non)-Cooperation among Italian Catholic and Communist Women's Organisations during the Early Cold War," *Gender & History* 23/2 (August 2011): 415–29; and Melanie Ilic, "Soviet Women, Cultural Exchange and the Women's International Democratic Federation," in *Reassessing Cold War Europe*, eds. Sari Autio and Katalin Miklóssy (London: Routledge, 2011), 157–74.

11 The report refers to a total of 600 delegates, representing 81,000,000 women in 35 countries. See United States, Committee on Un-American Activities, U.S. House of Representatives, 81st Congress, 2nd Session, *Report on the Congress of American Women* (United States Government Printing Office: 1950), 14, fn 22 for "truly astounding."

12 United States, Committee on Un-American Activities, 7.

13 *New York Times* (Feb. 22, 1947): 8; and *New York Times* (Nov. 22, 1946): 26.

14 Gerda Lerner, *Fireweed: A Political Autobiography* (Philadelphia: Temple University Press, 2002), 272.

According to Fanny Edelman, Argentine delegate and later secretary of the WIDF, the most important themes discussed at the conference were "peace and democracy." Edelman also describes Argentine delegates' contributions in Budapest, and their demands for the women's rights in Argentina. See Fanny Edelman, "El Congreso Mundial de Mujeres Fortalecerá la Causa de la Paz," *Orientación*, Dec. 11, 1948. For conference proceedings, see also WIDF, *Second Women's*

Fighting fascism 69

International Congress: Account of the Work of the Congress Which Took Place in Budapest (Hungary) from the 1st to the 6th of December, 1948 (Paris: WIDF, 1949).
15 Kate Weigand, *Red Feminism: American Communism and the Making of Women's Liberation* (Baltimore: Johns Hopkins University Press, 2001), 63–64.
16 For the important roles the Soviet-aligned peace movement and its anti-Soviet peace-counter-movement played in the ideological Cold War, see Patrick Iber's chapter in this volume. See also Helen Laville, "The Importance of Being (In) Earnest," in *The US Government, Citizen Groups and the Cold War: The State-Private Network*, eds. Helen Laville and Hugh Wilford (London: Routledge, 2006), 54–55.
17 Lawrence Wittner, *The Struggle against the Bomb* (Stanford, CA: Stanford University Press, 1993), 171. For context of Soviet peace movement, also see Patrick Iber's contribution in this volume.
18 Wittner, *The Struggle*, 175–77.
19 Wittner, *The Struggle*, 177.
20 For quotes from non-communist participants, see Wittner, *The Struggle*, 175–76.
21 For reference to the term "peace offensive," and discussion of its implications from a US perspective, see United States, *Report on the Communist "Peace" Offensive: A Campaign to Disarm and Defeat the United States*. 1951.
22 Wittner, *The Struggle*, 177.
23 Women's Affairs Section, Semi-annual report, 1 July–31 December 1949, as cited in Laville, "The Importance," 55, fn 21.
24 Laville, "The Importance," 55, fn 22.
25 For reference to the notion of women as prey see Yusta Rodrigo, "The mobilization," 54.
26 Laville, *Cold War Women*, 112.
27 WIDF, *We Accuse!: Report of the Commission of the Women's International Democratic Federation in Korea, May 16 to 27, 1951* (Berlin: WIDF, 1951), 6.
28 See Sahr Conway-Lanz, *Collateral Damage Americans, Noncombatant Immunity, and Atrocity After World War II* (New York: Routledge, 2006), 151–52.
29 For details on the reactions, see Helen Laville, "The Memorial Day Statement: Women's Organizations in the 'Peace Offensive'," in *The Cultural Cold War in Western Europe, 1945–1960*, eds. Giles Scott-Smith and Hans Krabbendam (London: F. Cass, 2003), 195–97.
30 As quoted in Laville, "The Memorial Day Statement,"195.
31 Helen Laville argues that this document, soon known as the "Memorial Day Statement," attempted to define proper peace initiatives, also shaped by the moral values of women in the US. Helen Laville, "The Memorial Day Statement," 196.
32 For information on the WUUN, see also Jennifer De Forest, "Women United for the United Nations: US Women Advocating for Collective Security in the Cold War," *Women's History Review* 14/1 (2006): 61–74.
33 Laville, "The Memorial Day Statement," 197.
34 Yusta Rodrigo, "The Mobilization of Women in Exile," 54; see also Mercedes Yusta Rodrigo, *Madres coraje contra Franco: la Union de Mujeres Espanolas en Francia : del antifascismo a la Guerra Fria (1941–1950)* (Madrid: Catedra, 2009).
35 Yusta Rodrigo, "The Mobilization of Women in Exile," 54.
36 For the changing US positions, see Joan Maria Thomas, *Roosevelt and Franco during the Second World War: From the Spanish Civil War to Pearl Harbor* (New York: Palgrave Macmillan, 2008), 3–24.
37 Walter LaFeber, *America, Russia, and the Cold War, 1945–1980* (New York: Wiley, 1980), 60.
38 For context see Dominic Tierney, *FDR and the Spanish Civil War: Neutrality and Commitment in the Struggle That Divided America* (Durham, NC: Duke University Press, 2007), especially 135–60.

39 For quotes see Greg Grandin, *The Last Colonial Massacre: Latin America in the Cold War* (Chicago: University of Chicago Press, 2004), 17; Susan Buck-Morss, *Dreamworld and Catastrophe: The Passing of Mass Utopia in East and West* (Cambridge, Mass.: MIT Press, 2000), 9.
40 "Yo no me lo podía creer. Me veía con mi máquina de coser en París, y de pronto estaba en medio de toda esa gente magnífica, todas esas mujeres, africanas, asiáticas, polacas, rusas [...]," as cited in Yusta Rodrigo, "The Mobilization of Women in Exile," 56.
41 Nina Popova, *Women in the Land of Socialism* (Moscow: Foreign Languages Pub. House, 1949).
42 Maxine Molyneux, "State, Gender, and Institutional Change: The Federación de Mujeres Cubanas," in *Hidden Histories of Gender and the State in Latin America*, eds., Elizabeth Dore and Maxine Molyneux (Durham, NC: Duke University Press, 2000), 299.
43 Scholars increasingly emphasize the diversity of feminist positions and the political lefts. See, for example, the collection of essays in Nancy Hewitt, ed., *No Permanent Waves: Recasting Histories of U.S. Feminism* (New Brunswick, NJ: Rutgers University Press, 2010).
44 For references to the 1959 WIDF congress in Santiago and its impact on women's political participation in Cuba see Barbara Nelson and Najama Caudhuri, *Women and Politics Worldwide* (New Haven: Yale University Press, 1994), 195–96.
45 Vilma Espín and Elizabeth Stone, eds., *Women and the Cuban Revolution: Speeches and Documents* (New York: Pathfinder Press, 1981), 40.
46 "... and Fidel provided the name: Federation of Cuban Women," Espín and Stone, eds., *Women and the Cuban Revolution*, 40–41.
47 Swerdlow, *Women Strike for Peace*, 37, as cited in de Haan, *Continuing Cold War Paradigms*, 548.
48 Flynn gave her first public speech at the age of 16, "What Socialism Will Do for Women," and started a feminist column for the *Daily Worker* in 1936. See Leila E. Villaverde, *Feminist Theories and Education* (New York: Peter Lang, 2008), 38.
49 As cited in Helen Laville, "Spokeswomen for Democracy: The International Work of the National Council of Negro Women in the Cold War," in *Cross-Routes: The Meanings of "Race" for the 21st Century*, eds. Paola Boi and Sabine Bröck-Sallah (Münster: Lit, 2003), 126–27.
50 Margot Badran, "Feminists, Islam, and the State in Egypt," in *Global Feminisms since 1945: A Survey of Issues and Controversies*, ed. Bonnie Smith (London: Routledge, 2000), 25.
51 Ann E. Towns, *Women and States: Norms and Hierarchies in International Society* (Cambridge: Cambridge University Press, 2010), 117.
52 For references to anti-colonial activism and the WIDF see Jacqueline Castledine, "'In a Solid Bond of Unity': Anti-colonial Feminism in the Cold war Era," *Journal of Women's History* 20/4 (2008): 57–81.
53 Cheryl Johnson-Odim and Nina Emma Mba, *For Women and the Nation: Funmilayo Ransome-Kuti of Nigeria* (Urbana: University of Illinois Press, 1997), 139.
54 Johnson-Odim and Mba, *For Women and the Nation*, 140. Also see the publication that resulted from her conference participation: WIDF, *That They May Live: African Women Arise* (Berlin: WIDF, 1954).
55 Johnson-Odim and Mba, *For Women and the Nation*, 145.
56 *Ibid.*
57 Johnson-Odim and Mba, *For Women and the Nation*, 148–49.
58 Ann Towns, *Women and States*, 117.
59 For some examples of the wide-ranging evidence of the maternalist component of WIDF activism, see WIDF, *For Their Rights as Mothers, Workers, Citizens*

(Berlin: WIDF, 1952); WIDF, *The Rights of Women, Defence of Children, Peace* (Berlin: WIDF, 1954); WIDF, *Protection of Motherhood, as a Right of Women and a Responsibility of Society* (Berlin: WIDF, 1958).
60 Nikolai Aleksandrovich Kovalsky and Elena Petrovna Blinova, eds., *Women Today* (Moscow: Progress Publishers, 1975), 301.
61 WIDF, *I Want to Live: Ban Atomic Weapons* (Berlin: WIDF, 1954), cover and p. 7.
62 For reprint, source of quote, and context, see James Rothrock, *Divided We Fall: How Disunity Leads to Defeat* (Bloomington, IN: Author House, 2006), 147, fn 21.
63 WIDF, "The Situation in the Countries of Indochina and Solidarity with their Peoples," *Council Meeting of the Women's International Democratic Federation, Budapest (5–9 October 1970)*. For an account of the meeting, also see Sheila Rowbotham, *Women, Resistance, and Revolution: A History of Women and Revolution in the Modern World* (New York: Pantheon Books, 1972), 218–19. Wolfson, at the time, was part of a group called D.C. Women's Liberation. See her testimonial account "Clenched Fist, Open Heart," in *The Feminist Memoir Project: Voices from Women's Liberation*, eds. Rachel DuPlessis and Ann Snitow (New York: Three Rivers Press, 1998), 268–83. For quote, see Rowbotham, *Women, Resistance, and Revolution*, 218.
64 Judy Tzu-Chun Wu, "Rethinking Global Sisterhood: Peace Activism and Women's Orientalism," in *No Permanent Waves*, ed. Nancy Hewitt, 193–220, for WIDF ref. see 215–16.
65 Fanny Edelman, "Entrevista en la Union de Mujeres de Viet Nam del Norte con la presidenta Ha Thi Kue," 1973, unprocessed material, Communist Party Archives, Buenos Aires, 3–4.
66 Hilkka Pietilä, *The Unfinished Story of Women and the United Nations* (New York and Geneva: United Nations, 2007), 38–39.
67 See Raluca Maria Popa's insightful chapter "Translating Equality between Women and Men across Cold War Divides: Women Activists from Hungary and Romania and the Creation of International Women's Year," in *Gender Politics and Everyday Life in State Socialist East and Central Europe*, eds., Jill Massino and Shana Penn (New York: Palgrave Macmillan, 2009), 59–74.
68 WIDF and World Congress for International Women's Year (IWY), *Bulletin*, November 4–5, 1974 (Berlin, GDR: Freda Brown and International Preparatory Committee for the World Congress for IWY, 1974), 1. For evidence of the wide range of participants, see also WIDF and World Congress for IWY, *Communique*, Berlin, Feb. 6, 1975, by the International Preparatory Committee for the World Congress for IWY (Berlin,1975), 2.
69 WIDF and World Congress for IWY, *Bulletin*, 4.
70 For long-term consequences of IWY, see Judith P. Zinsser, "The United Nations Decade for Women: A Quiet Revolution," *The History Teacher* 24 (Nov. 1990): 19–29.
71 United Nations, *World Plan of Action for the Implementation of the Objectives of the International Women's Year: A Summarized Version* (New York: United Nations, Centre for Economic and Social Information, 1976); see also Arvonne Fraser, "Becoming Human: The Origins and Development of Women's Human Rights," *Human Rights Quarterly* 21/4 (1999): 906.
72 See Popa,"Translating Equality," 59–74. Popa illustrates that in the 1970s, Romanian and Hungarian representatives to the UN's Commission on the Status of Women (CSW) were instrumental in pushing for IWY. Women from Eastern Europe were among those who actively promoted women's rights and gender equity.
73 Cynthia Enloe, *The Morning After: Sexual Politics at the End of the Cold War* (Berkeley: University of California Press, 1993), 18–19. For inspiration for a research frame of the subject, see also Charlotte Hooper, *Manly States:*

Masculinities, International Relations, and Gender Politics (New York: Columbia University Press, 2001).
74 Enloe, The Morning After, 18.

Selected bibliography

Castledine, Jacqueline, "'In a Solid Bond of Unity': Anticolonial Feminism in the Cold War Era," *Journal of Women's History* 20/4 (2008): 57–81.

——, "Continuing Cold War Paradigms in the Western Historiography of Transnational Women's Organisations: The Case of the Women's International Democratic Federation (WIDF)," *Women's History Review* 19/4 (September 2010): 547–73.

de Haan, Francisca, "Hoffnungen auf eine bessere Welt: Die frühen Jahre der Internationalen Demokratischen Frauenföderation (IDFF/WIDF) (1945–50)," *Feministische Studien* 27/2 (November 2009): 241–57.

Ilic, Melanie, "Soviet Women, Cultural Exchange and the Women's International Democratic Federation," in *Reassessing Cold War Europe*, eds. Sari Autio and Katalin Miklóssy (London: Routledge, 2011), 157–74.

Laville, Helen, "The Importance of Being (In) Earnest," in *The US Government, Citizen Groups and the Cold War: The State-Private Network*, eds. Helen Laville and Hugh Wilford (London: Routledge, 2006), 47–65.

——, "The Memorial Day Statement: Women's Organizations in the 'Peace Offensive'," in *The Cultural Cold War in Western Europe, 1945–1960*, eds. Giles Scott-Smith and Hans Krabbendam (London: F. Cass, 2003), 192–210.

Pojmann, Wendy, "For Mothers, Peace and Family: International (Non)-Cooperation among Italian Catholic and Communist Women's Organisations during the Early Cold War," *Gender & History* 23/2 (August 2011): 415–29.

Yusta Rodrigo, Mercedes, "The Mobilization of Women in Exile: The Case of the *unión de mujeres antifascistas españolas* in France (1944–50)," *Journal of Spanish Cultural Studies* 6/1 (March 2005): 53.

Part II
Separating enemies from friends: communism, anti-communism, and the construction of Cold War realities

4 Cold War happiness

Singing pioneers, internal enemies and Hungarian life under Stalinism

László Kürti

> Like a squirrel on the tree,
> The pioneer is just as happy,
> Singing songs endlessly.
> When he pitches a camp somewhere,
> All the small pals sing similarly,
> From dawn to dusk.
> Years pass under the summer trees,
> The singing is so happy,
> Happy melody forms the lines:
> Very good, this life is so happy.[1]
>   "Happy Pioneer"

In June of 1965 I was part of a pioneer school group heading for a vacation to the mountainous part of Hungary, singing our songs, including the "Happy Pioneer," over and over again all the way to the campsite, a six-hour journey, at least. At the time I did not fully understand this song's hidden significance, but was amazed at how long we were able to persist with our singing. Looking back, I am not sure why we sang the way we did, nor am I sure whether we were told to do so (most probably yes) – but we reached our campsite in fine spirits, totally exhausted and more than ready for a good night's sleep. Taking a closer look at that song, and its myriad of artistic ramifications in films, photographs, posters, music and fine art, one cannot but agree that the obviously banal message was simple: people under duress, like most Eastern Europeans after World War II, were not depressed, afraid, or lethargic. On the contrary, they were strong, brave, and ready to live in peace, and – above all – they all were extremely happy. This fabricated culture of happiness was one of the fundamental strategies introduced by Soviet Premier Josef Stalin and his followers during the period that has come to be known as the Cold War (*hidegháború* in Hungarian). To show how this culture of happiness functioned and why the construction of happiness was so important in shaping the Cold War atmosphere, I will investigate here the example of Hungary, a country that lost the war on the side of Nazi Germany but soon managed to become a staunch ally of the Soviet Union.

I start with the assumption that some 20 years after the official Cold War ended, and well over 60 years since it was invented, enough time has elapsed whereby we can now see that this period was not the homogenous era it was once imagined to be.[2] Whatever date we assign to the inception of the Cold War, the meeting at Potsdam in July–August 1945 brought into clear relief the tensions between U.S. President Harry Truman and Stalin.[3] Winston Churchill, for example, was already convinced that the Soviet Union, and with it communism, was an evil force, conflating Stalin with the Devil. As for Eastern Europe, Winston Churchill reckoned later that "police governments are prevailing in nearly every case, and so far, except in Czechoslovakia, there is no true democracy."[4] Not surprisingly, George F. Kennan's idea of "containment" of Soviet power was received with cheers in the West. The U.S. and its allies' ambitious efforts to install economic, military and spy operations in order to save the world from communist infiltration were part and parcel of Cold War ideology emanating from the West. As Harold Wydra writes, "The aggressive anti-communism of the United States in the absence of a concrete military conflict with the Soviet Union was based on the pervasive fear of contagion with the disease of communism."[5]

In this chapter, I argue that there were different Cold Wars after 1945, and that their single most important unifying element was the antagonistic and dualistic thinking characteristic of both the Western powers, led by the United States of America, and the Soviet Union headed by its leader Josef Stalin. Cold war, just like any war, has an internal (i.e., how we see them and what we do about it) and an external dimension (i.e., how they see us and what they do about it) that provides its structure and meaning. The external dimension can be best summed up as a feverish, if not furious, competition between superpowers, specifically the victorious Soviet Union and the United States. This resulted in an ideological, economic, militaristic and cultural bipolarization of the world into us and them. A subtitle in an article in *Life* magazine on February 26, 1945, describes the Big Three (Churchill, Roosevelt and Stalin) as those who will "shape the world's future."[6] Just how these leaders went about framing their own country's future has been the subject of many previous studies; therefore, I intend to focus on what I consider to be the two most important aspects of the Cold War in its East-Central European setting – the combined processes of fighting against the enemy both literally and through the workers' movement of Stakhanovism. All this was legitimated via a plan to obtain peace and social happiness through the Cold War personality cult of Stalin and his Hungarian double, Mátyás Rákosi (1892–1971).

Stalinism, fear and happiness

After 1945, Hungary was not in a good position to negotiate with anybody about anything. It was disliked by the victorious Soviets and Westerners, but it was even more hated by its neighbors. There were plenty of reasons for such antagonism.[7] Allied in both world wars with the losers and engaging in an irredentist and chauvinistic war from 1938 to 1941 to regain territories in Slovakia, Romania and Yugoslavia, Hungary had been a thorn in the side of her neighbors as well as the Western powers. After 1945, the presence of the Red Army in Hungary, together with hyperinflation and the war reparation payments to the Soviets, offered no other choice but to accept unconditionally the demands of the Kremlin.[8] Yet, in one way most of the East European countries were not saved from Stalinization that was more specific than just Sovietization. That meant not only a duplication of the political, economic and cultural models set up by the USSR, but also the acceptance of Stalin as the only authority, a supreme being whose words and deeds could not be questioned. In the Western world, Stalinization reinforced the conviction that Stalin embodied the Devil, responsible for all the evil standing in the way of progress, democracy and peace.[9]

There were several things that supported the Cold War – directly or indirectly – in Hungary. The first was the Stalinist version of Marxism–Leninism, the motivations of the communists during the period from 1947 to 1953, from the election when the Communist Party first gained a majority to the death of Stalin six years later. The megalomania of the Communist Party chief Mátyás Rákosi during his reign (1946–56) was another. Thirdly, Moscow and the presence of the Soviet army strengthened and supported movements to facilitate violent "revolutionary" policy, the "dictatorship of the proletariat" as it came to be called. The fourth had to do with the sheer number of police (both open and secret) and political cadres present not only on the streets but in schools and workplaces and on collective farms. The social and economic situation in Hungary, a weakened and war-torn country following the war, also contributed to the fear and terror as well as the creation of a new personality cult that would coalesce into an ideology of Cold War in Hungary following the rigged election in 1947.[10] When, on November 4, 1945, Hungary voted in its first free election after the war, the result was not unexpected: the Independent Smallholders Party (*Független Kisgazdapárt*) won 57 percent and the Soviet-backed Communist Party (*Magyar Kommunista Párt*) only 17 percent of the votes. It had begun to seem as if Hungary, despite occupation by the Soviet army, would be allowed to establish a truly democratic multiparty system, maintain its relative independence, and distribute land to needy peasants – in a word, to get on with a stable and normal life.[11] Yet in a matter of months it became evident that the coalition of peasant parties was on a steep uphill climb to make ends meet.[12]

With the escalation of Cold War hostilities, it became clear that the economic and political pressures did not go far enough to elicit the support from the population that the communist leaders felt was needed to build a strong Stalinist state.[13] Thus, to win over the masses, promises had to be made. One crucial aspect in formulating the culture of Cold War happiness had to do with the elimination of enemies, both real and fictitious, at home and abroad.

The original formulas of V. I. Lenin, that the "real enemy is in your own country," and the necessity to transform "the imperialist war into civil war," were aptly applied soon after the Soviet army occupied Eastern Europe. From the Soviet perspective, they were fighting against capitalist, mainly U.S., hegemony over the area, a concern that was not kept secret by either side, the U.S. and the Soviet Union. To be sure, the Yugoslav party boss, Yosif Broz Tito, was soon described as a servant of Western imperialism, hence his fashionable imagery as a "chained dog." Wholly under the sway of Cold War ideology, this is how the logic worked, according to the Hungarian party chief, Rákosi:

> The accomplices of the imperialists, and especially the right-wing Social Democrats must be exposed. The British Labour leaders Atlee, Bevin and others, Blum and his ilk in France, all of whom wear a democratic mask, are helping reaction, are inciting hatred towards the Soviet Union and the people's democracies and are trying to violate the unity of the working class. American reaction attaches the greatest importance to destroying the rights of the working people wherever possible. As a means towards its plans for world domination the Americans are trying to set up global military-strategic bases. They are taking over the strategic positions, which the weakened British imperialists can no longer retain. The Americans aim at turning the Western zones of Germany and Japan into military-strategic bases against the Soviet Union. They are trying to realise their imperialist designs through the economic enslavement of the weaker states. Greece, Italy, France, Turkey and Austria have received loans running into hundreds of millions of dollars, which have placed these countries in the front ranks of inflation.[14]

However, this was not the full story. Cold War ideology worked in a more complex fashion: to create fear in order to achieve victory was one thing, but to sell it – especially the threat of nuclear attack by the capitalist/imperialist enemy – an equally strong feeling had to be inculcated into citizens. To achieve that end, a promise had to be made of building a peaceful and economically sound as well as autonomous socialist society in which all would be happy. But the official discourse was even more sinister because it implied that anybody who was unhappy was also not a believer but an enemy of the system, its ideology and its leaders. And this is why the regime carried out its utopian goal of creating a happy society by instilling fear in its citizens that internal enemies would be outed and destroyed. Internal enemies had to be found first in the Communist Party for, according to Stalinist political demonology, the untrustworthy class enemy had "infiltrated the communist party."[15] As the writer-journalist Paul Ignotus (1901–78), who served a six-year jail sentence in Hungary between 1949 and 1956, wrote, anybody in the party could be an enemy described as "Titoist-Trotskyite-Clericalist-Zionist-Fascist-Racist-Nationalist-Cosmopolitanist-Imperialist-Capitalist scoundrels who had been in the pay of American, British, French, Yugoslav and (before 1945) German and Hungarian secret agencies."[16] They were not the same as those enemies on the right, since these internal enemies within the party were deemed to be traitors, a sin so grave in the eyes of the rulers that they all deserved harsh punishment, including the death sentence.

Soviet Stalinism simply meant, in the words of the philosopher Agnes Heller, "terrorist totalitarianism," which can be defined as the inculcation of fear and the use of violence to achieve desired ends.[17] Promulgating fear, as Montesquieu recognized centuries ago, is one of the best weapons in the hands of tyrants. Violence against certain groups of people and spreading fear in others had a very specific momentum and direction, yet it also worked in a random fashion, for "random selection inflicts general fear, for no one knows who comes next."[18] The new enemies had multiple faces: aristocrats, former military and police officers, youth, leftist subversive intellectuals, clerics, merchants and craftsman and, above all, peasants of the hinterland areas.[19]

Among the vestiges of the "bourgeois past" singled out for elimination in the new state was not only the retrograde peasant culture, but everything associated with it, most specifically religion and religious holidays, as religion still played a major role in people's lives in 1947.[20] Priests and devout church members, especially, faced extreme prejudice and were used by the party as scapegoats for Hungary's social problems. Young workers and intellectuals were urged to form "village brigades" (*falujáró brigádok*) to assist in rebuilding the devastated countryside and provide labor for the harvest and, undoubtedly, to re-educate the "untrustworthy peasants." Industrial plants were also in the forefront of such village brigades.

Happiness and prosperity were very much a central concept in building a new society in postwar Hungary. The notion of creating a country inhabited entirely by happy people was on the mind of the country's ruler from the beginning. Mátyás Rákosi, the first Communist Party secretary and a capable orator, loved to utilize in his speeches and writings the words "*boldog*" and "*boldogulás*" – meaning happy and prosperity respectively, although the root of the two words is the same. In a speech given to the miners (!) in 1947, he said of the new peasants: "All around the country, everyone speaks highly of those new farmers, still working the land with their ten fingers, and could not tell which plot was done by the old and which one by the new owners because both are tilled with love and care. All in all, this reveals that during our land distribution only those received land who love it and respect it. We want to make sure that all of them will become healthy and happy small farmers."[21] Speaking to intellectuals a few weeks later, Rákosi reiterated that the Communist Party "respects and values the work of intellectuals, its willingness in helping reconstruction, and with this progressive elite the party wants to work together to build a happier society."[22] Surely, there was something utopistic about communist happiness. Even though they promised happiness on earth, they did not envision that it would happen immediately or be within the reach of the masses. In 1948, Rákosi announced that "true advancement will start with our new five-year plan to make our homeland flourish and happy."[23] Even people who were youngsters at that time enjoying the momentary benefit of the land distribution felt the same way. One woman had this to say about the years following World War II: "Of course we were happy. Before the war, my parents only had about 1 acre land rented from a rich peasant. We couldn't make a living on that, so my parents were constantly in debt. Following the land distribution act after 1945, my parents received almost 4 hectares of land on which they were able to build a small farm. That is how we started a new life on our new plot."[24] Youth who were drafted into the army now belonged to the "people's army of peace and happiness."[25] And youth were also trusted because "youth and workers are pervaded with optimism."[26]

The industrial working class, the real bastion in the building of the new society, was also exuding happiness: "In this new country the industrial worker is not a proletarian anymore, he is not the exploited worker of the capitalist. His labor is not robot, but respect and glory. This worker will build his future and socialist homeland proud and happy."[27] Women, too, shared in this sense of well-being: "Women in this new country are different; they were liberated and made equal in every respect to men by people's democracy. Hungarian women are especially thankful for this dual liberation, which made them both as workers and women happy, with joy they take their place in labor, a space that was closed to them by the reactionary forces but which is now open to them all."[28] For instance, various advertisements that appeared in the villages were aimed directly at women to elicit their help in promoting the new three-year plan introduced in 1947. One such slogan read: "Hungarian mothers, Hungarian women, for the happiness of our families assist the 3 year plan!"[29]

Happiness, however, had a price. The well-known Cold War formula – work for peace by fighting the enemy – meant several things. Hungary's Cold War euphoria resulted, according to one ironic saying of party chief Rákosi, in "salami tactics," the elimination of the radical opposition and then of members of the moderate opposition. The untrustworthy peasant was first the rich peasant for whom the Russian expression "kulak" was borrowed, but anybody could be placed in this category described as the enemy of the system.[30] Such "*zsíros paraszt*" (literally: greasy peasant), as the derogatory term was used at the time, however, found every means possible to avoid paying taxes or fines instead of providing the specific produce for the established quota set by the local councils. Here is a testimony as to why it was impossible to fulfill the established quota:

> I declare that we do not have any means to work on the field, we are totally dispossessed. In 1945 I had only one horse which died, and all my money I had to use up to buy another horse without which I cannot do agriculture. In 1946 there was an incredible drought and what I harvested I had to sow immediately so I will have bread in 1947. At the same time,

there was an outbreak of a strange disease among the poultry and all of my chickens died. Thus, I am unable to pay any fine at this point.[31]

Another farmer also tried to get out of the established quota by arguing that "the pig bit his wife's one finger which makes working on the field difficult." Another man asked local leaders to be excused from having to pay a fine by explaining that he had just married his daughter off and her "dowry cost too much for him," a good reason, in his view, why he could not fulfill the established quota.

A baker and his wife also became declared enemies of the state for selling their bread above the price limit established by the state. Called *"feketézők"* (black marketers) in popular parlance, the couple received altogether a ten-year jail sentence. Their two teenage daughters wrote a letter requesting clemency to the president of the country, explaining their helpless situation:

> Since 16 November 1947, we live without our father and mother and keep our sick 72 year old incapacitated grandmother with us as well. We do not want to beg on the streets, and we are too young to work. I am only 12, and my younger sister is 11. We know that our parents committed their crime in order to buy us food and clothing, all in all to provide us with a decent living. We are also aware that our parents are very sorry for the crime they committed and they now want to be useful members of the working society and by so doing to assist our developing democracy.[32]

It is possible that this letter was the reason that the baker's wife was released a year later from jail.

In the first years of the Cold War era, elimination of the "enemy" was the battle cry of state propaganda and, as such, dominated political messages throughout the country. The one group the regime did not target as possible enemies of the state was children, primarily because party officials believed that they had not been tainted by the old bourgeois ideas of their parents. No wonder the first gesture to Hungarian children was the opening of the Pioneer Camp at Csillebérc in 1948, a beautiful site in the hill district of Budapest. When the camp was opened a large sign was put up at the entrance: "For our happy and joyous childhood, we thank the Party and Comrade Rákosi." From that time on, the camp grew into the most coveted summer resort for pioneer camping. Naturally, being from the countryside, this was not within people's reach; the Pioneer City, as it was called by the 1960s, became so important and coveted that small schools from villages simply could not obtain permission to visit it. What was the solution? Naturally, to build many more similar camps all around the country, for both the pioneers and their older schoolmates, the Komsomol (*KISZ* in Hungarian) youth. Party rulers also favored another type of camp, the so-called "work camp" (*építőtábor*), which also aided various construction and harvesting projects throughout the countryside as well as in neighboring socialist countries. By the time we went to school, Rákosi and his cronies were gone, but the Cold War remained, and the notion of happiness continued to linger in the air. As schoolchildren, we were told that if we studied hard and got good grades and behaved well, we would receive as a bonus a week or two at one of these summer camps. That was one incentive, the other was the price; it was virtually no cost to parents. I can speak only for myself, but most of my schoolmates felt the same way and we were really happy when we got the chance to leave our home village and go for the summer pioneer camp. So, why would we not sing?

Little did we know then that melodies and texts fashioned after the Soviet-written songs (*chastuski*) were embedded with satirical political rhymes aimed at bourgeois enemies and extolling the virtues of socialist reconstruction. One such song – "Let's Sing, Pal, about Our Beautiful Homeland, Hungary" – that was popular in those years and which we were made to sing describes children enjoying life and expressing happiness. And what is the best sign of happiness? A singing child, of course. At least this is what the leaders and the people alike believed.

> Let's sing, pal, about our beautiful homeland, Hungary,
> This is where our cradle rocked,
> Our mother raised us here.
> Let's sing, pal, about our beautiful homeland, Hungary,
> Our country giving us all its treasures.
> This land is ours, the forest, the meadow's ears,
> And all flowers bloom for us.

Why sing? The answer is provided by another favored Cold War song, "Our Lips Sing a Happy Song":

> Life is easier and so is production when we sing,
> Singing hails us forward when we go to fight,
> So long as our lips open for a song.
> This earth will be ours and no one can beat us in the entire world.

There were, of course, more serious songs with similar tropes such as the "coming of the new, beautiful world" (új, szebb világ), the rising of "the shining sun" (napfény) and "how beautiful is this life" (szép az élet), together with the constants, "competition" (verseny), "work" (munka), and "fighting" (harc). These last two had numerous variations: fight and work, or to work in order to fight, or fighting while working and the like.[33]

The adoption of the Stalin Cantata, originally written in 1938 by composer A. V. Aleksandrov with the text supplied by M. Inuskina, is a good example of the eagerness and willingness on the part of Hungarian intellectuals to live up to ideological expectations.[34] In the first verse of the song the chorus sings, "Our hearts open up upon hearing the word of Stalin, And happy is the man who sings of you." However, the following verses in Hungarian do not follow the original cantata. This is especially noticeable in the third verse, in which the Russian composer extols the virtues of the Chinese (communist) soldiers, whereas the Hungarianized version is nothing but a mediocre attempt at pleasing Stalin, as in the lines: "Because Stalin is our fight and Stalin is the peace, And with the name of Stalin the world will be better." The fact that there is no such lyric in the original Stalin Cantata is well worth pondering for a moment. How was it possible that a songbook with such a textual sabotage was allowed to pass censorship? Or was it the censors themselves who committed such a forgery? The answer probably is the latter: István Raics was asked to translate the first verse of the song faithfully, but instead of translating the rest he simply wrote verses two and three on his own about Stalin. This can be easily followed, for the editors decided to publish the original Russian text with the Hungarian, a task that aided major Hungarian choirs at that time that were required to sing in Russian as well as in Hungarian. No matter how fashionable it was, the Stalin Cantata went out of favor after the death of Stalin, and songs that we were required to learn as children did not include any reference to him. Yet, the desire to build a happy, new socialist society was still strong in the hearts of millions and commissioned artwork did not cease to be produced.

Indeed, Cold War ideology celebrated "the race for reconstruction" (*újjáépítési verseny*), which along with the slogan "Hurry, Give, Help" (*Siess, Adj, Segíts*), urged people to work together toward the building of a new socialist society. Nowhere is this summarized more beautifully than in the title of a fashionable song of the era, "The Future belongs to the workers" (*Munkásoké a jövő*), with the last two lines "The nation is building a new country, where the future belongs to the workers."

In ideology it was Stalinization all right, but the means to implement it was the work of Andrei Zhdanov, the chief theoretician of cultural production after 1946 in the USSR. *Zhdanovshchina*, or Zhdanovism, meant not only a total censorship of all artistic production but a constant reminder that it is social realism that serves the purpose of the socialist state. Moreover, Zhdanov asserted that Western art – immoral, antihuman and decadent – serves only the interests of the ruling class. Throughout this period, Soviet figures were used for propaganda purposes: pictures of Lenin, Stalin and Rákosi filled the screens of theatres, and were evoked in songs, all to remind the people of the values of socialism, the imminence of war and the pre-eminence of the Communist Party. The country's rulers advocated a new "socialist" popular culture and entertainment as vehicles for "justifiable" political indoctrination. The swift ideological programming of key propaganda tools such as movies, television, newspaper and radio, which took place from 1948 to1950, all helped to contribute to the goal of making "agitation propaganda work" more popular.

The blueprint of proletarian culture was handed over to Hungary by the Soviets. As early as 1923, Leon Trotsky, later an enemy of Stalin, had this to say about the future of proletarian culture: it will be "a society which will have thrown off the pinching and stultifying worry about one's daily bread, in which community restaurants will prepare good, wholesome and tasteful food for all to choose, in which communal laundries will wash clean everyone's good linen, in which children, all the children, will be well-fed and strong and gay, and in which they will absorb the fundamental elements of science and art as they absorb albumen and air and the warmth of the sun."[35] The leaders also assured the people that the dictatorship of the proletariat was only the first stage of the fight. In Trotsky's words: "The liberating significance of the dictatorship of the proletariat consists in the fact that it is temporary – for a brief period only – that it is a means of clearing the road and of laying the foundations of a society without classes and of a culture based upon solidarity."[36] No wonder, then, that happiness culture was based on such a vision!

In conjunction with this propaganda, not only cultural identities but gender identities were also drastically reorganized. The era's fashionable motto was "Fight" (*harc*), translated as men and women faithfully serving and fulfilling party incentives. "We are merely soldiers in a campaign," uttered Trotsky earlier in the 1920s, and Stalin believed this until the last day of his life. "Forward for the establishment of socialist culture," another popular slogan, extolled citizens to spend as much time as possible in an organized manner with fellow DISZ members. Young pioneers greeted each other with "Forward" (*Előre*), which was meant as both an exhortation and a sense of direction about the coming of the future communist society. Mass sports activities soon became the ideal way of educating oneself and keeping fit physically. Outstanding and "worthy" participants were awarded state honors such as the Prize for the Socialist Culture and, most prestigious of all, the Stalin Prize or Kossuth Prize. Cold War-era art was above all an ideological educational tool, an instrument to mould the consciousness of the individual socialist citizen. This utilitarian approach formed the foundation of the aesthetic of socialist realism, and indeed copied aesthetic trends present in popular (folk) music as well as that of Soviet culture. For poets and musicians, this provided an impetus to write music for the masses that was above all concrete and easily recognizable, like folk songs, and grounded in the plight of the socialist state. Obviously, they sought to communicate to a wide audience by drawing on the themes expressed in popular melody, such as happiness and optimism, as well as those endorsed by the Soviet Union (progress, industrialization, future). At the same time, in order to be coherent, and to avoid superficial imitation of folk music, they attempted to utilize the various forms of European music of the workers' movement. Composers were also involved with a critical *Kulturkamp* endeavor: to root out all styles of song and music that were deemed bourgeois, anti-Soviet and Western. Since the function of socialist art was to acculturate the young and ideologically re-educate the peasants and the intelligentsia, it followed that "false art" and pre-World War II musical culture had to be identified, so that they could be properly condemned and eliminated. The arts, including music, underwent a profound transformation in accordance with the cultural policy of the party.[37]

Literature, posters and films were under the ideological cultural-political sway of "socialist realism," fabricated to hail Soviet heroes. György Lukács observed in 1962: "All science and all literature had to serve exclusively the propagandistic demands formulated above, by Stalin himself. The understanding and spontaneous elaboration of reality by means of literature, was more and more strictly prohibited. 'Party' literature must no longer creatively reflect objective reality, but must illustrate in literary form the decisions of the Party."[38] This was equally true for cinema; as József Révai stressed, "From Hollywood we only get rubbish, from Moscow we get films teaching humanity ... It is not New York but Moscow, which teaches us the new, progressive, socialist culture expressing realism, educating the working masses and helping them in their fight and work – a culture for which the Hungarian people is longing."[39] Popular culture surely followed such central directives, with movies being singled out as the number one medium for carrying the message, providing rich evidence of film and music, all with the central themes of happiness. As in the pioneer song:

> This song is about our land,
> There is no more beautiful country,
> Our country is the land of peace,
> Its inhabitants are happy people.

To further inculcate awareness of communist Stalinism, clubs and "culture circles" were created under the aegis of socialist centralized cultural homes (*művelődési ház*).[40] Many of these buildings were prewar clubs and associations that were nationalized by the communists and had to be refurbished and painted accordingly. Women's and workers' poetry circles, brass bands, a youth folk dance ensemble, choirs, hiking and nature clubs, retired workers' associations and Esperanto clubs were established to serve the recreational needs of the people. Local theatre was reorganized out of the prewar workers' theatre to stage hundreds of "socially accepted and redeeming" plays, many of which followed the tradition that had taken shape during the 1919 Republic of Councils and ensuing decades. While some intellectuals were relocated to the countryside and to re-education camps in the areas of Hortobágy and western Hungary, socialist culture and progress became synonymous with hard-working men and women unselfishly – and in unison – building a socialist nation-state.

Cold War on the labor front

In order to fight the Cold War successfully, the state needed both machinery (technology) and manpower (indoctrinated citizens). The world of labor became a fierce battleground as the nonexistent socialist proletariat had to be created out of the prewar working classes at the same time as the rural underclasses, suspected of retrograde and clerical subversion against the state, had to be coerced into accepting the party line. The social and ideological pressure was immense for those who did not fulfill or comply with expected quotas. They were singled out and exposed as "enemies" of the socialist state.

The establishment of an official workers' movement and the elimination of previous means of production dramatically altered the fate of workers, as well as that of East European industry as a whole. The transition from prewar capitalism to a postwar Stalinist state fundamentally changed the nature of working-class relations and the way in which political socialization affected youth within the entire Soviet orbit. The brief period of transition, however, was the time during which Stalin and his party bureaucrats (known through the Russian word *apparatchik*) made their move to construct Bolshevik-style and Soviet satellite states in East-Central Europe. Between May 1945 and December 1947, the Hungarian Communist Party increased its membership from 150,000 to 864,000, constituting a massive show of support and a popular base for its legitimacy. After two years of struggle, political and religious factions were eliminated and the newly created communist Hungarian Workers' Party (*Magyar Dolgozók Pártja* or MDP) became the country's only party.[41] Similarly, large landed estates were removed from aristocratic ownership, to be redistributed among needy peasants. Those who were teachers, bureaucrats and white-collar workers before the war were also suspected of harboring antagonism against the new regime and were "B-listed." Everyone who was B-listed and held a job had to be checked as to his or her past involvement with fascist parties, trustworthiness and loyalty to the Communist Party.[42] With such state terror in full swing, no serious opposition to communist rule could emerge.

It soon became clear that the communists were not about to allow the proliferation of prewar youth organizations and, in keeping with the Soviet model of the *Komsomol*, a single association was created. The young János Kádár, Hungary's powerful future leader, presented a radical proposition in 1947 to eliminate "reactionary" and "rightist" factions by propagating a single-party system. Consequently, following the establishment of the Hungarian Peoples' Republic on August 20, 1949, all youth organizations not endorsed by the communists became illegal in March of 1950; in their place, a single youth group, the Workers' Youth Association (*Dolgozó Ifjúsági Szövetség*, or DISZ for short) emerged under the control of the Communist Party.[43]

To successfully create a communist generation, the regime was eager to be the prime mover, together with Moscow, of the socialist international youth movement; hundreds of trusted cadres were sent from Hungary to its biennial world meeting (known in Hungary through its abbreviation as VIT). It seemed that the communist victory following World War II was a victory both by and for the youth in the newly created Soviet bloc.[44]

Following the ideological agenda, the infrastructure was modernized according to principles of socialist urban planning; paved roads were built, electric and water lines were repaired and extended to include the new apartment complexes. Drawing on well-known Soviet socialization patterns of cooperative living, schools, day nurseries, kindergartens and medical facilities were also erected close to where people lived and worked.[45] Free education and health care were introduced as basic rights of citizens of the Stalinist socialist state. Outstanding workers and their families received premium vacations, often spent on the former estates of aristocrats, which now functioned as publicly owned holiday resorts, such as those on Lake Balaton, where not only leisurely activities but also political education were the order of the day. Was this all happiness? Obviously, it was for some.

The overtly ideologized Stalinist work tempo could not have been achieved without winning over the 1.5 million industrial workers under 30 years of age. These nation-wide changes in Stalinist schooling and socialization were felt immediately, as gains in Stakhanovite economic production did not go unnoticed by the state or its citizens. The symbolic significance of the glorification of laborers is well illustrated by the words of a Stakhanovite song crafted to the folk song melody "*Megismerni a kanászt*" ("You Can Recognize the Swineherd"):

> The Stakhanov movement is growing day-by-day,
> Our inventors help to materialize the five-year plan.
> Hey! We'll get ahead for the Soviets are sending us machinery
> And the workers of the world will benefit greatly.[46]

As Valuch explains, "Combativeness, heroism and self-sacrifice acquired high values. A mythologized community rather than the individual, centrally defined so-called community values rather than individual norms, were now posited as the desirable norms for everyday life and public thought."[47]

Work (*munka*, *dolog*) now became strictly "socialist work," following the party's directives. As opposed to the peasantry, which could not be trusted, industrial workers and miners were the primary social base of Stalinism. Wives of miners were especially urged to work as well as fight; as one political leader put it, "women's hands are not only made for gently stroking but they could turn the tools faster, and if needed they can also take up arms."[48] Moreover, women were useful not only for the battlefield and the world of labor but on the home front as well in order to discover enemies responsible for sabotaging the socialist "coal battle" (*széncsata*): "The miners' wives should help their husbands so they start their shift in the mines punctually every day. They should urge their husbands by being interested in their work, by asking them about whether they fulfilled the daily quota or not. The wives should not allow their husbands to stay home without a good reason, or to be late at the morning shift making them conscious that out of the 480 minutes of daily work not one minute is spent idly."[49]

This ideological Stakhanovite masculinization of Hungarian culture certainly stimulated some industrial production and aided the implementation of social policies. Equally extraordinary were the measures taken to curtail women's rights, sexual practices and family life, and the general subordination of women to men concomitant with the solidification of a masculine gender model. Michel Foucault's observation that the modern state attempts to regulate a specific sexual discourse is applicable to Cold War Stalinist-totalitarian states as well, where constraints were placed on fecundity and reproductive behavior.[50] Young females were viewed as essentially masculinized workers (*munkás*), an image reinforced by the blue overalls so visible in the popular media of the early 1950s.[51] Their individualistic desires and sexual pleasures were thought to require taming by the newly conjured citizen of the Stalinist state, replacing the purportedly selfish, egotistic, bourgeois personality. Young women were to bear children for Rákosi's homeland: "*Asszonynak szülni kötelesség, lánynak dicsőség*" – "For a married woman to bear a child is obligation, for a girl, it is honor." Such mothers were identified as progressive and socialist, receiving maternity leave, supplementary consumer goods and "multiple-child bonuses."[52] To achieve a communist utopia, abortion was outlawed, childless families were forced to pay a surtax (tax on childlessness), and contraception was available only in extreme circumstances. At the same time, women were encouraged to be educated – often only at the Marxist-Leninist High Schools of the Communist Party – and to take an active role in local and state-level politics. A national women's organization was created, MNOT (following the earlier Soviet pattern of the *zhenotdel*), to address the needs of all women in Hungary.

The ideological and economic pressure was extremely successful: to date, there have been only three years during which Hungary has witnessed a population boom (1952–54), when children were called "Ratkó kids," after the Stalinist Minister of Health Anna Ratkó. The demographic changes during the early 1950s are instructive indices of Stalinist redefinitions of gender roles and the ways in which these patriarchal tendencies simultaneously undermined and elevated the status of working women. The many inherent contradictions notwithstanding, it looked as if youth had been tamed to become the true vanguard of the Communist Party. Remarkably enough, the image of youth and the future was fused into one common mythic theme, as exemplified by the Democratic World Federation of Youth anthem extolling youth as the "rhythm of the future."[53]

Cold War personality cult

The making of a happy society could not be achieved without the help of Stalin – and his pupil Rákosi. In Rákosi's words: "The happier and freer the working people of Hungary are the more they will treasure the significance of liberation, and the more they will strive to express by all means their warm gratitude to the liberating Soviet Union, to the Soviet youth and the wise leader, the great Stalin."[54] The personality cult of Mátyás Rákosi served to cement ideology to action and at the same time expressed Hungary's unwavering loyalty to the Soviet Union. As one of the Moscow-trained ideologues, József Révai, wrote, "Mátyás Rákosi and we, all the Hungarian communists, all simultaneously Hungarian patriots and patriots of the Soviet Union."[55] To emphasize total submission to their leader, young pioneers sang a hymn of praise to Rákosi:

> We thank you comrade Rákosi,
> The pure flames of our gratitude burn for you,
> Seeing you, our faces become even more proud,
> We'll throw flowers wherever you go.
> We pledge to you comrade Rákosi,
> To take your road, just lead us forever!
> The spring beckoning childish song of ours,
> Will bow to you like a flowery branch.[56]

But the final verse causes a bit of a shock as we discover that the happy children singing their praises to Rákosi are living in a state foster home and their number is expanding:

> Sunshine jumps through the window of our foster home,
> Many clean little tables, many small chairs await us,
> Many new little comrades will join us,
> How good and how beautiful is the foster home!

The father-party-family was one of the symbols that assisted in the remaking of social relations. As Jeffrey Brooks writes, "The metaphor by which the Party became a surrogate family, though less common than the military metaphor, served to enhance the loyalties and priorities of activists."[57] Cold War identity legitimized the workers' state, whose leader had acquired mythical proportions, a feat achieved by well-paid intellectuals. Both the Hungarian party chief Rákosi and Stalin were idolized as "fathers," inspiring numerous novels, poems, films, songs and posters describing their heroic deeds for the "socialist patria." According to one slogan, "*Rákosi a legjobb apa, szereti is minden fia*" ("Rákosi is the best father to all his country's sons"). In 1952, when the country celebrated Rákosi's sixtieth birthday, well-known centres of folk art all around the country were asked to produce new folk art with pertinent socialist themes expressing the unflinching love toward "the greatest son of our beloved homeland."[58] Galvanizing the entire countryside, village artisans were commissioned to create objects with Rákosi, his name or the well-known national coat-of-arms (Rákosi címer) placed on them. The number 60 adorns the middle of several pieces of art, to signify the age of the country's celebrated leader. A carefully selected sample of these artistic objects was then exhibited for public viewing. Potters, carvers, and embroiderers were obviously told by the local leadership how to make these objects so they would pass the careful screening of censors.[59]

Stalin, the epitome of the aggrandizement of the self, stands alone among all of the other East European party chiefs of his time for his ability to maintain a personality cult based on both charisma and terror.[60] How did he achieve the status of a charismatic leader? Such a leader, according to sociologist Max Weber, possesses special gifts of grace that need to be openly offered to the public as proof of divine power. This was not a difficult task for the ideologues bent on dissolving churches, religious orders and Christian beliefs: they resorted to the image of the sacred father that Stalinists created for Stalin. In fact, the fabrication of Stalin/Rákosi as the father of the new socialist country recalls the "imperial cult of the divinely ordained Father of the Fatherland" of the Romanov tsars.[61] However, the cult of leader was not simply about just a father but, as John Schoberlein suggests, about an authoritarian father whose decisions, directions and leadership were never to be questioned.[62] György Lukács recognized this when he wrote after the twentieth congress of the Communist Party of the Soviet Union: "I pictured Stalin to myself as the apex of a pyramid which widened gradually toward the base and was composed of many 'little Stalins': they, seen from above, were the objects and, seen from below, the creators and guardians of the 'cult of the personality.' Without the regular and unchallenged functioning of this mechanism, the 'cult of the personality' would have remained a subjective dream, a pathological fact, and would not have attained the social effectiveness which it exercised for decades."[63]

The personality cult of Stalin and that of his Hungarian "pupil," Rákosi, bore a striking resemblance to nationalist and religious cults that are used by those in authority to solidify citizens.[64] Actually, cults centre on a single charismatic figure idolized out of proportion. Stalinism primarily served the purpose of keeping Stalin as the headman of a helpless heterogeneous tribe. The people were led to believe that it was their duty to recognize their leader as a real one, if not by nature then through political education and, if needed, by force. Weber writes of the charismatic leader that "it is the duty of those to whom he addresses his mission to recognize him as their charismatically qualified leader."[65] However, there is one important distinction: a true charismatic figure ("pure" charisma, according to Weber) is divine because the leader is naturally recognized as such a figure by the people. In creating a leader, Hungarian Cold War doctrine copied Stalinist charismatic leadership, and by so doing generated a structured ideology with its rituals, language and a whole bureaucratic organization to keep it going. But unlike Stalin, who could boast of victories both in the civil war of 1919–21 and in World War II, the Hungarian Rákosi could claim as his only achievement his success in purging the country of its internal enemies and creating a socialist happiness.

Coda

With Stalin dead in 1953, Rákosi gone from power after 1956, *Life* magazine belatedly announced in 1961 the removal of Stalin's body from the Lenin Mausoleum with the sentence "Stalinism was buried."[66] True, signs appeared on the horizon that in the Soviet Union and elsewhere in the East bloc Stalinism was laid to rest for good. Although Stalingrad was renamed Volgograd, the cult of leader has transmogrified into many facets. In a strange way, even Vladimir Putin understood that to work for the future, he had to turn back to the past: he restored the old Soviet national anthem, but with new words.[67] In Hungary, "Happy Pioneer" remained in the repertoire of the youth movement well into the 1970s and 1980s, with many similar songs written by eager composers.[68] While Stalinism itself was reduced to history, it seems that the cult of leader and the culture of the Cold War, for all their inherent danger, remain an inspiration for many.[69]

Notes

1. "Happy Pioneer" was commissioned sometime after the first months of 1946, when the official pioneer movement took off in Hungary. The music was written by István Loránd (1933–?), a composer of socialist and popular songs; the text is by the poet, translator and writer of children's literature, Lili B. Radó (1896–1977).
2. The historian Walter Laqueur has warned that, despite obvious similarities, each Soviet-bloc country should be seen as unique; *Europe in Our Time: A History, 1945–1992* (New York: Viking, 1992), 67.
3. Alan Wood, *Stalin and Stalinism*, 2nd edition (New York: Routledge, 2004), 62.
4. Winston Churchill presented his Sinews of Peace (the Iron Curtain Speech), at Westminster College in Fulton, Missouri on March 5, 1946.
5. Harald Wydra, "The power of second reality. Communist myths and representations of democracy," in Alexander Wöll and Harald Wydra, eds., *Democracy and Myth in Russia and Eastern Europe* (London: Routledge, 2008), 68.
6. *Life*, 26 February, 1945, 26.
7. Stephen D. Kertesz, "The methods of communist conquest: Hungary, 1944–47," *World Politics*, 1950, 3, 1, 20.
8. William A. Bomberger and Gail E. Makinen, "The Hungarian hyperinflation and stabilization of 1945–47," *Journal of Political Economy*, 1983, 91, 801–24.
9. Roy Medvedev points out that, "The first issue of 'Pravda' for 1934 carried a huge two-page article by Radek, heaping orgiastic praise on Stalin. The former Trotskyite, who had led the opposition to Stalin for many years, now called him 'Lenin's best pupil, the model of the Leninist Party, bone of its bone, blood of its blood'. ... He 'is as far-sighted as Lenin', and so on and on. This seems to have been the first large article in the press specifically devoted to the adulation of Stalin, and it was quickly reissued as a pamphlet in 225,000 copies, an enormous figure for the time." See Roy A. Medvedev, *Let History Judge: The Origins and Consequences of Stalinism* (London: Macmillan, 1972), 148. But others – like Nikita Khrushchev and Anastas Mikoyan – were also involved with creating the personality cult. Actually, it was Khrushchev who coined the term Stalinism and referred to the 1936 constitution as Stalin Constitution.
10. The election was preceded by the promulgation of a new law on 23 July 1947 which restricted the number of citizens allowed to vote. The list of eligible voters

92 *László Kürti*

was also manipulated; it left out about half a million voters, most of whom belonged to the peasant party or the social democratic party. On 31 August 1947, some voters cast their absentee ballots several times in different voting districts by presenting a temporary residency permit – the so-called "blue slip" – a reason why subsequently the election was termed the "blue slip election of 1947." On the history of what took place between 1945 and 1947, see the Hungarian works by S. Balogh szerk., *Nehéz esztendők krónikája, 1949–1953* (Budapest: Gondolat, 1986); I. Kovács, *Magyarország megszállása* (Budapest: Katalizátor Iroda, 1990). For English language studies, see László Borhi, *Hungary in the Cold War, 1945– 1956: Between the United States and the Soviet Union* (Budapest: CEU Press, 2004); and Miklos Molnár, *From Béla Kun to János Kádár: Seventy Years of Hungarian Communism* (New York: Berg, 1990). For the elimination of the peasant parties and the agricultural policies between 1945 and 1947, see Ferenc Nagy, *The Struggle behind the Iron Curtain* (New York: Macmillan, 1948); I. Csicsery-Rónay, *Saláta Kálmán, Fejezetek a Független Kisgazda Párt 1945-os Küzdelméből* (Washington, DC: Occidental Press 1989); F. Donáth, *Demokratikus Földreform Magyarországon, 1945–1947* (Budapest: Akadémia Kiadó, 1969), and I. Vida, *A Független Kisgazdapárt Politikája, 1944–1947* (Budapest: Akadémiai Kiadó, 1976).

11 This was certainly seen from the US; see, for example, the optimistic analysis of events by the political scientist Andrew Gyorgy, "Postwar Hungary," *The Review of Politics* (1947) 9, 297–21.

12 Aside from the Independent Smallholders Party there was a smaller party, the National Peasant Party (*Nemzeti Paraszt Párt*). For an excellent short English summary about the developments between 1945 and 47, see Nigel Swain, *Hungary: The Rise and Fall of Feasible Socialism* (London: Verso, 1992), especially pp. 35–40. On the nature of the social democratic party and its working during this time, see Ullin Jodah McStea, "Slowing Sovietization: The Labour Party, the Hungarian Social Democrats and the Elections of 1947," *European History Quarterly* 3 (2006), 350–70.

13 For an English description of Stalinist take-over in Hungary, see Joseph Held, "1945 to the Present," in Joseph Held, ed., *The Columbia History of Eastern Europe in the Twentieth Century* (New York: Columbia University Press, 1992) especially pp. 206–13. For an interesting comparative case, see, for example, on the establishment of Romanian national communism, Vladimir Tismaneanu, *Stalinism for All Seasons: The Political History of Romanian Communism* (Berkeley: University of California Press, 2003).

14 The speeches of Mátyás Rákosi, as well as his memoirs written originally in exile in the Soviet Union, are available in Hungarian. Excerpts in English can be found on the website http://www.revolutionatrydemocracy.org/archive/index. htm#pdhung (last accessed January 15, 2012).

15 Tismaneanu, *Stalinism for All Seasons*, 111.

16 Paul Ignotus, *Hungary* (New York: Praeger, 1972), 107.

17 Agnes Heller, "Legitimation deficit and legitimation crises in East European societies," in Vladimir Tismaneanu, ed., *Stalinism Revisited: The Establishment of Communist Regimes in East-Central Europe* (Budapest–New York: Central European University Press, 2010), 151.

18 Heller, "Legitimation deficit," 151.

19 On the trials of peasants – some 400,000 between 1948 and 1950 – see V. Révai, szerk., *Törvénytelen szocializmus* (Budapest: Zrinyi, 1991), 84–85.

20 According to a survey, 38 percent of those asked considered the Bible to be one of the most important books, and going to the movies was the most favored pastime among the citizens of Budapest. Tibor Valuch, "Changes in the structure and lifestyle of the Hungarian society in the second half of the XXth

century," in Gábor Gyáni, György Kövér and Tibor Vlauch, eds., *Social History of Hungary from the Reform Era to the End of the Twentieth Century* (Highland Lakes: Atlantic Research and Publications, 2004), 662.
21 From the speech of Mátyás Rákosi at the miners' meeting in Pécs, May 11, 1947. http://mek.niif.hu/04400/04493/04493.htm (last accessed February 26, 2012).
22 Rákosi's speech in Debrecen, August 20, 1947. http://mek.niif.hu/04400/04493/04493.htm (last accessed February 26, 2012).
23 Rákosi's speech in front of the Budapest communist selectmen on November 20, 1948. http://mek.niif.hu/04600/04670/04670.htm (last accessed February 20, 2012).
24 Interview with Julia Kiss Gálné, November 11, 2011.
25 Speech in the parliament, August 17, 1949. http://mek.oszk.hu/04300/04351/04351.htm (last accessed February 28, 2012).
26 Speech at the World Democratic Youth Forum, August 28, 1949. http://mek.oszk.hu/04300/04351/04351.htm (last accessed February 28, 2012).
27 Rákosi's speech at the Opera House for the fifth anniversary of Hungary's liberation, April 3, 1950. http://mek.oszk.hu/04300/04351/04351.htm (last accessed February 28, 2012).
28 Rákosi's speech at the Opera House for the fifth anniversary of Hungary's liberation, April 3, 1950. http://mek.oszk.hu/04300/04351/04351.htm (last accessed February 20, 2012).
29 Photos of such village brigades and their political messages can be viewed at http://server2001.rev.hu/oha/oha_picture_id.asp?pid=1672&idx=2&lang=h (last accessed February 25, 2012).
30 Actually, the official classification made a distinction between "*uribirtokos*" and "*kulak.*" To the former category belonged those land owners who were not of peasant origin, to the latter, land-owners with peasant origins who were not "working peasants" themselves, i.e. they did not do actual physical labor but only enjoyed the harvest.
31 Letter by Antal Német to the County Land Distribution Council, Délpestvármegyei Földbirtokrendező Tanácsnak Kecskemétre, Lajosmizse, December 26, 1946, Földbirtokrendező Tanács Kecskeméti Tárgyaló Tanácsa, Lajosmizse, Pest-Pilis-Solt-Kiskun vm.,45/1077., BKMÖL XVII. 501.
32 Letter to Zoltán Tildy, President of Hungary, by A. Kármán and I. Kármán, July 11, 1948, Köztársasági Elnök Úr! Kármán Aranka és Kármán Irénke levele Tildy Zoltánnak, 1948. július 1-én. Original letter in the archive of the historical collection of Lajosmizse, Helytörténeti Gyűjtemény, Lajosmizse.
33 István Raics (1912–86), pianist-composer, writer and translator had a special talent for writing the lyrics for such songs.
34 Rudolf Víg ed., *Népek dalai* (Songs of the Peoples) (Budapest: Budapest Székesfő város Irodalmi Intézete, 1949), 238–39.
35 Leon Trotsky, *What Is Proletarian Culture, and Is It Possible?* (1923), available at http://www.marxists.org/archive/trotsky/1923/art/tia23c.htm (last accessed January 12, 2012).
36 *Ibid.*
37 See Robert M. Slusser, "Soviet music since the death of Stalin," *Annals of the American Academy of Political and Social Science*, 303 (1956): 116. For example, the communists attempted to portray Béla Bartók's music as transcending Eastern and Western dialectics by being a true "example of the new socialist music." See Danielle Fosler-Lussier, *Music Divided: Bartók's Legacy in Cold War Culture* (Berkeley: University of California Press, 2007), 19.
38 Georg Lukács, "Brief an Alberto Carocci," available at http://www.marxists.org/archive/lukacs/works/1962/stalin.htm (last accessed January 15, 2012). For a discussion of Zhdanivsm and its criticism, see Ann Demaitre, "The Hungarian Shores of Realism," *Comparative Literature Studies* 1, 4 (1964): 311–23.

39 See Open Society Archives, http://files.osa.ceu.hu/holdings/300/8/3/text/29-4-72.shtm (last accessed January 12, 2012).
40 I have described these in much more detail in László Kürti, *Youth and the State in Hungary. Capitalism, Communism and Class* (London: Pluto Press, 2002) especially Chapter 4, 82–114.
41 The secret police (AVH) was one of the most important factors in assisting the establishment of the Stalinist order in Hungary, similarly to other East European countries. The *Stasi* in East Germany, the *Cheka* or later the *KGB* in the Soviet Union, the *Securitate* in Romania had the same role. They infiltrated all major institutions – schools, municipal administrations, factories, radio, television, newspapers and political parties – and instituted a reign of terror over the population. On February 27, 1947, the so-called "conspiracy trials" began, during which more than 200 people were sentenced before the People's Court. For a firsthand account of the trials, see Istvan Szent-Miklosy, *With the Hungarian Independence Movement, 1943–1947* (New York: Praeger, 1988), 151–54.
42 The communists, consciously or not, followed the example of 1922 when, during the first years of the regime of Admiral Miklós Horthy leftist and communist sympathizers were fired from their jobs. On the cult of Horthy and possible parallels see, Dávid Turbucz, *Horthy Miklós* (Budapest: Napvilág, 2011).
43 The Workers' Youth Association, DISZ (Dolgozó Ifjúsági Szövetség), was founded on June 16, 1950, with its purpose defined as follows: "The Workers' Youth Association is a non-party mass organization uniting the widest spectrum of working youth into a revolutionary association. It is the vanguard of the Hungarian working-class and the people, led indirectly by the Hungarian Workers' Party. All activities of the DISZ are determined by the victorious worldview of the working class, Marxism-Leninism." Even as late as 1986, at the Communist Youth League congress it was stated that there was a need to "build and defend a developed socialist society," see Kürti, *Youth and the State in Hungary*, 142.
44 Leerom Medovoi, *Rebels: Youth and the Cold War Origins of Identity* (Durham, NC: Duke University Press, 2005), 18.
45 Victor Buchli, *An Archeology of Socialism. The Narkomfin Communal House, Moscow* (Oxford: Berg, 1999), 28–30.
46 For a useful comparison see the detailed analysis of Stalinist popular music and the banal lyrics of mass songs in Soviet Russia by Richard Stites, *Revolutionary Dreams: Utopian Vision and Experimental Life in the Russian Revolution* (New York; Oxford: Oxford University Press, 1992).
47 Valuch, "Changes in the structure and lifestyle," 605.
48 Gyöngyi Gyarmati, "Nők, játékfilmek, hatalom," in Gyöngyi Garmati, Mária Schadt and József Vonyó szerk., *1950-es évek Magyarországa játékfilmeken* (Pécs: ASOKA Bt, 2004), 33.
49 *Ibid*, 37.
50 See, László Kürti "The Wingless Eros of Socialism: Nationalism and Sexuality in Hungary," *Anthropological Quarterly* 164, 1 (1991): 55–67.
51 Gyöngyi Farkas, "Gyertek lányok traktorra, női traktorosok a gépállomáson és a propagandában," *Korall* 13 (2003): 65.
52 Kürti, "The Wingless Eros of Socialism."
53 The "Anthem of Democratic Youth" was written by the noted Russian Anatoly Novikov (1896–1984), and transcribed into Hungarian by Endre Gáspár (1897–1955), an excellent translator and literary editor. The trite and overzealous text reads as follows: "We have one slogan: peace, / We'll go to war for a happy future. / For one grand goal advances our youthful army, / Wherever they live, whatever sky they are under, / The new generation of our struggling world is with us. / On the earth, in the sky, the new song is: / Youth, youth, youth! / Million

hearts throb its rhythm, rhythm, / There can't be no force defeating those fighting for the people, / And who sings the anthem of future: / Youth, youth!"
54 Speech at the World Democratic Youth Forum, August 28, 1949. http://mek.oszk.hu/04300/04351/04351.htm (last accessed February 25, 2012).
55 Excerpts of Révai's speeches and writings can be found on the home page of the Open Society Archives, http://files.osa.ceu.hu/holdings/300/8/3/text/29-4-72.shtm (last accessed January 12, 2012).
56 The Hungarian text can be accessed at http://www.justsomelyrics.com/950774/K%C3%B6sz%C3%B6nj%C3%BCk-n%C3%A9ked-R%C3%A1kosi-elvt%C3%A1rs-Lyrics; it can be listened as well, with some archival photos, at: http://karpathaza.network.hu/video/a_szocializmus_korszaka/koszonjuk_neked_rakosi_elvtars. It is also available on YouTube, but with different, sometimes funny, photos http://www.youtube.com/watch?v=MYGhcYJYtzU.
57 Jeffrey Brooks, *Thank You, Comrade Stalin! Soviet Public Culture from Revolution to Cold War* (Princeton: Princeton University Press, 2000), 25.
58 Quote from an editorial in the journal *Ethnographia*, official quarterly of the Hungarian Ethnographic Society, 63 (1952): 2. The editorial is anonymous but it can be fairly certain that the editor-in-chief, Gyula Ortutay, wrote it, or that he ordered somebody to write it. Ortutay was also the first Stalinist minister of religion and education between 1947 and 1950, then president of the Hungarian Ethnographic Society.
59 A few photos of these objects can be seen on the digitized version of *Ethnographia*, see http://www2.arcanum.hu/ethnographia/opt/a100602.htm?v=pdf&a=start_f.
60 The cults of communist leaders are discussed by Balázs Apor, Jan C. Behrends, Polly Jones and E.A. Rees, eds., *The Leader Cult in Communist Dictatorships: Stalin and the Eastern Bloc* (Houndsmill and New York: Palgrave Macmillan, 2004).
61 See, Ernest A. Zitser, *The Transfigured Kingdom: Sacred Parody and Charismatic Authority at the Court of Peter the Great* (Ithaca: Cornell University Press, 2004), 142.
62 John Shoeberlein, "Doubtful Dead Fathers and Musical Corpses: What To Do with the Dead Stalin, Lenin and Tsar Nicholas," in John Borneman, ed., *Death of the Father: An Anthropology of the End of Political Authority* (Oxford: Berghahn, 2004), 203–4.
63 Lukács published his reflections on the Twenty-second Congress of the Communist Party of the Soviet Union first in 1962, Georg Lukács, "Brief an Alberto Carocci."
64 Balázs Apor, "National Traditions and the Leader Cult in Communist Hungary in the Early Cold War Years," *Twentieth Century Communism*, 1, 1 (2009): 50–71.
65 Max Weber, "The Sociology of Charismatic Authority," in Hans H. Gerth and C. Wright Mills, eds., *From Max Weber: Essays in Sociology* (New York: Oxford University Press, 1958), 247.
66 "In Moscow a Plot Unfolds, A Despot Emerges. Big Pitch To Shake Up the Universe," *Life*, 10 November 1961, 32. See also Robert Payne, *The Rise and Fall of Stalin* (New York: Simon and Schuster, 1965), 713.
67 Robert Service, *Stalin: A Biography* (Cambridge: Harvard University Press, 2004), 596.
68 Just to name some of the most important collections of socialist song from post-Stalinist years, "Zúgjon dalunk, miként fergeteg" (Like thunder, roars our song), published in 1975; "Daloljunk, pajtás" (Let's sing, pals), published sometimes in the mid-1970s; and "Mint a mókus fenn a fán" ("Like a squirrel on the tree") appeared in 1971. The "Happy Pioneer" song has also been revived since 1990

and it is in the repertoire of a number of music bands and singers, all using it to parody socialism.
69 Balázs Apor, "The 'Secret Speech' and its Effect on the 'Cult of Personality' in Hungary," *Critique*, 35, 2 (2007): 229–47.

Selected bibliography

Apor, Balázs. "The 'Secret Speech' and its Effect on the 'Cult of Personality' in Hungary," *Critique* 35, 2 (2007): 229–47.
——"National Traditions and the Leader Cult in Communist Hungary in the Early Cold War Years," *Twentieth Century Communism* 1, 1 (2009): 50–71.
Apor, Balázs, Jan C. Behrends, Polly Jones and E. A. Rees, (eds.) *The Leader Cult in Communist Dictatorships: Stalin and the Eastern Bloc*. Houndmills and New York: Palgrave Macmillan, 2004.
Balogh, S. Szerk. *Nehéz esztendők krónikája, 1949–1953*. Budapest: Gondolat, 1986.
Boll, Michael M. *Cold War in the Balkans: American Foreign Policy and the Emergence of Communist Bulgaria, 1943–1947*. Lexington: The University Press of Kentucky, 1984.
Bomberger, W. A. and G. E. Makinen. "The Hungarian Hyperinflation and Stabilization of 1945–47," *Journal of Political Economy* 91 (1983): 801–24.
Borhi, Laszlo. *Hungary in the Cold War, 1945–1956: Between the United States and the Soviet Union*. Budapest: CEU Press, 2004.
Brady, Anne-Marie. *Marketing Dictatorship: Propaganda and Thought Work in Contemporary China*. Lanham: Rowman and Littlefield, 2008.
Brooks, Jeffrey. *Thank You, Comrade Stalin! Soviet Public Culture from Revolution to Cold War*. Princeton: Princeton University Press, 2000.
Buchli, Victor. *An Archeology of Socialism. The Narkomfin Communal House, Moscow*. Oxford: Berg, 1999.
Campeanu, Pavel. *The Genesis of the Stalinist Social Order: From Leninist Revolution to Stalinist Society*. New York: M. E. Sharpe, 1989.
Cox, Michael and Caroline Kennedy-Pipe. "The Tragedies of American Foreign Policy: Further Reflections," *Journal of Cold War Studies* 7, 1 (2005): 175–81.
Cronin, James E. *The World the Cold War Made*. London: Routledge, 1996.
Csicsery-Rónay, I. *Saláta Kálmán, Fejezetek a Független Kisgazda Párt 1945-os küzdelméből*. Washington, DC: Occidental Press, 1989.
Demaitre, Ann. "The Hungarian Shores of Realism," *Comparative Literature Studies* 1, 4 (1964): 311–23.
Donáth, F. *Demokratikus Földreform Magyarországon, 1945–1947*. Budapest: Akadémia Kiadó, 1969.
Farkas, Gy. "Gyertek lányok traktorra, női traktorosok a gépállomáson és a propagandában," *Korall* 13 (2003): 65–86.
Fosler-Lussier, Danielle. *Music Divided: Bartók's Legacy in Cold War Culture*. Berkeley: University of California Press, 2007.
Gaddis, John Lewis. *The Cold War A New History*, 2nd ed. New York: Penguin Press, 2005.
Gati, Charles. *The Bloc that Failed: Soviet–East European Relations in Transition*. Bloomington: Indiana University Press, 1990.
Germuska, P. "A magyar fogyasztói szocializmus zászlóshajói. Hadiipari vállalatok civil termelése, 1953–63," *Korall* 33 (2008): 62–80.

Gyarmati, Gy. "Nők, játékfilmek, hatalom", in Gy. Garmati, N. Schadt, J. Vonyó szerk., *1950-es évek Magyarországa játékfilmeken*, Pécs: ASOKA Bt, 2004: 41–67.
Gyorgy, Andrew, "Postwar Hungary", *The Review of Politics* 9 (1947): 297–21.
Hada, K. "The Origin of the Cold War and Eastern Europe – The Turning Points from 1946 to 1948, Investigating from Hungary," K-OMHP C3. 17. Paper Delivered at the 21st International Congress of Historical Sciences, Amsterdam, 2010.
Held, Joseph. "1945 to the Present," in Joseph Held, (ed.) *The Columbia History of Eastern Europe in the Twentieth Century*. New York: Columbia University Press, 1992: 204–28.
Heller, Agnes. "Legitimation Deficit and Legitimation Crises in East European Societies," in Vladimir Tismaneanu (ed.) *Stalinism Revisited: The Establishment of Communist Regimes in East-Central Europe*. Budapest and New York: Central European University Press, 2010: 143–60.
Hixson, Walter L. *Parting the Curtain: Propaganda, Culture and the Cold War, 1945–1961*. New York: St. Martin's Press, 1998.
Ignotus, Paul. *Hungary*. New York: Praeger, 1972.
Kertesz, Stephen D. "The Methods of Communist Conquest: Hungary, 1944–47," *World Politics* 3, 1 (1950): 20–54.
Kovács, I. *Magyarország megszállása*. Budapest: Katalizátor Iroda, 1990.
Kürti, László. *Youth and the State in Hungary: Capitalism, Communism and Class*. London: Pluto, 2002.
——"The Wingless Eros of Socialism: Nationalism and Sexuality in Hungary," *Anthropological Quarterly* 64, 1 (1991): 55–67.
Laqueur, Walter. *Europe in Our Time: A History, 1945–1992*. New York: Viking, 1992.
Leffler, Melvyn P. and Odd Ame Westad, (eds.) *The Cambridge History of the Cold War Vol. 1. Origins*. Cambridge: Cambridge University Press, 2010.
Mastny, Vojtech. *Russia's Road to the Cold War*. New York: Columbia University Press, 1979.
McStea, Ullin Jodah. "Slowing Sovietization: The Labour Party, the Hungarian Social Democrats and the Elections of 1947," *European History Quarterly* 36, 3 (2006): 350–70.
Medovoi, Leerom. *Rebels: Youth and the Cold War Origins of Identity*. Durham: Duke University Press, 2005.
Medvedev, Roy A. *Let History Judge: The Origins and Consequences of Stalinism*. New York: Alfred A. Knopf, 1972.
Mevius, M. *Agents of Moscow: The Hungarian Communist Party and the Origins of Socialist Patriotism, 1941–1953*. Oxford: Oxford University Press, 2005.
Molnár, Martin. *From Béla Kun to János Kádár Seventy Years of Hungarian Communism*. New York: Berg, 1990.
Mosely, Philip E. "Hopes and Failures: American Policy toward East Central Europe, 1941–47," *The Review of Politics* 17, 4 (1955): 461–85.
Mueller, Wolfgang. "Soviet Policy, Political Parties, and the Preparation for Communist Take-overs in Hungary, Germany and Austria, 1944–46," *East European Politics and Societies* 24, 1 (2011): 90–15.
Nagy, Ferenc. *The Struggle behind the Iron Curtain*. New York: Macmillan, 1948.
Payne, Robert. *The Rise and Fall of Stalin*. New York: Simon and Schuster, 1965.
Pető, Andrea. *Women in Hungarian Politics, 1945–1951*. Boulder: East European Monographs, 2003.
Puddington, Arch. *Broadcasting Freedom: The Cold War Triumph of Radio Free Europe and Radio Liberty*. Lexington: The University Press of Kentucky, 2000.

Raack, R.C. *Stalin's Drive to the West, 1938–1945*. Stanford: Stanford University Press, 2005.
Révai, V. szerk. *Törvényelen szocializmus*. Budapest: Zrínyi, 1991.
Service, Robert. *Stalin: A Biography*. Cambridge: Harvard University Press, 2004.
Shoeberlein, John. "Doubtful Dead Fathers and Musical Corpses: What To Do with the Dead Stalin, Lenin and Tsar Nicholas," *Death of the Father: An Anthropology of the End of Political Authority*, ed. John Borneman. Oxford: Berghahn, 2004: 201–19.
Slusser, Robert M. "Soviet music since the death of Stalin," *Annals of the American Academy of Political and Social Science* 303 (1956): 116–25.
Stites, Richard. *Revolutionary Dreams: Utopian Vision and Experimental Life in the Russian Revolution*. New York and Oxford: Oxford University Press, 1992.
Straus, Kenneth M. *Factory and Community in Stalin's Russia: The making of an Industrial Working-class*. Pittsburgh: The University of Pittsburgh Press, 1997.
Swain, Nigel. *Hungary: The Rise and Fall of Feasible Socialism*. London: Verso, 1992.
Tismaneanu, Vladimir. *Stalinism for All Seasons: The Political History of Romanian Communism*. Berkeley: University of California Press, 2003.
Turbucz, D. *Horthy Miklós*, Budapest: Napvilág, 2011.
Valuch, Tibor, "Changes in the Structure and Lifestyle of the Hungarian Society in the Second Half of the XXth Century," in Gábor Gyáni, György. Kövér, Tibor Vlauch (eds.) *Social History of Hungary from the Reform Era to the End of the Twentieth Century*, Highland Lakes: Atlantic Research and Publications, 2004: 511–71.
Vida, I. *A Független Kisgazdapárt politikája, 1944–1947*. Budapest: Akadémiai Kiadó, 1976.
Whitfield, Stephen J. *The Culture of the Cold War*. 2nd ed. Baltimore: The Johns Hopkins University Press, 1996.
Wood, Alan. *Stalin and Stalinism*. 2nd ed. New York: Routledge, 2004.
Wydra, Harald, "The Power of Second Reality. Communist Myths and Representations of democracy," in Alexander Wöll and Harald Wydra (eds.) *Democracy and Myth in Russia and Eastern Europe*. London: Routledge, 2008: 60–76.
Zitser, Ernest A. *The Transfigured Kingdom: Sacred Parody and Charismatic Authority at the Court of Peter the Great*. Ithaca: Cornell University Press, 2004.
Zubok, Vladislav M. *A Failed Empire: The Soviet Union in the Cold War from Stalin to Gorbachev*. Chapel Hill: The University of North Carolina Press, 2007.

5 New men of power
Jack Tenney, Ronald Reagan, and postwar labor anticommunism[1]

Jennifer Luff

By the fall of 1947, the wartime alliance between the Soviet Union and the United States had soured into an undeclared Cold War, turning American Communists into enemy combatants on the home front. Ronald Reagan urged Congress to respect the civil liberties of the Reds. Testifying before the House Un-American Activities Committee (HUAC) about Communism in the motion picture industry, Reagan urged against a ban on the Communist Party "on the basis of its political ideology." Reagan reassured Congress that "99% of us" in Hollywood were reliable anticommunists, and their fight to contain Communist influence in the movies showed that "democracy is strong enough to stand up and fight against the inroads of any ideology." Reagan showed real political courage to speak up for Communists' civil liberties as the red scare gathered steam.[2]

But Reagan declined to join a radio debate on the question, "Is There Really a Communist Menace in Hollywood?" California's legislature had been holding hearings to investigate Communist influence in Hollywood for its own "Fact-Finding Committee on Un-American Activities," headed by State Senator Jack Tenney. Since the early 1940s, the Tenney Committee had rivaled HUAC in its campaign against the "Communist menace," and Tenney often called for the Communist Party to be outlawed. In August 1947, Tenney agreed to argue the affirmative in the radio debate. Reagan begged off, claiming illness, and other staunch Hollywood anticommunists also refused, calling the venue "inappropriate." Tenney's reputation as a red-baiter prone to indiscriminate accusations made him dangerous, and Reagan knew better than to join him in a live broadcast.[3]

Ronald Reagan and Jack Tenney disagreed on how to handle Communism, but they shared a common background. Both men were veteran performers: Tenney as a musician, Reagan as an actor. And both men started out as liberal activists and New Deal Democrats in 1930s Hollywood. Above all, both were union leaders. Jack Tenney had served as the president of the Hollywood American Federation of Musicians chapter; Ronald Reagan was president of the Screen Actors Guild (SAG). They became anticommunists, and later Republicans, due to their experiences contending with Communism in the labor movement. As unionists in Hollywood, a site of perpetual labor turf battles, both men also saw how rival unions sought advantage by labeling their challengers as Communists.

Tenney and Reagan exemplify the American union leaders who became anticommunist activists in the years before McCarthyism swept American politics. Labor anticommunists developed a critique of Communism that was grounded in practical conflicts with Communists in their unions over politics, organizing, and bargaining. In the 1930s, labor anticommunism diverged into two types: liberal labor anticommunists like Reagan defended Communists' civil liberties, while conservative labor anticommunists like Tenney resorted to red baiting and endorsed broad restrictions on civil liberties.[4]

Labor anticommunists exerted influence beyond their unions, lobbying to shape federal policy on Communism and civil liberties in the 1920s and 1930s, when Communism was a marginal political issue, and they continued to do so during the early years of the Cold War. Tenney and Reagan differed from most labor anticommunists by holding elective office outside their unions. Reagan entered political life in 1966, when he was elected governor of California, while Tenney served in the California legislature from 1936 to 1952.

Looking at Tenney and Reagan as labor anticommunists helps explain their distinctive politics. Tenney belonged to the ranks of conservative labor anticommunists, and from his state senate seat, Tenney enacted many of the planks of their program. Reagan, on the other hand, was far more liberal than most labor anticommunists, and under his leadership, the Screen Actors Guild eschewed the antiradical excesses of mainstream labor anticommunism. Caught in the middle of complicated union jurisdictional disputes over the rights to represent Hollywood workers, Reagan publicly debunked dubious red smears. In contrast to his conservatism later in life, as a union president in the 1940s, Ronald Reagan stood to the left of the leadership of the American Federation of Labor.

The history of labor anticommunism recasts our understanding of the origins and development of American anticommunism and the Cold War. Historians have often treated the American labor movement as the victim of an anticommunist campaign concocted by hostile businessmen and politicians aiming to undermine unions' bargaining power, but as I show more fully in my book *Commonsense Anticommunism*, American union leaders were pioneering anticommunist activists. Decades before the Non-Aggression Pact, McCarthyism and NSC-68 (National Security Council Report 68), labor leaders and rank-and-file workers fought over foreign and domestic policy questions such as whether the United States should recognize the Soviet Union or if the Communist Party should be banned from the ballot. Seen from the perspective of conservative labor anticommunists, the American Cold War mobilization looked like a long-overdue response to a familiar threat, and many labor liberals had soured on Soviet Communism well in advance of Pearl Harbor.

Reconstructing the role that unions played in crafting American anticommunism shows that the Cold War was a project that began on factory shopfloors and picket lines as well as in Washington offices and corporate suites. And these decidedly local struggles over labor contracts and union leadership, motivated by a mix of expediency and genuine conviction, turned labor leaders into international anticommunist campaigners. In the end, labor anticommunism helped lay the groundwork for working-class conservatism and ushered many unionists, like Tenney and Reagan, into the new American right. Reagan became the most prominent member of a generation of American unionists who made up the labor wing of the American Cold War apparatus.

Unionists, Communists, and politics

In the late 1920s, when Jack Tenney became a union activist, the American Federation of Labor had declared itself the country's "first line of defense" against Communism. The Bolshevik Revolution turned many AFL leaders from staunch antisocialists into active anticommunists. A federal judiciary hostile to labor rights and a political system that discouraged third-party initiatives convinced them that socialism was infeasible in the American context. Instead they advocated robust craft unionism, premised on skilled workers' solidarity and militancy, as the best alternative for social redistribution. AFL founder Samuel Gompers explained in 1914: "The American Federation of Labor has some apprehension of placing additional powers in the hands of the government which may work to the detriment of working people, and particularly when the things can be done by the workmen themselves."[5] To antistatist union leaders, the seizure of the state by Russian revolutionaries and the subordination of Russian trade unions to party discipline was anathema.[6]

Many union members and non-union workers disagreed, and a vibrant Left thrived within most American unions. Radical workers centered in the Industrial Workers of the World and the Jewish needle trades, especially, embraced socialism and syndicalism, and the October Revolution drew many of them into the American Communist Party. Veteran organizers like William Z. Foster aimed to revolutionize American unions, in part by deposing conservatives like Gompers. "Working-class emancipation" would require unionists to replace the AFL's "reactionaries, incompetents, and crooks" with "militants," Foster argued.[7] With the assistance of the Soviet Union's Comintern, labor communists rocked the old order of the AFL throughout the 1920s.[8]

Federation leaders tolerated socialist and radical members while denouncing their dissenting views, but Communists' ties to an alarmingly powerful revolutionary state, and early successes in recruiting unionists, led the AFL to conduct a deliberate and devastatingly effective purge. John L. Lewis, president of the Mineworkers, led the anticommunist forces in the Federation; at the AFL's 1926 convention, he declared that "any man who believes in the least degree in the philosophy of communism and who lends that philosophy support of any character is simply driving a knife into the heart of his own organization and striking a death blow at the trade-union movement in America." Unions banned members from joining the Communist Party and expelled those who did.[9] And they ceaselessly crusaded against Communism, lobbying Congress against diplomatic recognition of the Soviet Union and warning that conservative unions formed the strongest bulwark against Communism's incursions on America's working classes. Unions waged an internal war, but they also turned to the state for help. During the WWI-era Red Scare, AFL leaders fed information about their challengers to the newly-created Department of Justice, helping federal agents arrest, prosecute, and imprison labor radicals, and they also received regular updates on party activities from police files.[10]

Nevertheless, the AFL defended Communists' right to advocate Communism. When Congress considered extending the Espionage and Sedition Acts into the 1920s, and other measures that would criminalize radical politics, they heard stout opposition from Gompers, who warned in 1920, "if the open meeting, assemblage, and freedom of the people are curbed, the underground, the secret assemblage, with all that breeds from secrecy and darkness and the feeling of suppression and denial of right will surely follow."[11] On repeated occasions, when proposals for such laws resurfaced in 1930, 1934, and 1935, AFL lobbyists turned up to testify against them. Federation leaders couched their defense of civil liberties in practical terms, arguing that legislative limits on political speech could easily be twisted to "apply to people engaged in labor organization work whom it was never intended to affect."[12] The AFL preferred to treat Communism as an internal union problem, using organizational tools like trials and membership bans to keep avowed Communists out of unions. Strong trade unions were the best defense against Communism, AFL President William Green told Congress in 1930, as they permitted working people "to express themselves through organizations of their own choosing." Free citizens could assess Communism for themselves, and gulled union workers quickly realized that "their doctrine is not on a sound basis, and they soon see what it all means, and then the Communist is done; he is driven out."[13]

This commonsense labor anticommunism contrasted sharply with the repressive policies advocated by the small, conspiracy-minded anticommunist network coalescing in these years. Activists in nationalistic groups like the American Legion and freelance researchers like Elizabeth Dilling warned of "red webs" linking figures like Robert M. LaFollette Jr. to Sinclair Lewis to Leon Trotsky. They conjured a vast Communist plot, as Michael Rogin put it, in a "countersubversive imagination," fed by a toxic brew of nativism and anti-Semitism. These armchair anticommunists favored authoritarian measures to contain Communism, calling for sedition laws, loyalty tests, and police crackdowns. Although AFL leaders sometimes shared information with the countersubversives, they largely abjured red-baiting and fervid hyperbole, sticking to straightforward denunciations of actually-existing American and Soviet

Communism. Labor anticommunists acted as a moderating check on efforts to curtail civil liberties, under the cloak of fighting Communism.[14]

By the eve of the Depression, labor conservatives had driven most Communists out of AFL unions, but they presided over a shrinking movement. The economy was transforming, eroding the AFL's traditional redoubts in skilled craft work. Factory workforces surged, and in California, the entertainment industry boomed. Jack Tenney's career track reflected the shift from the old economy to the new. His family moved from St. Louis to Los Angeles in 1908, when Tenney was ten years old. He got his first job as a telegraph operator in 1917, but when his stint in France for the American Expeditionary Force ended, Tenney came home and started a band. Tenney played piano and organ, and he tried to make a career of performing, traveling around southern California, Nevada, and Mexico throughout the 1920s. He had a moderate hit with his song "Mexicali Rose," but it was a tough existence.[15]

Tenney joined the American Federation of Musicians in hopes of getting more bookings and pay. The Musicians were facing the same sorts of challenges as other traditional craft unions. The AFM, organized in 1896, represented musicians who played in vaudeville shows, orchestras, and theaters. The invention of the gramophone, the rise of radio, and the creation of "talkie" movies all conspired to put musicians out of work. The 1920s saw a rapid decline in musicians' wages. The AFM had a hard time enforcing any kind of standards for its members. Tenney found the union to be often ineffectual: "so far as I could ascertain, the union was incapable of doing very much for its members," he recalled. But Tenney was an activist. While performing in Las Vegas in the early years of the Depression, he grew angry about the low pay. Tenney organized fellow musicians into a new local of the AFM. The Las Vegas musicians elected Tenney as their president, and he oversaw the establishment of a union wage scale, enforced with the help of a union walkout.[16]

Tenney had a talent for politics, and he returned to Los Angeles and attended law school while still working as a musician on the side. In 1936, he won a seat in the state assembly on the Democratic ticket. He embraced populist politics, supporting Upton Sinclair's antipoverty campaign and backing Cuthbert Olson's gubernatorial bid; he also took up labor causes, fighting for the pardon of Tom Mooney and the repeal of California's criminal syndicalism laws. Tenney also championed radicals like the Abraham Lincoln Brigade. All this attracted the attention of Martin Dies's Committee on Un-American Activities, which put Tenney on its list of suspected Communists.[17]

Meanwhile, Tenney kept his union membership active. In 1937, he became vice-president of Local 47 of the AFM, and in 1938 was elected to the presidency. In contrast to other locales, movie studios and radio broadcasters made Los Angeles a booming market for musicians. Local 47 had 6,000 members in LA, and a tradition of militancy that helped the union bargain good contracts with the entertainment industry. It was an excellent base for Tenney's budding political career, and his election was auspicious for the labor movement; the AFL, he recalled, "looked upon me as 'one of their own,' and fully expected me to 'rubber stamp' everything they demanded," but he was more sympathetic to the federation's radical challengers.[18]

Organizing Hollywood

Hollywood was a hotbed of unionism in the 1930s. Roosevelt's New Deal emboldened workers across the country to organize, and the National Labor Relations Act obliged employers to bargain with them. Cartoonists and screenwriters created new organizations, and stagehands and carpenters joined existing unions. But as new energy suffused the labor movement, old conflicts resurfaced. Liberal and radical unionists bolted from the AFL and created the Committee for Industrial Organization to organize new mass unions and shore up the New Deal state, while conservative leaders of the AFL tried to sustain existing unions and defend the principles of voluntarism. The National Labor Relations Board (NLRB), charged with adjudicating organizing efforts, increasingly found itself adjudicating disputes among unions as this institutional fight played out in countless local skirmishes. In Hollywood, established unions like the Carpenters and the International Association of Theater and Stage Employees had represented skilled workers in vaudeville and theater for decades. When film and radio transformed the entertainment industry, these unions claimed the right to represent its professional trades. Meanwhile entirely new unions organized along craft lines, such as SAG, started enlisting members. This flurry of organizing created a turbulent political atmosphere.[19]

Elsewhere in the country, the NLRB played a significant role in enforcing collective bargaining. Hollywood labor relations, by contrast, looked like a throwback to an earlier era. Hollywood unions struck backroom deals and elaborate alliances with studio heads and other union bosses, sometimes with the help of mob muscle. An older, craft-based style of unionism persisted in Hollywood, as elsewhere in Los Angeles. Historian Ruth Milkman has described this form of labor relations as an "L.A. Story," whose main features are occupational, not industrial unionism, sustained by workers' ability to take wages out of competition through occupational solidarity rather than governmental protection for bargaining. This form of organizing rarely relied on the government to certify unions or order bargaining; rather, bare-knuckled direct pressure on employers—and sometimes, collusive bargaining—ensconced unions. Los Angeles truck drivers, construction workers, and janitors all organized in this fashion.[20]

Hollywood unions followed the same approach. Skilled professional workers like actors, writers, and even directors formed "guilds," while set workers allied according to their occupation. Meanwhile, the arrival of organized-crime figures scrambled the situation further. In 1934, Chicago gangster

Willie Bioff appeared in Hollywood on behalf of the International Association of Theater and Stage Employees (IATSE), the theatrical workers union. After some menacing threats of violence against the studios, he quickly negotiated an exclusive union contract with the studios to recognize IATSE, and then simply bargained weak contracts but high dues for set workers, who never had the opportunity to vote whether to join the union. The studios paid regular kickbacks to Bioff, and enjoyed the protection against more militant unionism that IATSE provided (especially since its AFL affiliation meant that other AFL unions could not challenge its representational claims). Although Bioff and other IATSE mobsters were indicted in 1941 and removed from the scene, IATSE retained their corrupt bargaining practices. Most Hollywood unions were not mob controlled; many were traditional craft affiliates like the Carpenters and Painters unions that were accustomed to bargaining by banding together and controlling their skilled work. The problem was that in Hollywood, where industry employment grew very rapidly, and industry management was concentrated among relatively few employers, this profusion of small craft unions invited problems.[21]

The case of IATSE was the most visible, and extreme, example. IATSE became ensconced as the primary representative for set workers in 1935. However, IATSE had represented some studio workers since the 1920s, when it struck a deal with other skilled workers' unions, including the Carpenters, to divvy up workers whose proper union affiliation was unclear. Once IATSE won its corrupt closed-shop agreement, various union members sought to leave the union and join another. Meanwhile, other skilled unions looked with jealousy on IATSE's membership and invoked their jurisdictional rights, protected by the AFL, to claim some of them—for example, should interior decorators belong to the Carpenters, IATSE, or the Painters? Negotiations among unions to resolve these disputes could take years of argument and arbitration in Washington. In any case, each union could negotiate side deals and separate agreements with the studios, creating incentives for jockeying and corruption. Set designers and interior decorators were easier to replace than actors and writers, so craft unions sought alliances with the more-powerful SAG and the Screen Writers Guild. For their part, the professional guilds often sympathized with the struggles of the craft unions, but keenly desired that movie production continue, and sought their own advantage with studio employers. Finally, the entry of the Committee for Industrial Organization onto the scene in the mid-1930s created a whole new axis of conflict, as the CIO argued for industry-wide unions. The whole situation would have baffled Otto von Bismarck.[22]

Hollywood was an especially fertile ground for Popular Front politics, uniting the labor movement with the leftists who worked as screenwriters, set decorators, and actors in Hollywood studios.[23] Ronald Reagan fit right into this heady milieu when he arrived in Hollywood in 1937. Reagan was a confirmed liberal, having just graduated from a small Illinois college where he had helped lead students in a strike against the college administrators. Reagan signed on with the Warner Brothers studio, and he quickly signed a union card to join SAG. Hollywood actors had been trying to organize a union for years. Their efforts were impaired in part by the complexity of the movie industry workforce. The power of the studios made solidarity imperative for bargaining, but the diversity of movie industry jobs, and the numerous unions which represented them, made it easy for studios to play off groups of workers against each other. Three unions—Actors Equity, Associated Actors and Artistes of America, and SAG—vied for actors' loyalties, while IATSE jostled with the Carpenters Union and the Painters Union to represent set workers, and so on.[24]

In 1937, SAG merged with the Associated Actors and thus won a charter from the AFL, earning the right to jointly bargain with other AFL affiliates. One union, IATSE, had a favored position with the studios, having negotiated a poor contract for its members in exchange for kickbacks and bribes for the Chicago racketeers who ran the union. When IATSE backed SAG's demand for recognition in May 1937, the studios conceded—in part because SAG had just crossed the picket lines of strikers who competed with IATSE. The studios hoped that the actors' union would prove as tractable as IATSE.[25]

The turmoil in Hollywood was mirrored in Washington. As the NLRB intervened in internecine union battles, often ruling in favor of the CIO, labor conservatives came to believe (with some justice) that Roosevelt's administration promoted the CIO. Conservative unionists in the AFL soured quickly on New Deal labor policy. In 1938, the AFL began collaborating with the National Association of Manufacturers to lobby for amendments to the National Labor Relations Act that would undermine industrial organizing, and in the 1938 congressional midterm elections, the AFL campaigned against Roosevelt's endorsed candidates in the Democratic primaries. "This quarrel between the A.F. of L. and the CIO has divided labor's political strength and helped conservatives to gain office," remarked a contemporary observer; "A.F. of L. into G.O.P." said another.[26] The CIO was a stalwart defender of Roosevelt, but the conflict within the labor movement helped undermine Roosevelt's electoral majority and sap the energy of the New Deal order.[27]

Such conflicts were predictable: the vigorous new power of the New Deal state jolted the existing order, and unions habituated to the old regime struggled to adapt. The return of the Communist Party to the mainstream labor movement added a volatile new element. Stalin's declaration of a "Popular Front" in 1935 drove American Communists to resume their campaign to agitate within American unions, as well as support FDR and shore up the Democratic Party. In a strange coincidence, the CIO broke from the AFL just as the Popular Front got underway, and CIO head John L. Lewis, needing recruiters, enlisted Communist organizers to help launch the CIO. This new alliance flabbergasted conservative union leaders who had recently counted Lewis among their ranks.[28]

Communist organizers dedicated themselves to building up the CIO and the Democratic Party, in accord with Popular Front directives, and their diligence and militancy attracted new members and allies to the Communist Party in the 1930s. The CIO's alliance with the Communist Party was largely a marriage of expedience, and Communists and radicals also helped organize AFL craft unions like SAG. Increasingly, though, conflicts about Communism erupted within local unions as well as among national union leaders.

The success of CIO organizers and the Communist Party challenged the civil liberties commitments of conservative union leaders. Complaining about CIO incursions onto AFL territory aroused little sympathy from the public. Beginning in 1938, the AFL took another tack: it red-baited the CIO and the NLRB. Martin Dies's new Committee on Un-American Activities offered a free-wheeling arena, as Dies had few staff and needed material. Labor conservatives had been keeping tabs on Communist organizing for years, and they had fresh—and accurate—intelligence on Communist Party activities in unions. In August 1938, AFL leader John Frey opened the Dies Committee hearings with three days of testimony. The Communist Party had "failed to secure a foothold in an American trade-union movement," he said, "until the CIO was organized. Since then the Communist Party has become a definite factor in the American labor movement." Communists swarmed "every sitdown strike, every mass-picketing venture" and they "fostered violent disturbances" in the steel and auto industry. Their vehicle was the CIO, where Communists occupied senior positions. The sensational success of these early hearings helped establish the Dies Committee, which was later reconstituted as HUAC, in the Congress as a perch for attacking radicals, liberals, and the New Deal state.

Tenney's blue-collar red scare

The AFL's Dies Committee offensive was strategic, intended to discredit the CIO and the NRLB. But it also reflected some real frustration of unionists alarmed by the sudden strength and popularity of Communist and radical movements. Tenney's Local 47 was symptomatic of this dynamic. Tenney later explained that he had been recruited for the union presidency in the first place by Mischa Altman, a Communist violinist and member of Local 47. Once Tenney was installed, Altman squired him to various Communist Party meetings in Hollywood, including a private audience with John Howard Lawson, a leading party organizer. Tenney's amiable support of campaigns like the Abraham Lincoln Brigade likely persuaded Hollywood Communists that Tenney was a good recruit, but a veteran anticommunist informer later reported that the party also believed Tenney could be "successfully manipulated."[29] The head of the Los Angeles County Federation of Labor, J.A. Buzzell, was incredulous. He took Tenney to lunch and "tried to explain the strategy used by the Communists to involve innocent people," Tenney recalled, and "said that I was unwittingly helping them out in the council meetings."[30]

Soon after his 1938 election, Tenney noticed that a few activists had begun dominating union meetings, trying to push through resolutions to affiliate Local 47 to Labor's Non-Partisan League, political arm of the CIO. Their tactics—dispersing members throughout the hall, stalling deliberations and prolonging meetings until most members departed—enabled them to easily control the union's agenda. One member told Tenney that "he had never seen meetings so thoroughly manipulated by so few members before." Tenney was losing control of the local. "'Do you think, Jack,' the member asked, 'that we are being taken over by a bunch of communists?' There was a puzzled, almost pained expression on his face as he waited for my answer. I realized that he had almost humiliated himself in voicing the thought because a year before he would have denounced the question as 'red-baiting.'"

But the tactics on display in Local 47 were characteristic of some Communist unionists who did seek to take over leadership of union locals, and echoed descriptions of Communist practices dating from the early 1920s. Similar complaints were voiced by subway workers in New York City and auto workers in Detroit; at the Dies Committee hearing table, the United Auto Workers' Zygmund Dobrzynski complained that Communists kept up "3 or 4 or 5 hours of constant heckling, filibustering," until "the honest-to-goodness members of the organization become disgusted and walk out." Even at the height of the Popular Front, Communist sectarianism had the potential to alienate liberal and radical noncommunist unionists. Tenney was not alone in turning on them.[31]

He resorted to the techniques developed by a generation of labor conservatives: he sought help from the police to confirm his suspicions. In 1939, Tenney and his Local 47 staff prepared a list of the names of union members they suspected of being secret Communists, and they gave it to the Los Angeles police red squad, to check against police files. Shortly, Tenney received photostatic copies of police files on several Local 47 members, including party membership cards. He showed the cards to the union executive board, and began preparing his move against his Communist members. That September, at the convention of the California State Convention of Labor Tenney described his fight. Tenney said that in the past, "because of my record I was called a Communist," and "I did not believe much in the bogeyman of Communism. But I have seen Communism develop in Local 47." The Communist "fraction" members "formulate a policy to follow the party line and then go out in the general membership and by window dressing their activities bring those other brothers into the program who innocently carry on that plan to dominate every local in this State and in the nation." The threat was real, he insisted: "I assure you I am not being fantastic." He warned that "not only Organized Labor must get rid of Communists, but the Democratic Party must get rid of Communists."[32]

Tenney's reaction was visceral, and passionate. The officers of the California Federation shared his anticommunist fervor, and likely helped him formulate a plan to "smoke out" the Communist members. When he got back to Los Angeles, Tenney created a pledge card and mailed it to each member of the local, reading: "I affirm that I have never been and am not now a member of the Communist Party, either openly or secretly, and I do not espouse or advocate any philosophy of Fascism, Nazism or Communism. I solemnly promise to attend all meetings of Local 47 whenever physically possible to do so and to actively and vigorously oppose all Communistic, Fascistic and Nazistic groups and tactics."[33] The American Federation of Labor had formally banned Communists from membership in 1935, giving Tenney a pretext for expulsion. He estimated that "about ninety percent" of the membership signed the pledge; the remainder were expelled from the local that fall. But in December 1939, Tenney himself lost his seat in the election for Local 47's presidency. For the rest of his life, he would blame his loss on the "sinister subtlety" of Communist organizers.[34]

Years later, a number of members of Local 47's Communist cell, called "Branch O," recounted the same events to HUAC investigators. Many were recruited by Mischa Altman, who chaired party meetings and reproved members for skipping their assigned readings of Marx. Altman had been a longtime musician and Local 47 member, and he organized among his many contacts: "I have to give him an A for effort," recalled musician Judith Poska. One member, Don Christlieb, recalled that only about 20 people attended meetings, on average. Notably, Tenney was not among the many people named by HUAC witnesses as Party members. Branch O sought to influence decisions in Local 47—"all they did was talk Union matters," said musician David Raksin—but its small size made it hard to have much impact. As Tenney suspected, Altman indeed threw his backing behind Spike Wallace, Tenney's opponent, in the 1939 union election. But when asked by a HUAC investigator whether the Communist cell was "instrumental in getting [Wallace] elected," Raksin laughed. "Oh, no. Hell, no. This bunch of peanuts? They had no numbers," Raksin said. "He was elected because people liked him." Raksin left the party, like Poska and Christlieb, when he grew tired of the group's sectarianism and discipline. "If I wanted to go out on a date, I went regardless of the meeting," said Judith Poska, "for which they were pretty upset with me."[35] The experiences of Local 47 Communists resemble those of many other unionists who drifted through the party before the war.

As for Tenney, his own unpopularity, not Communist conspiracy, cost him his union presidency. Indeed, Tenney's increasing concern about a tiny group of radicals among a union membership of thousands likely alienated musicians more concerned about bread-and-butter issues. But the existence of an actual Communist cell in Local 47 made it easy for him to attribute his defeat to dark plotting.

Tenney had lost his union office, but he still held a seat in the state assembly. California had a strong conservative streak, and other legislators were also concerned about Communism. Public sentiment had turned sharply against the party in the summer of 1939, when Stalin and Hitler struck a separate peace with their Non-Aggression Pact, and American Communists immediately abandoned Popular Front politics and began agitating against American entry into the European war. In January 1940, the governor appointed Tenney and Sam Yorty, another Los Angeles Democrat, to a committee to investigate Communist infiltration of the State Relief Administration, which oversaw welfare funds. Tenney and Yorty discovered plenty of Communists in that agency and throughout the state government.[36]

In September 1940, Tenney returned to the California Federation of Labor convention to explain his new program. "There is absolutely no difference between Nazism, Fascism, and Communism," he said, and "American labor must particularly guard itself from Stalin's red termites." Tenney had just come from the legislature, where he helped engineer passage of a bill banning the Communist Party from California elections. But this would not suffice, as Communist "termites" would "continue to gnaw away at our unions and our Democracy." He cried, "Be vigilant and do not be deceived!" He vowed to carry on the fight to root out Communists in unions, and in the government.[37]

Tenney thus joined a campaign already launched by labor conservatives in Washington. In the summer of 1940, AFL leaders had renounced their long-standing opposition to antisedition laws and endorsed federal limits on free speech by supporting the Smith Act, which effectively criminalized the Communist Party. They had also backed the Hatch Act of 1939, which barred Communists from federal employment, and continued to lobby against the NLRB by alleging that Communist staffers influenced its decisions. "This is not hysteria. It is plain common sense," said AFL president William Green, endorsing the Smith Act in June 1940. "The time has come for us to identify the traitors in our midst. I believe the Communist Party and the Nazi Bund should be outlawed."[38]

As ever, the AFL was driven by a sincere aversion to Soviet Communism and frustration with Communist unionists. Indeed, many unionists in the CIO felt the same way, especially after the Non-Aggression Pact exposed the sectarianism of staunch Communists. In the late 1930s, a liberal version of labor anticommunism emerged among CIO leaders. They repudiated statutory limits on Communists or other radicals and opposed the Dies Committee, but moved to sideline Communist activists and instituted formal bans on Communist Party membership in numerous unions. In 1940, CIO convention delegates renounced "Communism, Nazism, and Fascism," as "foreign doctrines opposed to our concept of industrial and political democracy." The next summer, the UAW's convention banned Fascists and Communists from union office. A string of unions followed suit, from the Laundry Workers Joint Board in Brooklyn to the Marine Engineers' Beneficial Association.[39]

AFL leaders took a much harder line, and increasingly they resorted to red baiting, falsely imputing Communist sympathies to unionists who chose the

CIO. But AFL leaders were limited to lobbying. They governed their own unions, where they enacted bans on Communist membership such as Tenney's ban in Local 47, but they could only advocate from the sidelines for statutory limits on the Communist Party and the CIO. As a politician, Tenney could wield power directly. After his anticommunist conversion, Tenney became a newly minted labor conservative in power.

In January 1941, Tenney pushed through a resolution in the California legislature to establish a Fact-Finding Committee on Un-American Activities in California—a state replica of the Dies Committee—and was appointed its chair (which he remained even after moving to a seat in the state senate). Tenney made the committee his fiefdom: he "employed the committee personnel. He wrote or arranged for the writing of the reports. He gave out the press releases, carried on the correspondence, drafted the legislation, arranged for the hearings, decided on the witnesses, and conducted a substantial portion of the questioning."[40] The Tenney Committee's proceedings thus reflected his predilections.

Chief among the Tenney Committee's early subjects: the problem of Communists in labor unions. Tenney subpoenaed his old antagonist from the Musicians' Union, Mischa Altman, in the first days of the hearing. Altman denied having anything to do with the Communist Party, and Tenney took relish in interrogating him: "Do you mean to say that you didn't drive me out to [John Lawson's home] and introduce me to him?"[41] He explored the influence of Communists in recent Auto Workers strikes and waterfront conflicts. Early on, the film industry emerged as a particular focus. At a hearing in August 1941, an organizer for the American Federation of Labor warned that Communism was "particularly dangerous in the film industry because the screen educates people not only in the United States but throughout the world." Representatives from the Studio Utility Employees, Electrical Workers, Teamsters, and Studio Technicians Guild all complained of "red efforts to take over labor unions." One unionist accused of spreading Communism was Herbert Sorrell, the business agent for the Painters Union. He told the committee that he suspected that Disney had engineered his subpoena, for his role in organizing cartoonists at Disney Studio, but he insisted that he was a freelance radical. "I don't do what the Communists want me to do and I don't do what the others want me to do and so everybody is throwing rocks at me," he said.[42]

Sorrell always denied party membership, and he made numerous anticommunist statements over the years, criticizing the Soviet Union and naming other union activists as suspected reds—hardly the actions of a Communist Party loyalist. When the Taft-Hartley Act of 1947 required union leaders to submit anticommunist affidavits, Sorrell did so readily. Sorrell was a freelance radical, more of a syndicalist than a Communist. But his militant unionism often aligned with the Communist Party, which applauded efforts to unify Hollywood workers in industrial unions. Sorrell and other Hollywood labor radicals drew the particular ire of industry heads and AFL leaders not for espousing a Communist Party line, but for challenging the entrenched craft unions, especially the corrupt IATSE, and the sweetheart contracts they negotiated. The ideology of the CIO was far more disruptive in Hollywood than Communist doctrine. Tenney's committee swiftly became a useful venue for employers and craft unionists to smear strikers and rival union organizers as Communists.[43]

The Tenney Committee thus operated very much like the Dies Committee, which continued to meet in Washington, and indeed, the two committees often collaborated, sharing information and consulting on investigations.[44] Likewise, California adopted state versions of anticommunist federal legislation. California's 1941 Subversive Organizations Registration Act resembled the Smith Act in obliging organizations which advocated "overthrowing the Government by force" to register with state authorities. California also enacted the first in a series of loyalty-oath statutes for state employees.

Reagan and civil liberties

By late 1941, though, the Tenney Committee's anticommunist work dwindled. The Soviet Union's enlistment in the Allied coalition in World War II dramatically dampened the fervor of public and private anticommunism. Even Hollywood, whose movie studio heads banded together to create the Motion Picture Alliance for the Preservation of American Ideals, pumped out pro-Soviet films like *Mission to Moscow* and *Song of Russia*.

Ronald Reagan was drafted into active duty in April 1942. But Reagan spent the war years in Los Angeles, detailed to the Army Air Force's Motion Picture Unit. He narrated training films, and got a special dispensation to appear as a uniformed soldier in a feature film, *This Is the Army*. When Reagan was mustered out of the service at the end of the war, he was as liberal as ever. The Hollywood left thrived during the war, and Reagan remained active in it. He got involved with the Hollywood Independent Citizens Committee of the Arts, Sciences, and Professions (HICCASP), a remnant of the Popular Front era founded in 1938 by a Communist organizer. HICCASP held fundraisers and public events promoting liberal and left ideas, from price controls and minimum wage increases to supporting the United Nations. HICCASP also spoke up for civil liberties. It regularly denounced the Tenney Committee, which named HICCASP a Communist "front group." Reagan's left-wing associations caused the FBI to identify him as a possible Communist.[45]

Reagan stepped up his political activity after the war, joining HICCASP's board of directors in 1946. But HICCASP was fracturing under the pressures of US–Soviet conflict. When a faction of the board introduced a resolution to expressly repudiate Communism, the group split apart. Reagan caucused with the anticommunists who resigned from HICCASP. He had always been more of a New Deal Democrat than a radical, and he had no difficulty reconciling his liberalism with his anticommunism. He also got more active in the SAG.

He had joined SAG's board in 1941, describing himself as a "rabid union man."[46] In September 1946, he was elected as a SAG vice-president. It was a turbulent time to be a union officer anywhere in America. Pent-up industrial conflict exploded in 1945 and 1946, unleashing the biggest strike wave in the nation's history. As a SAG officer, Ronald Reagan was thus drawn into the nitty-gritty details of union bargaining when Hollywood erupted in its own strike wave in 1946.

The details of the conflict are dizzyingly complex, "almost beyond comprehension," according to one historian.[47] Essentially, Sorrell organized a new union coalition, the Conference of Studio Unions (CSU), which included craft unions such as the Carpenters and the Painters. IATSE and the studios regarded this development with alarm, as it raised the specter of a real challenge to IATSE's dominance. Sorrell was the public face of the CSU, and he provided a convenient foil for IATSE, which regularly denounced him as a Communist. But behind Sorrell lay the real power base of the CSU: the conservative craft unions, especially the Carpenters, which were delighted to back a militant organizer who could wrest work away from IATSE. The fact that the Carpenters was among the most reactionary and militantly anti-communist of unions did not seem to trouble either Sorrell or the Carpenters, but it did muddy the waters considerably for Hollywood leftists who struggled to understand which side they should support. At bottom, the labor dispute had little to do with Communism or any stripe of ideology; it was an instance of the bruising and frustrating jurisdictional battles among craft unions that had led to the creation of the CIO in the first place.[48]

SAG tried to stay above the fray. Its membership agreed that the fight was a jurisdictional war among unions, not a strike against studio management, and thus voted "overwhelmingly" to cross the picket lines and keep working. Most other Hollywood unions did the same. IATSE's longstanding corruption, and its obvious collusion with studio management, rankled many Hollywood activists who supported Sorrell's efforts, but the conservatism of the Carpenters was also unappealing. A panel of AFL arbitrators, appointed to decide how the Carpenters and IATSE should split up the work of constructing stage sets, issued several contradictory rulings, under duress from AFL union heads. It made no difference. Hollywood fractured into opposing camps. SAG leaned toward IATSE (which had helped SAG beat out competing actors' unions and win studio recognition in the 1930s). After a series of skirmishes, the situation dramatically worsened in late 1946, with picket lines turning violent and strikers demanding that actors and others respect their picket lines.

At that moment, Matthew Woll, an AFL official and longtime Carpenters' ally, denounced "treasonable stars and writers" in Hollywood. These "world-savers in grease paint find refuge in the Communist Party," Woll said. He urged the studios to expel "fifth columnists and fellow travelers" from the movies. SAG quickly retorted that "the high command of the American Federation of Labor might have been goaded into a denunciation of the actors and actresses because of their activities in the current jurisdictional strike in Hollywood." But Woll's accusation still stung. And as Cold War tensions with the Soviet Union mounted, it was dangerous.[49]

In the context of the strike, Woll's claim was ridiculous—after all, CSU was alleged to be a Communist union, and IATSE a decidedly anticommunist one. But his charges were characteristic of the way labor conservatives had strategically red baited their adversaries before. Woll resorted to an old tactic, recasting an organizational conflict as an ideological one. Woll's red baiting also revealed the underlying power dynamic within the labor movement: the Carpenters were the real engine driving the CSU fight, and as an old ally of William Hutcheson, the extremely conservative head of the Carpenters Union, Woll sought to pressure SAG to support the Carpenters and the CSU.

This was clear to SAG leaders, who went to the AFL's convention in Chicago in October 1946 to plead with the Federation to resolve the situation. "We had learned that one man was responsible for this situation," Reagan said, "Mr. Hutcheson." Ronald Reagan, Gene Kelly, Dick Powell, and other stars joined the delegation, hoping, as Reagan later said, to wield their star power—"our greatest weapon"—to compel settlement. Their efforts were fruitless. Days of shuttle diplomacy and negotiations with the union heads and arbitrators yielded little. AFL president William Green said, "I have no power to do anything," and Reagan recalled that "he was crying" as he said it. They got an audience with William Hutcheson, who told them that he would not be bound by any arbitrator's ruling, and insisted that his union retain jurisdiction over a small number of set-building jobs. He did not care how it occurred, and he told them that if IATSE would relinquish the claim to the work, "I will run Herb Sorrell out of Hollywood and in 5 minutes break up the Conference of Studio Unions." Hutcheson, Sorrell, and the CSU were merely instruments for the Carpenters' ends.[50] Sorrell surely understood this fact, and SAG leaders believed that Sorrell did much to prolong the conflict, sticking with the Carpenters despite Hutcheson's intransigence.

Although some Hollywood activists dismissed the claims by SAG and other unions that internecine union warfare, not Communism, was the main force behind the strike, AFL unionists knew better. SAG sent a delegation to the AFL convention, not the Kremlin, to negotiate a resolution, and no one at the AFL ever suggested that Communists were running the strike. AFL leaders certainly did not shy from exposing Communist influence in union affairs or strategically imputing red sympathies to their opponents. In this case, it was clear that whatever the allegiances of Sorrell or the aspirations of the Communist Party, a straightforward and familiar craft-union dispute was at play. The local IATSE official, Roy Brewer, ceaselessly repeated claims that Communists controlled the CSU, but the silence of other conservative anticommunists is telling.

The conflict dragged on for another year, while Reagan ascended to the SAG presidency in March 1947. Actors, along with the rest of Hollywood, remained divided; many liberals and leftists backed the CSU, due to Sorrell's radical reputation and the union's militancy, while conservatives tended to repeat IATSE's denunciations of the CSU as a Communist conspiracy. Liberals like Reagan were caught in the middle.[51]

Later in life, Reagan picked up the claim that Communism drove the CSU strikes, and traced his political awakening to those days. At the time, though, Reagan rarely interjected Communist charges into the debate. Testifying before a Congressional hearing on the strikes in 1947, Reagan spoke at great length about the details of the jurisdictional dispute, and defended the principles of unionism: while "the present Hollywood strike does not reflect glory" on the AFL, he said, "we should not let isolated incidents or individuals beguile us into a general attack on the labor movement."[52] In his testimony, he never suggested that Communism was at play in the strike. Later that year, when Reagan appeared before HUAC, he was asked directly whether "Communists have participated in any way" in the CSU/IATSE conflict. Reagan replied that "Sir, the first time that this word Communist was ever injected into any meetings concerning the strike was at a meeting in Chicago with Mr. William Hutchinson [sic], president of the carpenters union," who said that if Hutcheson could prevail on the jurisdictional issue, "he would run this Sorrell and the other commies out—I am quoting here—and break it up."[53] Given the opportunity to repeat anticommunist charges, Reagan instead implied that cynicism, not conviction, lay behind the conflict.[54]

Reagan's personal aversion to Communism certainly expanded during these years, and his castigation by Hollywood leftists pushed him farther toward the political right. In the politicized atmosphere of Hollywood, Reagan was becoming more conservative. But compared to other labor anticommunists, Reagan remained on the left in 1947. He stood up for the political rights of Communists in the labor movement and did not attempt to purge or expel Communists from SAG. Simply exposing Communist "propaganda" was enough to prevent Communists from winning supporters, he argued: "the best thing to do is make democracy work," by "ensuring everyone a vote." Thus Reagan opposed criminalizing the Communist Party, because the country "should never compromise with any of our democratic principles" due to "fear and resentment."[55] Having contended against Communists in union struggles, he believed that simple exposure to democratic debate defused their strength. Reagan echoed mainstream labor anticommunists who defended civil liberties even as they opposed Communism.

Jack Tenney, by contrast, had spun out into the wild yonder of red-scare politics. Since the end of the war he had been holding increasingly flamboyant hearings in Sacramento, hauling schoolteachers, judges, and the provost of the University of California before his committee to answer charges of Communist sympathies. The Tenney Committee discovered Communistic tendencies in school textbooks and sex education classes, and named the American Civil Liberties Union as a Communist front group. Communism in unions still occupied him, and Tenney proposed several bills guaranteeing unions the right to expel Communist members. The Tenney Committee weighed in on the Hollywood strike, of course, calling it "a Communist Party design for the destruction of the American Federation of Labor and the establishment of Communist influence and domination in the motion-picture industry."[56] Tenney's connection to the labor movement had become increasingly attenuated, though. Unmoored from the practical politics he learned in union struggles, Tenney slipped to the political fringe.

Tenney lost his committee chairmanship in 1949, when he publicized ill-advised accusations that leading California politicians, including many legislators, had Communist sympathies. His colleagues swiftly decided that it was "time to blow the whistle on the Tenney Committee," and forced him from the chair. Tenney stayed in the state senate until 1954, but his notoriety faded quickly. He left a legacy in the California code, however, having enacted legislation requiring loyalty oaths of state workers, which remains in effect to this day.[57] Tenney was on the leading edge of the rise of the new right in California. He had switched his party affiliation to the Republicans in 1944, renouncing the Democrats as "the New Deal–Hillman–C.I.O.–Marxist party determined to lead the United States into Socialism." His hearings helped catechize a generation of Californians in the anticommunism that, as Lisa McGirr puts it, would provide the "symbolic glue that united conservatives with divergent priorities and interests, bringing social and religious conservatives together with libertarians."[58]

Richard Nixon also rode to office on this Californian wave, arriving in Washington as a freshman Congressman in 1946. Nixon joined the House Committee on Education and Labor, which was debating the proposed Taft-Hartley bill to contain the national strike wave by limiting unions' rights to strike in sympathy with each other. The Hollywood strikes featured prominently in the debate. Studio head Cecil B. DeMille testified at length on the turmoil in Hollywood, complaining that "it is national insanity" to allow union strikes to "shut down this country so it would be as black as Russia." (DeMille refrained from red baiting the Hollywood strikers, however, characterizing the conflict as "entirely to settle jurisdiction, not between CIO and the A.F. of L., but entirely between two A.F. of L. unions.")[59]

The law also required union officers to submit affidavits swearing that they were not Communists. Nixon had a seat on the House Un-American Activities Committee, where he had listened to ample testimony about Communist organizing in unions. Nixon was one of the first Congressmen to float the idea of the anticommunist affidavits. The Taft-Hartley Act gave labor anticommunists a new tool to purge their unions, and within a year most Communist leaders had been evicted from the AFL and CIO alike.[60]

Ronald Reagan signed the affidavit as president of the SAG, which he remained until 1952. During his tenure at SAG he remained a reliable liberal, campaigning for Democratic candidates Hubert Humphrey and Helen Gahagan Douglas and joining Americans for Democratic Action, a progressive caucus founded by Eleanor Roosevelt and Walter Reuther. But his anticommunism deepened. Antiradicals like Roy Brewer and Reagan's new wife,

Nancy Davis, replaced his liberal confidantes and helped shape his thinking. He endorsed a voluntary oath for SAG members that repudiated "Stalinism and totalitarianism," and Reagan increasingly cast American Communists as disloyal "fifth columnists." Reagan was a committed anticommunist, but he continued to warn against excess in the Red Scare, criticizing HUAC and Senator Joseph McCarthy, and repeating his insistence that Americans should not be "so frightened that we suspend our traditional democratic freedoms."[61]

His shift to the right came gradually over the course of the 1950s. As Reagan's film career dried up, he found new work as a television host and corporate spokesman for General Electric (GE), and he grew close to GE's extremely conservative executives. As Reagan traveled to GE factories around the country, he talked to workers about his experiences fighting Communists in Hollywood, while learning the tenets of modern conservatism from their bosses. Reagan learned to distill his critique into a snappy 20-minute speech that could appeal to workers and managers alike. Like Tenney, his conservatism grew as he became unmoored from his union role, but his ongoing contact with workers helped him anchor his conservative views in popular sentiment. During the 1950s, Reagan became another charter member of California's new right, but one with a working-class touch. Over the next decades, Reagan would usher many working-class voters along the same path. And as President of the United States, Reagan remembered what he learned "from the experience of hand-to-hand combat" in the Hollywood strikes—that "America faced no more insidious or evil threat than that of Communism"—when he made American foreign policy.[62]

Notes

1. Acknowledgements: I would like to thank the members of the D.C. Labor and Working-Class History Seminar for their helpful comments and suggestions.
2. U.S. House, Committee on Un-American Activities, *Hearings Regarding Communist Infiltration of the Motion Picture Industry*, 82nd Cong., 1st sess., 217.
3. *Los Angeles Times*, August 29, 1947.
4. My discussion of labor anticommunism relies on my book *Commonsense Anticommunism: Labor and Civil Liberties between the World Wars* (Chapel Hill: University of North Carolina Press, 2012). This essay extends the ideas in that work, which closes in 1941, to consider domestic labor anticommunism and civil liberties in the postwar years. On styles of American anticommunism, see Ellen Schrecker, *Many Are the Crimes: McCarthyism in America* (Boston: Little Brown, 1996); Richard Gid Powers, *Not Without Honor: The History of American Anticommunism* (New York: Free Press, 1995). On labor anticommunism, see Ronald Radosh, *American Labor and United States Foreign Policy* (New York: Random House, 1969); Bert Cochran, *Labor and Communism: The Conflict that Shaped American Unions* (Princeton: Princeton University Press, 1977); and Harvey A. Levenstein, *Communism, Anti-Communism, and the CIO* (Westport, Conn.: Greenwood Press, 1981).
5. *The Double Edge of Labor's Sword: Discussion and Testimony on Socialism and Trade-Unionism before the Commission on Industrial Relations* (New York: Socialist Literature Company, n.d.), 100.

6 For the early political history of the American Federation of Labor, see especially Julie Greene, *Pure and Simple Politics: The American Federation of Labor and Political Activism, 1881–1917* (Cambridge: Cambridge University Press, 1998); Elizabeth Sanders, *Roots of Reform: Farmers, Workers, and the American State, 1877–1917* (Chicago: University of Chicago Press, 1999); Joseph A. McCartin, *Labor's Great War: The Struggle for Industrial Democracy and the Origins of Modern American Labor Relations, 1912–1921* (Chapel Hill: University of North Carolina Press, 1997); and Robin Archer, *Why Is There No Labor Party in the United States?* (Princeton: Princeton University Press, 2007).

7 William Z. Foster, "The Principles and Program of the Trade Union Educational League," *Labor Herald*, March 1922.

8 On Communist organizing and political tumult in the 1920s labor movement, see James A. Barrett, *William Z. Foster and the Tragedy of American Radicalism* (Chicago and Urbana: University of Illinois Press, 1999); Edward Johanningsmeier, *Forging American Communism: The Life of William Z. Foster* (Princeton: Princeton University Press, 1994); Selig Perlman and Philip Taft, *History of Labor in the United States, 1896–1932* (New York: Macmillan, 1935); and Irving Bernstein, *The Lean Years: A History of the American Worker, 1920–1933* (Boston: Houghton Mifflin, 1960).

9 U.S. House of Representatives, *Hearings Before a Special Committee on Un-American Activities*, 75th Cong., 3rd sess., vol. 1 (Washington: Government Printing Office, 1938), 164 (herein after cited as *Dies Committee Hearings*.)

10 Luff, *Commonsense Anticommunism*, 32–59; William Preston, Jr., *Aliens and Dissenters: Federal Suppression of Radicals, 1903–1933*, 2nd ed. (Urbana and Chicago: University of Illinois Press, 1963), 129.

11 U.S. House Rules Committee, Hearings on H. Res. 438, 66th Cong., 2nd sess. (Washington: Government Printing Office, 1920), 46; see also U.S. Senate, Judiciary Committee, Hearings on S.J. Res. 171, *Amnesty and Pardon for Political Prisoners*, 66th Cong., 3rd sess., 1921 (Washington: Government Printing Office, 1921). For an illuminating look at the organizing campaign against sedition legislation, in which the AFL was a somewhat late and reluctant participant, see Ernest Freeberg, *Democracy's Prisoner: Eugene V. Debs, the Great War, and the Right to Dissent* (Cambridge: Harvard University Press, 2008).

12 U.S. House, Special Committee on Un-American Activities, *Investigation of Nazi Propaganda Activities and Investigation of Certain Other Propaganda Activities*, 73rd Cong., 2nd sess., December 17 and 18, 1934 (Washington: Government Printing Office, 1934), 14.

13 U.S. House, Special Committee to Investigate Communist Activities in the United States, *Investigation of Communist Propaganda: Hearings on H. Res. 220*, 71st Congress, 2nd sess., June 9 and 13, 1930 (Washington: Government Printing Office, 1930), 78. On labor and civil liberties, see Luff, *Commonsense Anticommunism*; James Gray Pope, "Labor's Constitution of Freedom," *Yale Law Journal* 106, no. 4 (January 1997), 941–1031; and David M. Rabban, *Free Speech in its Forgotten Years* (Cambridge: Cambridge University Press, 1999).

14 A note on terminology: I use the term "red-baiting" to signify spurious imputations of Communism for strategic purposes, but not to describe accurate accusations of Communist sympathies. On American anticommunism in the 1920s, see Ellen Schrecker, *Many Are the Crimes: McCarthyism in America* (Boston: Little, Brown, 1998); Richard Gid Power's *Not Without Honor: The History of American Anticommunism* (New York: Free Press, 1995); Michael Paul Rogin, *Ronald Reagan, The Movie, and Other Episodes in Political Demonology* (Berkeley: University of California Press, 1988).

15 Jack Tenney, "California Legislator," v–vii, Special Collections, Young Research Library, University of California; on Tenney, see also Kevin Starr, *Embattled*

Dreams: California in War and Peace, 1940–1950 (Oxford: Oxford University Press, 2002), 301–8; M.J. Heale, "Red Scare Politics: California's Campaign against Un-American Activities, 1940–70," *Journal of American Studies*, 20, no. 1 (April 1986), 5–32; Ingrid Winther Scobie, "Jack B. Tenney and the 'Parasitic Menace': Anti-Communist Legislation in California 1940–49," *Pacific Historical Review*, 43, no. 2 (May 1974), 188–211.

16 Tenney, "California Legislator," 142; on musicians and the AFM, see James P. Kraft, *Stage to Studio: Musicians and the Sound Revolution, 1890–1950* (Baltimore and London: Johns Hopkins University Press, 1996).
17 Scobie, "Tenney and the 'Parasitic Menace,'" 191–92.
18 Tenney, "California Legislator," 323; Kraft, *Stage to Studio*, 89–90.
19 On union conflicts in the 1930s, see Walter Galenson, *The CIO Challenge to the AFL: A History of the American Labor Movement, 1935–1941* (Cambridge: Harvard University Press, 1960); Robert Zieger, *The CIO, 1935–1955* (Chapel Hill: University of North Carolina Press, 1995); Christopher L. Tomlins, "The AFL Unions in the 1930s: Their Performance in Historical Perspective," *Journal of American History* 65, no. 4. (March 1979), 1021–42. There is an extensive literature on Hollywood unionism; see especially David F. Prindle, *The Politics of Glamour: Ideology and Democracy in the Screen Actors Guild* (Madison: University of Wisconsin Press, 1988); Otto Friedrich, *City of Nets: A Portrait of Hollywood in the 1940s* (New York: Harper and Row, 1986); Gerald Horne, *Class Struggle in Hollywood, 1930–1950* (Austin, TX: University of Texas Press, 2001).
20 Ruth Milkman, *L.A. Story: Immigrant Workers and the Future of the U.S. Labor Movement* (New York: Russell Sage Foundation, 2006), 26–28; Prindle, *Politics of Glamour*, 25–31.
21 On IATSE's corrupt involvement with organized crime, see especially David Witwer, *Shadow of the Racketeer: Scandal in Organized Labor* (Urbana and Chicago: University of Illinois Press, 2009), 68–102; also see Prindle, *Politics of Glamour*, 31–36.
22 On the CSU, see especially Horne, *Class Struggle in Hollywood*.
23 Michael Denning, *The Cultural Front: The Laboring of American Culture* (New York: Verso, 1997), 18–19.
24 For Ronald Reagan's years in Hollywood, see especially Steven J. Ross, *Hollywood Left and Right: How Movie Stars Shaped Politics* (Oxford: Oxford University Press, 2011), 131–85; and Stephen Vaughn, *Ronald Reagan in Hollywood: Movies in Politics* (Cambridge: Cambridge University Press, 1994). On SAG's formation, see Prindle, *Politics of Glamour*, 16–34.
25 Prindle, *Politics of Glamour*, 30–31.
26 Joel Seidman, "Organized Labor in Political Campaigns," *Public Opinion Quarterly*, October 1939, 651; Kenneth G. Crawford, "A.F. of L. into G.O.P.," *The Nation*, March 11, 1939, 283. See also the essays by Peter Rachleff and Bruce Nelson in Kevin Boyle, ed., *Organized Labor and American Politics: The Labor–Liberal Alliance* (Albany: State University of New York Press, 1995).
27 On these struggles, see James A. Gross, *Reshaping of the National Labor Relations Board* (Albany: State University of New York Press, 1981); Luff, *Commonsense Anticommunism*.
28 On the Popular Front Communist Party, see Harvey Klehr, *The Heyday of American Communism: The Depression Decade* (New York: Basic Books, 1984); Barrett, *Tragedy of American Radicalism*.
29 Tenney, "California Legislator," 342.
30 Ibid., 338–39.
31 *Dies Committee Hearings*, vol. 2, 2211–12.
32 Officers' Reports and Proceedings of the California State Federation of Labor, September 25–29, 1939, 122.

33 Tenney, "California Legislator," 664–66.
34 Jack B. Tenney, *The Tenney Committee: The American Record* (Tujunga, Calif.: Standard Publications, 1952), 20.
35 U.S. House, Committee on Un-American Activities, *Investigation of Communist Activities in the Los Angeles, Calif., Area*, Part 9, 84th Cong., 2nd sess. (Washington: Government Printing Office, 1956), 3920–21; ibid, Part 11, 5776–78; U.S. House, Committee on Un-American Activities, "Testimony of David Raksin," [unpublished], September 5, 1951, 15, 18.
36 Scobie, "Tenney and the 'Parasitic Menace,'" 194–96; Heale, "Red Scare Politics," 11–12.
37 *Officers' Reports and Proceedings of the California State Federation of Labor*, September 23–28, 1940, 85, 94.
38 *New York Herald Tribune*, June 27, 1940.
39 Levenstein, *Communism, Anticommunism, and the CIO*, 94; Nelson Lichtenstein, *The Most Dangerous Man in Detroit: Walter Reuther and the Fate of American Labor* (New York: Basic Books, 1995), 192; *New York Times*, February 1, 1941; *New York Times*, January 31, 1941; Maurice Isserman, *Which Side Were You On? The American Communist Party during the Second World War* (Urbana and Chicago: University of Illinois Press, 1993), 76–79.
40 Edward L. Barrett, Jr., *The Tenney Committee: Legislative Investigation of Subversive Activities in California* (Ithaca, NY: Cornell University Press, 1949), 17–18.
41 *Los Angeles Times*, July 31, 1941.
42 *Los Angeles Times*, August 1, 1941.
43 On Sorrell, see especially Gerald Horne, *Class Struggle in Hollywood*, 15–19; *City of Nets*, 282.
44 Barrett, *Tenney Committee*, 20–21.
45 Ross, *Hollywood Left and Right*, 141–42; Vaughn, 121–32.
46 Ross, *Hollywood Left and Right*, 145.
47 Vaughn, *Ronald Reagan in Hollywood*, 136.
48 On the conservatism and anticommunism of the Carpenters' Union, see Robert A. Christie, *Empire in Wood: A History of the Carpenters' Union* (Ithaca: Cornell University Press, 1956), 253–68. On the Carpenters' involvement in the Hollywood studio conflict, see Walter Galenson, *The United Brotherhood of Carpenters: The First Hundred Years* (Cambridge: Harvard University Press, 1983), 290–95.
49 *New York Times*, October 1, 1946; Vaughn, *Ronald Reagan in Hollywood*, 140–41.
50 U.S. House, Committee on Education and Labor *Jurisdictional Disputes in the Motion Picture Industry*, 80th Cong., 1st sess. (Washington: Government Printing Office, 1940), 237, 239.
51 Reagan's liberalism stands in marked contrast to George Murphy, who had also served as SAG president and was a close friend of Reagan. As Steve Ross shows, Murphy preceded Reagan in moving from the SAG presidency, serving from 1944 to 1946, into electoral politics, winning one of California's seats in the U.S. Senate on the Republican ticket in 1964. Murphy was a committed conservative and dedicated anticommunist from the late 1930s. At the 1947 hearings before HUAC, Murphy supported the notion of outlawing the Communist Party, saying "I don't think that an agent of a foreign government should be able to hide under the guise that he is a member of a legal American political party." Historians sometimes treat Reagan's testimony as a cowardly concession to HUAC and red-scare politics, but in the context of the late 1940s, Reagan demonstrated a commitment to civil liberties that stood out, especially among union leaders. For Ross's illuminating discussion of Murphy and Reagan see *Hollywood Left to Right*, 131–85; for Murphy's testimony, *Communist Infiltration of the Motion Picture Industry*, 212.

52 *Jurisdictional Disputes*, 222.
53 *Communist Infiltration of the Motion Picture Industry*, 216.
54 The main source cited by historians to buttress claims that Reagan was motivated by anticommunism in the studio fight is the memoir of Jesuit professor George W. Dunne, written in the late 1960s after Reagan had become a prominent anticommunist activist. Dunne was an ardent Popular Front radical in the 1930s and 1940s (and red-baited by the House committee investigating the Hollywood strike). It should be noted that Dunne did not make such claims at the time. Testifying before Congress, Dunne said that Roy Brewer, the IATSE's representative, "has a very definite interest in trying to smear the Conference people as all Communists," but made no mention of Reagan as an anticommunist, although he discussed Reagan's involvement in the strike at length; *Jurisdictional Disputes*, 430. In a recent article, writer John Meroney reports that a trove of untapped documents shared by Roy Brewer reveals that in the course of the studio fight, Reagan, under the tutelage of Brewer, gradually developed suspicion and later, antipathy, towards Communists: Meroney, "Left in the Past," *Los Angeles Times Magazine*, February 2012.
55 *Communist Infiltration of the Motion Picture Industry*, 217. Reagan also met with FBI agents in 1947 and provided information about the activities of Communists in Hollywood; the extent of his contact with the FBI, and the exact information he shared, is unknown. Vaughn, *Ronald Reagan in Hollywood*, 130; Ross, *Hollywood Left and Right*, 142.
56 *Los Angeles Times*, February 20, 1946.
57 Scobie, "Tenney and the 'Parasitic Menace,'" 208; see also Edward R. Long, "Earl Warren and the Politics of Anti-Communism," *Pacific Historical Review* 51, no. 1 (February 1982), 51–70.
58 Lisa McGirr, *Suburban Warriors: Origins of the New American Right* (Princeton: Princeton University Press, 2001), 35–36; see also Becky Niolaides, *My Blue Heaven: Life and Politics in the Working-Class Suburbs of Los Angeles, 1920–1965* (Chicago: University of Chicago Press, 2002). Working-class conservatism remains understudied. For a recent survey of the scholarship, see Kim Philips-Fein, "Conservatism: A State of the Field," *Journal of American History*, December 2011, 723–72.
59 U.S. House, Committee on Education and Labor, *Amendments to the National Labor Relations Act*, 80th Cong., 1st sess. (Washington: Government Printing Office, 1947), vol. 3, 1171, 1176. On the influence of the Hollywood strikes on the Taft-Hartley debate, see Horne, *Class Struggle in Hollywood*, 15, and Witwer, *Shadow of the Racketeer*, 244–47.
60 U.S. House, Committee on Education and Labor, *Amendments to the National Labor Relations Act* (Washington: Government Printing Office, 1947) vol. 3, 1712. On the addition of the affidavit to Taft-Hartley, see Harry Millis and Emily Clark Brown, *From the Wagner Act to Taft-Hartley: A Study of National Labor Policy and Labor Relations* (Chicago: University of Chicago Press, 1950), 545–53.
61 Ross, *Hollywood Left and Right*, 156–57. On liberal anticommunism in the postwar years, see Jennifer Delton, "Rethinking Post-World War II Anticommunism," *Journal of the Historical Society* 10, no. 41 (March 2010), 1–41.
62 Ronald Reagan, *An American Life* (New York: Simon and Schuster, 1990), 115. The AFL-CIO (the two organizations merged in 1955) likewise played a prominent role in fighting Communism worldwide; on labor anticommunists in foreign policy, see Ted Morgan, *A Covert Life: Jay Lovestone, Communist, Anti-Communist, and Spymaster* (New York: Random House, 1999), and Edmund F. Wehrle, *Between a River and a Mountain: The AFL-CIO and the Vietnam War* (Ann Arbor: University of Michigan Press, 2005).

Selected bibliography

Cochran, Bert. *Labor and Communism: The Conflict that Shaped American Unions.* Princeton: Princeton University Press, 1977.

Luff, Jennifer. *Commonsense Anticommunism: Labor and Civil Liberties between the World Wars.* Chapel Hill: University of North Carolina Press, 2012.

Powers, Richard Gid. *Not Without Honor: The History of American Anticommunism.* New York: Free Press, 1995.

Prindle, David F. *The Politics of Glamour: Ideology and Democracy in the Screen Actors Guild.* Madison: University of Wisconsin Press, 1988.

Ross, Steven J. *Hollywood Left and Right: How Movie Stars Shaped American Politics.* New York: Oxford University Press, 2011.

Schrecker, Ellen. *Many Are the Crimes: McCarthyism in America.* Boston: Little, Brown, 1998.

Vaughn, Stephen. *Ronald Reagan in Hollywood: Movies in Politics.* Cambridge: Cambridge University Press, 1994.

Witwer, David. *Shadow of the Racketeer: Scandal in Organized Labor.* Urbana and Chicago: University of Illinois Press, 2009.

6 Female terrorists and vigilant citizens
Gender, citizenship and Cold War direct-democracy

Dominique Grisard

In the 1970s, terrorist attacks by communist and anarchist groups were a common occurrence in Central Europe. The most prominent of these groups was West Germany's Red Army Faction (RAF). Like other terrorist factions of the time, the RAF emerged from the radical periphery of the waning student movement of the 1960s.[1] It existed "underground," robbing banks, carrying out bombings and kidnapping high-profile public figures, until 1998. Its mission was to expose the democratic state's capitalist, imperialist and ultimately fascist agenda (such as supporting the Vietnam War and collaborating with the Shah of Iran, and silencing the Nazi past). The fact that some of the group's most active members were women – journalists regularly referred to them as "hyenas,"[2] "female supermen"[3] and "phallic women"[4] – was cause for great concern.

In Switzerland, it was anti-communist citizen watch groups who were particularly alarmed over the existence of female terrorists. One heavily debated question was whether the participation of women in terrorism was the result of women's liberation. The groups believed that these women were puppets of the USSR, their violence a product of the aberrant politics of communism and, by extension, a result of feminism. Citizen watch groups promoted a culture of watchfulness where both feminism and communism were deemed precursors to or inherent qualities of terrorism. Given that Swiss (male) citizens granted women the right to vote only in 1971, this commingling of feminism's struggle against patriarchy and terrorism's violence against the state is not surprising. It is testimony to the fragile state of women's (political) participation in German-speaking Europe, and Switzerland in particular.

This chapter discusses how citizens of a nation that hosted several Cold War peace summits shaped the Cold War phenomenon in markedly gendered ways. My aim is to show how the Cold War was not just a conflict between the USSR and the US. Indeed, the neutral direct-democratic country of Switzerland was much more than a passive bystander. What is more is that locating the Cold War in regular people's everyday practices will underscore how citizens – not just states – participated in Cold War politics. In the first section, I introduce the theoretical premises of this chapter by raising questions related to power. I then contextualize the Cold War in neutral Switzerland.

The third and main section discusses how anti-feminism and anti-communism conjoin in the citizen watch groups' image of the female terrorist other. The fourth section focuses on individual citizens' construction of that same figure. Finally, I delineate citizens' vested interests in participating in anti-communist and anti-feminist security discourse.[5]

Conceptualizing power: Cold War practices of othering and self-affirmation

In order to understand why regular citizens would actively single out and report people and behaviors they believed to be terrorist, it is necessary to clarify the position of the citizen in relation to (state) power. My research suggests that the Swiss state neither overtly nor covertly manipulated its citizens to engage in anti-communist policing practices, but that these citizens acted of their own accord. In fact, my empirical data leads me to conclude that the commonly held assumption that citizens were – in a case of false consciousness – led astray by a state's brain-washing scheme, misses the point. A notion of state power that works from the top down and in coercive or manipulative ways will not be able to get at what incentivizes certain citizens to take the law into their hands for the nation. A Foucaultian notion of power, on the other hand, is well suited to analyzing the intricate workings of power in a semi-direct democracy like Switzerland. Foucault introduces a notion of power that does not necessarily oppress or coerce. In his understanding, power works through a seemingly voluntary confessionary mode as well as through the production of knowledge. Foucault shows how power-knowledge in the shape of empirical data is an integral part of security discourses.[6] Those professing expertise about security threats are the ones shaping the discourse. Power must thus be thought of as productive: not only does it *produce* cohesion and/or exclusion, it also provides individuals with agency.[7]

Relocating the locus of power in the hands of citizens invites us to look at how anti-feminist and anti-communist discourses conjoined to empower certain actors over others; not just on the level of the state but on the street level of regular citizens. In this respect it seems important to note that the citizen is not a gender-neutral concept. Feminist theories of masculinity and citizenship remind us that most constitutional democracies initially conceptualized the citizen as a male landowner and protector of the nation.[8] They show how the concept of the citizen helped to construct the bourgeois division between the masculine public and the feminine private sphere. Feminist theories also shed light on how tying citizenship to military duties allowed it to remain an exclusively male privilege for such a long time.[9]

One central way that the Foucaultian notion of power-knowledge works is through practices of othering. Othering is a dividing practice: it marks something or someone in a pejorative way and thereby constructs difference while at the same time affirming one's own identity.[10] Othering must be understood as a mode of exercising power: it is implemented to establish one's culture as superior to others. A typical othering strategy is to feminize an opponent: whether the enemy is deemed external or internal to the nation doesn't really matter. Feminizing someone or something is a way of containing and mitigating a supposed threat. In contrast, masculinizing a person, thing or concept tends to keep the threat alive. When the first female Russian students were admitted to European universities in the mid-nineteenth century, the Swiss described these students as masculine in both habitus and attire: they smoked, talked boisterously, frequented the same venues as men and even met up with them without the supervision of a chaperone. In contrast, Swiss women were portrayed as docile, domestic housewives. The fact that female Russian students were othered as masculine and non-Swiss suggests that Swiss men felt threatened by women who appropriated masculine codes. Constructing a deviant or lesser other also affirms one's own cultural values and mores. Usually this process goes hand in hand with claiming certain virtues to be unique to one's own culture. Othering and self-affirmation are thus two sides of the same process. One obvious example that I will explore further in this essay is Swiss anti-communism, which allowed citizens to construct themselves as uniquely Swiss.[11]

The term "anti-communism" doesn't refer to a clearly defined ideology or goal, nor does it target a specific organization. Instead, anti-communism sets communism up as an antagonism in the sense of what Ernesto Laclau refers to as an "empty signifier."[12] As the term suggests, an empty signifier lacks content. Its emptiness allows different interest groups to organize around it. The meaning one group gives the signifier may be quite different from another interest group's definition and stakes. The disparate meanings, however, converge to produce a discursive formation. So in one and the same historical context, say 1970s Switzerland, many different groups rallied against communism. Anti-communism bound them together even though their definitions of communism and their threat scenarios differed significantly. In fact, it was the vagueness, or rather the emptiness, of anti-communism that served as a common ground. What held the different meanings together was that they were imagined to be in stark contrast to positively connoted values and beliefs about democracy, freedom and neutrality. Anti-communism was thus the empty signifier that was seen to prevent a Western democracy like Switzerland from being fully independent and neutral. In the words of Laclau, anti-communism was the antagonism that kept the political project from realizing itself completely.[13]

Similar to anti-communism, anti-feminist sentiments were prevalent among the right-wing elite and large parts of the population in 1970s Switzerland. Anti-feminism may be broadly defined as the production of vague fears of change in relation to the male/female, public/private binary. While anti-feminism posited itself in opposition to the organized actions of Second Wave feminism and the demands for equal rights, it envisioned a female/feminist threat that had little basis in real-life events or changes. Anti-feminism might have been an explicit and implicit reaction to the demands of women's liberation but, much like anti-communism, it thrived on the construction of a threat of mythical proportions. The Cold War image of the female terrorist, I argue in this paper, is the joint product of anti-feminism and anti-communism.

To be clear, anti-communism and anti-feminism are not products of the Cold War. Early twentieth-century constructions of the Russian in Swiss newspapers reveal that anti-communist othering practices are clearly less unique than is commonly assumed, or to put it more cautiously: 1970s counter-terrorist and late nineteenth- and early twentieth-century anti-Russian discourse relied on similar ways of affirming one's own culture. Indeed, anti-communism, as Patrick Iber underlines in this book, is much older than what is referred to as the Cold War era. In Switzerland, anti-communism is said to have originated in the 1840s – before communism was even a household name.[14] Anti-communist sentiments became more prevalent after the Russian revolution, when the government articulated the need for the "spiritual defense of the nation" (*Geistige Landesverteidigung*). It subsequently turned into a government program to symbolically fortify the Swiss nation against fascism, communism and national-socialism.[15] With the onset of the Cold War, the spiritual defense program focused more narrowly on communism: all Swiss citizens were called on to actively counteract a communist infiltration of Switzerland by protecting and cultivating all that which was considered to be truly Swiss, e.g. Swiss culture, direct democratic moral courage, armed neutrality and independence. Spiritual defense was thus a non-militaristic means of getting civilians involved in combating communism.

Goetschel et al. underline the anti-communist continuity in Swiss history: "The Swiss political elite's anti-communism became a long-term identifying feature from the Russian revolution until the end of the Cold War."[16] As historian Brigitte Studer comments, Swiss anti-communism was both a perception and a projection:[17] anti-communism was first and foremost the product of a bourgeois elite who saw its core values concerning family, gender relations and the nation threatened. An anti-communist world-view, however, permeated the wider fabric of Swiss society. Even certain social-democratic and union circles believed in and feared an international communist conspiracy.

Contextualizing the Cold War: neutral direct-democratic Switzerland

Throughout the Cold War Switzerland was fighting communism on both a national and an international level, and this despite its pledge of neutrality. In the Swiss context, neutrality may be loosely defined as the non-participation in wars initiated by other states and the defense of the nation against incursions resulting from foreign wars.[18] This "armed neutrality" allowed Switzerland to keep a conscript army, even if only for the purpose of defense.[19] One major impact that neutrality had on Switzerland seems obvious: the country stopped being officially involved in wars once its neutrality was established in the

Treaty of Paris in 1815. Indeed, neutrality may in part be responsible for the remarkable stability, tranquility and wealth of the semi-direct democratic nation-state.

This does not mean that Switzerland remained outside of the Cold War, though. In fact, the term "Cold War" is misleading. According to international law at least, the Cold War was not a war. Indeed, *de jure* the Cold War was considered a state of peace. In times of peace, Switzerland is prohibited aggression, military alliances and military bases by international neutrality law. However, this legal definition of the Cold War as a state of peace undermined the grave conflict that the Cold War symbolized for the Swiss, which is why a 1973 Swiss government report on homeland security re-framed the Cold War era as a state of "relative peace."[20] The term "relative peace" referred to both international and domestic instabilities: on the one hand it addressed the strong "ideological, power and socio-political tensions" between the two super-powers, the USA and the USSR, and alluded to the rise of international collaborations.[21] Domestically, the term expressed anxieties about young men's service to the nation.

In the 1960s, young people started to mobilize against the state, and the military in particular. As early as 1963, protesters at annual Easter marches campaigned against nuclear arms, and against the dominant view that those opposing arms build-up were also communist. In the late 1960s tens of thousands took to the streets to protest the war in Vietnam and the intervention of the Warsaw Pact powers in Czechoslovakia.[22] Around the same time, young people in Zurich got wind of the riots at the Sorbonne in Paris and started a protest of their own. They demanded youth centers that weren't under the auspices of the state, and were met with extraordinary police violence. These so called Globus riots mark the beginning of the 1968 social movement in Switzerland. Youth protests in smaller Swiss cities, demanding autonomous space for young people, followed.[23]

The army took center stage in these young people's critique of existing political, economic and social structures. Their goal was to achieve autonomy and liberation from state oppression, which for them necessarily entailed the refusal to serve in the military. Clearly, the 1968 protestors were not the first ones to claim conscientious objection. However, the social movement influenced young men to refuse to serve in the military at much higher rates.[24] Also, people protested against the export of weapons manufactured in Switzerland. Their protest was directed against the Swiss government and Buehrle, a noted Swiss weapons manufacturer who circumvented the 1963 United Nations arms embargo against apartheid South Africa with the help of high Swiss government officials, and in 1968 illegally exported canons to Nigeria when the country was involved in a civil war in Biafra. Swiss (armed) neutrality was thus a contested terrain: it worked both as a dividing and as a unifying force.

The sixty-eighters' attack on the army, a central pillar of the nation and its independence, only added to the sense of domestic instability on the far right.

Young men's increasing disinterest in serving in the military disconcerted even moderate circles. The already mentioned government report stated that subversion, upheaval and revolution were to be expected at all times, and this constantly looming threat was seen as disintegrating the "classic boundary between peace and war."[25] The government observed that the specific techniques of the Cold War were less discernible than those of classic warfare. To them, the blurred boundaries were best exemplified by the increase in domestic warfare-like protests since 1968. According to the government report, these instigators of terror and subversion acted under the "spell of foreign ideology." By "foreign" they meant communist. The protesters used these ideologies, the Swiss government noted, to foster "domestic antagonisms and all forms of political and social discontent in the population" in order to paralyze state institutions and democratic decision-making processes.[26] Again, the 1968 student riots were used to illustrate Swiss citizens' growing hostility towards the state. In their view, the students attempted "to abuse our democratic institutions and attainments in support of revolutionary goals."[27] The domestic and international instabilities responsible for Switzerland's inability to achieve complete peace (as opposed to "relative peace") were seen as intimately entwined. Neither of them was homemade, both of them endangered the Swiss credo of neutrality and independence.[28]

The relatively limited and limiting role of neutrality law in times of peace and the ostensibly growing domestic and international instabilities might be why, on a symbolic level, the need for neutrality was called on rather frequently in Cold War Switzerland. In fact, it was not until the onset of the Cold War that neutrality became a defining aspect of what it meant to be Swiss. While neutrality had been linked to the nation's independence prior to 1945, for example when it joined the League of Nations in 1920, during the Cold War it came to stand for independence and collective freedom *tout court*. The Swiss notion of independence was now seen in stark opposition to the dependence of the regimes that made up the Eastern Bloc. However, as Goetschel et al. note, it was also the dependence on the community of Western states that felt disconcerting to the Swiss and let them invoke neutrality and independence. "Neutrality, allied with marked anti-communism, was seen as a way to defend against presumed threats to independence – whether from the East or from international organizations."[29] Indeed, an exaggerated notion of neutrality was frequently invoked to prevent and slow down foreign policy. The insistence on Swiss neutrality promoted insular thinking and practices. It was, for example, instrumental in political campaigns against Swiss membership of the UN, not achieved until 2002. At the same time, Switzerland was happy to provide the neutral ground for the European headquarters of the UN and several important Cold War conferences such as the 1954 Indochina conference or the 1955 and 1985 Geneva peace summits. This said, it is a well-known fact that Switzerland maintained close ideological and economic ties to the West. Accordingly, Switzerland was generally considered to be "Western neutral."[30]

Neutrality law might have prevented Switzerland from officially joining forces with the West. However, it could encourage individual Swiss citizens' anti-communist activities. The Swiss acted on informal levels, namely through ostensibly apolitical business transactions or participation in private networks and organizations. To be clear, the vigilantes featured in this chapter didn't spy in any official capacity, but they were known to inform state officials about suspicious individuals, so they wouldn't be hired. As Cold War historian Luc van Dongen stresses, in Switzerland it is virtually impossible to disentangle state from private Cold War activities.[31]

"Everybody's terrorism": citizen watch groups' othering practices

The seemingly pervasive communist threat to Switzerland's neutrality–independence was quickly commingled with "everybody's terrorism." The term was coined by anti-communist Swiss citizen watch groups, who informed the general public about the kinds of people who were joining West-German left-wing terrorist groups: "From the communist activist, the women's libber to the dreamer, gay man or punk every age was represented."[32] For one, sexual and gender liberation movements were lumped in together with communism. What's more, participating in any social movement was believed to be potentially terrorist.

The citizen watch groups under scrutiny were founded shortly after the student revolts of 1968. Many of their members demonized foreign people and ideologies.[33] It was the threat that the upsurge of young people on the left posed to many conservatives that gained them the backing they needed. Their mission was to fight the ideological infiltration of communism. At the same time they filed initiatives to stop the influx of migrant workers and to decrease the number of foreign people living in Switzerland more generally. As I stressed earlier in this essay, anti-communism was no invention of the Cold War. Indeed, the nationalists in question could draw on a 100-year-old tradition of Swiss "spiritual defense of the nation" and the idealized notion of Swiss neutrality that took shape after World War II. In the view of these nationalists, neutrality was equated with independence and autonomy from what were considered oppressive, non-democratic regimes, such as the USSR.

Even though the 1968 revolt was a mobilizing factor for those on the right, they were not just alarmed by youth riots. They feared that the Left would leave a more permanent mark by undertaking what famed German student leader Rudi Dutschke called the "long march through the institutions":[34] Dutschke had advised the Left to find their way into institutions of power such as schools, universities, seminaries, newspapers, magazines, theater, radio, television, the cinema and the courts.[35] His call to take over and dismantle the pillars of power–knowledge production was taken very seriously by the bourgeoisie. The fact that this institutional strategy was nonviolent didn't make it any less threatening to them. If anything, changing the system from within appeared to eat away at bourgeois hegemony more profoundly than illegal violent attacks by radicals could. The "march through the institutions" was not just subtle and legal, it also promised to have a lasting effect. The threat that a takeover of state institutions by the Left exuded might be why the "long march through the institutions" and leftist terrorist attacks were often portrayed to be on a continuum, the difference from the former to the latter only gradual.

Ernst Cincera was undoubtedly the most visible vigilante in 1970s Switzerland. He was the owner of a small advertising agency, a charismatic politician, a prominent member of the Swiss trades and crafts association and an enthusiastic advocate of national military service. In April 1972, he co-founded the Group for Contemporary Critical Analysis, and two years later the Information Group of Switzerland. While the former procured information on suspicious individuals and groups, which it neatly archived in its database, the latter distributed and communicated the findings to relevant parties.[36] The members of these vigilante groups were middle and upper middle-class white men with at least four significant things in common: they were members of the Free Democratic Party of Switzerland (FDP), veered to the political right, advocated liberal economic policies and filled the higher ranks of the conscript army.

The Information Group of Switzerland published a monthly newsletter called *WhatWhoHowWhenWhere (WasWerWieWannWo)*. A board of 22 to 23 members – among them high military officials and well-known members of the Zurich section of the FDP, also known as the Zurich Economic Liberals – was responsible for the content of the newsletter. Until September 1975 the newsletter carried the subheading "Information about Agitation and Subversion of Political Extremism in Switzerland." In 1977 the name of the newsletter was changed to the more nondescript "Info-Switzerland." It is not clear whether this name change has anything to do with the national scandal that the Group caused a year earlier when the press got wind of its anti-communist spying. The Group had provided the Swiss government and private businesses with information on thousands of Swiss citizens whom it deemed subversive.[37] Not just those known to sympathize with communism figured among the suspects, but all those who dared to question the political status quo. The Group infiltrated non-governmental organizations, communes and political parties. The information gathered was recorded in a suspects' database.

In the first issue of its newsletter in 1975, the Group stated its interest in the close observation of political extremism in Switzerland.[38] Because "every citizen of a democratic state" has the right to build his own opinion about extremism, explained Cincera in a 1978 issue of the newsletter.[39] The debate about these issues had been too emotional in the past, Cincera claimed, which is why the Group deemed it necessary to intervene: "The following account, the publication of sources and the definition of terms, aims to contribute to the objectification of the debate."[40] Cincera and his Group legitimated their interest in exposing extremist and terrorist activity in Switzerland by explicitly drawing on science and empirical data, and by allegedly producing objective, rational knowledge. They claimed to stand for positively connoted values such as democracy and to criticize both leftist and rightist extremism. Their connections to various right-wing and liberal organizations and networks shows, however, that they were clearly biased. The Group was supported by influential military, political and business circles. This suggests that its anti-communist, anti-feminist stance was shared by large parts of the Swiss population.

Even though the 1976 scandal about the Group's private intelligence service led to a public debate about terrorism, homeland security and the role of civil society, Cincera was more present in the mass media after the scandal than ever before.[41] He was invited by all kinds of clubs and organizations, many of them not explicitly political.[42] Cincera's public appearances allowed him to reach a wide audience. A typical announcement for one of his talks would highlight his extensive expertise in security matters: "Ernst Cincera has dealt with the methods and techniques and the strategic and tactical goals of these conflict forms for many years. In his talk he will show the role espionage, subversion and agitation as well as international terrorism play."[43] In populist manner, he stylized himself as a dutiful citizen ready to serve his country, not just as a willing soldier but as a protector of the nation, alerting fellow citizens about the perils of terrorism.[44]

Anti-feminism and anti-communism: from hard to innocent, soft terrorism

Whereas Cincera made sure that the Information Group of Switzerland's anti-communist stance found its way into mainstream media, the contribution of the Institute for the Study of Contemporary Political Questions was more subtle. Its way of fostering anti-communist sentiments was no less substantial, though. The Institute was founded by the Action for a Free Democracy, an anti-communist association launched in 1966.[45] Similar to the Information Group of Switzerland, the Institute's members represented the military, economic and political elite of the time: "The Action for a Free Democracy is under the patronage of the 'Young Economic Chamber Switzerland' and enjoys the support of high ranked military officers, numerous businesses and other authorities."[46] Among the seven board members were bankers, insurance executives, CEOs of large corporations and academics. Cincera, as it happens, was also among the founding members of the Institute.[47]

The Institute's mission was to document and fight subversion in Switzerland, which it managed to do quite successfully. In 1978, the Institute's long-term director, Robert Vögeli, noted proudly that an increasing number of journalists, politicians and public speakers referenced the Institute's journal regarding homeland security issues.[48] He and his colleague Jürg Steinacher were responsible for most of the journal's issues on homeland security, subversion and terrorism.[49]

In the early 1980s, the Institute reported a disquieting change concerning the terrorist phenomenon: what had previously been identified as a "hard" kind of anarchist terrorism had turned into a less easily recognizable form of "soft" terrorism. This new type of terrorism called into question what one commonly thought a terrorist looked like. Up until now the figure of the "black bearded man with lit up, beady eyes, a dynamite stick in his hand" had personified terrorism in the Swiss cultural imaginary.[50] According to Rolf Tophoven, noted German terrorism expert, this image had to be revised. It didn't suffice anymore to just watch out for the obvious signifiers of the brutal terrorist about to plant a bomb.[51] Innocent looking women had to be distrusted just as much. In fact, "feminine attributes" gave the "bloody terrorist business new impulses," Tophoven proclaimed in a spring 1983 special issue on international terrorism of the Institute's journal.[52] In the same issue Tophoven pointed to the central role the USSR played in international terrorism. He believed that terrorist organizations such as the Palestine Liberation Organization (PLO) were controlled by Moscow.[53] Moreover, Tophoven stressed that the PLO's world-wide terrorist network deployed women because they were better equipped than men to commit terrorist acts:[54] "They are generally more inconspicuous, they integrate themselves seamlessly into any given society, they know how to pass wherever they go – their charm putting resistance to sleep."[55] He warned not to be fooled by female terrorists' friendly demeanor because their charm came with a Kalashnikov in tow. Tophoven claimed that this "soft" form of terrorism had become as prominent as older "hard" types, underlining his claim by recounting the story of a young "liberated" woman who had severed her ties to her family and decided to travel by herself. The young woman ended up falling prey to the brain-washing ploys of a North Korean terrorist camp run by the Russian secret service, the KGB. The moral of the story: young women who were too independent, too liberated and who dared to follow their dreams instead of remaining in the hearth of the family were in danger of being seduced by terrorism. Women's liberation, Tophoven suggested, directly led into the clutches of communist terrorist networks.

In this anecdote Tophoven doesn't refer to just any gun. He specifically names the Kalashnikov. The Soviet assault rifle quite obviously stands for the USSR and the KGB. The Kalashnikov, however, also symbolizes phallic violence. Tophoven's suspicion about female terrorists and their ability to charm, seduce and deceive unsuspecting men who then practically give out free passes to the women to wreak havoc, is reminiscent of the plot of many a Cold War film. In the 1963 classic *From Russia with Love*, for example, British agent James Bond is fighting the criminal organization Spectre, short for "Special Executive for Counter Intelligence, Terrorism, Revenge, Extortion."[56] Spectre is avenging the death of its infamous member Dr. No by using a Soviet decoding machine called Lektor as bait. Throughout the film James Bond is trying to get his hands on Lektor before Spectre does. When Bond comes face to face with a former KGB agent, he realizes that he is about to be lured into a trap. Indeed, she tries to kill him with her poison-tipped shoe. Bond needs to gather all his gadgets, tricks and skills to fight the enemy.

James Bond is probably one of the most prominent Cold War heroes in Western Europe. He would not be a hero though, were it not for the cutting-edge technological devices, flying car seats and spy toys. Queer theorist J. Halberstam describes James Bond as the prototype of "prosthetic masculinity,"[57] a term that describes how masculinity is constituted by the gendered objects that surround it. Indeed, "prosthetic masculinity" de-centers the male body as the "natural" indication of masculinity by pointing to the importance of masculine markers such as clothing, weapons and cars in constituting masculinity. When terrorist women adorn themselves with these masculine markers they challenge the assumption that masculinity is the domain of biological men. These women rupture the naturalized congruence of masculinity and the male body. More specifically, they call into question the commonly held belief that because of their physical make-up men are naturally prone to violence. In this sense, the figure of the female terrorist reveals the continuous work that male masculinity necessitates in order to appear natural.

Tophoven's anecdote about a girl caught in the throes of the KGB served several purposes, then: it tried to contain the threatening figure of the independent woman and warned young women and their families of the consequences of women's liberation. These women posed a threat to the nation because of their feminine exterior, which made them invisible when it came to detecting violence. Feminine self-presentation allowed them to "pass" as the girl next door.[58] Given the way these women adorned themselves with masculine markers, they challenged both women's and men's authenticity: despite their feminine exterior, these women were suspected to secretly want to be men. Their gender-conforming self-presentation was believed to be a cunning disguise that allowed them to remain undetected as terrorists.[59] The fact that masculinity is not inherent to men qua biology, but found in the many gadgets that men surround themselves with, allowed women to participate in the serious games of violence. For women to appropriate the gun, conventionally reserved to men, earned them slanders such as "phallic women." Robert Corber calls this the "epistemological uncertainty" of femininity, a lethal combination of secrecy and invisibility that may endanger unsuspecting citizens at any given time.[60]

The young woman's return to her family in Tophoven's anecdote not only alleviated her from any agency of her own. Her return home also reproduced the bourgeois distinction between dangerous outside world and familial safety and peace. Tophoven's story must thus be read as an attempt to restore the public/private, masculine/feminine binary, which of course had been fundamentally challenged by the women's movement and the New Left more generally. The anecdote also instructed individual citizens and states alike to be mindful of a new kind of terrorism that appeared in "camouflage battle dress."[61] By using the word "camouflage" Tophoven referred to Moscow's supposedly secret influence on the PLO. The phrase "camouflage battle dress," however, also implies the aforementioned "soft" version of terrorism in the guise of seemingly innocent young women. The women in disguise, or rather, "terrorists disguised as women," gave evidence of terrorism's all-pervasiveness. Not only did it penetrate all facets of Western culture, but it had turned into an "everybody's terrorism" that no longer relied on visible signs. In this logic, there were no discernable habitual or visual markers anymore to help identify a terrorist. In fact, terrorists could "pass" as the girl next door.

At first glance this new, deceivingly harmless feminine terrorist threat appears to be at odds with the then dominant – in conservative and government circles at least – understanding of terrorism as a war of aggression. A closer look reveals, however, that the two threat scenarios, terrorism as "soft," inconspicuous and pervasive, on the one hand, and terrorism as an overt declaration of war, on the other, were not so different after all. A conventional repertoire of classic warfare, military resistance and patriotic masculinity still prevailed in both government reports and citizen watch newsletters. The traditional repertoire was expanded by new metaphors such as "everybody's terrorism" and "relative peace," terms that expressed how uncertain and fickle the seemingly clear distinction between war and peace, homeland security and terrorism or the private and the public spheres actually was. Introducing new terminology may have amplified and mitigated the threat that women transgressing these boundaries posed. If women's everyday terrorism was responsible for today's "relative peace," achieving complete peace in the future would also hold the promise of clear divisions between women and men, the private and the public.

Dangerous amalgamation of the private and the political: terrorism as the flip side of women's liberation

In 1979, four years prior to Tophoven's article about how KGB-sponsored terrorist camps brainwashed young women, Hans Josef Horchem, a German terrorism expert and Hamburg head of homeland security, was interviewed for the same journal. The main topic of the interview: the unexpectedly high number of female terrorists in German activist groups.[62] Horchem was sure that the existence of terrorist women had to do with the "explosive emancipation of women."[63] He argued that women's newly gained right to "self-fulfillment" was not just responsible for invading universities and flooding the job market, it also promoted terrorism. In the same interview, Horchem claimed that women were more ferocious than men. This assumption was shared by numerous experts of the time. Indeed, the idea that women have a "greater capacity of being cruel" was neither new nor unique to counter-terrorist discourse.[64] Criminologists used these same arguments to explain the existence of women soldiers in World War II, for example. They back up this claim by drawing on the myth of the inherently peaceful woman and her counterpart, the gun moll. While Horchem conceded that there was something innately feminine about female terrorist violence, he also stressed that the German terrorists stood out. According to him, they showed an unusual "gift at improvising, acting at impromptu if needed, and at handling weapons confidently during a bank robbery or a kidnapping."[65] He thus associated the German terrorist women with masculine behaviors and skills. "This is an entirely new experience, possibly a sign of decadence of our times. Men have become mere manikins and women real viragos!"[66] In the interview, Hamburg's head of homeland security seemed to argue both in his role as an expert on terrorism and as a bourgeois man threatened by the recent changes in gender relations. Horchem demanded a return to traditional family values where women were still homemakers and men breadwinners, suggesting that a clear gender division, women to the private, men to the public sphere, would keep the terrorist threat at bay.

Conservative citizen watch members shared Hans Josef Horchem's anxieties about the blurred boundaries between the private and the public. In their view the danger lay in how terrorists turned their personal problems into a political mission. The authors who published in the conservative journal of the Institute for the Study of Contemporary Political Questions believed that the "true origin and motivating factor for terrorist violent acts were psychological defects and stress."[67] It was here that the Institute's journal authors saw a clear connection between the well-known women's liberation motto, "The Private is Political," and terrorist violence. One prominent person who, to the Institute, exemplified this connection, was Red Army Faction leader Ulrike Meinhof. As a terrorist, journalist and feminist, Ulrike Meinhof stood for the demands of the women's movement and the political claims of the New Left, and she advocated counter-state violence and armed struggle. The Institute for the Study of Contemporary Political Questions used her as an example to demonstrate how dangerous it was to amalgamate the private and the political, especially if one elevated one's personal problems to a "just cause."[68] According to the Institute, terrorists such as Meinhof objectified their subjective beliefs, which they deemed a pathological condition of young people raised in Western postwar affluent societies more generally.[69] Steinacher observed that it was those lacking identity who were susceptible to terrorism: "Lazy young people" who were used to fulfilling their every (consumer) wish now expressed an "irrational" longing to be part of something.[70] What Steinacher and others bemoaned was the younger generation's supposed loss of traditional values – a sense of duty to serve the nation and a clear distinction between the public and the private spheres.

The problems that arose from commingling private and political matters were far-reaching, the authors of the Institute for the Study of Contemporary Political Questions' journal emphasized. They described the case of a professor whose political views veered to the left and claimed that his inability to properly separate the private from the political led to sexual impotence. In other words, he mistook orgasm for class struggle. It was impossible to him to sleep with a "conservative woman" because he desired a socialist formation.[71]

In the view of these authors, men on the left had taken the political claims of the feminist and the socialist movement too seriously and let their well-being depend on their partner's politics. Lefty men were stylized as castrated.[72] Pathologizing the feminist slogan "The Private is Political" was the Institute's way not just of denouncing women's liberation but of feminizing and thus devaluing the Left altogether.

Individual citizens' surveillance practices

These public and secretive doings of private guardians of the state would not have been thinkable, however, had they not been able to fall back on a tightly knit network in business, institutional politics and the military, and the watchful eyes and support of regular citizens. In their publications, Ernst Cincera and others appealed to citizens' duty to secure the nation. These calls are surprising insofar as they seemed to preach to the converted. Individual citizens had actively contributed to this counter-terrorist security discourse all along. In 1977, the federal police files give testimony of a growing number of telephone calls and letters to the police: Swiss people reported daily observations or thoughts in connection with terrorism, information about suspicious neighbors or work colleagues, out-of-the-ordinary behaviors at customs, critique or praise of state measures against terrorism, and ideas on how to protect potential victims of kidnappings, bombings and robberies. To give just a few examples: in 1978, a person who wished to stay anonymous and signed her letter with "wife" informed the police about a potential terrorist hideout.[73] She felt the need to report her suspicions, she explained, because she was convinced that a South-East Asian spiritual guru practicing in Switzerland was taking in "terrorists in need":[74] "It is easy to hide people here," she wrote in her letter to the federal police, "because this particular religious community hosts so many foreigners."[75] She did not want to hurt the guru, the self-proclaimed "wife" emphasized, but had written the letter out of a sense of duty to her nation. After all, the security of the "Swiss people" was at stake.[76] The security of the Swiss people was also what motivated her to criticize the sloppy border control of Swiss customs officers. Compared to the West-German passport inspection, the Swiss were inattentive, if not to say careless, she complained. She and her husband had recently observed their negligent work while at a café near the border. In closing, she encouraged the government to mobilize Swiss citizens in its fight against terrorism. "What if the police keep placing ads in newspapers, and ask those to step forward who might know about terrorist hideouts? If terrorists don't find hiding places anymore and nobody gives them money – they won't be able to cause as much damage."[77] It seemed clear to her that regular citizens played a vital part in enabling and/or disabling terrorism.

Similarly, a male caller, who did not want to identify himself to the Zurich police because he feared revenge, invoked the "Swiss people" as his reason for making the call.[78] He reported a woman whom he suspected of having been part of a bomb threat. The caller not only gave the police her name and address. He also stressed that she was a radical feminist and a lesbian. The police looked into the matter and, among other things, interrogated the woman's employers: "Her employers were happy with her job performance but they reported recurring tensions with the 'menfolk' and women with a normal disposition."[79] In the end, the police could not find evidence of a connection to terrorist networks. Even so, presumably as a preventive measure, the information gathered on the woman was neatly documented and archived in their "terrorist files."

The police also checked up on a letter writer or caller's neighbor if they suspected them to be terrorists or sympathizers of terrorists. Usually the neighbors in question were foreigners. In one example the police inquired into the lives of two female students from France and Japan after having received an anonymous note that they were Red Army Faction sympathizers.[80] In one case the police decided against following up on an observation, however. A prisoner had seen something suspicious from the window of his cell and reported it to the police.[81] In his letter he insulted the police for putting away the small fish – him – while letting terrorists get away. His complaint was seen as an affront by the police, both for who he was, a prison inmate, and for the tone of the letter.

The letters and transcribed telephone conversations to state officials reveal that the finger was mainly pointed at foreigners, young people, lefties, communards, lesbians and feminists and at all those who lived alternative lives and/or practiced a non-Christian faith. Clearly, the letter writers felt they had the right to make xenophobic, sexist, homophobic and otherwise defaming statements. The callers and letter writers were no homogenous group, however: letters were written by women and men, prisoners, blue-collar workers and established lawyers, even though letters by Swiss men from the middle and upper middle classes prevailed. The informers did have one thing in common though: they seemed to generally feel the need to justify why they were sharing their worries and advice with the police. This suggests that turning to the state might have been controversial. Indeed, it was the appeals to the welfare of Switzerland that served to bolster these watchful citizens with the necessary legitimacy: citizen watch in the name of the nation.

The opportunity to report was seized by people who were able to call themselves Swiss citizens. It is not surprising, then, that women seemed to claim the right to lodge a complaint less frequently. Indeed in my research I came across only one long letter written by a woman, the self-proclaimed "wife." As her letter suggests, women's relation to citizenship and to the state more generally was an indirect one, in her case one that was mediated through the husband. Considering that women's suffrage was only recently introduced in Switzerland, it may not be surprising that only a few women voiced their concern outside of the privacy of their home.

The self-imposed duty of notifying the police was regaled with considerable interpretative authority, the power of defining communism and feminism as terrorism. In short, those who reported what was deemed out of the ordinary also defined and othered the out of the ordinary. Furthermore, writing or calling in the conspicuous confirmed the citizen in his or her individuality. As an individual "I," the citizen felt empowered to point to certain people and their life-style practices as potentially threatening to the Swiss. Admitting to his or her fears, and identifying the conspicuous and other, constituted and confirmed the individual letter writer as a citizen. It was in these acts of naming the other that Swiss citizens also subjected themselves to the state's power-knowledge regime. The framing of events as suspicious, on the one hand, and the state's recognition of the worries of citizens, on the other, empowered the individual person and the state alike. By reporting their observations to state officials, the individuals in question affirmed their status as diligent Swiss citizens, while they provided the federal police with the necessary information and confidence to fulfill their role as the central archive on Swiss citizens.

The informal and formal networks of citizen watch groups, individual citizens, and the state proved to be incredibly strong and sustaining. The fact that support for citizen watch groups did not subside after Cincera's private intelligence agency was uncovered in 1976, gives evidence of that.

Conclusion: bolstering the old boys network

Taking a closer look at citizens' activities revealed that the Cold War phenomenon had not only seeped into the state's security discourse. Swiss citizens actively contributed to the re/production of the Cold War conflict by reporting on communists-feminists-terrorists. Their practices also show how anti-communist, anti-feminist and counter-terrorist ideology relied on each other – on an individual, symbolic and institutional level:

1. Those who were granted a subject position in the counter-terrorist discourse – journal authors, experts and well-to-do citizens – tended to be white professional men. These bourgeois men were used to fraternizing amongst themselves. One telling example of the homosocial culture favored by the two citizen watch groups described in this article, is that women – with the exception of the yearly Christmas dinner – were not welcome guests. The sense of fraternity that underwrote the collaboration between citizen watch groups, state officials and individual citizens was severely called into question, however, once the left embarked on its "long march through the institutions"[82] and Swiss women entered institutional politics.[83]
2. Citizens' spying and reporting on each other contributed to the larger struggle for hegemony at a time when state institutions such as the military and parliamentary politics came under attack. The vigilantes were thus busy securing their position institutionally: they bolstered a labor market that catered to the male breadwinner, praised the virtues of compulsory military service for all Swiss male citizens and fostered homosocial bonds

in professional clubs such as the Information Group of Switzerland. Most notably, though, vigilante citizens cemented white bourgeois masculinity by circumventing institutional politics whenever it pleased. At a time when parliamentary politics had just opened its doors to women, citizens' clandestine extra-legal practices kept women out of decision-making processes in the public sphere.
3. On a symbolic level, this counter-terrorist discourse propagated an ideology with clearly demarcated roles and areas of responsibility: the public sphere was reserved to men, the private arena to women. The fact that it was mostly female terrorists who were featured in the publications of the Information Group of Switzerland and the Institute for the Study of Contemporary Political Questions was no accident. It was part of a strategy of giving terrorism a facelift: by shifting the image of terrorism away from the easily identifiable foreign, black-bearded anarchist, vigilantes prepared their readers for an international "everybody's terrorism" in the guise of seemingly innocent young women. Citizen watch groups coded the terrorist as feminine, and in doing so, they promoted the idea of the ubiquitous nature of terrorism: terrorism could surface anywhere, even in the privacy of one's home. This "soft" type of terrorism did not call for visible evidence, the black beard, for example, to legitimate calls for the expansion of homeland security.

In this chapter it will have become clear that Swiss citizen watch groups were not just trying to contain left-wing terrorism. Their larger concerns were anti-feminist and anti-communist in nature. Implicitly, they reacted against the disconcerting changes in gender relations, which in their view went hand in hand with the spreading of communism and/or socialism in Switzerland. Their fear of communism not only revealed the frailty of the independence-neutrality myth of the Swiss nation, it also increasingly revealed how blurry the boundaries between the seemingly separate spheres of the private and the political were.[84] In their perspective, female terrorists threatening to eradicate the state and lefty politicians threatening to infiltrate state institutions were evidence of unnatural developments. Indeed, Western democracies' allegedly natural gender order was pitted against the perverted gender relations in communist states and terrorist cells.

It is thus safe to conclude that both the counter-terrorist security discourse described in this chapter and the communist-feminist-terrorist other it produced fortified the figure of the masculine citizen, a combination of heroic lone wolf and soldier fulfilling his duty. This figure of the citizen ready to take the law into his own hands, if only for nationalist reasons, was the cement that glued together citizen watch groups, individual citizens and state interests. It also empowered certain citizens to seize the opportunity to define and contain terrorism-communism-feminism. Let's not forget that Swiss professional men and a few women not only shaped counter-terrorist politics but also affirmed their status as exemplary Swiss citizens along the way. Indeed, citizens' policing and reporting of fellow citizens must be considered a mode of ruling the Swiss social body. By drawing boundaries around all that which in their view did not pertain to the neutral-independent Swiss nation, by stigmatizing those within Switzerland who seemed to withdraw from traditional bourgeois duties such as serving the nation or taking care of the family, citizens collaborated with the state in stabilizing and reaffirming Cold War bourgeois masculine hegemony.

Notes

1 Leith Passmore, "The Art of Hunger: Self-Starvation in the Red Army Faction," *German History* 27.1 (2009): 34; Patricia Melzer, "Death in the Shape of a Young Girl: Feminist Responses to Media Representations of Women Terrorists during the 'German Autumn' of 1977," *International Feminist Journal of Politics* 11.1 (2009): 35–62.
2 "Frauen der Gewaltszene. 'Wenn Weiber zu Hyänen' werden ...," *St. Galler Tagblatt*, September 17, 1977.
3 "Frauen im Untergrund: 'Etwas Irrationales,'" *Der Spiegel*, August 8, 1977, 22.
4 Margarete Mitscherlich-Nielsen, "Hexen oder Märtyrer," in *Frauen und Terror. Versuche, die Beteiligung von Frauen an Gewalttaten zu erklären*, ed. Susanne von Paczensky (Reinbek/Hamburg: Rowohlt-Taschenbuch, 1978), 19.
5 Methodologically, this chapter pursues a close reading of the concerns voiced by citizens in letters and telephone calls made to the local or federal police or to the executive council in 1970s and early 1980s Switzerland as well as the monthly newsletters and journals published by two citizen watch groups called Information Group Switzerland and Institute for the Study of Contemporary Political Questions. In addition, the journal contributions by Hans Josef Horchem and Rolf Tophoven, two internationally acclaimed terrorism experts, and the unpublished talks by Ernst Cincera, the most prominent vigilante in Switzerland at the time, figure prominently in my analysis.
6 Michel Foucault, "Vorlesung I. Sitzung vom 11. Januar 1978," in *Geschichte der Gouvernementalität I. Sicherheit, Territorium, Bevölkerung. Vorlesung am Collège de France 1977–1978*, ed. Michel Foucault (Frankfurt a.M.: Suhrkamp, 2004), 25.
7 See Michel Foucault, "Nietzsche, Genealogy, History," in *The Foucault Reader*, ed. Paul Rabinow (New York: Vintage, 1984), 88, also 95; Dominique Grisard, *Gendering Terror. Eine Geschlechtergeschichte des Linksterrorismus in der Schweiz* (Frankfurt a.M.: Campus, 2011), 33.
8 Ute Frevert, *Ehrenmänner. Das Duell in der bürgerlichen Gesellschaft* (Munich: C.H. Beck, 1991), 120; see also Carole Pateman, "Gleichheit, Differenz, Unterordnung. Mutterschaftspolitik und die Frauen in ihrer Rolle als Staatsbürgerinnen," *Feministische Studien* 10.1 (1992): 54–69.
9 See Ute Frevert *"Mann und Weib, und Weib und Mann". Geschlechter-Differenzen in der Moderne* (Munich: C.H. Beck, 1995), 120; Ute Frevert, *Die kasernierte Nation. Militärdienst und Zivilgesellschaft in Deutschland* (Munich: C.H. Beck, 2001), 179–81; Frevert, *Ehrenmänner*, 117–18.
10 Stuart Hall, "Introduction: Who needs 'Identity'?," in *Questions of Cultural Identity*, eds. Stuart Hall and Paul Du Gay (London: Sage, 1996), 4–6; Dominique Grisard, "Ein Terroristenprozess als Medienereignis. Die Konstruktion von Nation in der Schweizer Presse in den späten 1970er-Jahren," *Traverse* 3 (2006): 138–39; Grisard, *Gendering*.
11 Laurent Goetschel et al., *Swiss Foreign Policy. Foundations and Possibilities* (London/New York: Routledge, 2005, 16).
12 Ernesto Laclau, *Emancipation(s)* (London and New York: Verso, 1996), Ch. 3.
13 Laclau, *Emancipation(s)*, 44.

14 Brigitte Studer, "Antikommunismus," in *Historisches Lexikon der Schweiz*, March 23, 2009, accessed July 1, 2010, http://www.lexhist.ch/externe/protect/textes/d/D27836.html.
15 Stefanie Frey, *Switzerland's Defence and Security Policy during the Cold War, 1945–1973* (Lenzburg: Verlag Merker im Effingerhof, 2002), 238.
16 Goetschel et al., *Swiss*, 17.
17 Studer, *Antikommunismus*.
18 Daniel A. Neval, *'Mit Atombomben bis nach Moskau': gegenseitige Wahrnehmung der Schweiz und des Ostblocks im Kalten Krieg 1945–1968* (Zurich: Chronos, 2003), 182–83; Jürg Stüssi-Lauterburg and Stefanie Frey, *Unvollständiges Protokoll eines Krieges, der nicht stattfand: schweizerische Militärgeschichte aus Sicht westlicher Quellen von 1944 bis 1973* (Lenzburg: Verlag Merker im Effingerhof, 2009), 55–57.
19 Eric Flury-Dasen, "Kalter Krieg," in *Historisches Lexikon der Schweiz*, Oct. 9, 2008, accessed Oct. 25, 2011, http://www.hls-dhs-dss.ch/textes/d/D17344.php.
20 Bundesrat, "Bericht des Bundesrates an die Bundesversammlung über die Sicherheitspolitik der Schweiz (Konzeption der Gesamtverteidigung) vom 27. Juni 1973," *Bundesblatt* II (1973), 119.
21 Bundesrat, *Bericht*, 125.
22 René Lévy and Laurent Duvanel, *Politik von unten: Bürgerprotest in der Nachkriegsschweiz* (Basel: Lenos Verlag, 1984), 205.
23 Lévy and Duvanel, *Politik*, 171.
24 Emanuel Moecklin, *Militärdienstverweigerung. Über die Ursachen der Militärdienstverweigerung in der Schweiz. Eine explorative Studie* (Soziologisches Institut, Universität Zürich: unpublished Master's thesis, 1998), 70.
25 Bundesrat, *Bericht*, 119.
26 Bundesrat, *Bericht*, 120.
27 Bundesrat, "Zwischenbericht zur Sicherheitspolitik vom 3. Dezember 1979," *Bundesblatt* I (1980), 364.
28 Alois Riklin, "Neutralität im Kalten Krieg," in *Historisches Lexikon der Schweiz*, Nov. 9, 2010, accessed Oct. 25, 2011, http://www.hls-dhs-dss.ch/textes/d/D16572.php; Mauro Mantovani, "Sicherheitspolitik," in *Historisches Lexikon der Schweiz*, July 4, 2011, accessed Oct. 25, 2011, http://www.hls-dhs-dss.ch/textes/d/D8679.php.
29 Goetschel et al., *Swiss*, 23.
30 Flury-Dasen, *Kalter*.
31 Hartmann, Dominique, "Internationaler Antikommunismus," *Horizonte* 2 (September 2011), 24.
32 Info+ch 44, "'Jedermann-Terrorismus' für den Alltag" (October 1982), 2; Hans Josef Horchem and Robert Vögeli, "Verfall des Staatsschutzes und die Konsequenzen," *IPZ-Information. Dokumente/Zitate/Analysen/Kommentare*, E/10 (October 1980), 28.
33 Goetschel et al., *Swiss*, 16.
34 Hans Josef Horchem, *Extremisten in einer selbstbewußten Demokratie. Rote-Armee-Fraktion. Rechtsextremismus. Der lange Marsch durch die Institutionen* (Freiburg: Herder, 1975).
35 Rudi Dutschke, "On Antiauthoritarianism," in *The New Left Reader*, ed. Carl Oglesby (New York: Grove, 1969), 243–53.
36 Jürg Frischknecht et al., *Die unheimlichen Patrioten. Politische Reaktion in der Schweiz. Ein aktuelles Handbuch*, 2nd edn (Zurich: Limmat, 1979); Jürg Frischknecht et al., *Die unheimlichen Patrioten. Ergänzungsband 1979–1984* (Zurich: Limmat, 1984).
37 Daniela Niederberger "Staatliche Lizenz zu Spitzeln. Der Cincera-Skandal," in *Die Schweiz und ihre Skandale*, eds. Heinz Looser and Hansjörg Braunschweig

(Zurich: Limmat, 2005); also Georg Kreis et al., *Staatsschutz in der Schweiz: die Entwicklung von 1935–1990. Eine multidisziplinäre Untersuchung im Auftrage des schweizerischen Bundesrates* (Bern: Haupt, 1993).
38 WasWerWieWannWo 1 (Feb. 1975), 1.
39 nfo+ch 16, "BI = Bürgerinitiative: Legaler oder illegaler Widerstand?" (May 1978), 1.
40 Info+ch 13, "Terror" (Oct. 1977), 1.
41 Günter Stratenwerth, "Beschränkter Persönlichkeitsschutz," *Die Weltwoche*, Dec. 1, 1978; Walter Haller, "Kein Raum für private Nachrichtendienste," in *Die Weltwoche*, Dec. 8, 1976.
42 Frischknecht et al., *Ergänzungsband*, 256; Niederberger, *Staatliche*.
43 ACH (Archive for Contemporary History), Premortem Bequest Cincera: Talks, Manuscripts. Anonymous: Zum Referat von Nationalrat Ernst Cincera "Die nichtmilitärischen Bedrohungsformen," undated.
44 Info+ch 44, "'Jedermann-Terrorismus' für den Alltag" (October 1982), 1.
45 The Action for a Free Democracy continued the work of another group called Action of Free Citizens, which had disbanded in 1965; see ACH, IPZ-Archive, 1970–92, accessed July 22, 2010, http://onlinearchives.ethz.ch/ReportViewer.aspx?obj=189e6bca96b94d729776a59344c3da4f&format=PDF.
46 In 1982, the Action for a Free Democracy changed its name to Association for the Institute for the Study of Contemporary Political Questions.
47 Ernst Cincera, *Unser Widerstand gegen die Subversion in der Schweiz* (Lugano: Athenäum, 1976).
48 ACH, IPZ-Archive, Flyer "Das IPZ im Dienste der freien Marktwirtschaft," 1978.
49 Robert Vögeli, "Stadtguerilla," *IPZ-Information. Dokumente/Zitate/Analysen/Kommentare* R/1 (July 1971); Robert Vögeli, "Stadtguerilla in Europa," *IPZ-Information. Dokumente/Zitate/Analysen/Kommentare* R/2 (May 1972); Robert Vögeli, "Stadtguerilla in der Schweiz," *IPZ-Information. Dokumente/Zitate/Analysen/Kommentare* R/3 (November 1973); Robert Vögeli, "Neue Linke und Anarchismus," *IPZ-Information. Dokumente/Zitate/Analysen/Kommentare* PP/2 (April 1974); Robert Vögeli, "Vom Guerilla-Konzept zum Terrorismus," *IPZ-Information. Dokumente/Zitate/Analysen/Kommentare* R/4 (November 1977); Jürg Steinacher, "Neue Linke und Anarchismus," *IPZ-Information. Dokumente/Zitate/Analysen/Kommentare* PP/2 (April 1974); Jürg Steinacher, "Terror," *IPZ-Information. Dokumente/Zitate/Analysen/Kommentare* PP/4 (January 1975); Jürg Steinacher, "Die Jugendunruhen und ihr gesellschaftspolitischer Stellenwert," *IPZ-Information. Dokumente/Zitate/Analysen/Kommentare* G/4 (April/May 1982).
50 Steinacher, *Neue*, 6.
51 Rolf Tophoven, "Die Internationale des Terrorismus," *IPZ-Information. Dokumente/Zitate/Analysen/Kommentare* R/8 (May 1983), 12.
52 Tophoven, *Die Internationale*, 15–16.
53 Tophoven, *Die Internationale*, 11.
54 Tophoven, *Die Internationale*, 15.
55 Tophoven, *Die Internationale*, 12.
56 *From Russia with Love* (1963), dir. T. Young, 115 min., USA.
57 Judith Halberstam, *Female Masculinity* (Durham and New York: Duke University Press, 1998), 3–4.
58 Robert J. Corber, *Cold War Femme: Lesbianism, National Identity, and Hollywood Cinema* (Durham and London: Duke University Press, 2011), 3.
59 Corber, *Cold*, 19.
60 Corber, *Cold*, 21.
61 Tophoven, *Die Internationale*, 32.
62 Hans Josef Horchem and Robert Vögeli, "Probleme des Terrorismus in Europa," *IPZ-Information. Dokumente/Zitate/Analysen/Kommentare* R/7 (September 1979).

Female terrorists and vigilant citizens 143

63 Horchem and Vögeli, *Probleme*, 14.
64 Horchem and Vögeli, *Probleme*, 16.
65 Horchem and Vögeli, *Probleme*, 16.
66 Horchem and Vögeli, *Probleme*, 16.
67 Steinacher, *Terror*, 2.
68 Steinacher, *Neue*, 17.
69 Steinacher, *Neue*, 17.
70 Steinacher, *Terror*, 13.
71 Steinacher, *Neue*, 16.
72 Steinacher, *Terror*, 15.
73 BAR (Swiss Federal Archives), E 4320 (C), 1995/390, 264 (0)39/758/1, April 25, 1978, 2.
74 BAR (Swiss Federal Archives), E 4320 (C), 1995/390, 264 (0)39/758/1, April 25, 1978, 2.
75 BAR (Swiss Federal Archives), E 4320 (C), 1995/390, 264 (0)39/758/1, April 25, 1978, 1.
76 BAR (Swiss Federal Archives), E 4320 (C), 1995/390, 264 (0)39/758/1, April 25, 1978, 3.
77 BAR (Swiss Federal Archives), E 4320 (C), 1995/390, 264 (0)39/758/1, April 25, 1978, 3.
78 BAR (Swiss Federal Archives), E 4320 (C), 1994/121, 73 (236:0) 39/324, July 21, 1978.
79 BAR (Swiss Federal Archives), E 4320 (C), 1994/121, 73 (236:0) 39/324, July 21, 1978, 2.
80 BAR (Swiss Federal Archives), E 4320 (C), 1995/390, 255 (0)39/608, Nov. 1, 1977.
81 BAR (Swiss Federal Archives), E 4320 (C), 1994/121, 73 (236:0) 39/324, Sept. 18, 1978.
82 Horchem, *Extremisten*.
83 Regula Ludi, "Gendering Citizenship and the State in Switzerland after 1945," in *Nation and Gender in Conemporary Europe*, eds. Vera Tolz and Stephenie Booth (Manchester: Manchester University Press, 2005).
84 Grisard, *Gendering*, 204–7.

Selected bibliography

Cincera, Ernst. *Unser Widerstand gegen die Subversion in der Schweiz*. Lugano: Athenäum, 1976.

Corber, Robert J. *Cold War Femme: Lesbianism, National Identity, and Hollywood Cinema*. Durham and London: Duke University Press, 2011.

Dutschke, Rudi. "On Antiauthoritarianism." In *The New Left Reader*, edited by Carl Oglesby, 243–53. New York: Grove, 1969.

Foucault, Michel. "Nietzsche, Genealogy, History." In *The Foucault Reader*, edited by Paul Rabinow, 76–100. New York: Vintage, 1984.

——"Vorlesung I. Sitzung vom 11. Januar 1978." In *Geschichte der Gouvernementalität I. Sicherheit, Territorium, Bevölkerung. Vorlesung am Collège de France 1977–1978*, edited by Michel Sennelart, 13–51. Frankfurt a.M.: Suhrkamp, 2004.

Frevert, Ute. *Mann und Weib, und Weib und Man. Geschlechter-Differenzen in der Moderne*. Munich: C.H. Beck, 1995.

——*Die kasernierte Nation. Militärdienst und Zivilgesellschaft in Deutschland*. Munich: C.H. Beck, 2001.

Frey, Stefanie. *Switzerland's Defence and Security Policy during the Cold War, 1945–1973*. Lenzburg: Verlag Merker im Effingerhof, 2002.

Frischknecht, Jürg, Ueli Haldimann and Peter Niggli. *Die unheimlichen Patrioten. Politische Reaktion in der Schweiz. Ein aktuelles Handbuch*, 2nd edn. Zurich: Limmat, 1979.

Goetschel, Laurent, Magdalena Bernath and Daniel Schwarz. *Swiss Foreign Policy: Foundations and Possibilities*. London and New York: Routledge, 2005.

Grisard, Dominique. *Gendering Terror. Eine Geschlechtergeschichte des Linksterrorismus in der Schweiz*. Frankfurt and New York: Campus, 2011.

Halberstam, Judith. *Female Masculinity*. Durham and New York: Duke University Press, 1998.

Hall, Stuart. "Introduction: Who Needs 'Identity'?" In *Questions of Cultural Identity*, edited by Stuart Hall and Paul Du Gay, 1–17. London: Sage, 1996.

Horchem, Hans Josef. *Extremisten in einer selbstbewußten Demokratie. Rote-Armee-Fraktion. Rechtsextremismus. Der lange Marsch durch die Institutionen*. Freiburg: Herder, 1975.

Kreis, Georg, Jean–Daniel Delley and Otto K. Kaufmann. *Staatsschutz in der Schweiz: die Entwicklung von 1935–1990. Eine multidisziplinäre Untersuchung im Auftrage des schweizerischen Bundesrates*. Bern: Haupt, 1993.

Laclau, Ernesto. *Emancipation(s)*. London and New York: Verso, 1996.

Lévy, René and Duvanel, Laurent. *Politik von unten: Bürgerprotest in der Nachkriegsschweiz*. Basel: Lenos Verlag, 1984.

Ludi, Regula. "Gendering Citizenship and the State in Switzerland after 1945." In *Nation and Gender in Conemporary Europe*, edited by Vera Tolz and Stephenie Booth. Manchester: Manchester University Press, 2005.

Melzer, Patricia. "Death in the Shape of a Young Girl: Feminist Responses to Media Representations of Women Terrorists during the 'German Autumn' of 1977." *International Feminist Journal of Politics*, 11.1 (2009): 35–62.

Mitscherlich-Nielsen, Margarete. "Hexen oder Märtyrer." In *Frauen und Terror. Versuche, die Beteiligung von Frauen an Gewalttaten zu erklären*, edited by Susanne von Paczensky, 13–23. Reinbek/Hamburg: Rowohlt-Taschenbuch-Verlag, 1978.

Neval, Daniel A. *Mit Atombomben bis nach Moskau: gegenseitige Wahrnehmung der Schweiz und des Ostblocks im Kalten Krieg 1945–1968*. Zurich: Chronos, 2003.

Niederberger, Daniela. "Staatliche Lizenz zu Spitzeln. Der Cincera-Skandal." In *Die Schweiz und ihre Skandale*, edited by Heinz Looser and Hansjörg Braunschweig, 119–30. Zurich: Limmat, 2005.

Passmore, Leith. "The Art of Hunger: Self-Starvation in the Red Army Faction." *German History*, 27.1 (2009): 32–59.

Pateman, Carole. "Gleichheit, Differenz, Unterordnung. Mit Mutterschaftspolitik und die Frauen in ihrer Rolle als Staatsbürgerinnen." *Feministische Studien*, 10.1 (1992): 54–69.

Riklin, Alois. "Neutralität im Kalten Krieg." In *Historisches Lexikon der Schweiz*, November 9, 2010, accessed October 25, 2011, http://www.hls-dhs-dss.ch/textes/d/D16572.php.

Studer, Brigitte. "Antikommunismus." In *Historisches Lexikon der Schweiz*. March 23, 2009, accessed July 1, 2010, http://www.lexhist.ch/externe/protect/textes/d/D27836.html.

Part III
Rethinking opposition and conformity

7 Making sense of "China" during the Cold War
Global Maoism and Asian studies

Fabio Lanza

> Ah ça, dit Truptin, mais voulez parler de Mao de la révolution culturelle, *tageming*? ... Invention, madame mademoiselle, invention de journaliste, tout ça, moi en Chine, jamais rien vu tout ça. Chine, invention française, parisienne même, tous des ignorants, ignorant la langue, l'écriture et ça parle, ça parle puisque ça ne sait pas lire. ... Permettez-moi de vous dire, madame, permettez mois de vous dire, la Chine n'existe pas.[1]

In May 1968, a slim, almost artisanal publication appeared out of Cambridge, Massachusetts. First labeled simply as a *Newsletter*, it quickly evolved into a *Bulletin*, conveying the voice of the newly formed Committee of Concerned Asian Scholars.[2] CCAS was an organization of young professors and graduate students who were vociferously critical of US policies in Vietnam and throughout Asia, of the complicity of the field of Asian studies with these policies, as well as of the very intellectual constitution of the field itself. Between 1968 and 1979, the Concerned Asian Scholars (CAS) mounted a sweeping attack on the academic, political, and financial structure of Asian studies in the United States. The journal the group published—still in existence, albeit under a different name—the *Bulletin of Concerned Asian Scholars* (*BCAS*), was radical, vibrant, at times excessive, and always politically minded.[3]

The field of Asian studies, like all area studies, had been created and shaped by the Cold War. Funded and expanded as part of a government mission, its practitioners had been both objects of purges during the McCarthy era and willing (or unwitting) collaborators with US policies in Asia, including the very real wars that were being waged in the 1960s. CCAS represented the first collective attempt to unveil the Cold War connections between state and academia hidden behind the neutrality of scholarship and to show how these connections had influenced both US policies in Asia and the very ability of their academic field to account for what was happening there. To reach these goals, these young scholars challenged directly the authority, the politics, and the scholarship of their own teachers, the founding fathers of the field; they renounced the funding provided by major institutions; and ultimately, they risked and often gave up their academic careers.

A double disappearance

"Concerned" is quite an unusual characteristic for a scholar to use in order to self-define, and even more so for a group of scholars: it implies a subjective commitment, a direct involvement in the issue at stake—and it further suggests that there exist scholars who are *not* concerned, but rather indifferent. In the case of the CCAS it also implied the possibility of a collective concern, of a positioning vis-à-vis politics and knowledge, in particular the politics of knowledge embedded in the profession and the field of Asian studies. It pointed to and even called for a political militancy in the arena of intellectual production.

The *Bulletin* conveyed concern about, and opposition to, the Vietnam War.[4] It proposed a radical rethinking of scholarly and political approaches to Japan, South Korea, and South Asia. But the CAS also argued for a complete re-evaluation and re-assessment of Maoist China and, in particular, of the politics and policies of the Cultural Revolution. China figured as the necessary "positive" side of the *Bulletin*'s harsh attack on Asian studies and the US government: it offered the possibility of alternative development, a more humane economy, and peaceful policies. This ended in 1976. Between 1976 and 1981 only a handful of essays on the People's Republic of China (PRC) were published in the *Bulletin* and only one of them addressed directly the radical shift in Chinese politics that began with Mao Zedong's death.[5] China basically "disappeared" from the journal's pages; it became a conspicuous absence, the veritable elephant in the room. When it reappeared, in a double issue in 1981, the contributors to the *Bulletin* struggled to cope with the new China and the very different evaluation of Maoism it presented. Gone was the optimism toward the Chinese model, gone was the possibility of alternative policies, but also gone was the grounding that since 1968 had provided a foundation to the collective subject of the Concerned Asian Scholars. The Committee had already disbanded in 1979.

There was also another, more personal disappearance. While most of the CAS who specialized in Japan or Korea went on to prestigious and well-deserved careers, the "China side" of the Concerned Scholars was decimated by the late 1970s. Many of the China scholars dropped out of academia completely, did not get tenure, or suffered other personal losses.[6]

I examine the case of the *Bulletin* and the CCAS to explore a larger moment of transition in Cold War international politics, the role of China in that transition, as well as the history of Asian studies in the US. Given the massive effects that the end of the Chinese revolutionary experiment had on the *Bulletin* and the very enterprise of the CAS, I argue that "China"—and specifically the Cultural Revolution—was fundamental to the collective concern embodied by the CCAS. It was only by taking seriously and personally the political issues that the Cultural Revolution presented and by making those issues central in their daily lives as scholars, teachers, students, and activists, that the CAS could articulate, albeit briefly, a collective position.

However, while the Cultural Revolution was essential for the activism of CCAS, it was also a critical point of tension. Maoism challenged the role of intellectuals and universities in the production and transmission of knowledge and the CAS struggled with being at the same time scholars *and* activists, sometimes paying a very high professional price. In the Cultural Revolution, the personal, the everyday was political: and so it was for the young CAS. This was one of the reasons for both the political commitment of these young scholars and the devastating effects of its end. An emphasis on China produced tensions within the larger group and made activism often dependent on the vagaries of Cold War diplomacy, especially after the Nixon rapprochement in 1972. Also, for many of these young scholars, "China" was both the name of a political alternative, a distant object of desire, and the topic of their professional research, literally their "field." The tensions between these different meanings exploded when CCAS groups were allowed to visit the People's Republic of China in 1971 and 1972, and debates over their relationship with China figured prominently in the life of the group, until its dissolution.[7]

The case of CCAS illustrates how China played a crucial and global role in the Cold War era, one that cannot and should not be restricted to international diplomacy. Maoist China, studied, (mis)perceived, or imagined, was not only and not simply the location of a utopia that could be deployed by idealistic youth to define other and more local political goals;[8] nor was it just the exotic destination of dreamy left-leaning tourists who saw in it whatever they wanted to see.[9] Rather, "China" was the name of a short-lived radical political alternative, one that forced those people who took it seriously to rethink their relationship to work, social roles, and the production of knowledge. From today's perspective one can easily dismiss "global Maoism" as a juvenile illusion based on an invented Shangri-La, but its effects in the political practices it produced worldwide were real enough.

Within the field of Asian studies, CCAS presented the first instance of an organized challenge to a mode of knowledge production about Asia that predates the Cold War but that had become absolutely dominant after 1949. By making China into a possible model, the CAS unmasked and reversed the prevalent "Cold War Orientalism"[10] of the field and, by doing so, produced new approaches to the study of Asia, in some cases opening the way for further developments in the following decades. Therefore, the CCAS illustrates how, within the Cold War, "Maoism" and "China" were also the names under which major political and scholarly discoveries could be globally articulated.

America's China

So, what did "China" mean for these young scholar-activists?

First, very practically, in the context of both an active war in South-East Asia and the Cold War, China seemed to provide a possibility for moderation. Since the 1950s, China had moved to a position declaredly removed from the Cold War dualism, and its opposition to the US policy of aggression was justified as an opposition to any policy of aggression anywhere.[11] To the CAS, this perceived Chinese attitude provided a starting point from which to state that a radical alternative to the status quo of global war was possible. On the one hand, this meant a constant call to alter the China policy of the US.[12] On the other hand, the CAS pushed public opinion to consider the particular position of China as a rational, viable stance. In the general resurgence of militarism that affected other Asian nations (Japan and South Korea, for example), they depicted China as pursuing a completely different path. Taking the Chinese perspective as a real, existing standpoint allowed the CAS to stake a position that was not simply anti-war but also disengaged from the brutal duality of enemy–friend, while supportive of development and independence in Asia.[13] For example, the *Bulletin* constantly cautioned against underestimating the real situation of encirclement and insecurity in which China lived, which was usually dismissed in the US as cultural paranoia. China was justifiably worried, they argued, but even in those circumstances—and unlike the US—China continued to pursue a policy of dialogue, anti-aggression, and anti-imperialism. CCAS thus subverted one of the tropes of Cold War Asian scholars: China, for the first time, could be seen as rational, while it was the US that was irrationally fearful, ideologically motivated, and prone to indulge in nightmarish fantasies.

"China" functioned as a possible model in a more radical sense. The CAS singled out the late 1960s, the era of radical Maoist reforms, as a paradigm in the field of education, health care, gender equality, treatment of the elderly, etc., an example that they proposed to a US society struggling with similar problems.[14] If we look closely at the first decade of the *Bulletin*, it is evident that it was precisely through a "triangulation" with the Chinese experience that the Concerned Scholars could call for a radical rethinking of national and international politics, as well as of the very figure of the (Asian) scholar.

For China to be accepted as a model, the CAS had to first and foremost debunk the Cold War perspective of the PRC as the "irreducible Other" and show how that very framework was merely a way to legitimize US policies. The discourse of Asian "irrationality," they argued, provided a cover and a disguise for the very real practices of foreign and military policy, and made it impossible to even question the rationality and morality of American objectives.[15] In the words of Mark Selden, "to recognize the role of Asian scholarship in providing a rationale at home for American military expansion in Asia, and for the propagation abroad of liberal capitalism and American protection as the royal road to development and social change, is merely the beginning of the effort to create a more truthful and humane scholarship."[16] Rather than stress the cultural alterity of a "Confucian Asia," it was necessary instead to make evident the biases implicit in the US scholarly perspective. But it was not enough to affirm that China, as Ric Pfeffer put it, was not "a freak show in the world."[17] Rather, CCAS called on the necessity to evaluate China (and other Asian countries) less in terms of the international communist menace and more in terms of the immense problems confronting the poverty-stricken nations of the world and the human cost of varying approaches to social change; the imperative to critically re-evaluate the origins of cold and hot war in Asia and the nature of American domination with greater attention to the perspective of Asian nations rather than through the glowing rhetoric of democracy and reform emanating from Washington.[18]

The phrase "varying approaches to social change" referred mainly to the egalitarian experiments of the Great Leap Forward and the Cultural Revolution. The CAS looked at these experiments as something completely new; they were "perhaps the most interesting economic and social experiment ever attempted, in which tremendous efforts are being made to achieve an egalitarian development, an industrial development without dehumanization, one that involves everyone and affects everyone."[19] It was on the basis of these perceived successful political realities that a challenge to a hegemonic model of society and of intellectual analysis could be launched. In the view of the CAS, Maoist China promised and, at least in part, had realized a model of development, both economic and social, that was not only based on local realities and on the people, but was also human and egalitarian and therefore fundamentally different both from capitalist markets and from Soviet dirigisme.

Significantly, the Maoist model was also avowedly not "Chinese," in the sense of being culturally or ethnically defined; rather, it was thought to be relevant worldwide *and* in the US. Education figured prominently among the possible lessons of the Maoist revolution. China, Jonathan Unger observed, was going through "perhaps the most important innovations in education ... since Dewey came along,"[20] and yet "American students of China ridiculed the Chinese efforts."[21] If, as many CAS argued, during the Great Leap Forward, China changed its educational system because it was unfair toward a large section of the population (the poor, the rural), why couldn't this be a serious model for the US society "faced now with the demand of Black America for justice"?[22] Chinese educational reform, then, Unger proclaimed at a meeting in the Bay Area, could be "of use not only to people in the Third World, in organizing education and really changing the attitudes of people in villages, in ghettos, but it's also for education right here at Berkeley."[23] And yet, they asked, where was the scholarship on this particular topic, why wasn't anybody looking at this "China?"

CCAS skewered the supposed blindness of the established Asian studies scholars in particular vis-à-vis the successes of Chinese economic reforms. The prejudices inscribed in the field, the CAS argued, made them incapable of taking into consideration something absolutely factual, like the improvement in the lives of millions of Chinese under Maoism.

The result has been supposedly objective research on China which actually accepts the official misrepresentation of the Chinese Revolution as a "tragedy" and of the People's Republic as "aggressive." We believe, on the contrary, that the Chinese Revolution led by Chairman Mao Tse-tung has been immensely beneficial for the Chinese people and serves as an inspiration throughout the world.[24]

It was precisely the perceived success of the Maoist economic experiments that made them a palatable model for other Asian countries, like India, which could be used as negative proof that "without socialism there is no economic development."[25] Clearly, the CAS were making clear-cut and enthusiastic statements about the successes of the Chinese revolution, and especially of its most radical experiments, like the Great Leap Forward, without much support in terms of real data. Despite that, they were quite accurate—certainly more accurate than many of their opponents—and it would be difficult for any honest scholar today to deny, as John Gurley wrote in 1969, that "China over the past two decades has made very remarkable economic advances (though not steadily) on almost all fronts. The basic, overriding economic fact about people in China is that for twenty years they have all been fed, clothed, and housed, have kept themselves healthy, and have educated most."[26] However, Gurley's next sentence, where he affirms that "millions have *not* starved," cannot but make one cringe, given what we now know about the death toll of the post-Great Leap famine—a number that probably exceeds 15 million. This will be eventually one of the issues behind the "end" of the CAS: how can an alternative model of society survive the recognition of a disaster of such massive proportions? What can be rescued of "China" when its practical success is challenged?

However, it is crucial to stress that CCAS analysis of China was much more complex and more interesting than the simple interpretation of economic figures. To the China studies "establishment" (John K. Fairbank, Lucian Pye, etc.) that primarily affirmed how communism does not work, the CAS did not respond simply "it does," but rather, as we have seen in the cases of education and foreign relations, they challenged the very understanding of what "to work" meant. And that required them to rearticulate the connection between economy and politics, between development and social justice. The Maoist experiments of the 1950s and 1960s were important and new not so much because they had been hugely successful in strict economic terms—growth, development, GDP—but rather, because they embodied the stubborn (and global) search for an "economy" whose success was measured not simply in production numbers but also in the radical reduction of social inequalities. It was precisely that aspect that made "China" incomprehensible to the majority of US analysts, trained and operating under the framework of modernization theory.[27] As Chuck Cell contended, "These scholars have wondered why, after the 50's [*sic*] when the Chinese seemed to do so well, they went off on such a silly tangent as the Great Leap when everyone knows something like that is going to do nothing for economic growth. This brand of thinking is unable to recognize that socialist human relations are compatible with economic growth."[28] Then, Cell explained, the US scholars' denial of any economic growth under the Chinese model—which was factually wrong, to be sure—should be viewed as the product not of an objective analysis, but of the political need to take away any credit to an equalitarian vision of social relations. Denying Maoism its economic success was a means to erase any relevance it might have as a radical alternative to the existing organization of society. In other words, the experiments of the Cultural Revolution were interesting also because, unlike the various Five Year plans, they went beyond economics and state building. They tried to address the integration of work and ideas, of production and the production of knowledge, of intellectuals and a revolutionary society, all issues that were crucial to the Concerned Scholars. In this sense, they served as a model not so much of possible policies, but of politics *tout court*.

Rethinking the field

It was the utter incommensurability of these political experiments in China with the dominant scholarly and governmental practice in the US that provided the CAS with a logical justification for launching a radical challenge to the framework of Asian studies, the profession, and the very status of universities. The criticism of the CCAS engaged first and foremost a field that had been created and shaped by government support and showed how Asian studies was still framed by the imperative "know thy enemy." That is to say, by a strictly state-based and military directive.[29]

The *Bulletin* traced the genealogy of Modern China studies and the involvement of a generation of academics (often, the CAS' own teachers) in government organizations born directly out of the Cold War effort (the Joint Committee on Contemporary China, the Social Sciences Research Council), whose goal was to direct and control the whole China field.[30] This massive government funding, "impelled by the concept of China as a mortal enemy of the United States," it was argued, had had a strong effect on *everything* the field had produced,[31] and the field was therefore "due for a self-conscious probing, and uncompromising self-examination."[32]

In such a heavily "embedded" field, it was impossible to be an "expert" without being reduced to a "mental technician" at the call of the state.[33] The question that was incessantly asked in the pages of the *Bulletin* concerned the scholar's moral responsibility for the knowledge he or she produces. "You refuse to inquire into the purpose of scholarship"—this was addressed to John K. Fairbank in 1968—"when all around you are signs that much of the research on China and Southeast Asia is being grotesquely misused. Never the gut question, i.e. 'what is it all for?'"[34]

The CAS dismissed with irony any defense of the field based on the idea of the neutrality and objectivity of scholarship. "Its euphemistic clarity," wrote

Jon Livingston, "is like that of a mountain stream: crystalline and shallow at the same time."[35] Established scholars, it was argued, "did not withdraw from political involvement. It was the style and type of involvement, the internalization of the rightist world view, that is the continuing legacy of McCarthyism."[36] Political bias was deeply embedded in the field; it was constitutive of the profession itself. It was not relevant whether the Asian scholars viewed themselves as instruments of the US government or whether they were involved in actual policy making, "they nonetheless proved influential in justifying America's policies. This was not because many approved of the actual course of American policy toward China after 1949, but because by the work they did not do they upheld significant portions of the official definition of reality and, by the work they did, even elaborated upon it."[37]

Not only was the approach that had dominated China studies in the postwar period at the service of state policy, the CAS argued, but it was also one that could not provide any true understanding of modern and contemporary China. China had been portrayed as the realm of the irrational, the atavistic, the traditional, and the totalitarian. "Simply put," wrote Jim Peck, "social change and revolutionary transformation were understood primarily through leadership techniques of control and domination. Revolutionary spirit merged into an examination of charismatic leadership; political subjects became manipulated objects."[38] Because imperialism (past and present) could only be denied, the evolution of Chinese society could be described only as a failure to follow the forces of Western modernization. Communism, if studied, could be viewed only as yet another form of administration, the Chinese people as objects of bureaucracy, not subjects of politics.[39] "In most of the published research," argued Stan Lubman, China "seems to somehow lack people and is full of faceless cadres and crowds doing strange irrational things."[40]

The new position articulated by the CAS through the triangulation with the Chinese experience allowed them to produce seminal insights, which in many cases anticipated future development in the field by at least a couple of decades. By taking the experience of Chinese communism as something relevant politically and historically—and not as an aberration on the natural path of development—the CAS were able to argue a more cogent and constructive case against modernization theory, which was revealed not as an objective, value-free description, but as the ideology of a specific path of development forcefully imposed on other nations. This approach had obvious effects in the study of Japan, which had been framed during the Cold War as a potential counter-model for revolutionary China.[41]

By taking Maoist China as a "rational" model of society, the CAS undermined the psychological tropes used by modernization theorists: they painstakingly pointed out how in the paternalistic discourse of both the US government and the Asian scholars, the Chinese were not dedicated but "obsessed," their leaders were "bosses,"[42] and Asian nations were reaching "maturity." In revealing and debunking this attitude, the CAS brought forth the novel assumption that "what is revolutionary need not be irrational or inefficient,"[43] but also, more importantly, they reversed the psychological attack, by pointing at the ideological and emotional core of postwar scholarship on Asia. As James Peck maintained, "For though American China watchers have sought to explain how and why the theories of American imperialism and revolutionary Marxism were so emotionally satisfying to the Chinese, it is our theory of modernization which could be understood as a 'psychologically' comforting rationalization of America's imperial role and its consequences."[44]

CCAS started by debunking the Cold War view of the PRC and traced it back to a larger orientalist perspective, pervasive in the entire Asian Studies field. Notably, CAS were the first to offer a counterargument to the theory of "China's world order." According to that view, China had always functioned as "the Middle Kingdom," structuring its relations to the rest of the world not on the basis of rational diplomacy and commercial benefit, but through the distorted perspective of rituals, so that foreigners could only be viewed either as representing a tributary state or as "barbarians."[45] By revealing how this unchangeable and ritualistic China—in its imperial and communist versions—was mainly a product of the policy needs and the colonial tropes of the western nations, CCAS fashioned, without the support of Said's Orientalism and of Foucault's notions of power/knowledge, an argument that predates more sophisticated analyses by about 20 years.[46]

Finally, in a connected maneuver, the CAS proposed a kind of scholarship that moved away from the practice of Asian studies, where "priority is given to the discovery of new materials and sources rather than to the activity of thinking."[47] Restoring priority to the act of thinking meant, on the one hand, reflecting on one's own scholarly practice and, on the other, paying attention to the thinking of others. In the case of China, that signified essentially a focus on politics: the CAS studied and wrote of Asia, and China specifically, by taking politics as a central determinant, a shared commitment, and not as a smoke screen to be dissipated in order to reveal a more empirical truth, a power struggle, or an irrational leaning. In that, the CAS offered some of the finest examples of a history of politics as politics.

"China" as a place of desire: the China trips

"China" was the necessary grounding for the collective position of CCAS, but it also represented a continuous source of tensions. For the China scholars within CCAS, the People's Republic of China was an object of study, a subject of politics, but also an unreachable place. China students did their language training in Hong Kong or Taiwan[48] and their archival research in Japan. Although they wrote extensively about the PRC, restraints imposed by the Cold War meant that they had no realistic chance of ever crossing its borders. This intellectual, political, and psychological conundrum was described in a short, humorous text, "The China Scholar as a Legume," published in the April 1973 issue of the *CCAS Newsletter*.

> In Laymens [*sic*] terms schizofrenia [*sic*] can be defined as a type of psychosis characterized by a loss of contact with the environment, with the here and now. What better way to describe a China scholar, lost as he is in a fiction, a dream which bears no fruit in the Americo-Nightmare machine. We all know that true knowledge can only be gotten via experience, thru practice (see Mao). But where does his knowledge come from [?] Intuition, history, politics and all that, but no experience—there is no true carnality in his existence. He is imprisoned then, lost in a false world of kung-fu movies and take out noodle shops where the help only speak Cantonese. He lives in the Middle Kingdom between his ears, a dreamer with an empire to manipulate, but an empire of smoke and kingdom of phantoms—all second or third rate reality—he must be a madman ... too bad.[49]

US China scholars continued to live "in the Middle Kingdom between their ears" at least until 1971, when a delegation of CAS studying in Hong Kong were invited to visit the PRC. They toured the major cities, saw schools and factories, spent some time in a commune, and even met Zhou Enlai.[50] Despite the fact that the visit lasted only one month and could be considered, at best, a well-guided tourist trip and, at worst, a staged display of Potemkin villages, it was in many ways a breakthrough. It was the first time a US-based group of scholars had access to the PRC and it opened the possibility that CCAS—in large part because of its "radical" status, or so the members thought—could become the conduit through which more trips and possibly a more continuous and regular path of exchanges would be organized.

The first trip had not been a "national" initiative of the Committee: members happened to be in Hong Kong for study, approached or were approached by Chinese representatives, an invitation came and was readily accepted. The CCAS national coordinator was alerted at the last minute and the national organization came to play a role only in the aftermath, when the participants of the China trip traveled all over the US for a lecture tour. An instant book, *China! Inside the People's Republic*, was published the following year, presenting an overwhelmingly positive view of the PRC. To use the measured words of other CCAS members, the first friendship delegation "failed on many occasions to maintain a critical and objective perspective about their knowledge of China."[51]

The first delegation had left China with a standing invitation from Zhou Enlai to more CCAS members, and a second trip was planned for the following year. This was a better-organized and less starry-eyed group—apparently they got into trouble for irreverent references to the Mao cult—but it had its own share of problems, aptly summarized in a report: "insufficient language, relatively little representation of Asian-Americans, lack of preparedness and skill in interviewing, insistence on visiting some places (prisons, mental hospitals) where delegation members had insufficient expertise and where our hosts were unaccustomed to dealing with foreigners and answering their questions."[52] The report was dated 1973 and a third trip was planned for the same year, but postponed indefinitely.

The second trip opened the Pandora's box of how to select the small delegation of lucky travelers (30 in total) out of the many CAS who longed to visit the PRC. Immediately after the first trip, members started debating not only who should do the selection but also how to do it. Should preference be given to China specialists and Chinese speakers? Or maybe people with knowledge of "socialism" should have top priority? Should the delegation be an accurate representation of the complex constituency of CCAS? And finally, as CAS stubbornly defined themselves as both scholars and activists, should activism be weighted in the selection? And if so, how?[53]

Looking at the *CCAS Newsletter* and at the members' correspondence, it is apparent that the planning for the China trips took an inordinate amount of time, effort, and energy in the period 1971–73, and that it generated a fair amount of internal dissent and acrimony. The timing could not have been worse: this debate took place just as the United States and China were normalizing their relationship and, in the eyes of many activists, China seemed to abandon its commitment to a "third world" and to its South-East Asian allies. CCAS members became concerned that "China might be undercutting the Vietnamese struggle for its own reasons and that publicity about China might damage the antiwar movement in the US."[54] Many CAS questioned an excessive focus on China "to the detriment of work on the war, Bangladesh, Japan, Korea, U.S.'s South Asian/East Asian policies, etc."[55] They complained that too much emphasis was being placed on the China trips, trips which could only be viewed as "a fiasco."[56] In April 1972 many local chapters reported that they were dealing with extreme cases of China-itis.[57]

The harshest criticism came from the Stanford chapter, which drew a connection between the spreading enthusiasm for China (both within and without CCAS) and the general decline of activism in the US.

> [O]ur gradually growing uneasiness about the general drift in our chapter, and the directions evidenced in the national retreat, toward an emphasis on China at the expense of continued work on the Indochina War, has brought us to the point of concluding that the general Nixon thaw in US–China relations has in effect defused the antiwar movement in the United States ... [O]ur attention has for too long been focused on large, splashy ventures which appear worthwhile on the surface, but which have taken us away from the area in which we have been especially effective in the past. This is the area of local activity ... In short, we find we have been failing, due to the euphoric climate surrounding US–China relations at this point, to continue to bring the war and US imperialism home. ... China will be there for a long time; it is up to us to see that the US is not in Indochina much longer.[58]

Not everybody shared this bleak view, and several members argued that "the trips had encouraged CCAS to avoid becoming a single-issue which might fold after the war's end and to move from simply an anti-war position to a broader anti-imperialist one which had increased the life expectancy of the organization."[59] Although this was in part the case—CCAS was truly "Asian" in its range of interests and had tried for years to define itself as more broadly "anti-imperialist"—a declared and centered focus on China meant a redefinition in terms of both organizational and political coherence. With the waning of the anti-war passion, some of the scholars stressed that the organization was going to be increasingly concerned with "the meaning of socialism" and with "acting politically as socialists."[60] In that perspective, China clearly played a central role and the China trips, while unsatisfactory as investigative expeditions, could be rethought as "friendship" exchanges.[61] However, that would have required a complete redefinition of the functioning of CCAS—from an open-ended, loosely structured, anti-war organization of Asian scholars to one that furthered and investigated "socialism"—and a shift from the ambivalent status of scholar-activist to an unequivocally and more strictly political one.

The China trips, then, stood at the intersection of scholarly need, political passion, international diplomacy, and the very meaning of the organization at a time when the balance of Cold War diplomacy was shifting. The simple possibility of going to China put the CAS in an unsolvable bind: the emotional need to see the land that they had studied and the political system that they had supported conflicted with the risk of damaging their long-term political efforts. In all these ways the China trips uncovered some of the hidden contradictions and tensions within the group: between being anti-war and embracing socialism, between individual pursuit and collective loyalty, between foreign relations and subjective politics, and between activism and scholarship.

To study (and to make) revolution

To take Maoist China seriously could not but imply a rethinking of the very position of the scholar, as intellectual and political being. It was the need to understand Chinese politics "in interiority," in and of itself, and not merely as a distorted reflection of US interests, that led CCAS to pursue a radical re-evaluation of the field of Chinese studies, and Asian studies in general. When John K. Fairbank accused Jim Peck, on the pages of the *Bulletin*, of being "primarily concerned not with understanding Chinese realities but with combatting American Imperialism"[62] he was not off the mark. What Fairbank did not want to understand was that the two ventures—understanding China and combating imperialism—were tightly connected; there were no "Chinese realities" out there that did not in some way involve imperialism, either as a factor or as an object of political rethinking and criticism. And if we take Fairbank's accusation of combating imperialism as meaning "a political militancy," the case of contemporary China showed precisely how politics was and *had to be* part of a project of economic and social transformation. In a field whose methodology had been shaped under the financial and intellectual backing of imperialism, a "re-orientation of the scholarship and teaching" could not proceed without "a commitment to the need for revolutionary change in Asian land."[63]

Only by researchers taking a political stance, by being "concerned," could the Maoist experiments of the Cultural Revolution be evaluated, studied, and appreciated, because these experiments, if taken seriously, questioned the politics of the researcher directly.

China's Cultural Revolution displayed a completely new relationship between intellectuals, work, production, and politics, and this clearly reflected and was reflected in how scholar-activists in the US considered themselves. The first issue of the *BCAS* framed the problem in terms of the relation between scholarship and politics: the question was how to be intellectuals *and* politically relevant. French scholar Jean Chesneaux used Maoist terms when he called for the radical historian to "lean on one side," to probe into history's meaning and direction. The radical historian, he argued in the *Bulletin*, must concern himself with the people and must in the broadest sense "serve the people."[64] And the CCAS chapter at Columbia University called for Asian Scholars to "reach the great majority of the American people, and break out of the elitist confines of academia which have separated *us* from *them*."[65] It was not the will to take an active role in someone else's revolution, but the realization that the issues were similar, that many things that had happened in the Chinese twentieth century—and in particular since 1966—were crucial and meaningful even for the students and teachers at Harvard and Columbia.

By calling themselves "concerned," these young scholars were also stating the necessity to reinsert a political commitment into their professional lives, something that was theoretically unavoidable but practically extremely dangerous. "Emotion," argued Jon Livingstone, "*cannot* be extracted from the debate, and in fact *should not be*."[66] And "emotion" here means political passion, a declared and outspoken militancy, something that clashed loudly with the requirements of objectivity and detachment that academia demanded (and in some ways, still demands) from its members.

Orville Schell, in a 1969 issue of the *CCAS Newsletter*, highlighted the conundrum facing many Asian scholars. "If one becomes a scholar of Asia," he wrote, "and if one has strong feelings and convictions about what has happened and is happening in Asia, one ends up with a severe case of schizophrenia; one's life becomes divided between two essential human functions, namely thinking and acting. ... Rapidly the world divides into scholars (the researchers) and the actors (the political men). Each side deprives the other of an essential part of its being. Each accuses the other of being misled." If the breach between studying and living is not compounded, then we will lose the finest members of academia and, worst of all, the pointless division in the lives of scholars will continue. "Universities will become the refuge of those who escape from reality and real knowledge into the world of theory and magnificent irrelevance. And finally, Asian scholars will have no alternative but to sit in their offices studying the second hand shadows of revolutions that others make."[67]

The Cultural Revolution had shown that it was impossible to be an intellectual in one's office or classroom and an activist in the streets: politics had to permeate and alter the very fabric of daily life, the structure of the professions, the framing of one's intellectual activity. It was in this particular aspect (the inseparability of politics from culture) that the example of the Cultural Revolution resonated deeply within the experience of the CCAS. The debates and discussions within CCAS, their continuous wrangling over the different requirements and temporalities of cultural production and political activism, and even the organizational tensions that fractured the Committee show the enormous difficulties implicit in the particular position that these young scholars had taken. The historian Rebecca Karl has suggested that central to the failed project of the Cultural Revolution was "the attempt to reconcile and bring coherence to the asymmetries between and within politics and culture, understood in their revolutionary forms as mass activity transformed into and actualized through individuals' everyday life."[68] In other words, the Cultural Revolution represented the attempt to actualize in the now of the transformed everyday (in the breaking of boundaries between the manual and the intellectual, the scholarly and the practical) the political promises of the future, always displaced by a lagging cultural change. From this perspective, the difficulties and divisions among CCAS reflect these scholars' commitment—and ultimate failure—to make the issue at the center of the Cultural Revolution a principle of everyday practice. In that, the CAS embody a much more complex understanding of the role of Maoist China for the global activism of the 1960s and 1970s, a role which goes way beyond the promise of a communist promised land.

The end of concern?

The demise of Maoism after 1978 and the absolute negation of all the political experiments of the previous era under which Deng Xiaoping's reform policies were predicated could not be without consequence for the position of the CAS. In 1978, the Committee seemingly dissolved: that was the year when the last national convention took place and when the *Newsletter*, which had been regularly sent to all members, ceased publication. In print, the first response of the CAS when faced with the Dengist condemnation of the previous decade took the form of a veritable silence. As I mentioned at the beginning, between 1976 and 1981 very few essays on China were published in the *BCAS* and only one of them addressed in some way the "Thermidorean" reaction of 1976.[69] It was not just a simple question of assimilating new information, or exploring new possibilities of research and on-site investigation, but rather a massive tectonic shift, and one that had invested and consumed the political and intellectual subject identified as CAS.

Two special issues on China were finally published in 1981 and present quite a surprising array of texts. With the notable exception of two short, op-ed-like pieces by Edward Friedman, most of the essays dealt with very specific points of economic and administrative planning. In all but one of these essays—with variations in tone and emphasis—the reform policies, the return to administrative discipline and individual responsibility, are all viewed as necessary or indeed beneficial. The shift from previous contributions on China was dramatic, not only in content, but also in tone. The question is, then, "why such a radical change?"

As I mentioned, one major realization was that the Maoist experiments had not worked and that people had, in fact, starved and suffered. Strangely for scholars who had previously stressed repeatedly the value of the political, in 1981 they measured the Maoist failure strictly in administrative-economic terms, never once in political terms: indicators used in the previous decades were highly misleading and the policies of the Cultural Revolution brought "either limited gains in peasant income or led to actual declines. ... There was, in other words, a *policy* failure during the Cultural Revolution which must be explained."[70]

Deng Xiaoping found the reasons for this failure to be rooted in the equalitarian politics of the Cultural Revolution and, as such, he pursued a complete de-politicization in the name of the stability of the party-state and administrative efficiency. The 1981 issues of the *BCAS* did not surrender to this total de-politicization: some essays predicted the resilience of the Maoist communes or considered how egalitarianism might be reformulated rather than erased. What these essays show, however, is an obvious retreat from the political to the strictly economical and administrative. There was a clear awareness, a recognition, and an acceptance that, after 1978, politics had taken a back seat; or that what was happening resonated "to the declining importance in post-Mao China of political considerations and power in almost all spheres of social, cultural and economic activity, including socialist productive relations such as ownership, organization, planning, regulation, distribution, and redistribution."[71]

Curiously, faced with the massive shift in China, it seemed that the only possible solution for the *BCAS* was to take refuge in an abstract idea of objectivity, one that had been criticized and vehemently attacked in the *Bulletin* in the early years. Friedman's 1981 essays exemplify this shift in the most manifest way. In one, he describes Claudie Broyelle's disavowal of her 1973 book on women in China and her revisionist condemnation of the Cultural Revolution policies as murderous to women. She argued—Friedman quotes—that she needed to take sides in 1973 and that a "radical intellectual's job was not to tell mere present-day truths but to identify with and promote the potential forces of liberation in China and the world."[72] And while Friedman cherishes this shift from "political lies to political truths," one wonders if, in that sobering turn, we don't see the exhaustion not merely of a form of propaganda but also, perhaps, of the very possibility of that collective identification for radical intellectuals.

The only discordant and very wary voice in the 1981 special issues deals with, not surprisingly, women and the issue of gender equality in the post-Mao era. Phyllis Andors in her essay "The Four Modernizations and Chinese Policy on Women" decries the complete cancellation of the egalitarian measures of the late 1970s and observes how the return to the family as the main unit of production reinforced once again "traditional roles" for women.[73] In the end, she concludes, "it is clear that the present Hua–Deng leadership perceives socialist development more as technologically solvable issues of economic growth than its predecessor, which viewed the social revolution as an integral part of the process of economic modernization."[74] The "Hua–Deng perception" Andors excoriates was indeed not far from the position adopted by most essayists in the 1981 special issues of the *BCAS*. And although the focus on administration, growth, and technology hid perhaps an effort to salvage some sort of commitment to the previous period, the general acceptance of the demise of egalitarian politics after 1978 clearly signaled a shift in the perspective of the CAS. It is significant that after 1978 there was a general realignment in the scholarly and intellectual approaches to the PRC precisely along the lines of the old Cold War/Orientalist approach criticized by CAS; in this sense, the Cold War paradigm in China studies came to be reaffirmed precisely at the time when the actual Cold War was declared to be ending.[75]

In the 1980s the *Bulletin* published several other essays on China, more or less in support of the Dengist reform policies, with caution in some cases, with passion in others. But that is not particularly relevant; what seems evident to me is that, at least since 1978, it has become impossible to conjure again that collective position largely constructed in relation to China. This does not mean that activism or individual involvement has withered. Many of the former CAS have continued to be politically active in some form. But not anymore, or not significantly, in the forms subsumed under the name "Concerned Asian Scholars." And not because of lack of will, but rather, due to sheer impossibility. The conditions, the metaphorical ground for that kind of activism have disappeared and faithfulness to that enterprise has meant reinvention.

In that perspective, the name change from *Bulletin of Concerned Asian Scholars* to *Critical Asian Studies* in 2000 was long overdue. What disappeared from the title was precisely a "subject," the Concerned Asian Scholars, who had embodied in 1968 the "interconnections between scholarship and activism."[76] The collective subject was substituted by the object, the activity, which in a sense implies a fragmentation of the approaches, of possible political and intellectual positioning. Gone, rightfully, was also the concern, which was, as I have argued, inscribed in a particular relationship with the international situation and the localized political experiments of the time.

The story of the CCAS was also symptomatic of a global development. In their analysis of China, the CAS had tried and in part succeeded to account for the political, to look at the Maoist project as a rational, thinkable political sequence. By 1978, under Deng, the sequence had been declared "unthinkable," had been once again subsumed under the category of pathology, and politics had once again been reduced to governance, administration, efficiency. The Dengist reforms were predicated precisely on what Alain Badiou calls a Thermidorean reaction, that is, a subjectivity at the end of a political sequence that makes the political sequence unthinkable.[77] And one of the things that ended, that was made unthinkable, or, worse, irrelevant, was the possibility of thinking of oneself, individually *and* as part of a collective, *both* as a scholar *and* as an activist, of framing one's militancy in both intellectual and political terms. That this possibility was foreclosed in coincidence with the failure and collapse of a specific meaning of "China"—and that this happened globally (albeit in different forms)—is not insignificant: it reveals how the Cold War included also a search for political and intellectual alternatives under the name of Maoism and it shows how Maoism, invented or imagined, did produce its own reality. It proves that "China," at least for a brief time, existed.

Notes

1 "'Ah then', said Truptin, 'you want to talk about the Cultural Revolution, *dageming* [the great revolution]? An invention, madame, miss, a journalistic invention, I have never seen such things in China. China is a French invention, or rather a Parisian invention; all those ignorants, who don't know the language, who don't know the writing and yet they speak, they speak because they can't read. Let me tell you, madame, let me tell you that China does not exist.'" Natacha Michel, *La Chine européenne*. Paris: Gallimard, 1975: 44–45. I am thankful to Alessandro Russo for pointing out this novel and this specific passage. Truptin is the not-so-veiled caricature of the sinologist Jacques Pimpaneau.
2 The CCAS was founded in March 1968 in Philadelphia. On the founding, see Choy Cheung Ching, "Shadows and Substance: The Formation of a Radical Perspective in American China Studies, 1968–79" (M.A. thesis, University of Melbourne, 1987), chap. 1.
3 The *Bulletin* changed its name to *Critical Asian Studies* in 2000.
4 CCAS was not the only group to show "concern." There were also, for example, organizations such as the Concerned Psychologists and the Clergy and Laymen Concerned About Vietnam.
5 Stephen Andors, "The Political and Organizational Implications of China's New Economic Policies, 1976–79," *BCAS* 12:2 (April–June 1980): 44–57.
6 There are successful China scholars among former CCASers, like Victor Nee, Ed Friedman, and Mark Selden. The latter, however, "branched out" of the China field and has since worked on Japan and Asia in general. Several former CCASers survived the end of Maoism and remained in the China field but dramatically shifted their intellectual and political positions. It was a different "disappearance."
7 The organization disbanded in 1979, but the *Bulletin* continued until the change of title in 2000.
8 Examples of this particular approach in the French case are Christophe Bourseiller, *Les maoïstes. La folle histoire des gardes rouges français* (Paris: Plon, 2008) and

Richard Wolin, *The Wind from the East: French Intellectuals, the Cultural Revolution, and the Legacy of the 1960s* (Princeton: Princeton University Press, 2010).

9 See François Hourmant, *Au pays de l'avenir radieux. Voyages des intellectuals français en URSS, à Cuba et en Chine Populaire* (Paris: Aubier, 2000).
10 See Daniel F. Vukovich, *China and Orientalism: Western Knowledge Production and the P.R.C.* (New York: Routledge, 2012).
11 Committee of Concerned Asian Scholars Friendship Delegation to China, "Interview with Chou En-lai," *BCAS*, 3:3–4 (Summer–Fall 1971): 50.
12 "Purpose and Policy Statements," *BCAS* 2:1 (October–December 1969): 9.
13 Edward Friedman, "China, Pakistan, Bangladesh," *BCAS* 4:1 (Winter 1972): 99–108.
14 Mark Selden, "Introduction," in *America's Asia: Dissenting Essays on Asian-American Relations*, ed. Edward Friedman and Mark Selden (New York: Pantheon, 1971): xv.
15 Herbert Bix, "A Critical Review of some Anti-Communist Perspectives in American Policy Towards Asia," *BCAS* 1:2 (October 1968): 2.
16 Mark Selden, "Toward the Revitalization of Asian Scholarship," *BCAS* 1:2 (October 1968): 6.
17 Transcripts of the "Wither Chinese Studies" panel (1970): 5, CCAS Archives.
18 Selden, "Toward the Revitalization of Asian Scholarship."
19 John Gurley, "Capitalist and Maoist Economic Development," *America's Asia*: 348.
20 Transcripts of the "Wither Chinese Studies" panel: 11.
21 Selden, "Introduction," xv.
22 *Ibid.*
23 Transcripts of the "Wither Chinese Studies" panel: 11.
24 "Harvard chapter report," *CCAS Newsletter* (May 1969): n.p.
25 Gail Omvedt, cited in "CCAS Convention Report, Boston, March 30–April 4 1974," *CCAS Newsletter* (May 1974): 11.
26 Gurley, "Capitalist and Maoist Economic Development:" 345. Lin Chun, in her reassessment of Chinese socialism corroborates large parts of John Gurley's argument. Lin Chun, *The Transformation of Chinese Socialism* (Durham: Duke University Press, 2006): 50–51.
27 For a critical analysis of modernization theory see Nils Gilman, *Mandarins of the Future: Modernization Theory in Cold War America* (Baltimore and London: Johns Hopkins University Press, 2003).
28 Charles Cell cited in "CCAS Convention Report, Boston, March 30–April 4 1974," in *CCAS Newsletter* (May 1974): 13.
29 Angus McDonald, "The Historian's Quest: Joseph R. Levenson," *BCAS* 2:3 (April–July 1970): 71.
30 See the supplement on Modern China Studies, *BCAS*, 3:3–4.
31 Thomas M. Engelhardt, "Letter to Dean Phelps," *BCAS* 1:1: 8. Emphasis mine.
32 Leigh Kagan, "A Statement of Directions," *BCAS* 1:1: 1.
33 Jim Peck, "An Exchange: The CIA at Harvard": 6–7.
34 Jon Livingston, "An Exchange: The CIA at Harvard": 9.
35 *Ibid.*: 11.
36 John K. Fairbank and James Peck, "An Exchange," *BCAS* 2:3 (April–July 1970): 56.
37 James Peck, "The Roots of Rhetoric: The Professional Ideology of America's China Watchers," in *America's Asia: Dissenting Essays on Asian-American Relations*, ed. Edward Friedman and Mark Selden (New York: Pantheon, 1971): 51.
38 *Ibid.*: 64.
39 Richard M. Pfeffer, "Revolution and Rule: Where Do We Go from Here?" *BCAS*, 2:3 (April–July 1970): 91.
40 Transcripts of the "Wither Chinese Studies" panel: 1.

41 On Japan and modernization theory see the brilliant introductory essay by John Dower, "E. H. Norman, Japan and the Uses of History," in *Origins of the Modern Japanese State: Selected Writings of E. H. Norman* (New York: Pantheon Books, 1975).
42 Gurley, "Capitalist and Maoist Economic Development," 343.
43 Stephen Andors, "Revolution and Modernization: Man and Machine in Industrializing Society, The Chinese Case," in *America's Asia: Dissenting Essays on Asian-American Relations*, ed. Edward Friedman and Mark Selden (New York: Pantheon, 1971): 395.
44 Peck, "The Roots of Rhetoric": 50–51. It is worth noting that a quite exasperated Fairbank, in a 1971 special issue, accused his CAS students of "a psychological Freudian impulse to kill their fathers." John K. Fairbank, "Comment," *BCAS* 3:3–4 (Fall 1971): 52.
45 The theory is most closely associated with John K. Fairbank. See his edited volume *The Chinese World Order: Traditional China's Foreign Relations* (Cambridge: Harvard University Press, 1973).
46 James Hevia, *Cherishing Men from Afar. Qing Guest Ritual and the Macartney Embassy of 1793* (Durham: Duke University Press, 1995).
47 Jean Chesneaux, "Approaches to the Study of China," *BCAS*, 1:4 (May 1969): 32.
48 See Richard C. Kagan, "Can We Study Chinese in Taiwan?" *BCAS* 1:2 (October 1968): 5.
49 *CCAS Newsletter* (April 1973): 14.
50 The interview with Zhou Enlai was published in *BCAS* 3:3–4 (Fall 1971): 31–60.
51 "An Evaluation of CCAS Friendship Delegations to China and Recommendations for a Third Trip," *CCAS Newsletter* (January 1973): 7.
52 *Ibid.*: 13.
53 "CCAS Goes to China: Questions and Future Relationship," *CCAS Newsletter* (July–August 1971).
54 "CCAS Members attend the world assembly of Paris for peace and the independence of the Indochinese peoples," *CCAS Newsletter* (March 1972): 6.
55 "Report on Plans for Chinese Visit to the US," *CCAS Newsletter* (March 1972): 2.
56 "1972 CCAS Summer Retreat," *CCAS Newsletter* (August 1972): 3.
57 *CCAS Newsletter* (April 1972).
58 "Stanford Statement on National Priorities," *CCAS Newsletter* (November 1971): 10.
59 "An Evaluation of CCAS Friendship Delegations," 10.
60 "CCAS Summer Retreat," *CCAS Newsletter* (October 1972): 8.
61 "Responses to initial report of the China exchange committee," *CCAS Newsletter* (March 1973): 10.
62 "John Fairbank: A Reply," 117.
63 Leigh Kagan, "Proposals," *BCAS* 1:1 (May 1968): 7.
64 Jean Chesneaux, "Approaches to the Study of China," *BCAS* 1:4 (May 1969): 33.
65 CCAS Columbia, "Asia Scholars to End the War," *BCAS* 2:3 (April–July 1970): 109. Emphasis mine.
66 Jon Livingston, "An Exchange: The CIA at Harvard," n.p.
67 Orville Schell, "Learning by Doing," *CCAS Newsletter* (January 1970): 9–10.
68 Rebecca E. Karl, "Culture, Revolution and the Times of History: Mao and 20th-Century China," *The China Quarterly*, 187 (2006): 695.
69 Stephen Andors, "The Political and Organizational Implications of China's New Economic Policies, 1976–79," *BCAS* 12:2 (April–June 1980): 44–57.
70 Victor Lippit, "The People's Commune and China's New Development Strategy," *BCAS* 13:3 (July–September 1981): 21, 23. Emphasis mine.
71 Mitch Meisner and Marc Blecher, "Rural Development, Agrarian Structure and the County in China," *BCAS* 13:2 (April–June 1981): 16.

72 Edward Friedman, "Learning about China after the Revolution ... for the first time!" *BCAS* 13:2 (April–June, 1981): 42. Claude Broyelle's first book was published in English as *Women's Liberation in China* (Atlantic Highlands, N.J.: Humanities Press, 1977). The second (revisionist) book was Claudie Broyelle, Jacques Broyelle, and Evelyne Tschirhart, *China, a Second Look* (Brighton, Sussex; Atlantic Highlands, N.J.: Harvester Press; Humanities Press, 1980).
73 Phyllis Andors, "'The Four Modernizations' and Chinese Policy on Women," *BCAS* 13:2 (April–June 1981): 44–56.
74 *Ibid.*: 56.
75 Daniel Vukovich analyzes the resilience of the Orientalist paradigm in Western knowledge production on the PRC after 1978 in his *China and Orientalism*.
76 Tani E. Barlow, "Responsibility and Politics: An Interview with Mark Selden," *positions*, 12:1 (2004): 254.
77 Alain Badiou, *Metapolitics* (Verso, 2005): 136.

Selected bibliography

Allen, Douglas and Vĩnh Long Ngô. *Coming to Terms: Indochina, the United States, and the War*. Boulder, Colo.: Westview Press, 1991.

Barlow, Tani E. "Responsibility and Politics: An Interview with Mark Selden." *positions* 12:1 (2004): 247–59.

Choy, Cheung Ching, "Shadows and Substance: The Formation of a Radical Perspective in American China Studies, 1968–79." MA thesis, University of Melbourne, 1987.

Committee of Concerned Asian Scholars. *The Indochina Story: a Fully Documented Account*. New York: Pantheon Books, 1970.

——*China! Inside the People's Republic*. New York: Bantam Books, 1972.

Connery, Christopher. "Editorial Introduction: The Asian Sixties: An Unfinished Project." *Inter-Asia Cultural Studies* 7, no. 4 (Dec 2006): 545–53.

Dower, John. "E. H. Norman, Japan and the Uses of History," in *Origins of the Modern Japanese State: Selected Writings of E. H. Norman*. New York: Pantheon Books, 1975.

Fairbank, John King. *Chinabound: A Fifty-Year Memoir*. 1st ed. New York: Harper & Row, 1982.

Friedman, Edward and Mark Selden, (eds.) *America's Asia: Dissenting Essays on Asian-American Relations*. New York: Pantheon, 1971.

Gilman, Nils. *Mandarins of the Future: Modernization Theory in Cold War America*. Baltimore and London: Johns Hopkins University Press, 2003.

Hourmant, François. *Au pays de l'avenir radieux. Voyages des intellectuals français en URSS, à Cuba et en Chine Populaire*. Paris: Aubier, 2000.

Lin, Chun. *The Transformation of Chinese Socialism*. Durham: Duke University Press, 2006.

Madsen, Richard. *China and the American Dream: A Moral Inquiry*. Berkeley: University of California Press, 1995.

Vukovich, Daniel F. *China and Orientalism: Western Knowledge Production and the P.R.C.* New York: Routledge, 2012.

Wolin, Richard. *The Wind from the East: French Intellectuals, the Cultural Revolution, and the Legacy of the 1960s*. Princeton: Princeton University Press, 2010.

8 Anti-Communist entrepreneurs and the origins of the cultural Cold War in Latin America

Patrick Iber

The year was 1950, and the Colombian liberal intellectual Germán Arciniegas was writing a letter to the American ex-Trotskyist James Burnham. Burnham would later gain renown as one of the intellectual forefathers of neoconservatism but was, at the time, serving as an advisor to the CIA. "We have responsibilities as writers," wrote Arciniegas, "and we must recall to our companions in all the intellectual, artistical and scientific activities that our main goal now is to survive as free men in a free world. We have to put the word freedom before the word peace."[1] Arciniegas believed that the ideas of peace and freedom were in tension not because of some leap in logic, but because he was living in New York City, and had, a few months earlier, attended a gathering known as the Cultural and Scientific Congress for World Peace, held in the Waldorf-Astoria hotel. That gathering, part of a worldwide campaign for "Peace," blamed Cold War tensions solely on the United States and praised the cultural climate under Stalin, which appalled Arciniegas.[2] He was inspired by a counter-demonstration led by the anti-Communist philosopher Sidney Hook to attend the inaugural meeting of the "Congress for Cultural Freedom," which Hook and Burnham helped organize, in West Berlin in 1950. The Congress proved the mirror image to the Soviet-aligned and financed "Peace" campaigns in more ways than one: it was sponsored, from its inception until 1965, by the CIA, and Burnham, in his organizational role, was trying to involve Arciniegas in planning a meeting in the Western hemisphere. Burnham passed Arciniegas' positive reply to a CIA officer in Mexico City (who happened to be future Watergate burglar E. Howard Hunt), but they could not find a suitable host for their conference in Latin America and their plans were put on hold.[3]

Organizing under the rubric of the "Peace" Movement and anti-Communist counter-mobilization are generally taken to mark the beginning of the engagement now known as the "cultural Cold War." (It might better be called the "ideological Cold War," for though many artists and writers participated in it, many of its combatants were professional ideologists, not necessarily "cultural" figures as such.) This chapter will describe four attempts at Partisans of Peace organizing in Latin America—Brazil and Mexico in 1949, Uruguay in 1952, and Chile in 1953—and the anti-Communist counter-organizing they engendered. In so doing, it explains how these parallel movements emerged in Latin America, and in the process contributes to de-centering traditional narratives of the Cold War both geographically and causally.

To begin with geography: although scholars have become increasingly aware that the Cold War system was one that touched all parts of the globe, the vast majority of the discussion about the cultural dimensions of the conflict remains anchored to Europe and the United States. This chapter shows the geographical limits to that logic, for the shape of the ideological conflict of the early Cold War was much the same in Latin America as it was in Europe. That an apparently "peripheral" region to the Cold War should be the contemporary of Europe in these matters shows the manner in which the Cold War was created out of a confluence of local, national, and international interests—the combination that gave the Cold War its global reach. At the same time, many but by no means all of the most dedicated Cold War ideologists living in Latin America were Spaniards living in exile, for whom the fate of Europe remained the central moral issue of the conflict.

The Partisans of Peace Movement that had struck Arciniegas as so partial was indeed a Soviet-aligned project, which had taken shape at a series of conferences involving greater and lesser degrees of Soviet coordination: at Wroclaw, in Poland, in August 1948; the Cultural and Scientific Conference for World Peace held at the Waldorf-Astoria hotel in New York in March 1949; the World Congress of Partisans for Peace held in Paris that April; and the Continental Congress for Peace held in Mexico City that September. In November 1950, the Cominform declared that the struggle for peace against imperialist aggression and in defense of the USSR was the most important task of the Communist movement worldwide. The movement was institutionalized in the World Peace Council in 1950, operating on the Popular Front model of outreach to as broad a progressive alliance as could be assembled. It enlisted the support of intellectuals from around the globe in campaigns against US imperialism, militarism, and war crimes. Yet with Soviet funding and orientation, it excused similar behavior by the Soviet Union.[4]

Although anti-Communists were correct in seeing the Peace Movement as part of the Soviet Union's efforts to enhance its diplomatic leverage and its prestige among intellectuals at home and abroad, they often misread and overstated the movement's potential power. The House Committee on Un-American Activities (HUAC) called the Peace Movement "the most dangerous hoax ever devised by the international Communist conspiracy," and warned that its goals were to sap American morale, taking advantage of good-will and hatred of war to secure converts to treason.[5] Since the Partisans of Peace movement was interpreted by the US government as a problem of national security, the CIA came to support the creation of the anti-totalitarian Congress for Cultural Freedom to counter its influence among intellectuals.[6] The Congress was the most important of the CIA's Cold War projects of aid to "civil society" groups.[7] Where the World Peace Council blended advocacy for peace with the defense of Soviet interests, the Congress for Cultural

Freedom was often similarly guilty of associating cultural freedom with US interests. With the interests of powerful states clearly at hand, it is tempting to give them full responsibility for the conflict. But, as this chapter shows, the US government also relied on existing networks of anti-Communists to bring the ideological civil war among the left-wing intellectuals into the official Cold War. In part, the "anti-Peace" campaign depended on the interests of local and national governments whose actions were sometimes prodded, but not necessarily determined, by US government action. Fundamentally, it required networks of anti-Communists who had been active for many years and now found a new patron in the US government. To describe the anti-Peace Movement campaign as "US-orchestrated" would be to miss the degree to which anti-Peace campaigning, and the ideological Cold War in general, depended on the voluntary action of individuals who sought US support for their plans and schemes, rather than the other way around: individuals engaged in what might be called *anti-Communist entrepreneurship*.

Some of this "entrepreneurship" was purely opportunistic, but much of it married opportunity to conviction. In time, some of these "entrepreneurs" would become part of an established anti-Communist propaganda apparatus, their work institutionalized and professionalized. Those who had no other identifiable form of work would be called, usually derisively, "professional anti-Communists." (The parallel structure to Lenin's "professional revolutionists" was not intended to be flattering.) But, when it came to propaganda, the late 1940s and early 1950s was a less professional and a more entrepreneurial time: in both the labor and cultural fields, the networks that would sustain ideological anti-Communism were just being brought closer to the state interests of the US government. The purpose of introducing the notion of the *anti-Communist entrepreneur* here is neither to flatter entrepreneurs (whose behavior can be rent seeking and predatory as well as socially useful) nor anti-Communists (who could be unscrupulous, short sighted, and worse), but to suggest that, like entrepreneurs in business, these anti-Communists took advantage of new opportunities to provide a service—where the consumers were, in this case, political interests. What was new about the Cold War was not the anti-Communist activism, which had deep roots, but that the United States government's entry into the marketplace for their services expanded opportunities for these political entrepreneurs; indeed, over time, it grew into a quasi-monopsonistic purchaser of their services.

But the United States was not, of course, the only place in the world in which Communist ideas, including the Partisans of Peace campaign, were considered dangerous and destabilizing by powerful social forces, and so the anti-Peace campaign was carried out by newspapers, police forces, local officials, and intellectuals around the world. US embassies sometimes acted as clearinghouses, but other governments, at municipal, state, and national levels, had anti-Communist and other agendas that resulted in their taking actions to attempt to foil the activity of the Partisans of Peace. Furthermore, networks of anti-Communists, including those on the political left who had been engaged in anti-Communist campaigning for years, mobilized to respond to Peace Movement propaganda, often volunteering their services to assist the US government in matters of mutual concern.

The first attempt to establish a Peace Movement in Latin America took place in Brazil, where it was blocked from growing larger than it might have. A substantial portion of the Brazilian political class shared the view of Communism as a threat to order, pointing as evidence to the 1935 uprising led by Luís Carlos Prestes of Brazil's Communist Party (PCB). When that uprising failed, Prestes was imprisoned and the Brazilian state enhanced its anti-subversive policing capacity, capturing and torturing left-wing political prisoners and enacting harsh censorship of the press.[8] Near the end of World War II, when democratizing pressures were high, political prisoners, including Prestes, were granted amnesty and the PCB was allowed to participate in elections. In 1945, the PCB had enough strength in the major cities to elect one senator (Prestes, from the Federal District of Rio de Janeiro) and four federal deputies from São Paulo. But the government undertook many actions to ensure that the PCB did not grow too powerful. In 1946, the Brazilian government established the *Serviço Social da Indústria* (SESI) as a way of coordinating efforts with industry to combat Communist influence in the Brazilian labor movement. In elections in 1947, the PCB maintained its level of support—nine percent of the overall vote—and made gains at the state level in São Paulo. But later that year, Brazil's Superior Electoral Tribunal, under pressure from the executive, voted to cancel the legal registration of the party, and the government again undertook a campaign of anti-Communist repression, also moving to restrict the action of leftist labor unions whether or not they included Communists. Hundreds of labor leaders were removed from office, and, in September of 1947, the Brazilian Congress voted to remove the mandates of elected Communists.[9]

For Brazilian Communists, then, Peace campaigning was a way of undertaking political action when electoral and labor routes were, at best, highly constrained. From April 3 to 5, 1949, a São Paulo State Congress for Peace met, with the goal of establishing the Peace Movement in Brazil and intending to organize a larger conference in Rio de Janeiro. To check the growth of the Peace Movement, US government officials coaxed the appropriate Brazilian authorities to conclude that Peace campaigns were nothing more than a front for Communist activity. The US Consulate General spoke to the head of SESI, and had one of his employees place an article in the *Diario de São Paulo*, portraying the peace congress as a Communist-front organization.[10] Many posters, both in favor of and against the *Congresso*, appeared on the streets prior to the event (Figures 8.1 and 8.2), sometimes with a pro-*Congresso* poster covering an anti- to obscure its message, or vice versa.

The Congress for Peace in São Paulo, however, was held as scheduled, with delegates pronouncing in favor of nationalist and anti-imperialist themes. Marxist historian Caio Prado Júnior—one of the São Paulo Communist politicians whose electoral mandate had been cancelled—spoke against the North Atlantic Treaty (signed on April 4, 1949, during the Congress for Peace), arguing that the UN already existed to keep the peace and that the Atlantic Treaty would pull Brazil into a capitalist war. The US consulate tried to amplify independent anti-Peace developments: when a group of intellectuals (including socialist literary critic António Cândido) signed a bill criticizing the Congress as a Communist front, the consulate copied and distributed 3,000 copies of the statement without attribution.

A police investigation reached the same conclusions about the nature of the Peace Congress as had Cândido's group, forwarding the results of its investigation on to the authorities in Rio, where the police announced that any meeting would be disallowed.[11] The US maintained pressure on the Peace group, using a printer who was a friend of a member of the US Information Agency staff to produce an anonymous pamphlet called "What is a Peace Congress?" which described the Eastern European origins of the campaigns. It was distributed, confidentially, to a list of known sympathizers with the São Paulo Congress for Peace who were believed by the department not to be Communists, and who might be expected to be turned off by exposure of the Communist direction within the movement.[12] Further conferences, planned for 1952, were similarly disallowed, and the Peace Movement never gained much purchase in Brazil. Its most important participating artist, the novelist Jorge Amado, was living in semi-exile in Europe, where he penned a nearly unreadable trilogy, *Os subterrâneos da liberdade*, in the style of the official artistic ideology of the Soviet Union, socialist realism.

Peace organizers had better luck in Mexico, where the ruling party's approach to managing the Left featured a mixture of repression and inclusion. Mexican president Miguel Alemán (1946–52) and his government repressed and co-opted labor groups and oppositional elements of the Left, as in Brazil. Both the government and the conservative press increasingly made anti-Communism a part of official discourse in this period, and in 1950 Alemán disallowed Communists from holding dual membership in the ruling Partido Revolucionario Institucional (PRI).[13] Nevertheless, the PRI was ideologically heterogeneous, and Alemán allowed the Left its symbolic gestures from time to time. Though he gave the Partisans of Peace no official support, they were permitted to hold a major Peace conference in Mexico City from September 5 to 10, 1949. Forced into a sports arena because of a lack of government endorsement, the Continental Congress for Peace, as it was known, brought together thousands to hear criticisms of the trampling of Latin American sovereignty by Yankee imperialism. There was a joint appearance by the muralists David Álfaro Siqueiros and Diego Rivera—the latter tried to use his support for the Peace Movement to gain re-admission into the Communist Party, from which he had been expelled for "Trotskyism" in 1929. Poet Pablo Neruda, in exile from his native Chile and involved with the Partisans of Peace since its April meeting in Paris, derided the books of "Western culture" as the drugs of a dying system. Neruda also directed an

Figure 8.1 A poster advertising the *Congresso Paulista pela Paz* stands outside the bookstore of the Editoria Brasilense, owned by Caio Prado Júnior; São Paulo, 1949. It reads "Fight for Peace." Image courtesy of US National Archives at College Park; attachment to 800.00B/4–1849.

evening of performance in which he performed a section of his in-progress *Canto general* set to modern dance. The poem he performed, *Que despierte el leñador*, is, in part, a plea for the United States to return to the spirit of Abraham Lincoln and put an end to the blight of racism and warmongering that Neruda saw as typifying the United States of the late 1940s.[14]

In advance of the 1949 Peace Congress, the dominant anti-Communist and conservative press in Mexico took its customary approach to reporting on the activities of the Mexican Left by ignoring, minimizing, and trying to discredit the event. A small amount of US embassy-provided information ensured dissemination of the "right" messages, but anti-Communist activity that had nothing to do with the embassy dominated the response. Embassy officials, in the course of regular meetings with editors and journalists of major Mexican periodicals, offered their interpretation of events, which was generally reproduced in the papers. When one conversation led to a piece in the magazine *Todo*, the embassy noted that the editor was probably already disposed toward an anti-Communist interpretation of the Peace Congress, but that nevertheless it seemed like a good example of "press cooperation."[15] The *Todo* article, "¡Mucho cuidado con el próximo Congreso Continental de la Paz!"—which declared that the organizers of the "Red Congress" were no longer Mexican but, rather, Soviet men—was reproduced as a

Figure 8.2 An anti-Communist poster depicting Joseph Stalin as angel and devil, his militarism hidden behind an apparent offer of peace. The top text reads "The Angel of Peace: Inside and Out." Image courtesy of US National Archives at College Park; attachment to 800.00B/4–1849.

large poster and pasted on walls throughout the city in advance of the Congress.[16]

Two members of a small group known as the Grupos Socialistas de la República Mexicana, Benjamín Tobón and Rodrigo García Treviño, approached the embassy on their own initiative. In the 1930s, Tobón and García Treviño had formed a minority anti-Communist socialist group within Mexico's dominant labor confederation.[17] García Treviño, a veteran of the Mexican Revolution and an ex-Communist, was one of the best-educated Marxists in Mexico and had been involved in heated polemic with the Party over doctrinal matters for years, drawing close to Trotsky during his Mexican exile. In approaching the US embassy prior to the 1949 Peace Congress, he documented his long history as an active anti-Communist, and then asked the embassy to provide him with information about the Communist affiliations of foreign delegates to the Peace Congress, which he believed he could use to discredit the Peace Congress in a credible way that would not appear to come from the US government. Embassy officials liked the idea of criticism from the Left, since most of the anti-Congress propaganda to that point had been from conservative sources, and delivered the requested information. García Treviño was able to distribute it widely, attributing the intelligence regarding the Communist affiliations of conferees to "socialist allies" in other Latin American countries.[18] When the Congress for Cultural Freedom was later created and extended to Latin America, García Treviño would be given responsibility for its Mexican operations, but the grievances that led him to seek out the United States as an ally in his personal struggle against Communism were, in 1949, already more than a decade old.

The establishment Mexican press responded to the event itself with practiced scorn. The newspaper *Novedades*, for example, covered some of the proceedings but paired almost all articles with exposé-style coverage of Soviet involvement in the Peace Movement. The tabloid *La Prensa* ran screaming headlines about Communist plots. *Excélsior*, instead of covering the Peace Congress, explained what anti-Communist groups (such as students who were planning to go out and take down any Peace-related posters they found around the city) were doing to combat its influence. The official government paper, *El Nacional*, demonstrated its particular genius for calculated indifference regarding an event that it wanted neither to support nor to antagonize. It ran one piece by Marxist writer and historian José Mancisidor—who remained close to the PRI—that both announced the Peace Congress and complimented President Alemán for his recent statement that what was needed was a "just and lasting peace in the world." After that, the paper ran only modest and neutral announcements of the activity of the Peace Congress.[19] The US embassy, judging that the conference was getting little traction and little coverage outside of the minor left-wing press, decided not to release its own counter-propaganda.

Outside of Mexico, where Peace Movement activity continued to draw support through the early 1950s, Latin American organizing provided difficult. Another major international conference, in Montevideo, was scheduled for March 11–16, 1952. Although Uruguay possessed a comparatively robust welfare-state democracy and laws favoring political tolerance, on March 10 the chief of police in Montevideo refused to sign the application that would have permitted the conference to convene. Two days later, the minister of the interior sustained the police chief's decision. With such a late-breaking prohibition, many of the delegates from neighboring Argentina had already arrived, and an impromptu assembly was held, in spite of the cancellation. Prohibited from meeting inside, it gathered on the street on March 15, where about 1,000 people assembled in front of a makeshift stage to hear the delegates. Because of the police chief's legal decision, the speakers defensively emphasized that their gathering was *not* the planned conference but a simple street meeting to which no one could object, in spite of the large banner bearing a white dove behind them.[20] Its approximately 300 delegates felt that they had some kind of small triumph, though they were again ignored by all but the far-left press.

The prohibition sparked a debate in the Uruguayan chamber of deputies and in the press: could the cause of free speech be served by prohibiting speech? Many in Uruguay argued that while they did not support the Peace Conference, they thought it was a dangerous abridgement of democratic freedoms to prohibit the gathering.[21] A similar debate emerged during the planning stages to the Continental Congress for Culture (CCC), held the next year, 1953, in Santiago. The CCC, organized by Pablo Neruda, proved to be the most important Latin American gathering of the Peace Movement since Mexico in 1949, and the last major one for some eight years.

Pablo Neruda, in exile from his native Chile because of his Communist politics, spent a great deal of his time in the early 1950s in the Soviet Union, China, and the Eastern bloc, and was made representative of the World Peace Council to the United Nations. He participated in every major European reunion of the Partisans for Peace. Following a meeting in Vienna, held in December 1952, he sought to organize his own conference in Santiago.[22] After another trip to the Soviet Union, in January 1953 he returned on Chile, where the political climate suggested greater tolerance might make possible a major event. All the same, organizing did not prove easy. According to the CIA, in 1950 Neruda had privately expressed that the "[Peace] campaign in Latin America had been a complete failure." But he pressed on, hoping without success to receive funds for his Congress while in European exile.[23] Even without outside funding, and following several delays, the "Continental Cultural Congress (CCC)" met in Santiago, from 26 April to 3 May 1953, opening less than a month after the death of Stalin.[24]

Still, the mayor of Santiago was opposed to allowing the gathering to meet in the Teatro Municipal, the only suitable space in the city for a gathering of the expected size. Neruda had to call on a friend, who pressed President Carlos Ibáñez del Campo to persuade the mayor to allow the event to proceed, in light of the important guests who would be attending.[25] Even still, Ibáñez did not fully endorse the proceedings; the visas for the Soviet and Chinese delegations were granted only at the last minute, making it impossible for the Soviet delegates to attend.[26] Harassment continued: following the second day of the Congress, a judge ordered *El Siglo*, the newspaper of the still illegal Communist Party, be closed for ten days, citing its campaign of "permanent conspiracy." The bourgeois and government press also refused to report on the event, creating a kind of news blackout during the days of actual meeting.[27]

In response to the climate of suppression, Neruda promised that the CCC would offer culture and not politics, but echoes of the language of earlier

Peace congresses were unmistakable. The Santiago Congress was a last gasp of cultural Stalinism, not yet brought to an end by the policies of Stalin's successor in the Soviet Union, Nikita Khrushchev. Speaking first, Chilean writer Fernando Santiván spoke in favor of cultural exchange among the American republics, but wondered whether the nations of Latin America were allowed an independent economic and spiritual existence. He answered his own question in the negative, implicating the United States in rhetorically asking:

> And isn't it true that the [United States] influences decisively so that [Latin American] cultures cannot develop themselves as we all want them to? And doesn't that block them from exercising their necessary influence and are seen to be prevented from conserving and defending their traditions and their patrimony and from developing their national characteristics?[28]

The folk singer Betty Sanders, the only US delegate to be granted a visa to attend, received a standing ovation when she criticized her government's consistent efforts to obstruct the free flow of people and ideas.[29]

Neruda had promised to keep "politics" out of the CCC, but it was absurd to imagine that he could have done so. As one critic of the proceedings, Christian Democratic philosopher Jaime Castillo Velasco, observed, the US was consistently criticized, the Soviet Union frequently praised. "I know and admire the Soviet people," Neruda said at the Congress,

> and its leaders for their extraordinary deeds, indelible in human history. But what I most admire in that land is its dedication to culture. Perhaps above all else, this is the most fundamental and impressive feature of Soviet life, with the full flowering of the individual, as never before achieved in history.

The CCC concluded that the arts should be free in the Americas, but made no mention of the state of artistic control that existed in the Eastern bloc. According to this reasoning, Castillo wrote, "Politics begins, in effect, in Berlin. On this side of things, it is called culture."[30]

When the CCC ended, the Communist newspaper *El Siglo* claimed victory, saying that it had not been what its enemies had said it would be. They noted that anti-Communists and non-Communists had been allowed to speak freely, citing one of two available examples, and declared the CCC "free in all aspects."[31] Thus, declared the newspaper, those who had attacked the Congress, and would not now recognize their error, must have attacked it in bad faith. This was no surprise, for, according to *El Siglo*, "the entire campaign against the Congress, here in Chile, has been carried out by international foreign agents." *El Siglo* and the CCC claimed nationalist ground for themselves, wanted their critics to be seen as foreign and therefore part of an illegitimate, non-Chilean line of criticism.[32]

El Siglo was not wholly wrong: there were foreign agents involved in the campaign against the CCC; there were also many others. As the date of the CCC had approached, many non-Communists found evidence of Communist involvement unsettling. A group of politically centrist figures, many associated with the "social Christian" tradition within Chile's Falangist party, publicly sought an accommodation with the CCC while still making known its reservations regarding Communist control.[33] Putting together a small position paper, these figures argued that because Communism placed politics above all other spheres of life, it would be naïve to participate in a "cultural" congress sponsored or organized by Communists. But, they acknowledged, the positions of both the Communists and their critics had some merit. "Communism," they wrote,

> is presenting a problem to culture, and that problem should be addressed. For many, the concepts put in practice in Communist countries constitute the only possible way of progressive development. For others, they represent a disastrous rehearsal of "directed culture" that will irredeemably impoverish the cultural tradition of those countries in which it is developed, and that threatens, for that reason, the common destiny of culture around the world.

Those who signed this manifesto declined to participate in the Continental Cultural Congress, asking for a larger debate on the issues of culture and Communism. So long as the CCC, by committing not to include political topics and sticking only to "culture," did not intend to create a forum to discuss the issues of directed culture, they would not participate. Affirming the importance of the "liberty of man's creative spirit," they asked for a forum to discuss these important issues and the role of culture in a conflicted world.[34]

To the young Chilean writer Jorge Edwards, in spite of his growing friendship with CCC organizer Pablo Neruda, this seemed a reasonable position to take. It was the first manifesto he had ever signed, and the consequences of his decision would give him pause whenever one was presented to him again. His decision brought rebuke from Neruda. "That manifesto," he scolded Edwards, "was only a scheme to destroy our congress." When Edwards protested, Neruda replied: "What is going on is that you are very naive. You still lack political experience." Edwards called it one of his first political disappointments, but, looking back as he wrote his memoirs, he defended his position as honorable. There *was* a need to discuss the intersection of culture and politics under Stalin, he thought, and such a meeting might have been useful. But that was not the purpose of the CCC. Edwards tried to act in good faith in a terrain strewn with bad, but that made Neruda right: he was naïve. Of his experience with the CCC, he wrote:

I was a neophyte, a new arrival, and I had gotten involved among older people, people who knew that a declaration, beyond that which was said in the words according to the dictionary, was equivalent to a move on a chessboard. The move provoked the expected reaction, and the masters, those who knew the art, proceeded to make the second move ... [35]

There were indeed many savvy players of the game, and by 1953 the United States had a much more sophisticated and professional operation in place to counter Communist front activity. Aware that their plans were at risk if they were too closely associated with Communism, the CCC organizers sought to avoid controversy by including greater intellectual diversity. They invited two men—the lawyer Francisco Walker Linares and the composer and musicologist Juan Orrego Salas, both known to be opposed to Communism—to participate in the organization of the event. As Tobón and García Treviño had in Mexico, these men then approached the US government of their own volition: in this case by walking into the office of the United States Information Service (USIS) in Santiago. What, they wanted to know, should we do? USIS advised Orrego Salas to continue to serve on the organizational committee of the CCC, in an attempt to steer it away from its state of Communist domination. Expecting this to fail, USIS advised that they could then resign their positions shortly before the CCC and publicly denounce it as Communist inspired—all of which came to pass. In the meantime, Walker and Orrego Salas could provide information about committee proceedings to USIS, which could then pass them to other US government agencies. Through this contact, the US embassy in Santiago learned that the CCC was having trouble raising funds, which it had hoped to be forthcoming from the Kremlin or the Cominform. USIS passed this information to *El Mercurio* columnist Carlos de Baráibar, a Spanish socialist living in Chilean exile, well known to the embassy as an anti-Communist and as "a steady and willing 'customer' for USIS materials."[36] The anti-Communism of Spanish exiles like Baráibar was hard earned; their Cold War politics were, to rudely paraphrase von Clausewitz, a continuation of the Spanish Civil War by other means. Though Baráibar continued to see himself as a socialist, making common cause with more conservative anti-Communists, like his employers at *El Mercurio*, became *de rigeur* during the Cold War. In late 1952 and early 1953, furnished with information from USIS, Baráibar's position at *El Mercurio* provided a regular platform for anti-CCC information. In contact with US officials and other anti-Communist Spanish Republicans in exile, Baráibar and his friends formed a kind of informal intelligence network.

With its contacts on the organizational committee and a partner in Baráibar, the United States Information Service and the Chilean embassy launched a continent-wide campaign to discredit the Continental Cultural Congress. They passed off Baráibar's clips as independent reporting, sending them via wireless file and to Voice of America stations throughout the region, where they were republished in other newspapers and broadcast on radio.

This created the illusion of an independent source establishing the Communistic nature of the CCC, and succeeded in getting potential delegates from other countries, including Alfonso Reyes of Mexico and Érico Veríssimo of Brazil, to withdraw their support. In the end, the State Department was satisfied with its strategy, adopting the curious position that its campaign of denunciation had forced the Communists to include more dissenting viewpoints and created something that, in the end, resembled a genuine exchange of ideas.[37]

USIS and State Department actions were generally reactive, assisting where they could in operations to further the interests of the United States. Deflating Peace campaigns, USIS complained, would require "gray" and "black" propaganda operations, which it was not, by law, supposed to carry out.[38] The organization responsible for that kind of work was the CIA, and it too had taken a particular interest in influencing intellectuals.[39] It had cultivated an instrument for doing precisely that—the Congress for Cultural Freedom (CCF). Sometimes described as both a Deminform (a Democratic counterpart to the Cominform), or an intellectual counterpart to the Marshall Plan, it began, more concretely, as a response to the Peace Movement.

The organization of the Congress for Cultural Freedom features the same mixture of anti-Communist voluntary action based on long-standing commitments and tentative support from the US government as had the wider story of anti-Peace campaigning here. The story has been told many times. Anti-Communist entrepreneurs in the United States and Europe, incensed by the partiality of the Peace Movement, mobilized counter-demonstrations. The recently formed CIA began to support the efforts financially and organizationally, sometimes with and sometimes without the knowledge of the intellectual organizers. The inaugural "Congress for Cultural Freedom" was held in West Berlin in 1950. In his opening address, Sidney Hook, one of the conference organizers, expressed his hope for clarity on a single point:

> [t]he fundamental distinction of our time must be drawn not in terms of [economic or social] programs, about which we may legitimately differ, not in terms of a free market in goods or a closed market but only in terms of a free market in ideas.[40]

Although its author did not attend, a paper contributed by German philosopher Karl Jaspers offers the best concise description of the Congress's self-justification:

> Propaganda, at first an instrument of ruse used to spread untruths that were seemingly favorable, has now become also an indispensable means for enforcing truth. Just as not only wrong but also right needs a lawyer, in order not to succumb, so is truth now in need of propaganda.[41]

For more than two decades the CCF tried to mitigate the intellectual appeal of Communism and to strengthen an anti-totalitarian "vital center" of generally liberal political opinion among the intelligentsia of Europe and the rest of the world, all the while receiving the majority of its funding from the CIA. Following the West Berlin congress, the CCF established its headquarters in Paris, organized other cultural and political symposia, and begin to publish its flagship magazines of politics and culture: *Encounter* in English and *Preuves* in French. Attempts to extend Congress operations to Latin American began almost from its earliest days, but, like the outreach to Germán Arciniegas described at the beginning of the chapter, they were initially ineffective.

The man who came to lead Latin American division of the Congress was Julián Gorkin. Gorkin, born in 1901, had been one of the first Communists in Spain: he founded the Communist Party of Valencia, and had trained with the Comintern in Moscow in the mid-1920s. Born Julián Gómez, he had chosen his *nom de guerre* as the concatenation of the names of Lenin and the Soviet writer Maxim Gorki.[42] Gorkin broke with the Comintern relatively early, in 1929: in his account, the result of disillusionment with the growing bureaucratization and Stalinization of the state apparatus.[43] Briefly a Trotskyist, in Spain Gorkin joined the tiny dissident Marxist party known as the Partido Obrero de Unificación Marxista (POUM), which, alongside anarchist groups, fought pitched street battles against Communists in Barcelona during May 1937. When the leader of the POUM, Andreu Nin, was kidnapped and executed by Communists, Gorkin became one of the most important remaining members. He spent 18 months in prison and was fortunate to escape Spain, making his way to Mexico via New York in 1940 with the help of anti-Communists in the American Federation of Labor.[44] Throughout the 1940s Gorkin moved in exile circles in Mexico, where he became a naturalized citizen. When Trotsky was murdered, Gorkin used his connections with the Mexican police to expose the responsibility of Stalin's agents.[45]

Gorkin resettled in Paris in 1948, and began to find multiplying opportunities in the field of anti-Communist propaganda. At the turn of the decade, Gorkin's most important work was ghostwriting for Valentín "El Campesino" González. El Campesino, who had fought Franco's forces as a Communist and might have killed the POUMist Gorkin during the Civil War if he had had the chance, had escaped to the Soviet Union when the war was lost, then broke with Communism and escaped from a Soviet prison camp on foot through Iran. Gorkin, along with the CIA, helped shelter the illiterate general in Western Europe and then took him on a tour of Latin America and eventually to Mexico.[46] At a CIA safe house in Cuernavaca (where he was secretly kept even as the FBI sought him so that he could testify before the US congressional subcommittee investigating international Communism), El Campesino told Gorkin his life story, which Gorkin formed into a book and saw published the following year in multiple languages.[47]

Gorkin had a prodigious memory, but he also had a reputation as a fabulist, someone who would tell elaborate stories as if he had been an eyewitness, and as someone who sometimes strained the truth.[48] "A rumor has been spread by word of mouth that [El Campesino] and I are American agents," he wrote to a friend around the time when they were working in a CIA safe house together. "American agents! We who have never received help from the United States for the work we are doing, and who would surely be denied a visa to enter the United States!"[49] On the matter of the visa, he was correct—he had been denied a visa in 1941 when he had attempted to testify before the Dies committee investigating international Communism. Had he merely maintained his indignation at being designated an American agent, he might at least have defended himself on the grounds that he maintained his independence, whomever he worked with. Like other anti-Communists who entered into relationships with US intelligence services, Gorkin seems to have been capable of believing that he was using the CIA as much as it was using him.[50] But if he was not exactly an American agent, most of his argument was nonsense: he had received help from the United States, would continue to do so for years, and surely knew it.

The Cold War provided Gorkin with new opportunities, and, as his work with the CIA and El Campesino shows, he was in no way confused about the nature of his partners. His political priorities now coincided with those of a powerful state, and his skills as an editor and an organizer made him the choice for director of the Congress for Cultural Freedom's Latin American division. Although there is no direct evidence that he understood the Congress for Cultural Freedom's links to the CIA, it is clear that he knew whom he was working "with"; he had regular strategy meetings with the cultural and labor attachés of US embassies in the context of his work for the Congress.[51] He was sent by the CCF on a tour of Latin America in mid-1952, and his travels convinced him that anti-imperialist rhetoric served as a pretext for Stalinist propaganda. "Nevertheless," he wrote, "the general sentiment of intellectual elements in Latin America is anti-totalitarian, anti-reactionary and profoundly liberal and democratic." Gorkin advised that

> [t]he Congress should be based on the liberty and universality of Culture—"Culture has no boundaries"—that it is necessary to defend against all totalitarianisms that threaten it and against all ambition to the management of thought or the submission of it to a political party.[52]

He recommended the creation of a magazine in the style of *Preuves* and national committees in Mexico and Chile (which he saw as the keys to their respective regions). He also advised taking advantage of the Spanish refugees working in universities and publishing houses across Latin America to promote the idea of universal culture through writing on Europe. The Congress brought out the first number of its Spanish-language magazine, *Cuadernos*, in March 1953, under Gorkin's editorial direction.[53]

Whatever lack of enthusiasm the CCF felt about extending its operations too deeply into Latin America, all doubts were overcome when the threat of Communist cultural organizing came into focus: during Neruda's Continental Congress for Culture in 1953. Making another tour of Latin America for the Congress, Gorkin—not by coincidence—arrived in Santiago a few days prior to the Continental Cultural Congress, and immediately made a series of radio broadcasts denouncing the Communist sponsorship that its programs attempted to conceal. Carlos de Baráibar, Gorkin's friend and fellow exile from the Spanish Civil War, helpfully "reported" on his activities in *El Mercurio*.[54]

Gorkin had a constructive agenda in addition to the goal of undermining the CCC: he wanted to create the first national chapter of the Congress for Cultural Freedom anywhere in Latin America. The signatories to the independent manifesto that Neruda had upbraided Jorge Edwards for signing—who had called for a forum to discuss issues of politics and culture—made up just the sort of anti-Communist center-left he sought. While in Chile, he spoke tirelessly about this new "Congress for Cultural Freedom" as a forum in which issues of culture and politics could be explored honestly. Before leaving, he put Baráibar in charge of hand picking the members of the new Chilean committee of the CCF. Baráibar carefully balanced secular and Christian, government and opposition, and professional responsibilities in choosing the committee, but remained the *éminence grise* of the Chilean committee of the CCF for years.[55] In September, the newly formed committee celebrated the opening of a library and conference space, inaugurating the first national center of the CCF in Latin America.[56]

The CIA had come to support a patchwork group of intellectuals, trying to amplify their criticisms of Communism, and at the same time making it clear that anti-Communism should not be the exclusive prerogative of reactionaries. In time, the CCF provided permanent employment for anti-Communists like Gorkin, professionalizing what had been more haphazard work. But, as this chapter has made clear, the US government campaign to discredit the Peace Movement depended on the voluntary actions of many entrepreneurial anti-Communists, as well as the initiative of foreign governments at the municipal, state, and national levels. In Chile, the power behind the national CCF branch was Carlos de Baráibar, a committed anti-Communist since the Spanish Civil War; in Mexico, it was Rodrigo García Treviño, the former associate of Trotsky who had approached the US embassy to offer to help it discredit the Peace Congress of 1949. Both had sought to use the US in *their* campaigns against the Peace Movement, and, within a few years, the US government was secretly paying for them to devote themselves to that cause. The cultural Cold War was created not merely by superpower conflict, but by the divergences between Communists and their rivals. In this fight, the US government was very much later to the game than the networks of entrepreneurial anti-Communists on which it came to rely.

Notes

1 Arciniegas to Burnham, 20 September 1950, James Burnham papers, box 11, folder 2, Hoover Institution Archives (HIA).
2 Arciniegas to Daniel Cosío Villegas, 30 March 1949 and Cosío Villegas to Arciniegas, 7 April 1949, Daniel Cosío Villegas papers, box 12, folder 71, El Colegio de México.
3 Arciniegas to Burnham, 20 September 1950, and Burnham to E. Howard Hunt, 27 September 1950, James Burnham papers, box 11, folder 2, and Burnham to Frank Wisner and Gerald Miller, 11 December 1950, box 11, folder 3, HIA.
4 The literature on the World Peace Council remains underdeveloped. Major sources are listed in the selected bibliography. On the Partisans of Peace Movement in Latin America, my dissertation, on which this chapter is based, may be helpful: Patrick Iber, "The Imperialism of Liberty: Intellectuals and the Politics of Culture in Cold War Latin America" (Ph.D. dissertation, University of Chicago, History, 2011).
5 U.S. House of Representatives Committee on Un-American Activities, "Report on The Communist 'Peace' Offensive: A Campaign to Disarm and Defeat the United States," (Washington, D.C.: USGPO, 1951), 1–3.
6 In Europe and the United States, writing on the Congress is substantial. Major references are listed in the selected bibliography.
7 Scott Lucas has described the amalgam of state and private interests created by the US government at the beginning of the Cold War as the "state-private network." Scott Lucas, *Freedom's War: The American Crusade Against the Soviet Union* (New York: New York University Press, 1999), 2; Helen Laville and Hugh Wilford, "The US Government, Citizen Groups and the Cold War: The State-private Network" (London; New York: Routledge, 2006).
8 Stanley E. Hilton, *Brazil and the Soviet Challenge, 1917–1947* (Austin: University of Texas Press, 1991); William Waack, *Camaradas: nos arquivos de Moscou, a história secreta da Revolução Brasileira de 1935* (São Paulo: Companhia das Letras, 1993), 38–65.
9 The law was implemented in January of 1948. Leslie Bethell, "Brazil," in *Latin America between the Second World War and the Cold War, 1944–1948*, ed. Leslie Bethell and Ian Roxborough (Cambridge: Cambridge University Press, 1992), 33–65.
10 See "A campanha pela paz do mundo," *Diario de São Paulo*, 25 March 1949 and Cecil M. P. Cross (American Consul General) to Secretary of State, 25 March 1949, 800.00B/3-2549, National Archives and Records Administration (NARA). Advertisements for the congress were placed in the *Folha da Manhã* and the *Folha da Noite*, which, in an interview with Alderman Jânio Quadros (who would serve as Brazil's president for part of 1961), who urged people to participate in the Peace Congress. A preparatory meeting was attended by about 1,200 people, including Quadros and the Marxist historian Caio Prado Júnior, as well as a substantial number of common laborers that the Consul General described as a "motely [sic], unwashed crowd."
11 "Seria proibido, no Rio, o Congresso Pró-Paz," *Folha da Noite*, 7 April 1949.
12 "São Paulo State Congress in Defense of Peace," 12 May 1949, 800.00B/5-1249, NARA.
13 Elisa Servín, "Propaganda y guerra fría: la campaña anticomunista en la prensa mexicana del medio siglo," *Signos Históricos* 11 (July 2004): 9–39.
14 For more on the rhetoric of the Peace Movement, see Iber, "The Imperialism of Liberty," 137–223.
15 Embassy dispatch No. 1076, "Brief Summary of Press Comment and Reaction Concerning the American Continental Congress for Peace," 22 August 1949, 810.00B/8-2249, NARA.

16 "Mucho cuidado con el próximo Congreso Continental de la Paz," *Todo*, 18 August 1949, 10.
17 That group had been known as the *Grupos Socialistas de la CTM*. There, Tobón especially worked directly with Vicente Lombardo Toledano, the pro-Soviet labor leader instrumental to the creation of the CTM. Lombardo Toledano was one of the principal organizers of the 1949 conference and one of the leading "Partisans of Peace" in Mexico.
18 On Rodrigo García Treviño, see Olivia Gall, *Trotsky en México y la vida política en el periodo de Cárdenas, 1937–1940* (México, D.F.: Ediciones Era, 1991), 86–87. The information he published with embassy support was printed widely prior to the meeting of the Continental Congress for Peace, including "Quinta columna de Stalin, en México," *Excélsior*, 12 August 1949; Embassy dispatch No. 1145, "Enclosing Clippings on Communist Identification of Supporters of Peace Congress," 6 September 1949 and Parke D. Massey Jr. to the ambassador, "Conversation with Benjamín Tobón and Rodrigo García Treviño concerning Anti-Communist Activity," 29 August 1949, both filed at 810.00B/9-649, NARA.
19 José Mancisidor, "La paz en México," *El Nacional*, 5 September 1949, 3; "Clausura del Congreso Continental por la Paz," *El Nacional*, 13 September 1949, 4.
20 Frank J. Devine, "Meeting of Peace Conference Delegates at Agraciada and Colonia on March 15, 1952," 27 March 1952, 700.01/3-2752, NARA.
21 Wallace W. Stuart (First Secretary of Embassy, Montevideo) to Department of State, "Communist Sponsored Continental Peace Conference," 27 March 1952, 700.01/3-2752, NARA.
22 David Schidlowsky, *Las furias y las penas: Pablo Neruda y su tiempo* (Berlin: Wissenschaftlicher Verlag, 1999), 1246–52.
23 See page 5 of the "Latin American Participation in the World Peace Movement" section of "Prometheus Bound," accessed 1 May 2006, CIA-RDP78-02771R0005005 00004-5, CIA Research Tool (CREST), NARA.
24 Among the important members of the presídium of the CCC were Jorge Amado, Benjamín Subercaseaux, Diego Rivera, Nicolás Guillén, Pablo Neruda, René Depestre, María Rosa Oliver, Ary de Andrade, Salvador Allende, and José Mancisidor.
25 Schidlowsky, *Las furias y las penas*, 772.
26 Jaime Castillo Velasco, "El Congreso Continental de la Cultura de Santiago de Chile," *Cuadernos*, no. 2 (June–August 1953): 85.
27 Castillo Velasco, "Congreso Continental," 85.
28 "Fernando Santiván informa en el Congreso de la Cultura," *El Siglo*, 28 April 1953, 1.
29 "Tres Dimensiones del Congreso de la Cultura," *Vistazo*, 5 May 1953, 16, 19.
30 Jaime Castillo, "El Congreso Continental de la Cultura de Santiago de Chile," *Cuadernos*, no. 2 (June–August 1953): 84–87.
31 The writer Benjamín Subercaseaux, an admirer of André Gide, had attended.
32 Juan de Luigi, "Los Hechos de Hoy," *El Siglo*, 9 May 1953, 4.
33 Chile's *Falange Nacional*, so named in 1936 after formation the previous year, became the *Partido Demócrata Cristiano* in 1957.
34 "Sus reservas frente al Congreso de la Cultura plantean intelectuales," *La Nación*, 24 April 1953, 6. The manifesto was signed by, among others, Eduardo Anguita, Eduardo Barrios, Enrique Bunster, Jaime Castillo Velasco, Jorge Cash, Jacques Chonchol, Eduardo Frei, Alejandro Magnet, Georg Nicolai, Chela Reyes, Andrés Santa Cruz, Radomiro Tomic, and Gabriel Valdés Subercaseaux.
35 Jorge Edwards, *Adios, poeta ... : memorias* (Barcelona: Tusquets Editores, 1990), 46.

36 "Continental Cultural Congress," 24 December 1952, 398.44-SA/12-2452, NARA.
37 Sims to Clarence A. Canary, 3 July 1953, and Embassy Dispatch no. 1250, 12 May 1953, 398.44-SA/6-853, NARA. Chilean poet Gabriela Mistral also refused any active involvement. Chilean writer Benjamín Subercaseaux, one of the non-Communists who did attend, also had regular contact with the US embassy.
38 "Communist Peace Propaganda," 17 May 1951, 700.001/5-1751, NARA. The USIA's domain was so-called "white" propaganda, in which the author of the propaganda is identified (the Voice of America and *Pravda* are examples). In "gray" propaganda, the author is concealed. "Black" propaganda involves active misdirection and misinformation.
39 "Prometheus Bound," accessed 1 May 2006, CIA-RDP78-02771R000500500004-5, CREST, NARA.
40 Sidney Hook Address at CCF Opening Session, Hoover Institution Library Society Publications, Congress for Cultural Freedom, 2.
41 Karl Jaspers, "On Dangers and Chances of Freedom," Congress Paper no. 17, Hoover Institution Library Society Publications, Congress for Cultural Freedom, 17.
42 Pepe Gutiérrez-Álvarez, *Retratos poumistas* (Sevilla: Espuela de Plata, 2006), 169.
43 Julián Gorkin, *El revolucionario profesional: testimonio de un hombre de acción* (Barcelona: Aymá, 1975).
44 David Wingeate Pike, *In the Service of Stalin: The Spanish Communists in Exile, 1939–1945* (New York: Oxford University Press, 1993), 304.
45 Leandro A. Sánchez Salazar and Julián Gorkin, *Ainsi fut assassiné Trotsky* (Paris: Éditions Self, 1948); Julián Gorkin, *Cómo asesinó Stalin a Trotsky* (Buenos Aires: Plaza & Janés, 1961).
46 E. Howard Hunt and Greg Aunapu, *American Spy: My Secret History in the CIA, Watergate, and Beyond* (Hoboken, N.J.: John Wiley & Sons, 2007), 56.
47 Valentín R. González and Julián Gorkin, *El Campesino: Life and Death in Soviet Russia* (New York: G. P. Putnam's Sons, 1952).
48 Gutiérrez-Álvarez, *Retratos poumistas*, 171.
49 Gorkin to Serafino Romualdi, 12 September 1951, Jay Lovestone papers, box 296, folder 2, HIA.
50 Gutiérrez-Álvarez, *Retratos poumistas*, 195.
51 Julián Gorkin, "Report," 18 July 1953, International Association for Cultural Freedom (IACF) papers, series II, box 205, folder 1, University of Chicago Special Collections Research Center (UC-SCRC).
52 Julián Gorkin, "Pour un Congrès pour la Liberté de la Culture en Amérique Latine," 30 May 1952, IACF series II, box 204, folder 5, UC-SCRC.
53 The full, official, and utterly unused name of the magazine was *Cuadernos del Congreso por la Libertad de la Cultura*.
54 See, for example, Julián Gorkin, "Detrás del telón de hierro se oculta la realidad de la experiencia soviética," *El Mercurio*, 29 April 1953, 1.
55 Carlos de Baráibar to Michael Josselson, 5 July 1953, IACF series II, box 204, folder 6, UC-SCRC. Important members of the committee included future president Eduardo Frei, Jaime Castillo Velasco, Alejandro Magnet, Hernán Díaz Arrieta, Chela Reyes, and Hernán Santa Cruz.
56 Germain to Josselson, 5 October 1953, IACF series II, box 204, folder 6, UC-SCRC.

Selected bibliography

Brogi, Alessandro. *Confronting America: The Cold War between the United States and the Communists in France and Italy*. Chapel Hill: University of North Carolina Press, 2011.

Coleman, Peter. *The Liberal Conspiracy: The Congress for Cultural Freedom and the Struggle for the Mind of Postwar Europe.* New York: Free Press, 1989.

Desanti, Dominique. *Les Staliniens, 1944–1956: une expérience politique.* Paris: Fayard, 1975.

Edwards, Jorge. *Adios, poeta ... : memorias.* Barcelona: Tusquets Editores, 1990.

Franco, Jean. *The Decline and Fall of the Lettered City: Latin America in the Cold War.* Cambridge, Mass.: Harvard University Press, 2002.

Grémion, Pierre. *Intelligence de l'anticommunisme: le Congrès Pour la Liberté de la Culture à Paris (1950–1975).* Paris: Fayard, 1995.

Lieberman, Robbie. *The Strangest Dream: Communism, Anticommunism and the US Peace Movement 1945–1963.* Syracuse Studies on Peace and Conflict Resolution. New York: Syracuse University Press, 2000.

Pinault, Michel. *Frédéric Joliot-Curie.* Paris: O. Jacob, 2000.

Prince, Robert. "Following the Money Trail at the World Peace Council." *Peace Magazine* 8, no. 6 (December 1992).

Santamaria, Yves. *Le parti de l'ennemi? le Parti communiste français dans la lutte pour la paix, 1947–1958.* Paris: Armand Colin, 2006.

Saunders, Frances Stonor. *Who Paid the Piper: The CIA and the Cultural Cold War.* London: Granta Books, 1999.

Schidlowsky, David. *Las furias y las penas: Pablo Neruda y su tiempo.* Berlin: Wissenschaftlicher Verlag, 1999.

Scott-Smith, Giles. *The Politics of Apolitical Culture: The Congress for Cultural Freedom, the CIA, and Post-war American Hegemony.* Routledge/PSA political studies series. London; New York: Routledge, 2002.

Wilford, Hugh. *The Mighty Wurlitzer: How the CIA Played America.* Cambridge, Mass.: Harvard University Press, 2008.

Wittner, Lawrence S. *One World or None: A History of the World Nuclear Disarmament Movement through 1953.* Stanford, CA: Stanford University Press, 1993.

9 A "new man" for Africa?
Some particularities of the Marxist *Homem Novo* within Angolan cultural policy

Delinda Collier

In 1978, a group of young artists from Angola converged on the city of Havana to take part in a youth conference for visual artists and writers. After returning to Luanda, the visual artists began to write the cultural policy for the newly independent Angolan nation, using the language of the *Homem Novo* [New Man] and applying it to the particular situation of Africa and Angola. The New Man was a collage of ideas that the artists and authors drew from Marxist theory, Négritude, Western anthropology, and Latin American cultural theory. Their unique application of this cultural theory during the later years of the Cold War reflects both the limitations of dominant chronologies and geographical demarcations in Cold War studies, and the relative autonomy with which many revolutionaries in Africa selected ideas from both sides of the global ideological divide.

If we understand the Cold War in part as a process of thickening global networks and their discursive "brands," the New Man discourse allowed for many interpretations and contingencies to intersect. In Angola, the New Man was used to indicate the universalist notion of developmentalism, held in tension with the particulars of Africanity and Angolanity. This chapter will introduce early documents of Angolan cultural activists who attempted to connect up with these global networks while fiercely defending and uniting Angolan art. The documents reflect a desire to connect to classical pro-communist ideals of collectivism, while retaining a pragmatic view of its application in Angola. Their dates are key to the discussion of chronology of the Cold War. As lusophone colonies in Africa did not gain their independence until the mid-1970s, their heavy reliance on Marxist theory demonstrates its reverberations within so-called peripheral nations struggling to overthrow colonial capitalism. The present discussion will culminate in a discussion of one particular artwork and how it embodies in many ways the paradox of Angolan socialism.

The 1978 founding statement of the National Union of Angolan Visual Artists conceives of revolutionary art as both "new" in its anti-bourgeois formalist tendencies and, perhaps more importantly, tied to the original meaning of the avant-garde as a site of military battle. The opening sentences of the proclamation read, " ... art is one of the fronts of combat of the

Angolan People in this critical phase of the Angolan Revolution ... art is a natural necessity of the human being and not simply an activity of leisure or luxury."[1] Later, the proclamation speaks of a change in consciousness that is brought about by both artistic and military struggle. The unanimous rejection of colonial appropriation of Angolan art, it declares, shall be harnessed in the creation of a New Man, with the People of Angola as the subject and object of artistic production. This term "New Man" was a theory of subjectivity as well as a set of policy statements that reflect a geopolitical alignment with other nominally Marxist governments in South America, and to a lesser extent, Eastern Europe and the USSR.

When Portugal finally withdrew from Angola in 1974, it made no attempt to organize a peaceful transition of power, leaving the country instead to a "coalition" government of the three anti-colonial parties. The method of Portugal's exit from Angola exacerbated a volatile situation, as the Portuguese nationals who controlled virtually all of the major industries abandoned Angola and took with them every item of machinery that could be exported. This exodus amounted to a near-complete collapse of the Angolan economy at the beginning of its independence. By then, three major factions of the anti-colonial struggle fought for leadership of the newly independent Angola: Movimento Popular de Libertação de Angola (Popular Movement for the Liberation of Angola, MPLA), União Nacional para a Independência Total de Angola (National Union for the Total Independence of Angola, UNITA), and Frente Nacional de Libertação de Angola (National Front of Liberation of Angola, FNLA). Their divisions were based on ideology, ethnicity, region, social class, and race.

The first president of Angola, Agostinho Neto, declared independence on 11 November 1975, "in the name of the Angolan people, the Central Committee of the People's Movement for the Liberation of Angola [MPLA]."[2] He conflated the Angolan people and the MPLA, while also indicating the tenuousness of the MPLA's ascendancy to power and the unity of Angola, as he referred to the "struggle we are still waging against the lackeys of imperialism." Without naming the organization he spoke of, out of a stated respect for the occasion, Neto referred to MPLA internal enemies as well as UNITA, which party was at the time increasingly making military pacts with the Portuguese army in the hinterlands. The MPLA had been already fighting a civil war with the FNLA and UNITA. According to William Minter, by the late 1960s "UNITA clashes with the MPLA were at least as common as its confrontations with Portuguese troops."[3] The MPLA's declaration of victory, not only over the Portuguese but also over opposing factions, was at best fragile. The divisions erupted into civil war that escalated in violence and resulted in an incredible destruction of life, land, and infrastructure.

The official ceasefire was not until 2002, when UNITA's leader, Jonas Savimbi, was killed in battle. Estimates vary as to the death toll of the civil war, from 750,000 to one million. An untold number of Angolans were injured by landmines, which, at the height of the conflict, numbered one to two for every person in the country.

Angolanidade and the New Man: these two political slogans helped Angolan nationalist artists (mostly MPLA members) negotiate the construction of African identity and international scientific socialism in the moment of independence. In their official usage, *angolanidade* and the New Man can be understood in terms of a cultural expression of Angolan exceptionalism and international socialism, respectively.

Angolanidade began as a student literary movement in 1948 in Portugal at the Casa dos Estudantos do Imperio. The movement was first titled "Let's Discover Angola!," with writers looking to the specific cultural attributes of Angola for their material and method of writing. Mário Pinto de Andrade, Viriato da Cruz, and first Angolan president, Agostinho Neto, wrote affectionately of Luanda's *musseques*, or shantytowns, as the birthplace of Angolan national culture. The choice of their language, syntax, and tone characterized the vibrancy of *musseque* life, countering the Angolan colonial government's descriptions of its squalor and crime. The authors' publication of *Mensagem* in 1951 marks, as Patrick Chabal argues, "the beginning of a self-conscious Angolan literature."[4] "Let's Discover Angola!" adapted a conception of Angolan cultural hybridity formulated during Angolan resistance to Dutch occupation in the seventeenth century. Heterogeneity was a natural fact of the urban and *assimilado* [assimilated] population of Luanda, a city formed by the slave trade in the sixteenth century.[5] Within the pages of *Mensagem* was a language that attempted to perform the hybridity and *creolité* of the *musseques* and urban Angola. Though *Mensagem* was short lived, running only four issues, the movement influenced a later wave of more militant nationalist writing in the late 1950s and 1960s, on the eve of the fully militarized independence war.

At the height of the independence struggle in 1960, Agostinho Neto, an early poet of Angolan nationalism, wrote "Havemos de Voltar [We Shall Return]." In it he advocates a return to the culture of Angola embodied in masquerade and music, coterminous with the return to material resources of Angola such as diamonds, oil, and soil. As the first president of Angola and the author of many of the early policy decisions on national culture, Neto was the symbol of the transition from an embattled nationalism via Portuguese imperialism to the MPLA as the harbinger of national culture in its statecraft.

The trope of return was essentially Neto's demand for repatriation, a communal circumscription of resources, traditional culture, and "our land, our mother."[6] His longing for the primordial and the communal was a feature of nationalist thought. Jacqueline Rose describes this fantasy as progressive in the sense that it is "always heading for the world it only appears to have left behind."[7] Angola's rich postcolonial cultural production was born from a search for the "real," conditioned of violently forced alienation from land and resources. Luandino Vieira, whom Chabal considers one of the two "central pillars of *angolanidade*" along with Neto, wrote about the visceral experience of space and time of Africa. His novels, rich in description of the loss and longing for the land, present "the Angolan landscape as a synecdoche for Angola itself; man and nature constitute the country."[8] Integration with "the land" marks peaceful social relations with a shared history and culture, and is also a search for the real.

To the extent that Neto borrowed from négritudist theories I would argue that it was in his search for a type of universal exceptionalism, a way to elucidate the condition of the victim as an embattled figure of "Africa." Black communalism with nature is, for Neto, a metaphor for utopia. On the other hand, arguing against the necessity of blackness as an identifier of Africa, Vieira claimed that "[c]ertainly a white man can be an African writer ... I am an Angolan writer, therefore an African writer."[9] This definition of the urban white and creole as Angolan is precisely what UNITA later used to mount a political attack on the MPLA, claiming that the party was made up of an intellectual international elite and therefore inauthentic.

"Home" came to be characterized in Angolan literature, art, and political discourse as the rural masses, the peasant workers with whom the intellectuals in the MPLA sought to identify. It was a strong fantasy in the face of the reality of a severely fractured nationalism, which formed in large part along the rural/urban divide. In a sense, the MPLA's intense level of adherence to the Marxist language as it formulated its civil policy suppressed the chaos it faced in its implementation.

The New Man was a concept adopted after these Angolan nationalist writers and visual artists came into contact with the network of socialist activists, most notably those operating in Cuba; it helped them transition to becoming leaders of their newly formed state. The New Man was a concept developed in Marxist writings, usually by functionaries of postcolonial states, those attempting to govern difficult post-revolution era lands. That is, while writers like Frantz Fanon wrote of the new man that emerged out of the violent overthrow of the colonial oppressor, the figure of his famous *tabula rasa*, the formalized New Man, represents the branding of a methodology: the scientific socialist method of state formation circulated within an increasingly networked set of countries.

Additionally, the New Man discourse helped newly independent countries to rein in regional disputes under the auspices of unities of all tribes under one national identity, in some cases an unfortunate retreat from pluralistic democracy. For instance, in Mozambique, the FRELIMO party under Samora Machel made a rather sudden about-face between the years of 1969 and 1971, from Mozambican nationalism to a state-directed "unity" of all Mozambicans. While on the one hand a matter of practical governance and the transition to an independent state, Michael Mahoney argues that Machel's reason for systematically purging the country of all ethnic divisions (read dissent) was power consolidation.[10] A similar situation developed in Angola, as the MPLA worked to purge its own party and the rest of the country from resistance to their policies and procedures.

The New Man discourse is born of one of Marxism's foundational ideas: consciousness arises from material conditions. It originated in 1920s Soviet political theory, in which the actual personality of the individual is changed, given the correct material conditions. For African independence activists, the same who became postcolonial state leaders, the ultimate goal was a renewal of "man" and to re-center society on the wellness of each person and mass consciousness. By the 1960s, the New Man was a key phrase of a networked discourse, a new theory of "humanism" that spread in various speeches and political declarations as a signal of political alignment. The two thinkers that most influenced Angolan and other Luso-African intellectuals were Brazilian scholar Paulo Freire and friend of the Angolan revolution Che Guevara. Both were important figures in south–south networks; both traveled extensively in Africa, helping to organize and implement a type of scientific socialism with military support in nearly or newly independent countries. For Freire, the New Man is formed when the oppressed develop a critical consciousness that makes them aware of both themselves and their counterparts. His *Pedagogy of the Oppressed* was based on a dialogical approach to education, where constant questioning leads to a progressive enlightenment of the masses.

Che addressed the New Man in terms of art that is tied to "old" ideas of realism—old conceptions of form and content. The New Man is one of two pillars of construction in the new socialist society, along with technological development.[11] In his theorizing, the New Man was a generic term for the reordering of consciousness, while being a general term of socialist revolution. During the 1960s, Havana became a node of the New Man discourse, hosting several conferences that included Lusophone Africa. Amilcar Cabral, anticolonial activist in Portuguese Guinea and Cape Verde and leader of the African Party for the Independence of Guinea and Cape Verde, spoke of the nature of this network in a speech he delivered at the first Tricontinental Conference of the Peoples of Asia, Africa, and Latin America in 1966. In his speech, "The Weapon of Theory," Cabral pays linguistic homage to the Cuban revolution in his mention of the New Man, "fully conscious of his national, continental, and international rights and duties."[12] Cabral goes on to affirm the deep connection between Africans and Cubans, both ancestral and contemporary, before arguing that each location and revolution has to happen from the inside, based on intimate knowledge of the specificity of the country.

For eager Marxist artists and writers in Angola, the camaraderie that resulted from the actualization of these networks in meetings and educational exchanges shaped and animated the language of founding proclamations of state-sponsored artist unions. At the same time, the texts show a struggle to maintain the particularities of Angola, to negotiate scientific socialism and *angolanidade*. The New Man appears in the declaration of the first artist union in Angola, the National Union of Angolan Plastic Artists [UNAP], written by a contingent of artists who had just returned from a youth festival in Cuba in 1978. UNAP's stated objective was to "contribute to the progressive transformation of the legacy of colonial domination, which made the values of African culture a mere bourgeois commodity, so that [art] can be harnessed in the creation of the New Man."[13] The document goes on to declare art as a key tool in transforming consciousness, "to educate and stimulate the public taste for works of art, channel their desire for intelligence in the sense of participation in the artistic process and thus the resulting art can be integrated in the dynamic transformation of our own minds."[14] Thus the New Man within visual arts discourse encompasses the public and the private, the (correct) structure of the state and the affective response of each individual in a new society. It was, for the artists and administrators, nothing less than reordering subject/object relationships in Angola. How exactly that art would look was less important to how it was framed.

The 1979 MPLA Museum Manual states that after independence, museums must always improve themselves, "to be assessed by dialectical materialism, in the experience of our People and in Universal concert of progressive culture."[15] This statement contains the descriptive and prescriptive functions of scientific socialism. The museum was to be a laboratory through which to observe the processes of change and progression to a new and better standard of living for Angolans.

In proposals for a new museum system found in official documents, the MPLA names the inhabitants of the hinterlands as the People. The MPLA publications attempt to circumscribe them through educational programs and a pledge of respect for their cultures. In order for this to succeed, the authors explain, officials in Luanda must work in concert with the various local chiefs and power structures. The MPLA's attempt to culturally integrate rural Angolans coincided with the historical struggle to gain control over all of the sectors of Angolan society, including agriculture, mining, industry, and so on. The urgent need to unify Angola in the face of serious fracture caused the MPLA to shift from the revolutionary side of Marxism-Leninism to the implementation of "scientific socialism," with the goal of transcending divisions of race, ethnicity, tribe, and ideology.

Part of the MPLA's anti-colonial challenge in the 1960s, as in all socialist movements, was to educate the peasantry of their status as Angolans. Speaking of the MPLA's Centers for Revolutionary Instruction, party leader Sparticus Monimambu explained, "we are trying to give people a consciousness of themselves as Angolans. We put on theatrical performances showing the people what it was like before the Portuguese came to Angola, how the people were living, what their societies were like."[16] The definition, idealization, and subsequent instrumentalization of the peasantry became characteristic of the ideological battle among the anti-colonial factions. Under the MPLA's scientific socialism, the peasants were the rural Angolans who had been forced to labor under colonialism, alongside the urban proletariat in Luanda, Benguela, and other cities. Both the FNLA and UNITA countered that the MPLA did not represent the "true" peasant masses, those ethnic groups in northern and southern Angola. UNITA characterized the MPLA as an urban party of elite and upper-class, privileged Angolans who were educated abroad and therefore had no connection to "real" Angolans. UNITA's bifurcation of Angolans was in itself an attempt to claim the hinterlands.

The shift to statehood for the MPLA accompanied a sudden shift in defining the enemy of Angolan nationalism, from the Portuguese to what MPLA members called the puppet regimes of the Portuguese, FNLA and UNITA. Angolan nationalist artists, especially those in the MPLA, faced a complex transition from anti-colonial nationalists to state workers charged with initiating a cultural infrastructure and a practice of collectivity. Until independence, the nationalist arts community was underground, embedded in the *musseques*, exiled in Portugal, Cuba, and other countries, or imprisoned in Tarrafal prison in Cape Verde. Many from this same community, including Neto himself, were now in administrative positions and faced with the task of preserving that unifying language of nationalism while structuring a state. The rhetoric of anti-imperialism did not leave Angolan nationalists, but rather, *angolanidade* was defined anew.

Instead of identifying with the Portuguese metropole, as many of the prominent postcolonial French intellectuals did with Paris, throughout the 1970s and 1980s Angolan artists and writers were increasingly influenced by their ideological counterparts in Cuba, the USSR, and East Germany. In addition to their strong linguistic and revolutionary ties with Guinea Bissau, Brazil, Cape Verde, and Mozambique, many visual artists, including the founding members of UNAP, left Angola and trained in the School of Fine Arts in Havana. In the end, however, many of them found that the socialist realism they learned while abroad did not fit the context of Angola and indigenous Angolan culture(s). In UNAP's 1977 inaugural proclamation, the signatories speak of the necessity of art that can interact with the people in order to better the behavior, consciousness, and material situation of the "everyday Angolan."[17]

Under the 80th decree on September 3, 1976, all cultural patrimony was declared the property of the People of Angola. The re-appropriation of Angola's cultural "patrimony" accompanied a detailed program for the newly nationalized museums. Museums were to play an important role in unifying the nation culturally, an intellectual and practical endeavor and a matter of cultural infrastructure. A publication by the MPLA's National Department of Museums and Monuments claims the People as the author of the artwork in museums and of the museum itself. In fact, the museum manual is one of the clearest statements on the MPLA's cultural program at the time of independence. At once celebratory and sober, it explains that museums are the storehouse of cultural capital—the objects of culture—and the educational apparatus that spread cultural capital to the Angolan people.

The anonymously authored museum publication was written in 1979 at the apex of the MPLA's power, when internal dissent in the party had been (violently) silenced and the party had established itself as the controlling party of Angola. The manual reflects the fervor with which the MPLA conceived of the state's responsibilities and functions. The preface argues that museum collections offer material proof of advancement and good in society. It argues that museums must be of a sound conception so as to powerfully demonstrate the depravity of all other political systems before socialism. Under the MPLA's authorship, museums must always teach about "the victory against colonialism, the victory against imperialist invasion, divisions practiced at times by the People, by tribalists (Unita, Fnla, and today's outlaws), racist factionists, leftists, and neocolonialists."[18] The conceived network includes, among others, museums of anthropology, nature, slavery, archaeology, the armed forces, and colonial history.

The museum manual echoes the call by party officials to educate the masses about their role as Angolans and their position in the new society. As functionaries of the revolution, museums had a pedagogical role as presenting objective proof of Angola's superior genealogy. The MPLA declared that with objects, "it is difficult to lie about the ingenuity of man, about material progress, about human sensitivity and the social consciousness of artists. ... "[19] The role of pedagogy was particularly urgent for the MPLA as it fought to circumscribe the vast territory of Angola and all of the political, ethnic, and social factions within it. The strident rhetoric of revolution would not yet be abandoned and in some cases contradicts the proclamations of open authorship and inclusivity.

The rigid museum program was in part a response to the violent cultural and social heterogeneity of Angola. In the museum program the party acknowledges that there is no "natural" communalism. Following classic Marxism-Leninism, however, MPLA officials asserted that all art production aided the revolution, and therefore cultural divisions could be bridged if all Angolans were conceived of as one class. In a speech given to the Angolan Writers' Union, Agostinho Neto referenced Lenin's theory of cultural nationalism, stating, "[m]ay I recommend to my esteemed comrades and colleagues that they take every advantage to those conditions that will permit our writers to work and produce and observe every nook and cranny of our national geographic sphere as they live the lives of the people."[20] In this speech Neto refers to the superiority of socialism in correctly utilizing culture and the importance of research in constructing and perpetuating the "soul" of the Angolan people.

This negotiation of universalist and specific notions of culture, both inclusive and repressive, was in some ways read as proof of the need to educate the masses, to improve their conditions before they could be enlightened. Neto claims that to move Angolan culture away from the emulation of Portuguese standards and towards nationalist standards would only happen "when material conditions are sufficiently determinant of a new consciousness."[21] Thus, veering away from his earlier interest in the spiritual communalism of blackness, President Neto invokes the Marxist materialist leveling of society and shaping of culture. The MPLA museum manual, as government policy, had to engineer artistic unity very carefully in order to preserve the spirit of nationalism. If a tension was present between individualism and communalism, there was likewise an inter-ethnic tension that the authors had to attend to. For example, the manual proposes an "Experimental Museum," in which any Angolan may mount an exhibition, as opposed to only institutionalized officials. There are a few guidelines as to what is permissible, the key one being that the exhibition "not have content contrary to the political agenda of the MPLA—*the Workers' Party.*"[22] Here, curation is understood as engineering content and not form under the strict purview of the Angolan state as defined by the MPLA.

The key cultural functionary of the visual arts was Victor Manuel "Viteix" Teixeira, founding member of the National Union of Angolan Plastic Artists. He was also a scholar; he completed his PhD at the University of Paris and wrote a dissertation on Angolan art, the most complete overview of Angolan art to date. *Theory and Practice of Angolan Plastic Art* answered Neto's call to research every nook and cranny of Angolan culture. Viteix (1940–93) was an anti-colonial activist who took refuge in Paris before independence. There, he and two other Angolan art students mounted an overtly anti-colonial exhibition in 1973 called "Angola—Art, Combat, Popular Music, Painting, Sculpture." That same year he finished a master's degree in Visual Arts in Paris, also having studied the visual arts in Portugal. Between the time of independence in 1975 and 1983, when he took his doctorate at the University of Paris, he trained the first batch of instructors at the former Barração (Shed) in Luanda. Following his PhD training, Viteix remained in Angola, where he was director-general of UNAP from 1987–89.

Theory and Practice of Angolan Plastic Arts was written in 1983 when Viteix returned to Paris after his tenure as teacher and Director of the Visual Arts Sector of Angola. In part, *Theory and Practice* is a summation of the work that Viteix completed under the employ of the MPLA as he worked to establish a post-independence body of visual art and practice. Like the MPLA museum policy, Viteix in *Theory and Practice* takes on the task of defining and describing Angolan visual art. But because his focus is on plastic (visual) art, he has a special task in defining not only the social history and function of art in Angola but also any unifying visual characteristics of this body of work. He takes on this challenge, suggesting throughout the book that there is an underlying logic of Angolan art that does not necessarily manifest in stylistic affinities.

Viteix's book uses functionalist and structuralist anthropology, ethnology, and art history. But his is a professed "ideo-sociological (*idéo-sociologique*)" work, both describing the various ideologies behind the art he presents, and prescribing a new Angolan art practice. This dual descriptive/prescriptive approach is important to note. He states that it is less important to him to operate within a single methodology, since the types of art and their contexts are so varied. The affinities between various types of art are more important to his project, so that they may be rightfully placed in the "new" Angolan society. Unlike the methodological pretenses of objectivity in anthropology, Viteix states the ideological platform of his cultural theory. He desires to instrumentalize culture for the advancement of Angolan people and maintains the importance of the MPLA in leading this project.

Viteix's theories are comparable to Che, in that he viewed socialist realism and other highly programmed art expression to be constrictive and detrimental to a truly nationalist art. In his warning against such "realism at any cost," Guevara posited instead that "the probabilities that important artists will appear will be greater to the degree that the field of culture and the possibilities for expression are broadened."[23] He maintained that adherence to party and artistic free expression were mutually compatible, even beneficial. If the MPLA reiterated that its leadership was really leadership by the everyman Angolan, it did not matter what the art looked like, it was at base "realism," a polemical term in socialist art. In language similar to that of the MPLA museum manual, UNAP "proclaim[ed] its decision to enter into and to contribute to a Society guided by the ideology of the Working Class and to support and defend the political line and the clear direction of the revolutionary vanguard of the Angolan People, the MPLA."[24]

MPLA activists also had ties to members of the African National Congress in South Africa [ANC]. The ANC had similar debates about the place of cultural production in the struggle, which were later articulated in an influential essay written by Albie Sachs in 1989, "Preparing Ourselves for Freedom."[25] Sachs argues against the use of art as propaganda, such as illustrating guns, and instead for understanding art as an activity that can open up to the possibility of complexity and contradictions. After all, he explains, the struggle is about winning the freedom of expression and humanity. In one important section, Sachs argues that the party guidelines should not be applied to the sphere of culture, but rather that culture should influence the party guidelines.[26] This viewpoint was somewhat exceptional within the ANC, and it is distinct from the MPLA rhetoric of culture in the struggle. Whereas both Neto and Sachs contend that propaganda is harmful to the culture of the people, Neto and the MPLA saw the value in pedagogy as a preliminary step in changing the consciousness of the people.

Theory and Practice is a product of a particular hermeneutic. Viteix begins by revealing his sources, for him an important aspect of his methodology. Viteix elaborates:

> [s]ome parts of this research have been conducted on site relying on local sources of local information on the subjects that concern us: artisans, artists, people, with or without prestige and great authority, diverse documents whether in Portuguese or other languages (see bibliography), our own experience in the field of education and artistic practice, some anthropological data and, conclusively, the continuation of our own observation and reflection.[27]

Viteix is partial to oral information, as he claims that it is the most pure source of information. However, throughout the text anthropological sources are treated as parallel information with local knowledge and oral history. He notes that the interlocutor will give him different types of information, depending on the context and "personalities," which then necessitates his own interpretation and his creation of connections between various sources. After all, he explains, his is a sociological study of plastic art in Angola.[28]

As it is a sociological study, Viteix takes on the major challenge to any argument for artistic nationalism: to properly contextualize provincial art production. His text demonstrates the difficulty in arguing for a unified "Angolan" national art, as he is faced with an array of art production and various histories of that production. First, however, he takes what he calls a detour through religion, philosophy, politics, etc., that follows a lengthy, conventionally written section on the history and geography of Angola. His history starts with European contact and its encounters with established kingdoms like the Kongo. He also goes to great lengths to bring history to the present and to include the anti-colonial struggle as the key point—and possibly the only one—of Angolan nationalism. In all, the introductory sections of *Theory and Practice* are the most telling of his challenge to argue for a unified Angolan plastic art while acknowledging, and even embracing, its contradictions.

Viteix explains that his "ideo-sociological" system of classification arises from his belief that political action is the original function of art.[29] It is an appeal to an ethical humanism in which all of the variegated histories of each ethnic group and colonial influence become part of the "new socio-cultural dimension of the country."[30] Part of the reversal of the colonial hermeneutic involves, for Viteix, the refusal to obfuscate the present condition of Angolans in his claim for their primordial rights to the land. If a study and/or practice of art is to be called "Angolan," it must address the current needs and desires of Angola's people. Indeed, as the title of his study argues, it must be a practice and not thought of as a natural law, one that integrates mind and body. Thus, hermeneutic practice of description precedes the construction of a new artistic practice. Angolan nationalists sought somehow to reintegrate the body, if only in the beginning the body politic.

Viteix then performs the collection and systemization of visual art production within the geographical boundaries of Angola in what amounts to securing the cultural capital of Angola. Viteix uses a structuralist approach not only to typologize the art, but more importantly to establish a network of Angolan artists, especially as seen in Section Two, the "Creator Groups of Plastic Arts." The first subsections of the second section consist of his listing the types of art produced by various "groups," which Viteix defines as both ethnic and territorial. In this, he notes the extreme difficulty in demarcating these groups, but its necessity in simplifying his study. This section also demonstrates Viteix's challenge in adopting the techniques of anthropology that he states have been so damaging in their colonial use, that is, the tribalization of Angola. Here he also faces the challenge of integrating the production of artists and artisans and including so-called decorative and functional arts into Angolan plastic art.

This theoretical system included a genealogy of art forms, not unlike most postcolonial nationalist art theories claiming a "primordial" nationalism. Viteix begins *Theory and Practice* with a lengthy discussion of ancient rock art in Angola. This section exists, as he explains in the introductory paragraph, to "reconstruct in part the ancientness of the human presence in Angola. ... "[31] Later on in his analysis, Viteix declares that the knowledge of this history is more than just a reconstruction of the genealogy of Angola; it is also an art history that post-independence artists can look to for formal tools. Here he quotes Senegalese painter Papa Ibra Tall's contention that African artists have the advantage of making a "pilgrimage to the sources" of African art in order to find the technical tools for expressing a contemporary reality.

Viteix points to the functional affinities of rock art to contemporary public art. For instance, Viteix explains that the format of the mural in rock art is a natural precursor to the MPLA political murals in Luanda. Departing from the voice of empirical anthropology, Viteix argues that all art, ancient rock art included, is made out of a social necessity, "created under the immediate influence of historic and social facts."[32] However, some of its functional value lies for Viteix in its "magical" content, where the image serves to infuse the material world with immaterial powers. For Viteix, cave painting and its related forms in Egypt is motivated art work, and any formal changes represent a change in worldview and the needs of the population; even magic arises from historical contingency.

Two influences run through Viteix's theory of artists' relationship to Angolan cultural heritage: Agostinho Neto and Vladimir Lenin. From Lenin, Viteix adopted ideas about how to institutionalize art and his theories on the role of the state in perpetuating artistic production. He cautiously agrees with Lenin's theories, as he does with all socialist theories. He refuses to be in any way dictatorial about artistic production, even when placing it under the umbrella of the state. From Neto, he draws the spirit of the work by including themes of Africanity and the brotherhood arising from a shared African history and experience. He is also influenced by Neto's desire to attend to the cultural heritage of Angola through the active preservation of cultural patrimony. He then draws the tenets of that practice from various sources. *Theory and Practice*, recall, was written more than 20 years after the majority of nationalist texts on art during the 1960s independence decade in Africa. He also had at his disposal a developed body of literature on Luso-African nationalism that reached back as far as the late nineteenth century, starting with the subversive writings of José de Fontes Pereira. In addition to these, Viteix cites a wide swath of theorists such as Theodor Adorno, William Fagg, Ernst Fischer, Romano Luis, Ferreira Sousa, and Adolf Jensen.

A "new man" for Africa? 199

Regardless of, or perhaps due to, the eclecticism of his sources, Viteix's study is at base pragmatic and concerned with the systematic logic of Angolan art. *Theory and Practice* is an attempt to demystify Angolan art, to examine its basic elements in order to propose a functional future. From heterogeneity comes unity, and unity can be achieved only through the everyday actions of the "people." One section is telling in this regard. After his discussion of the various creator groups and their characteristics, Viteix transitions to the crucial part of Section Two entitled "Elements of Visions and Perceptions," where he makes the following introductory remarks:

> We are going to summarize some different domains of expression and of the realization of a traditional Angolan conception of World. We study modestly some of these elements from a religious setting to a more banal everyday setting.[33]

Viteix makes a tremendous claim here, the existence of an Angolan worldview. He presents such things as games, proverbs, religion, magic, and beliefs in order to demonstrate a unifying logic—the Angolan worldview is at once universal and specific.

The most powerful moment of this discussion directly follows his statement to look at the more mundane aspects of this worldview, or the everyday life of the "Angolan." Viteix discusses at length the various instances of games in Angola, countering a conclusion reached by Claude Lévi-Strauss in *The Savage Mind* that positions games against ritual. Ritual is structured to join together asymmetrically arranged groups, while games, inversely, go from symmetry to asymmetry, with a clear winner and a loser.[34] Viteix argues the obverse of Lévi-Strauss's conclusion, explaining that in Angola games require neither a winner nor a loser. Viteix seems to want to assign games the same purpose as Lévi-Strauss assigns to ritual—the binding of groups—without the supernatural associations of ritual. It is the everyday secular elements of games that Viteix suggests have the most binding power for Angolans, in that they employ a shared logic or structure.

Viteix discusses the example of Txela, which is a variation of mancala marble game found throughout the world. Viteix focuses on the Angolan identity of the game, stating, "the game of Txela confirms the relevance of the notion of unity in the Angolan territory."[35] He goes on, " ... it seems significant that this game represents, without elitism, the unanimity of preference in Angola." Here, he enacts exclusion in order to formulate national identity. Regardless of mancala's being found throughout the world, Viteix underscores the logical and popular *Angolan* aspects of the game based on both geography and shared sensibility—the existence of a commonality without the imposition of religion, ritual, or any form of governance. It is for this reason that Viteix points out the absence of a winner in these games. The realm of games and "fun" lacks any type of power play whatsoever. Thus the Angolan worldview is egalitarian. Viteix's conclusion concerning games in Angola:

"this exercise is the culmination of an attitude towards the universe, life and society, it represents a direct expression or compensation of daily behavior."[36] Like his vision of a new society, a New Man, the games are participatory and, most importantly, operate at the level of everyday behavior, or habit.

The sixth, seventh, and eighth parts of the book set out actual practices, after arguing the necessity of contemporary Angolan art. These sections include a discussion highly indebted to a classic text, Ernst Fischer's *The Necessity of Art: A Marxist Approach* (1963). After arguing that art represents the human ability to transform nature "through creative work and using the tools of labor," Viteix lays out concrete plans on how the government might facilitate art production.[37] Under this mandate, Viteix explains, the MPLA established the União Nacional Artistas Plasticos in 1977. He elucidates the goals of UNAP as described by the MPLA Worker's Party: to involve the public in Angolan art in order to transform Angolan mentality, to progressively transform heritage from bourgeois goods to serve a new society, and to create the conditions or infrastructure to transmit these ideas.[38] Viteix identifies three impediments to UNAP: lack of materials, lack of participation by the 120 members across the country, and lack of qualified teachers. All three of these impediments were devastating to UNAP's ambitious program, which in *Theory and Practice* includes plans to include painting, design, sculpture, to host conferences, and to exhibit artists from Nigeria, Yugoslavia, the Soviet Union, Cape Verde, Italy, Romania, Portugal, Mozambique, and Congo.

Like the two strains of *angolanidade* embodied by the work of Neto and Vieira, Viteix's study proposes the "path towards socialism," while also presenting the sobering realities of a struggling new nation. Additionally, Viteix avoids dogma of any kind and instead celebrates the debates that occur within the arts community. Such debates, he explains, are signs of democracy. *Theory and Practice* itself is dialectical in its description and its prescription alike: art and everyday life, the banal and the exceptional, Western art and traditional art, bourgeois art and popular art, and so on. Though Viteix strongly warns of the continuing "threat" of the West to Angolan art, his causes for concern stem from intent and power relations, and not necessarily from any inherent problems with form or medium.

Even as Viteix describes his view for revolutionary art in *Theory and Practice*, he concedes that "art cannot transform society, it can only raise awareness of its present state."[39] It is a stand-alone paragraph that contains only one other sentence and indicates Viteix's assertion of the limits of political art, which is presaged in his book by his criticism of the didacticism of socialist realism. The rest of this section is devoted to art in its power to create a new subjectivity, one that inevitably happens with socio-political sea changes and therefore the audiences for art. Bourgeois subjects in art will be replaced by images of workers, peasants, and the downtrodden. Viteix references Fischer's book *The Necessity of Art*, particularly the section in which

A "new man" for Africa? 201

Fischer declares that each change in power brings a spontaneous change in subjects, without theory or constraint. Viteix implies that this "new" art for the people is actually a return to art's primordial purpose, the necessity of art to create a mass consciousness. By making the masses the subject of art, the masses experience a new subjectivity.

Viteix does not ever truly define his use of the term "subject." Instead he positions the subject in Angolan art against the anti-colonial stereotype of Western art as bourgeois, illusionistic, and hopelessly wedded to photographic realism. He goes on to argue that "[t]he confusion between art and the representation of nature or of life is recent in the West and has contaminated all judgments and erected an impenetrable barrier between Art and the people."[40] Earlier in *Theory and Practice* Viteix argues against the view that Western art is the enemy to Angolan art, in that it provided certain formal tools for the African artist. Here, his attack is instead directed toward the illusionistic creation of the subject itself. The subject that is figured in this way, he suggests, is objectified, "reduced to figuration, to a faithful copy of forms condemned to immobility ... the values of photographic accuracy led the subject to be lost within [representations of] nature."[41] Thus, for Viteix, photographic realism operates from a logic of static relations that stymie dynamic social exchange, instead positioning subject and object on two sides of a falsely created reality. The very idea of representational art, therefore, was shot through with a politics that objectified whole populations.

Viteix's condemnation of Western illusionistic representation is dialectically related to his praise of African art, in which art we read that "the goal was never to satisfy a vain desire of imitation, and the figures of men or animals were never embedded in nature; if an element of landscape was used it was a symbol and to complete the meaning of the work. ... "[42] This piquing statement concerning vain imitation is one of the only clear definitions of what he means by the Western treatment of the subject, and helps unlock some of what is in his own art production. Instead of decrying what colonial anthropologists saw as the shortcomings of native representational techniques, Viteix understands the symbol itself as being a powerful visual communication device to unify the people. The very existence of the symbol, Viteix suggests, is indigenous to African art and indicates a shared knowledge that can be deployed by anyone who shares that logic.

Viteix's collaging of elements of representation, expressionist flux and ordered pictographic language can be related to something Ernst Fischer writes about art in his *Art Against Ideology* (1966):

> With the increasing division of labour, with the beginning of authority, the division into ruled and rulers, into those who serve and those who enjoy, into haves and have-nots, the memory of a lost paradise, or a golden age, of a time when work was not a curse but a humanizing personal activity, becomes an inexhaustible source for the imagination.[43]

One way of understanding the new humanism inherent in the idea of the New Man discourse could be understood as "imagination" as collage. To bypass a relatively short historical period of industrial capitalism, to resuscitate a memory believed to already exist in the minds of the people, opens up the imagination not to one particular style or idiom, but to a condition of artistic utopia where art was freed of its class-based constraints and the perils of ideology.

Fischer's evocation of labor is important here. In one particular artwork, Viteix addresses labor as dually utopian and dystopian. *Construção Civil (Antonio Cardoso) Tarrafal 2/10/71* (1985) [hereafter *Civil Construction*] (Figure 9.1) is an adaptation of the poem by anti-colonial activist poet Antonio Cardoso. Cardoso's poem addresses the labor of writing, its metaphorical connection to nation building, and the melancholy that accompanies doubt over the effectiveness of such work. Cardoso suggests that in this state of emergency, the vacuum of meaning, the writer doubts the effectiveness of words to describe his experience, but it is "by dreams and deeds only that I measure the path." He goes on, "And the words, I undertake to write … / Is not only for me that shared grief, / but I will also be in the promised / future that will for us be realized."[44]

Figure 9.1 Viteix, *Construção Civil (Antonio Cardoso) Tarrafal 2/10/71* (1985). Ink on paper, 65 by 50 cm. Author's photograph.

Viteix's adaptation of the poem consists of a type of construction scene within the grid frame in a style that recalls socialist realist or even futurist art and its commemoration of the worker. Various free-floating Chokwe pictograms—line, dot grid, target, chevron—indicate the work of linguistic production, the tie to Cardoso's poem. Viteix illustrates labor as a shared activity, a civil construction, with a definite structure. As his allusion to Cardosos' poem about writing affirms, signification is an important part of the subject matter of Viteix's paintings. His focus on the linguistic process capitalizes on the state of its emergency. Not only is each symbol given a framed space, but also, each symbol is drawn as a closed form with ambient space of color. His near-ritualistic placement of the symbols along the dimensions of the canvas and paper comes to attain in the course of this series a preciousness that marks again and again the loss of tradition. By remembering ethnic, or "Angolan," tradition, Viteix is also mourning the trauma of its near extinction by the Portuguese. He laments, "throughout the colonial period, there was an effort to devalue the high aesthetic of popular national creation, to reduce this creation to a simple exotic, primitive, and commercial element."[45] Art is not an abstract theoretical idea, but a power struggle with dire consequences for life and limb.

Viteix's *Civil Construction* is the work that best reveals the line that Angolan Marxists straddled: while Viteix's *Civil Construction* echoes socialist realist scenes of the heroic worker, labor itself becomes the subject of the work. Labor as pre-commodity, the process that in traditional economics determines the value of the commodity, is one of the baseline activities that unites Angolans and their socialist comrades. The extended title, which refers to the Tarrafal prison in Cape Verde where Cardoso wrote the poem, delivers a shock of irony when we realize that these workers could be forced laborers. In fact, irony was endemic to Tarrafal; it was in the village of Chão Bom [Good Ground] and on one of the lushest islands of Cape Verde; Cardoso describes his cell as a barren surface onto which he projects hope for a free Angola. Warning against the simplistic content of propaganda, Viteix instead illustrates the dangers of nominal political gestures in art, or in creating scenes that mask power relations and their ultimate consequence for the body. Viteix illustrates this bodily process, showing the workers undergoing action in *Civil Construction*. The bodies are integrated within the grid of the composition to the point of being inseparable from it. Like Cardoso, Viteix portrays the conditions out of which such heterogeneity arises in *Civil Construction*, which can be anything but unified and peaceful.

For Viteix, as for Cardoso and other anti-colonial activists who straddled a time of Portuguese state repression and the establishment of a new state, he was articulating the very language that would be "sayable" within a new regime, while acknowledging that those articulations could constrict the possibilities for artists. Within Viteix's own art, this reference to the corporeality of vision and meaning had another valence as his new nation was enduring the devastating corporeal results of a geopolitical conflict between "East and West," spoken of in terms of the Iron Curtain and all of its associations.

Maria Gough writes of the impulse to judge the failure or success of politically programmatic art in her narrative of Constructivist art in 1920s Soviet Russia, providing a useful perspective with which to end this chapter. She cites the three critical problems that historians frequently use to judge political art: formalism, functionalism, and failure.[46] In order to bypass such pitfalls of judgment, especially after revolutions are usurped and/or "fail," Gough instead turns her attention to how an artist's relationship to her/his work is reoriented and how that itself is revolutionary. Within the cultural statements, poetry, and visual art, Angolan activists attempted to reconfigure the conditions of representation, artistic and political. As in the title of Amilcar Cabral's 1966 speech, "The Weapon of Theory," Viteix and other anti-colonial activists and MPLA functionaries understood conceptual work as a key front of the struggle for independence. Visual artists used the (fictional) neutral space of the canvas to pictorially describe current conditions of Angola, and, as in *Civil Construction*, how developmental projects and politics engineered the body.

The strength of the rhetoric was inversely related to the weakness of the state. Any systematic social cohesion that the MPLA attempted was increasingly challenged by the violent clashes with UNITA. During the 1980s UNAP suffered from lack of materials and patrons as artists in Angola struggled to keep alive the idea of a unified cultural production, to even be able to envision the "people" within a violent civil war. Viteix passed away in 1993, having become a major figure in Angolan art, his murals and visage now part of a contemporary landscape in Angola that includes monuments made by North Koreans, gunshot-marked colonial buildings, and Mercedes dealerships—a collage of politics and perceptions, slogans, and bodies. We could say that this collage is the condition of post-socialism, but it also reflects Angola's history as the chaotic hotbed of the Cold War.

Notes

1. União Nacional de Artistas Plásticos (U.N.A.P.), "União Nacional de Artistas Plásticos – U.N.A.P.: Proclamação." Reprinted in *África: literatura: arte e cultura* 1:2 (October–December 1978).
2. Agostinho Neto, "The Proclamation of Independence," Speech given on 11 November 1975 in Luanda, Angola.
3. William Minter, *Operation Timber: Pages from the Savimbi Dossier* (Trenton: Africa World Press, 1988), 13.
4. Patrick Chabal, "Aspects of Angolan Literature: Luandino Vieira and Agostinho Neto," *African Languages and Cultures* 8:1 (1995): 34.
5. The bulk of critical writing on these early movements of Angolan nationalism has been on its literature, a preferential treatment that Marissa Moorman has lamented in its incomplete picture of early Angolan nationalism. Marissa Moorman, *Intonations: A Social History of Music and Nation in Luanda from 1945 to Recent Times* (Athens, Ohio: Ohio University Press, 2008), 57–58. Her important book

A "new man" for Africa? 205

and Adriano Mixinge's historiography of Angolan visual artists and their role in nationalism have helped us to fill out the picture of Angolan nationalism as a concerted effort to amass cultural capital in all of its forms.
6 For a more extensive examination of the trope of "return" in postcolonial literature, see Vera Mihailovich-Dickman, *Return in Post-Colonial Writing: A Cultural Labyrinth* (Amsterdam: Rodopi, 1994).
7 Jacueline Rose, *States of Fantasy* (Oxford: Clarendon Press, 1996), 3.
8 Donald Burness, *Fire: Six Writers from Angola, Mozambique, and Cape Verde* (Washington, D.C.: Three Continents Press, 1977), 7.
9 Quoted in Burness, xiii.
10 Michael Mahoney, "*Estado Novo, Homem Novo*: Colonial and Anti-colonial Development Ideologies in Mozambique, 1930–77," in Michael Latham et al. (eds), *Staging Growth: Modernization, Development, and the Globalization of the Cold War* (Amherst: University of Massachusetts Press, 2002).
11 Ernesto Che Guevara, "O Socialismo e o Homem em Cuba," Texto dirigido a Carlos Quijano, semanário Marcha, Montevideo. Março de 1965.
12 Amilcar Cabral, "The Weapon of Theory," address delivered to the first Tricontinental Conference for the Peoples of Asia, Africa and Latin America, Havana, January, 1966.
13 União Nacional de Artistas Plásticos (U.N.A.P.), "União Nacional de Artistas Plásticos – U.N.A.P.: Proclamação."
14 Ibid.
15 Departmento Nacional de Museus e Monumentos, "Manual de Museologia" (Luanda: Instituto Angolano do Livro, 1979), n.p.
16 Don Barnett and Spartacus Monimambu, *Interviews in Depth. MPLA-Angola #1: Sparticus Monimambu* (Richmond, B.C.: LSM Information Center, 1973), 25.
17 União Nacional de Artistas Plásticos, "União Nacional de Artistas Plásticos – U.N.A.P.: Proclamação."
18 Departmento Nacional de Museus e Monumentos, "Manual de Museologia," (Luanda: Instituto Angolano do Livro, 1979), 12.
19 Ibid., n.p.
20 Agostinho Neto, "On National Culture," Speech given to UAE January 8, 1979. Compiled in Agostinho Neto, *On Literature and National Culture* (Luanda: União dos Escritores Angolanos, 1979), 30.
21 Neto, "On Literature," speech given at UAE November 24 1977, 12.
22 Departmento Nacional de Museus e Monumentos, "Manual de Museologia," 26.
23 Ernesto Che Guevara, "El socialismo y el hombre en Cuba," in *Escritos y discursos*, vol. 8 (Havana: Ministry of Culture, 1977), 266–67.
24 "União Nacional de Artistas Plásticos – U.N.A.P.: Proclamação."
25 Albie Sachs, "Preparing Ourselves for Freedom: Culture and the ANC Constitutional Guidelines." Reprinted in *TDR* 35:1 (Spring 1991), pp. 187–93.
26 Ibid., 190.
27 Vitor Manuel Teixeira, *Pratique et Theorie des Arts Plastiques Angolais*. Departement Des Arts Plastiques. (Saint Denis, Universite de Paris VIII: Doctorate, 1983), 12.
28 Ibid., 10.
29 Ibid., 10.
30 Ibid., 10.
31 Ibid., 14.
32 Ibid., 81.
33 Ibid., 55.
34 Claude Lévi-Strauss, *The Savage Mind* (Chicago: University of Chicago Press, 1962), 32.
35 Teixeira, *Pratique et Theorie*, 55.

36 Ibid., 57.
37 Ibid., 287.
38 Ibid., 216.
39 Ibid., 243.
40 Ibid., 241.
41 Ibid., 241.
42 Ibid., 241.
43 Ernst Fischer, "Productive Memory," from *Art Against Ideology*, reprinted in Maynard Solomon, ed., *Marxism and Art: Essays Classic and Contemporary* (Detroit: Wayne State University Press, 1979), 272.
44 António Cardoso, "Construção Civil," *21 Poemas da Cadeia* (Luanda: União dos Escritores Angolanos, 1979), n.p.
45 Teixeira, *Pratique et Theorie*, 285.
46 Maria Gough, *The Artist as Producer: Russian Constructivism in Revolution* (Berkeley, CA: University of California Press, 2005), xiii.

Selected bibliography

Birmingham, David. *Empire in Africa: Angola and Its Neighbors*. Athens, OH: Ohio University Press, 2006.

Burness, Donald. *Fire: Six Writers from Angola, Mozambique, and Cape Verde*. Washington, D.C.: Three Continents Press, 1977.

Freire, Paulo. *Pedagogy of the Oppressed*. New York: Continuum Press, 2005 (30th anniversary edition).

Mihailovich-Dickman, Vera. *Return in Post-Colonial Writing: A Cultural Labyrinth*. Amsterdam: Rodopi, 1994.

Mixinge, Adriano. *Made in Angola: Arte Contemporânea, Artistas, e Debates*. Paris: L'Harmattan, 2009.

Moorman, Marissa. *Intonations: A Social History of Music and Nation in Luanda from 1945 to Recent Times*. Athens, Ohio: Ohio University Press, 2008.

10 The Cold War and Orange County

Dimitri Papandreu

Business is ~~business~~ politics

In 2010, at the largest public university in Orange County – California State University, Fullerton – in prelude to the laying off of scores of teachers, cancelling of hundreds of classes, cutting of all employees' salaries and increasing of students' tuition fees, a series of Strategic Planning Documents were circulated among administrators outlining measures to make the university more "competitive" in the academic "marketplace."[1] Although the documents advocated cutting programs in the Humanities, they made ample use of arguments and analogies from the Humanities curriculum in presenting their case. Of particular import was a certain esoteric analogy made between the United States' successful conduct of the Cold War and the conduct of a successful business:

> During the Cold War, strategists such as Dean Acheson and George C. Marshall realized that the economic defeat of the Soviet Union was just as important strategically as the threat of force. In doing so, they expanded the notion of strategy.[2]

The intended analogy was that the public university (now conceived as a commercial enterprise) should also realize that the "economic defeat" of its competitors (other universities) in the struggle to attract more "consumers"[3] (students) is just as important strategically as the threat of a serious education. In doing so, it would expand the notion of education to include "an Amazon like interface where students use shopping carts to select courses while observing the ratings presented by other students" and "dynamic" classrooms in which "students use handheld devises to interact with professors."[4] In this scenario befitting science fiction, public universities are markets for high-tech companies whose products are surrogates for the work of teaching and learning; education is defined in the terms of a consumer experience, with a stream of busy-work tacked on for the sake of keeping up the appearance of standards. The university's workforce (its teachers) is brought into line with the norms of neoliberal labor policies (precarious employment outweighing secure employment), and its principal duty becomes that of maintaining the "positive" customer service ambiance that is intended – like the fanfare of a fast-food restaurant – to distract the consumers from the fact that the commodity they are buying lacks any nutritive substance. But not to worry, according to the Strategic Planning Documents, students "do not understand the meaning of general education and they don't care too much."[5]

Dwelling upon historical themes, the Strategic Planning Documents make further disclosures regarding the Cold War, its outcome and its effect on the American public education system. In the succinct tone of serious business they convey the bottom line of the Cold War: capitalism won and socialism lost. For the sake of precision and not verbosity, let it be added that *neoliberal* capitalism won, and that this victory is evidenced not only in the defeat of socialism but also in the dismantling of workers' rights and public programs in the core capitalist countries – for example the system of public education in the United States. The Strategic Planning Documents are compelled to acknowledge that a significant de-investment from public education has indeed occurred in recent decades, and they contrast this to the policies of earlier times when, "faced with the Sputnik scare [...] better planning for higher education reached a desperate stage."[6] If it seems peculiar that the word "desperate" would be used to designate the period of better public funding for public education, let it be recalled that such ominous language is consistent with neoliberals' intent of casting a shadow of danger over all public services, which on more vociferous occasions they have simply referred to as "creeping communism." Continuing on, the Strategic Planning Documents recognize that the recent de-investment from public education has been predicated upon a broad cultural consensus that is "ideologically opposed to public education";[7] quite true, and indeed almost Gramscian in its recognition of the connection between cultural consensus and political policy. But by what means was this neoliberal cultural consensus formed? Here the historical analysis expounded by this business-educational document hits the brick wall of its own partisanship, which it can scarcely acknowledge in a bureaucratic discursive space that claims to "not deal with politics." The cultural consensus against public education was advanced not least of all by neoliberals using the public education system itself as an instrument to teach "ideological opposition" to public education. If one of the first steps in this strategy was the pre-emptive defunding of public education to validate the neoliberals' claim that public programs were inherent failures, the strategy's cornerstone in the past 20 years has been to transform the public school into a market space for corporations, where they have been able not only to sell their products but also to promote their "culture" – the culture of corporate integration – whose cost-efficient view of the world has carried the weight of an unequivocal reality principle. In other words, the cultural consensus against public education has been advanced in the public education system itself by pursuing the very strategies advocated in the Strategic Planning

Documents. While claiming to follow only a pragmatic approach to customer service (giving students the Bread-and-Circus education they demand) and to public service (complying with the "social mandate"[8] against public education), the Strategic Planning Documents inadvertently reveal the extensive preparatory work that neoliberalism has devoted to moulding the customers and the social mandate that it needs, that will be ventriloquists for its own ambitions.

The campuses of California State University, Fullerton and of Orange County's other public university, the University of California, Irvine, look like the hundreds of business parks and strip malls that cover their vicinities – with the same repressive "security" regulations in place that curtail free socialization, free speech and any other type of behavior that is not in line with corporations' atrophic vision of how a population should behave. In this uniform landscape that knows only differences of degrees (from wealthy to poor, but always under the same auspices) the tale of one corporation is worth that of a thousand others, as they are all animated by the same logic. The meaning of the events that transpire at California State University, Fullerton is no different from the stories that could be told by the workers in the business park down the street. Indeed, the ability to transpose the alienating experiences of the corporatized university to the corporate workplace proper is one of the main lessons imparted by this model of education. The essential features of the Strategic Planning Documents, with their fetish of technology, their biblical adherence to "private enterprise," their taste for military metaphors, their aggressive espousal of conformist behaviors and their transparent cynicism are indicative of the general quality of life in Orange County: they are a panegyric to its most ubiquitous "street level experiences." During the Cold War, when Orange County became an epicenter of the anti-communist proto-neoliberal Right, it also became a capitalist caricature of the very totalitarianism that its zealots railed against, no doubt as a diversionary measure. If once upon a time Orange County could distinguish itself from its liberal southern California neighbours by its conservative fanaticism, today the "Orange Curtain" that surrounded the county has receded into memory, together with that other curtain of Cold War notoriety: if not Orange County's right-wing fanaticism, then certainly the actual policies which it advocated – neoliberalism – have redefined the political, economic and cultural mainstream of American life since the presidency of Ronald Reagan.

The prophecies of Orange County

During the Cold War a chorus of writers reiterated one consistent assessment of Orange County's place in American history: its current state was a reliable prophecy of what awaited the nation at large. "Orange County may just possibly be the pattern of the far-out future,"[9] wrote *Newsweek* magazine in 1966; "Orange County is not so much joining the mainstream as charting its new direction,"[10] wrote the political scientist Karl Lamb in 1974; "Orange County is being held up as a model for the future development of Western

Civilization,"[11] wrote the cultural anthropologist Dean MacCannell in 1983. The art of prophecy began with an attention to the visceral in Orange County: the feeling of its streets, the physical presence of its residents and the content of their speech. From this pallet of impressions what awaited America was described as a "lunatic landscape,"[12] "a commercial for itself, endlessly replayed,"[13] where "everything is possible and nothing is real,"[14] and where "you learn to live without freedom while pretending otherwise."[15] The actual future that Orange County revealed was the one determined by the outcome of the Cold War, in which the struggle against communism was inseparable from the most reactionary capitalists' struggle against workers' rights and progressive social legislations in general. This important connection which defined anti-communism was made abundantly clear in the anti-communists' own pronouncements and policies. Take for example the words of R.C. Holies, the anti-communist editor of Orange County's largest newspaper, *The Register*:[16] "Tax supported schools violate the Ten Commandments and the Golden Rule," he said in 1966, and then advised that "the entire public-school system be handed over to private enterprise."[17] Or take the example of Jim Sleeper, a homespun local historian who in 1971 expressed Orange County's dominant political outlook in these terms:

> We are not fighting communism. We are promoting it – by political spending which punches hard at self-reliance, programs which aggressively make state dependents out of larger and larger parts of our population, tax laws which to a major degree nationalize property and wages, and by the veiled drive into welfare-state socialism which is, in fact, the over-all objective.[18]

The future that has come to pass with the defeat of "communism" (meaning everything that stood in the way of pathological capitalist accumulation) is one of depreciated wages and job insecurity, where all of culture is open to commercial speculation, where corporations are subject to no higher governing power, and where society is constantly being distracted from pursuing a sober understanding of itself: in a word, the neoliberal era. This is the America, and indeed the world, that Orange County prophesized and that its cold warriors fought hard to make a reality in their struggle against socialism, against concessions to the working class, against state regulation and against basic common sense.

But now, 20 years after the Cold War's end, triumphant neoliberalism has devolved into a catastrophic economic crisis that is confirming to the letter the essential features of another prophecy which the victors of the Cold War thought they had buried once and for all: that of Marxism. The inherent contradictions of capitalism have been given all the freedom they need to fully matriculate in the neoliberal era; indeed, this is what the previous era of capitalism – that of state monopoly regulation – sought to avoid. In developing its contradictions, neoliberal capitalism has conducted a most effective propaganda campaign against itself: it is held responsible for staggering levels of unemployment, for the "shrinkage of the American middle class," and for the perennial cloud of uncertainty that hangs over many people's heads. Even public opinion polls conducted by the pro-business magazine the *Economist* show that Americans' belief that "the free market system is the best" has fallen substantially from the end of the Cold War to the onset of the current crisis.[19]

Orange County, once a showpiece of homogeneous middle-class affluence, has not been immune from the current crisis. This is because Orange County's former affluence was made possible by the very policies which neoliberalism has dismantled: state subsidies and state investment in the economy. The suburban sprawl that began to cover Orange County at the dawn of the Cold War was inhabited by beneficiaries of the G.I. Bill, who received state assistance to buy homes and to pursue an education. The high-paying jobs in Orange County's gigantic military-industrial complex were also contingent upon lucrative government spending. The restaurants, amusement parks and shopping malls that proliferated here during the Cold War were directly dependent on the spending prowess of the core employment constituency in the military-industrial complex. The reversal in Orange County's fortunes can be dated specifically to the end of the Cold War and the abrupt withdrawal of state-dependent manufacturing from southern California. In 1988 military-related industries reached the pinnacle of their employment numbers, almost 100,000, making them by far the largest employers in Orange County.[20] Twenty years later, Orange County's largest employer was Disneyland, with 23,000 employees. According to Orange County's most recent "Community Indicators Report," the wages paid by Disneyland and other locally-based service industries are well below the prerequisite cost of living.[21]

In the post-Cold War era Orange County has become the object of a new kind of prophecy concerning America's future: that of increasing economic polarization. This polarization is evidenced along the county's north–south divide, where "you have areas of poverty and areas of great affluence and less of a middle,"[22] according to Michael M. Ruane, the director of the Orange County Community Indicators Project. In the southern cities with median family incomes over $100,000, like Irvine, Mission Viejo and Newport Beach, gated enclaves of bourgeois ennui have congealed around a cluster of new "high tech" industries and powerful real estate corporations. "High tech" in Orange County has always been synonymous with the production of weapons, and if during the Cold War these were weapons of war, today they are weapons of culture intended to impose an artificial model of life onto the popular mind. The leader of Orange County's new high-tech industries is Allergan Incorporated, the number one manufacturer of Botox in the world. It is closely followed by an entourage of video-game manufacturers, pharmaceutical companies and specialists in surgical weight loss and penis "enhancement." In the area of real estate, the Irvine Company and the Mission Viejo Company (a subsidiary of the Philip Morris Company) have built and governed entire "planned cities" along actual totalitarian lines, where every detail of life is set in accordance with the need to maintain inflated housing prices. While these real estate companies have been able to advertise their cities in the recent Botox-drenched television shows set in south Orange County,[23] the south county's most organic cultural product has been the barely articulate moan of alienation resounding from its young people who have looked for ways to escape from the velvet cage of total corporate control. The overriding sentiment of their hymns to despair is expressed by the artist Melanie Kloetzel, who writes that in Irvine "there is no experience of leaving the system, no ability to escape the eye of state control, no true space to wander."[24]

In the northern cities with poverty rates over 10 percent, like Santa Ana, Fullerton and Anaheim, low-paid service workers have made their homes in the former stomping grounds of the military-industrial complex's labor aristocracy. The majority of these new workers are Mexican-Americans of the first and second generations. They, together with a large contingent of Asian immigrants (including many refugees from the losing side of the Vietnam War) have consigned whites to a minority status in post-Cold War Orange County. As the *New York Times* reported in 2010, this demographic change is connected to "how the regional economy has changed, with the shrinking of the aerospace industry, which supported the once dominant, mostly white middle-class community here. That has largely been taken over by service [and] tourism."[25] Mexican and Asian immigrants have been present in Orange County since the late nineteenth century, when they formed the core of the agricultural working class in what used to be a county covered in orange groves. If during the Cold War the military-industrial complex and its accompanying suburban sprawl eclipsed agriculture and its low-paid immigrant workers from the landscape, in recent times the class and race relations of the pre-Cold War era have saliently reappeared: now as then, Mexican-Americans constitute a core element of the Orange County working class, whose lower wages and diminished rights are reinforced by this reactionary citadel's pervasive racism. "Hate Mexicans? *Hola* – that's the *real* county faith,"[26] writes the local historian Gustavo Arellano, referencing a prolific history of racism that he has brought to the public eye: from the 1920s, when the Ku Klux Klan held a preponderant number of local public offices to the 1990s, when the anti-immigrant – and anti-constitutional – California State Proposition 187 was spawned in Orange County. While being the consistent object of racism, the Mexican-American working class has also been the most progressive force in Orange County's history: from initiating the county's largest-ever strike in the 1930s, to leading the desegregation campaign in public schools in the 1940s,[27] to leading the rent strikes in Santa Ana's barrios in the 1980s,[28] to currently populating Orange County's universities with the common sense of its sons and daughters, who have most tenaciously seen through the contrived rhetoric of California State University, Fullerton's Strategic Planning Documents and their like.

"Orange County is the Ellis Island of the twenty-first century. What we've experienced in our century-and-change of official existence is coming to your town, if it's not there already,"[29] writes Arellano. The demographic changes that have occurred in Orange County since the end of the Cold War are indicative of a national trend: Latinos are the fastest growing ethnic group in America – from comprising 9 percent of the national population in 1990 they now comprise 17 percent.[30] Will the heirs to a proud tradition of resistance and alterity, now stronger in numbers, be able to alter the political balance of forces upon which neoliberalism is based, or will the ubiquitous instruments of cultural-ideological assimilation, of which Orange County is renowned, be able to neutralize their potentiality? This glimmer of hope, perhaps only a vain illusion, is the matter for another prophecy.

The nightmare of the Cold War

When George Orwell coined the term "Cold War" in 1945 he at once "de-centered" its concept from the prevalent understanding of the conflict between the two superpowers. The central conflict in the Cold War, according to Orwell, was not between the United States and the Soviet Union as the representative leaders of two qualitatively different social systems, but between the social categories of *oligarchy* and *the people*, which existed in both superpowers in undifferentiated form. Victory in the Cold War, Orwell warned, would belong to the more clever and efficient of the two oligarchies: the one most adept at dominating its own people in prelude to dominating the world. What most intrigued Orwell in this scenario, leading him to write *Nineteen Eighty-Four*, were the "ideological implications" of a successful oligarchical-totalitarian state, "at once *unconquerable* and in a permanent state of 'cold war' with its neighbors," in which "world-view," "beliefs" and "social structure" would all be determined by the caprices of an irrational central command composed of technocrats, military representatives and fanatical ideologues.[31]

In 1947 the liberal writer Walter Lippmann introduced Orwell's term to America by identifying its conceptual relevancy to specific features of American society: Lippmann identified the military-industrial complex (though not yet named) as the main oligarchically inclined force threatening "the American constitutional system"[32] of government, and he identified conservative evangelical Christianity (epitomized in the belief that "Providence"[33] guided America's crusade against communism) as the main ideology buttressing the military-industrial complex's oligarchical ambitions. Although Orwell's and Lippmann's founding texts on the problems of the Cold War can be criticized from a number of angles, they still succeed in presenting a clear picture of the Cold War's most impending nightmare, beyond the apocalypse of nuclear extermination: namely, the extermination of popular sovereignty and of common sense by fanatical militarized regimes intent on making Doublespeak the order of the day. While it would be patently false not to acknowledge the totalitarian features of the Soviet Union and its satellite states, it would be equally false not to acknowledge now, with the benefit of 20 years' hindsight, that they were comparatively less advanced than in the leading capitalist states that have survived the Cold War. The ease with which the communist regimes fell is indicative of their state ideology's comparatively weaker grip on the popular mind and of their police apparatuses' comparatively weaker resolve to engage in popular repression. Is a "transition to democracy" even imaginable today in a place like Orange County, where behind the veneer of democratic elections and a contented populace there clearly exists a capitalist oligarchy that acts with impunity, and a pervasive feeling of alienation and malice among its compliant subjects?

Orange County's neoliberal prophecy and Orwell's Cold War nightmare are one and the same thing. The paths of their historical realization are adjoined by aligning their most essential concepts. The history of capitalism's transparent political dictatorship in Orange County and its corresponding forms of cultural domination run parallel to the fulfilment of the successful oligarchical-totalitarian state envisioned by Orwell. This synchronicity, which has been recognized in both historiography and fiction, finds its clearest expression in Orange Countians' proverbial capacity for Doublespeak, that is, to make pronouncements that are strikingly irrational and self-contradictory. Orange County is "the place one immediately thinks of on hearing the phrase 'nut country,'"[34] wrote *Fortune* magazine in 1966; "the Orange County mind defends itself against the requirements of clear thinking,"[35] wrote Dean MacCannell in 1983. The flagship statement of Orange County's Doublespeak was its loud objection to "proto-communist big government," when in fact the federal military budget was the main source of the county's prosperity.[36] In studying the causes of Orange County's Doublespeak, even liberal non-Marxist writers were compelled to acknowledge the pervasiveness of *false consciousness* and to concede that the local form of self-understanding was warped by reactionary capitalist ideologies and the quarantine against challenging ideas.

An assault upon the people of Orange County

In 1981 *National Geographic* described Orange County as a blend of "feudal ranch life and Orwellian futurism."[37] Developing the meaning of this observation is the guiding thread of the following survey of Orange County history and of the writings devoted to it. The vestiges of feudal ranch life are to be found in the patriarchal authority of local capitalists and their orchestration of a religious form of cultural hegemony that allowed their opponents to be attacked with the same fervour as medieval heretics. These regressive features of Cold War Orange County life were inherited from the previous era in its history, when agriculture predominated. The class and race relations in Orange County's citrus groves were akin to those of the Confederate plantations from where many of Orange County's first capitalists came.[38] These capitalists' political sovereignty was predicated upon two things: the racist denial of elementary rights to the Mexican agricultural working class and the ideological indoctrination of whites into biblical submission by distinctively Southern means, namely evangelical Baptist churches and the Ku Klux Klan. There is an illustrative example of this point, whose recounting foretells the political and cultural arrangements that prevailed during the Cold War.

In the city of Fullerton in 1904 the powerful agricultural capitalist Charles Chapman was elected mayor after having financed the construction of the city's First Christian Church. By the 1930s Chapman had so impressively expanded his land holdings as to earn the title "Father of the Valencia Orange" and to be able to finance the construction of Orange County's first university, the California Christian College (later renamed Chapman University).[39] The capitalist propaganda that emanated from his church's pulpit and his university's classrooms came to be of crucial use to Chapman and his fellow landowners when, in 1936, a strike for improved wages and union recognition was organized by Mexican agricultural workers in the Fullerton-Anaheim area. Not only was the entire apparatus of state repression set in motion against the strikers, but also, to the amazement of the historian Carey McWilliams, who witnessed the strike, "400 special armed guards" composed mostly of "high school and college youngsters"[40] volunteered to assist the police in its campaign of reprisals. McWilliams marvelled at "how quickly social power could crystallize into an expression of arrogant brutality in these lovely, seemingly placid, outwardly Christian communities."[41]

The defeated strike of 1936 set the mould of Orange County's class relations for decades to come. The agricultural capitalists who had experienced a moment's fear during the strike took precaution against any future mobilization by farm workers: in 1942 the Bracero Program was inaugurated at their behest, which reduced the living and working conditions in agriculture to a carceral state while significantly increasing profit margins.[42] The Bracero Program was not repealed until 1964, by which time real estate investors had become the new masters of the land in Orange County. By explicitly undemocratic means the agricultural working class was denied political representation in Orange County, while the capitalists, supported by their loyal congregations, made the local government their exclusive country club. When the military industrial complex and its suburban accoutrements transformed Orange County's physical landscape in the 1960s they did not transform the essence of its political landscape. The oligarchical structure of feudal ranch life was preserved perfectly intact as the older generation of agricultural capitalists yielded the reins of power to a new generation of capitalists in industry, real estate and the service sector. The historian Spencer Olin characterized this transition as "intraclass conflict," noting that in Cold War Orange County political conflicts did not exist between "an owning class and working class," but only "within the owning class itself."[43] This was because the local capitalists, despite their differences, "had sufficient class consciousness," to understand that "the role of municipal and county governments in the capital-accumulation process [had to] be insulated as much as possible from popular political challenge."[44] In other words, the working class was still excluded from Orange County politics, whose parameters were defined solely by the conflicts between different factions of capital. On the American political map these conflicts were largely confined to the space between the moderate and extreme wings of the Republican Party. The older generation of agricultural capitalists congregated around the Republicans' extremist wing, where they espoused an "anti-statist" position in line with the tenants of contemporary neoliberalism. In the 1950s and 1960s this position was represented by the local congressman James B. Utt, whose family owned extensive orange groves in the city of Tustin.[45] In 1970 Utt bequeathed his congressional seat to the John Birch Society member John Schmitz, whose family developed business relations with the military-industrial complex. The new generation of capitalists tended to favor the Republicans' moderate wing, whose national spokesman was the Orange Countian Richard Nixon. These conflicts were eventually reconciled in the figure of Ronald Reagan, whose "moderate" Hollywood smile made his extremist agenda more palatable to a television-entranced electorate.[46] Reagan was unanimously endorsed by Orange County's leading capitalists, from the amusement park owner and John Birch supporter Walter Knott, to the fast-food chain owner and fellow John Birch supporter Carl Karcher, to the real estate tycoons Donald Bren of the Irvine Company and George Argyros of Arnel & Affiliates, all of whom made significant financial contributions to Reagan's presidential campaigns.

The strike of 1936 also marked the first appearance of anti-communism in the official Orange County lexicon, where it would remain a prominent fixture throughout the Cold War. "The whole strike is now an assault upon the people of Orange County by communist agitators,"[47] asserted Orange County Sheriff Logan Jackson, who was also the owner of abundant citrus groves in the vicinity of the strike. Regarded as a discursive act, anti-communism's meaning in Orange County can be explained by identifying who was talking to whom about whom: the accusation of communism was an ideological call-and-response, or rather a call to arms, issued from the pulpits of local capitalists to their flock of believers, who had been trained to understand the term as meaning "godless," which in their fanatical minds meant the object of legitimized and unrestrained violence. The actual targets of this accusation were not communists, since there were never many to be found in Orange County, but *the working class* and other progressive forces who dared to exist outside of the flock's ideological parameters, or, in what amounted to the same thing, outside of the capitalists' balance sheets. This scenario was replayed ad nauseam during the Cold War, when progressive educators were branded as communists simply for espousing secular ideas and supporting racial integration.[48] The prevalence of communist accusations against liberals was even parodied in the 1990s by the journalist Rebecca Schoenkopf, who anticipated the response to her liberal column in the *OC Weekly* with the title "Commie Girl in the OC."[49]

While anti-communism is essentially an anti-working class ideology, there were indeed many workers who participated in Orange County's anti-communist crusades. Anti-communist churches and their armed militia, the Ku Klux Klan, had a sizable working-class following in the years surrounding the strike of 1936.[50] During the Cold War these same churches operated a network of prayer groups inside weapons factories,[51] where high-paid workers were taught to identify American imperialism's global war against communism as the source of their personal prosperity.[52] Anti-communist workers conceived of their beliefs as adhering to their self-interests, and also as adhering to their desire for self-improvement, which typically meant accessing the individualistic dream of upward mobility. Although these beliefs bespeak an enormous amount of ideological indoctrination, it is nonetheless important to identify the material bases upon which they could stand their ground. Anti-communism in Orange County was the most successful in attracting a working-class following when it addressed categories of privileged workers whose self-interests could be narrowly construed as being in opposition to the most starkly exploited categories of the working class as a whole. The clearest manifestation of this cleavage within the working class, which anti-communism exploited to the fullest, was in the institution of white privilege. The defense of white privilege was used to turn white workers against "communist" Mexican workers when the latter mobilized for their rights, as was the case in the strike of 1936.[53] In a less transparent form, the defense of white privilege on a global scale informed the anti-communism of workers in the Cold War's military-industrial complex. These labor aristocrats of American imperialism earned their high standard of living by manufacturing weapons targeted not only against the Soviet Union, but also against revolutionary workers in Asia and Latin America who, in fighting for their countries' independence from Euro-American domination, were also fighting against the historical foundations of white privilege.

Besides opposing workers' solidarity through its attachment to white privilege, anti-communism strongly influenced the way workers conceived of their self-interests by reinforcing the religious veneration of wealth. In the moral universe constructed by the dominant institutions of culture in Orange County, cautionary tales of communist atrocities were paired with capitalist success stories of the Horatio Alger type. From elementary school to the university level, Orange County students were taught to admire and emulate the local "food visionary"[54] Carl Karcher of Carl's Jr. Enterprises, in whose official rags-to-riches biography there appeared no mention of his contributions to obesity and minimum-wage employment. In Orange County's most prominent churches, where the "Gospel of Wealth" was preached, workers learned that capitalists were "chosen people" and that their path to salvation consisted in emulating the capitalists.[55] In Orange County's two historical amusement parks, Disneyland and Knott's Berry Farm, idealized re-enactments of the golden ages of capitalist individualism were performed – from the colonial New England township to the nineteenth-century Western frontier – for families to discuss at home in conjunction with the anti-communist literature that was provided at the turnstiles.[56] In this environment, where the affirmative, pro-capitalist side of anti-communist ideology assumed the status of a cult, workers were compelled to measure not only their self-interests but also their self-worth according to an ecclesiastical model of virtue whose incarnate was the successful self-made man. This venerated figure was purportedly accessible to all, if only they heeded the "good news" of self-help books, positive-thinking advocates and motivational speakers.[57] However, these evangelists' teachings could easily transform into instruments of self-hatred, by the logic of their own unattainable standards. Financial success, held on a par with salvation, carried no material threshold whose crossing could be quantified in a given annual income: there was always more that *could* be attained, no matter how much was already attained. Financially well-off workers could scarcely count their blessings before doubts emerged regarding the veracity of their salvation, that is, the reliability of their generous sources of income.[58] In 1985 the *Orange County Register* reported that "money worries" were "the main cause of mental depression in Orange County," and that the way Orange Countians generally relieved their depression was "by going shopping."[59] The perennial clouds of insecurity and self-admonishment that hovered above the local cult of wealth were not there by chance. They were there by design, to ensure that workers who strived to join the company of the elect remained complacent and subservient to capitalist authority – the real dispensator of their religion – which cleverly advanced *its* self-interests through the perceived self-interests of others.

The smile

The qualities of Orwellian futurism that emerged within Orange County's oligarchical political framework can best be apprehended by proceeding from the question asked by Dean MacCannell after his visit to the corporately planned fiefdom of Irvine in the early 1980s: "what sort of humanity will this type of community produce?"[60] For a highly regulated social environment such as Irvine to unequivocally produce a new type of humanity according to its specific criteria implies a scenario that is deeply Orwellian in nature, namely, the obliteration of all pre-existing cultural values through which the immediate environment could be critically appraised and its direct encoding onto consciousness could be reasonably filtered. Yet this state of cultural vulnerability to the most transparent forms of social engineering is exactly what characterized the two million new arrivals to Orange County's expanding Cold War job market. Notwithstanding churches' attempts to foster a sectarian version of "cultural community" among the new arrivals,[61] their overriding experience was to live as "non-citizens" who, like "career military men," understood themselves only as "citizens of the industry in which they work, not of the particular community they happen to be in," according to the political scientist Richard Baisden.[62] Pursuing a solitary existence amidst millions of other isolated people, with their minds compactly immersed in the circuit board of work and domestic privacy, these new residents gradually severed their living connections to any cultural formation that preceded their immediate existence. In their depersonalized state of unmitigated exposure to the surrounding environment, which was amplified among their children who had never known anything else, the prevalent logic of commodity production could stamp itself firmly onto consciousness, rendering their thoughts and behaviors a mirror image of the corporate landscaping, fast-food products and advertisements that enveloped them.

The priority of exchange value over use value in commodity production was resonated in consciousness by the fetishistic concern for appearances over actual content. "What is socially important in Orange County is not actual values, but the public expression of inflated values. [...] In this system of expression, auto-referentiality is all that counts. We are to accept everyone's public self-accounting at 'face value', never subjecting the circumstances of life to alternative re-interpretation,"[63] writes MacCannell, accurately conveying the essence of the "Orange County state of mind." Orange Countians understood the difference between a hamburger's glossy billboard image and the muted colors of its physical reality, just as they understood the difference between a corporate suburb's superficial ambiance of serenity and the anxieties which it concealed in every household, but, in their self-presentation, they also understood that this difference was essential to maintain if they were to successfully "sell themselves" to others in social transactions. Hence their speech became an instrument for advertising a product – a life, a self – which possessed none of the qualities that it purported, or rather, possessed them only in the most nominal form – in the form of souvenirs rather than the accumulated experiences of a life's journey. This vacuous and cynical mode of existence was portrayed in Philip K. Dick's novel *A Scanner Darkly*, set in Orange County in the 1970s. Dick's character Donna Hawthorne confesses:

> "I am warm on the outside, what people see. Warm eyes, warm face, warm fucking fake smile, but inside I am cold all the time, and full of lies. I am not what I seem to be; I am awful." The girl's voice remained steady, and as she spoke she smiled. Her pupils were large and mellow and without guile. "But, then, there's no other way. Is there? I figured that out a long time ago and made myself like this. But it really isn't so bad. You get what you want this way. And everybody is this way to a degree."[64]

Jean Baudrillard, who visited Orange County several times during his American sojourns, parodied the depthless pretensions of this simulated smile:

> The smile of immunity, the smile of advertising: "This country is good. I am good. We are the best." [...] Smile and others will smile back.

> Smile to show how transparent, how candid you are. Smile if you have nothing to say. Most of all, do not hide the fact you have nothing to say nor your total indifference to others. Let this emptiness, this profound indifference shine out spontaneously in your smile. *Give* your emptiness and indifference to others, light up your face with the zero degree of joy and pleasure, smile, smile, smile ... Americans may have no identity, but they do have wonderful teeth.[65]

In Baudrillard's strategy of forcing simulations "into an over-existence,"[66] "the smile of advertising" is deliberately reduced to the most superficial dimension of its auto-referentiality, it is taken to hide nothing – unlike in Dick's writing, where the "real" Donna Hawthorne is still acknowledged beneath the opacity of her smile. By accelerating the logic of fake appearances to their most nihilistic conclusion, in which the critical capacity is yielded to purely aesthetic considerations, Baudrillard forebode a world akin to *Nineteen Eighty-Four*, where the ability to discern meaning beneath propagandistic images is also conspicuously absent. The same cautionary tone resounds in Kim Stanley Robinson's 1988 novel *The Gold Coast*, in which Orange Countians are "sleepwalkers" who respond mechanically to the solicitation of images: "It's all aesthetics for you. I don't suppose you really believe in anything at all. It's just whatever attracts the eye,"[67] says the protagonist to his friends, while actually directing his admonishments to himself. Later in the novel, when he is in a less self-righteous mood, the protagonist concedes that there is in fact no escaping from the Orange Curtain's vortex of images:

> You can pretend not to care about the image, but that's as far as the culture will let you get. Inside you have to feel it; you can fight it but it'll always be there, [in its] contemptuous dismissal of you.[68]

The production of false consciousness in Orange County is the central theme of both *A Scanner Darkly* and *The Gold Coast*. In both novels the main characters are young Orange Countians whose drug-induced states of altered reality are allegorical of the general state of impaired perception. In *A Scanner Darkly* the drug "Substance Death" provokes a neurological disassociation that differs by only a few degrees from the "normal" condition of Orange Countians accustomed to living a double life between their public persona and real self. In *The Gold Coast* the main characters are never without eye-droppers containing a drug that distorts their vision in unison with the "bald-faced denial of reality" and "group hallucination shared by everyone in America."[69] At the conclusion of both novels it is revealed that the drugs are manufactured by state-affiliated corporations who deploy them as instruments of social control; their purpose is to deprive their consumers of the ability to comprehend themselves and their society in equal measure, thereby rendering them politically powerless. The characters' cognitive enclosure in the drugs' subjective experience, which makes them oblivious to the drugs' objective political meaning, is a metaphor of the false consciousness propagated by the wall-to-wall advertising, solitary suburban confinement, religious fanaticism and anti-communism that distinguished Cold War Orange County as a harbinger of the neoliberal future. In that future, an oligarchy of smiling businessmen and statesmen endeavored to achieve the Orwellian nightmare of reducing an entire population to pure and utter passivity, or worse, to unconscious participation in their own enslavement. In 1966 the most mainstream of magazines, *Newsweek*, offered this bleak summary of Orange County's political life, which still holds true today:

> Almost nobody presses the powers in Orange County. Almost nobody cares to. The basic thing about most Orange Countians is that they have turned inward, toward their own families, their own jobs, on matters of civic interest they allow themselves to be led by those who care. And in Orange County, those who care can give those who don't just about whatever they want.[70]

That joke isn't funny anymore

The fact that Orange County could be described as "something of a joke"[71] by even *Fortune* magazine in the 1960s implies that the way Orange Countians understood themselves was not yet shared by a definitive portion of the American public. The coalition of feudal ranch life and Orwellian futurism that prevailed in Orange County was rarely accepted on its own terms by non-indoctrinated observers; its façade of obsessive normality did not so much shield its cultural problems from scrutiny as stand out as one of their most obvious expressions. If the Orwellian nightmare was easily detectable in Cold War Orange County, a qualitative leap in its realization occurred when its detection fell out of vogue, that is, when Orange County's cultural anomalies were no longer recognized as such but were instead taken at their most ingenuous face value. In the body of literature devoted to Cold War Orange County, this dramatic shift in perspective occurred after the Cold War's end, when cautionary tales of the most advanced forms of capitalist alienation began to give way to flaccid reassurances that Orange Countians were in fact rational people. The direction of this shift, in which critical distance disappeared into the obliviousness of self-referentiality, was indicative of the general cultural realignment that accompanied neoliberalism's political triumph. The cultural decline of Marxism that paralleled the political defeat of communism saw the emergence of new methodological approaches in scholarship – such as postmodernism and a redundant form of empiricism – whose strategies of "empowering" their objects of research differed very little from the clichés of advertising agencies. In the writings devoted to Cold War Orange County these historically contingent methodological shifts were apparent in the move from *false consciousness* to *conservatism* as the axiomatic question of Orange County's cultural life. To assert that Orange Countians were simply "conservative" by rational choice or by virtue of their Midwestern and Southern roots, while downplaying the intensive ideological manipulation to which they were subject, was to endow the locally prevalent form of self-understanding with a coherency that, by any critical standard, it did not merit – and yet this is exactly what several recent historians of Cold War Orange County have done, most notably Lisa McGirr in her indulgent family portrait of the local "grassroots" "community" of reactionary fanatics, *Suburban Warriors*.[72] The fulfilment of Orange County's neoliberal prophecy has seen the edification of new cultural norms for which Orange County itself is the prototype. In passing from laughing stock to mainstream, the path that Orange County has followed has been paved by the dismissal of the critical capacity and the erasure from memory of the many warning signs posted by writers of the previous decades. Today, as Orange County is besieged by a new set of problems that have issued forth from its own neoliberal hand, it can only struggle to maintain its normative ambiance by enforcing an ever more draconian conspiracy of silence – to which there are few objectors.

Notes

1 Michael Parker, "Strategic Planning Activities 10-08 to 9-09," California State University, Fullerton, 2009, pp. 3–4. Online. Available at http://www.fullerton.edu/wasc/cpr/CWP/CWP-3_Summary_of_Strategic_Planning_Final.pdf (accessed 7 July 2010).
2 Parker, "Strategic Planning Activities 10-08 to 9-09," p. 4. The nature of this "economic defeat" is not specified, but it can be inferred from the historical record that it consisted of the escalation of the arms race (of which Orange County, the home of a large branch of the military industrial complex, was a chief beneficiary) and the stimulation of the consumer economy (a *cultural* strategy, also pivotal to Orange County).
3 Parker, "Strategic Planning Activities 10-08 to 9-09," p. 92.
4 Michael Parker, "President's Planning Retreat, Pre-event Readings," California State University, Fullerton, 20 January, 2010. Online. Available at http://makebelievecommittee.wordpress.com/2010/02/23/csuf-planning-committee-deems-humanities-esoteric/ (accessed 7 March 2010).
5 Parker, "Strategic Planning Activities 10-08 to 9-09," p. 33.
6 Parker, "Strategic Planning Activities 10-08 to 9-09," p. 9.
7 Michael Parker, "Integrated Strategic Plan," California State University, Fullerton, March 10, 2011, p. 26.
8 Parker, "Integrated Strategic Plan," p. 10.
9 "Orange County – A Little Piece of America," *Newsweek*, 14 November, 1966, p. 32.
10 Karl Lamb, *As Orange Goes: Twelve California Families and the Future of American Politics* (New York: Norton, 1974), 5.
11 Dean MacCannell, *Empty Meeting Grounds: The Tourist Papers* (New York: Routledge, 1992), 79.
12 Sheldon Zalaznick, "The Double Life of Orange County," *Fortune*, October 1968, 140.
13 Philip K. Dick, *A Scanner Darkly* (New York: Pantheon Books, 2006), 31.

The Cold War and Orange County 223

14 Edward Soja, "Inside Exopolis: Scenes from Orange County," in M. Sorkin (ed.) *Variations of a Theme Park: The New American City and the End of Public Space* (New York: Hill and Wang, 1992), 121.
15 MacCannell, *Empty Meeting Grounds*, p. 85.
16 In 1985 *The Register* was renamed *The Orange County Register*.
17 "Orange County – A Little Piece of America," 32. Inspired by Holies' ideas, the Orange County-based Howard Jarvis Taxpayers Association spearheaded the 1978 campaign to pass California State Proposition 13, which significantly reduced the funding to public schools derived from property taxes. The astronomical decline of California public schools that resulted from this measure, which is evidenced in virtually every national survey of public education, contributed to the growth of private schools – just as Proposition 13's partisans had intended.
18 Jim Sleeper, *Jim Sleeper's 1st Orange County Almanac of Historical Oddities* (Trabuco Canyon, CA: Ocusa Press, 1971), 17.
19 "Capitalism's Waning Popularity," *The Economist*, 7 April 2011. Online. Available at http://www.economist.com/node/18527446 (accessed 2 March 2012).
20 Spencer C. Olin, "Globalization and the Politics of Locality: Orange County, California, in the Cold War Era," *The Western Historical Quarterly* 22, no. 2 (May 1999): 152.
21 Orange County Community Indicators Project, *Orange County Community Indicators 2011*, pp. 22–23. Online. Available at http://egov.ocgov.com/vgnfiles/ocgov/CEO/Docs/2011%20Community%20Indicators.pdf (accessed 5 January 2012). The state's role in the local economy was further diminished when Orange County declared bankruptcy in 1994. The bankruptcy was used as a pretext for privatizing many of the county's public services. M. Davis, "Rotten Orange County: Bankruptcy on the Backs of the Poor," *The Nation*, 30 January 1995, pp. 121–22.
22 Adam Nagourney, "Orange County is No Longer Nixon County," *New York Times*, 29 August 2010. Online. Available at http://www.nytimes.com/2010/08/30/us/politics/30orange.html?_r=1&emc=eta1 (accessed 5 November 2010).
23 Most of these television shows have the words "real" and "OC" in their titles.
24 Melanie Kloetzel, "A Trek through Pseudo-Utopia: Irvine, CA and Beyond," *EnterText* 5.2 (Winter 2005). Online. Available at http://arts.brunel.ac.uk/gate/entertext/issue_5_2.htm (accessed 12 July 2011).
25 Nagourney, "Orange County is No Longer Nixon County."
26 Gustavo Arellano, *Orange County, A Personal History* (New York: Scribner, 2008), 11.
27 The 1946 federal court case of Mendez v. the Westminster School District was a decisive event in the desegregation of public schools in Orange County. G. Arellano, "OC's Famous Desegregation Case Finally Gets Its Historical Due, But One Family Feels Left Out," *The OC Weekly*, 5 November 2009. Online. Available at http://www.ocweekly.com/2009-11-05/news/mendez-estrada-guzman-palomillo-ramirez-westminster-santa-ana-garden-grove-el-modeno-school-districts/ (accessed 7 March 2010).
28 Lisbeth Haas, "Grass-Roots Protest and the Politics of Planning: Santa Ana, 1976–88," in *Postsuburban California: the Transformation of Orange County since World War II*, (ed.) Rob Kling, Spencer Olin and Mark Poster (Berkeley: University of California Press, 1995), 254–80.
29 Arellano, *Orange County, A Personal History*, p. 13.
30 United States Census Bureau, "The Hispanic Population: 2010," May 2011. Online. Available at http://www.census.gov/population/www/socdemo/hispanic/hispanic_pop_presentation.html (accessed 10 January 2012).

31 George Orwell, "You and the Atomic Bomb," *The Tribune*, 19 October 1945. Online. Available at http://tmh.floonet.net/articles/abombs.html (accessed 14 July 2011).
32 Walter Lippmann, "The Cold War," *Foreign Affairs* 65, no. 4 (Spring 1987): 872. Lippmann's warning was echoed in Dwight Eisenhower's 1961 Farewell Address to the Nation, in which he coined the term *military industrial complex*.
33 "It may be that Mr. (George Kennan) has read the mind of Providence and that he knows what history plainly intended. But it is asking a good deal that the American people should stake their 'entire security as a nation' upon a theory which, as he himself says, cannot be proved and cannot be disproved." Lippmann, "The Cold War," 871.
34 Zalaznick, "The Double Life of Orange County," 138.
35 MacCannell, *Empty Meeting Grounds*, 78.
36 "[Orange County] conservatives' ideological attack on 'big government' is a simple displacement, a pre-emptive strike against the government as a way to avoid having to credit government for schemes and accomplishments they want to call their own." MacCannell, *Empty Meeting Grounds*, 80. "The contradiction between conservatives' anti-statist rhetoric and their embrace of a strong defense was easily elided in a land whose prosperity was built on the military-industrial complex." Lisa McGirr, *Suburban Warriors: The Origins of the New American Right* (Princeton, N.J.: Princeton University Press, 2002), 174. "Until recently [Orange County] was [...] to a large extent, dependent on massive federal military expenditures (a fact that is strikingly at odds with its laissez faire political culture.)" Olin, "Globalization and the Politics of Locality," 145.
37 Judith and Neil Morgan, "Orange, a Most California County," *National Geographic*, December 1981, 750.
38 Gustavo Arellano, "The KKK Took My County Away: Meet the Klansman Who Helped to Found Orange County," *The OC Weekly*, 17 April 2008. Online. Available at http://www.ocweekly.com/2008-04-17/news/the-kkk-took-my-county-away/ (accessed 7 January 2010).
39 Susie Dittmar, "C. C. Chapman: A True Fullerton Story," *Fullerton Stories*, 19 March 2011. Online. Available at http://fullertonstories.com/c-c-chapman-a-true-fullerton-story/ (accessed 4 December 2012).
40 Carey McWilliams, *Factories in the Field, the Story of Migratory Farm Labor in California* (Berkeley: University of California Press, 1999), 250.
41 Carey McWilliams, *Southern California, an Island on the Land* (Santa Barbara: Peregrine Smith, 1973), 220.
42 Lisbeth Haas, *The Bracero in Orange County: A Work Force for Economic Transition* (San Diego: Program in United States-Mexican Studies, University of California, San Diego, 1981).
43 Spencer Olin, "Intraclass Conflict and the Politics of a Fragmented Region," in *Postsuburban California: the Transformation of Orange County since World War II*, 223–24.
44 Olin, "Intraclass Conflict and the Politics of a Fragmented Region," 225–29.
45 McGirr, *Suburban Warriors: The Origins of the New American Right*, 33.
46 Mike Davis, "The New Right's Road to Power," *New Left Review* 128 (July–August 1981): 28–49.
47 Gustavo Arellano, "Gunkist Oranges," *The OC Weekly*, 8 June 2006. Online. Available at http://www.ocweekly.com/content/printVersion/47719/ (accessed 15 November 2011).
48 Particularly infamous is the case of Joel Dvorman, who was branded a communist-sympathizer and recalled from the Magnolia School District's board of trustees in 1960 after hosting an event of the American Civil Liberties Union at his home. R. Bernhagen, "The Magnolia School District: A Case Study in Neo-McCarthyism

The Cold War and Orange County 225

in Contemporary America," Master's thesis, California State College, Fullerton, 1966.
49 Schoenkopf's articles have been published in a book by the same name. Rebecca Schoenkopf, *Commie Girl in the OC* (New York: Verso, 2008).
50 Christopher N. Cocoltchos, "The Invisible Empire and the Search for the Orderly Community: The Ku Klux Klan in Anaheim, California," in *The Invisible Empire and the West: Toward a New Historical Appraisal of the Ku Klux Klan of the 1920s*, (ed.) Shawn Lay (Urbana: University of Illinois Press, 1992), 97–120.
51 Darren Dochuk, *From Bible Belt to Sunbelt: Plain-Folk Religion, Grassroots Politics, and the Rise of Evangelical Conservatism* (New York: Norton, 2011), xiv.
52 McGirr, *Suburban Warriors: The Origins of the New American Right*, 29–30.
53 McWilliams, *Southern California, an Island on the Land*, 219–20.
54 Mimi Ko Cruz, "The Carl's Jr. Legacy," *Inside California State University, Fullerton*, 30 March 2010. Online. Available at http://calstate.fullerton.edu/news/Inside/2010/carls-jr-legacy.html (accessed 5 April 2010).
55 Barbara Ehrenreich, *Bright-Sided: How Positive Thinking Is Undermining America* (New York: Metropolitan Books, 2009), 97–146.
56 McGirr, *Suburban Warriors: The Origins of the New American Right*, 99–100.
57 Ehrenreich, *Bright-Sided*, 147–76.
58 Zalaznick, "The Double Life of Orange County," 184–86.
59 MacCannell, *Empty Meeting Grounds*, 77.
60 MacCannell, *Empty Meeting Grounds*, 88.
61 Dochuk, *From Bible Belt to Sunbelt*, xxiii.
62 Zalaznick, "The Double Life of Orange County," 184–89.
63 MacCannell, *Empty Meeting Grounds*, 77–78.
64 Dick, *A Scanner Darkly*, 257.
65 Jean Baudrillard, *America* (New York: Verso, 1988), 34.
66 Jean Baudrillard, *The Ecstasy of Communication* (New York: Semiotext(e), 1988), 97.
67 Kim Stanley Robinson, *The Gold Coast* (New York: ORB, 1995), 40.
68 Robinson, *The Gold Coast*, 285.
69 Robinson, *The Gold Coast*, 243.
70 "Orange County – A Little Piece of America," 32.
71 Zalaznick, "The Double Life of Orange County," 140.
72 McGirr, *Suburban Warriors: The Origins of the New American Right*, 4–11. Other recent historians of Orange County who have assumed a normalizing tone in their writings are: Christopher Cocoltchos in "The Invisible Empire and the Search for the Orderly Community: The Ku Klux Klan in Anaheim, California," and Darren Dochuk in *From Bible Belt to Sunbelt: Plain-Folk Religion, Grassroots Politics, and the Rise of Evangelical Conservatism*.

Selected bibliography

Arellano, Gustavo. *Orange County: A Personal History*. New York: Scribner, 2008.
Batalov, Eduard. *The American Utopia*. Moscow: Progress Publishers, 1985.
Baudrillard, Jean. *America*. New York: Verso, 1988.
Ehrenreich, Barbara. *Bright-Sided: How the Relentless Promotion of Positive Thinking Has Undermined America*. New York: Metropolitan Books, 2009.
Hargrove, Kristin. "Sunpist: Exploring the Alienation Resulting from Orange County's Post-World War II Development." Master's thesis, California State University, Fullerton, 2005.

MacCannell, Dean. *Empty Meeting Grounds: The Tourist Papers.* New York: Routledge, 1992.

Nikitin, Vyacheslav. *The Ultras in the USA.* Moscow: Progress Publishers, 1981.

Olin, Spencer, "Intraclass Conflict and the Politics of a Fragmented Region," in R. Kling, S. Olin and M. Poster (eds.) *Postsuburban California: the Transformation of Orange County since World War II.* Berkeley: University of California Press, 1995.

Robinson, Kim Stanley. *The Gold Coast.* New York: ORB, 1995.

Sogomonov, Y. and Landesman, P. *Nihilism Today.* Moscow: Progress Publishers, 1977.

Index

Italicised page numbers refer to figures.

ABCC (US Atomic Bomb Casualty Commission), 23–24
activism
   attempts to establish a Peace Movement in Latin America, 170–78, *172*
   after the Bikini Incident, 20–24
AFL, and labor communism, 101–3, 110–11
Aflatun, Inji, 61
Altman, Mischa, 109
American Federation of Musicians (AFM), 103–4
Andropov, Yuri, 3
Angola
   angolanidade, 189
   civil war, 188–89
   cultural policy, 195–201
   Mensagem, 189
   museum program, 192–98
   UNAP, 191–92
   withdrawal of Portugal, 188
angolanidade, 189
anti-communism
   and female terrorists, 131–34
   in Mexico, 171–74
   use of term, 125–26
   see also communism
anti-feminism
   and female terrorists, 131–34
   use of term, 125–26
   see also feminism
anti-feminist communists, 59–62
anti-imperialism *see* imperialism
anti-nuclear movement
   affiliated constituencies, 21–22
   after the Bikini Incident, 20–24

Arciniegas, Germán, 167
Asia–Africa Conference (Bandung 1955), Suharti's speech, 38–39
Asian studies
   and China, 153–55
   field of, 151–52
Atomic Bomb Casualty Commission (ABCC), 23–24
atomic bomb, meanings attached to, 18–20

Baráibar, Carlos de, 178
Baudrillard, Jean, 219–20
Bikini Incident
   anti-nuclear protests following, 20–24
   and Test Bravo, 18–20, 41–42
Bioff, Willie, 105
bombs *see* atomic bomb
Bond, James (fictional character), 132–33
Brazil, attempt to establish a Peace Movement in, 170–71, *172*
Broyelle, Claudie, 161–62
Bulletin of Concerned Asian Scholars (*BCAS*), 147–48
   see also Concerned Asian Scholars (CAS)
Burnham, James, 167

Cabral, Amilcar, 191
California State University, Fullerton, as a commercial enterprise, 207–9
   see also Orange County
El Campesino, 180–81
Cell, Chuck, 152–53
Chapman, Charles, 215
"Che" Guevara 6, 191

Index

Chesneaux, Jean, 159
Chile
  attempt to establish a Peace Movement in, 175–78
  Project Camelot in, 1–2
China
  and Asian studies, 153–55
  Cultural Revolution, 148–49
  as a destination, 155–58
  as a model, 149–53
  post-Mao, 160–63
  women in, 161–62
Cincera, Ernst, 130–31
citizen watch groups, and female terrorists, 129–31
citizens, individual
  and the image of female terrorists, 134–36
  surveillance practices of, 136–38
Civil Construction (Viteix 1985), *202*, 202–4
civil liberties, and Reagan, 112–17
clubs, and "culture circles", 85
colonialism, in Indonesia, 32–38
Committee of Concerned Asian Scholars (CCAS), 147–63
Committee on Un-American Activities of the US House of Representatives *see* House Un-American Activities Committee (HUAC)
communism
  and feminism, 59–62
  and happiness, 80
  in Indonesia *see* PKI
  in Japan, 24
  and the labor movement, 85–88
  views of, 22
  women's activism perceived as, 54–55
  see also anti-communism
communist unions, and Tenney, Jack, 107–12
Concerned Asian Scholars (CAS), 147–63
Conference of Studio Unions (CSU), 113–14
Confrontation campaign, 43
Congress for Cultural Freedom (CCF), 179–82
Construção Civil (Antonio Cardoso) Tarrafal 2/10/71 (Viteix 1985), *202*, 202–4
Continental Cultural Congress (CCC), 175–79
Cuba, anti-feminist communists in, 59–60

cultural identities, in Hungary, 84–85
Cultural Revolution, in China, 148–49
culture circles, 85

Deng Xiaoping, 161
Dick, Philip K., 219
Dies, Martin, 107
Dutch Women's Movement (*Nederlands Vrouwen Beweging*), support for Indonesia, 41
Dutschke, Rudi, 129–30

Edelman, Fanny, 64–66, *64*
Edwards, Jorge, 177–78
enemies of the state, elimination of, 80–82
Espín, Vilma, 59–60

Fact-Finding Committee on Un-American Activities, 99
Fairbank, John K., 158–59
fascism, in Spain, 58–59
father-party-family, symbolism of, 89–90
female terrorists
  and citizen watch groups, 129–31
  and individual citizens, 134–36
  surveillance of, 136–38
feminism
  and communism, 59–62
  and internationalism, 46
  see also anti-feminism
feminization of opponents, 125
Flynn, Elizabeth Gurley, 60
FMC, 60
Foucaultian notion of power, 124–25
FRELIMO party, 190
From Russia with Love (1963), 132–33

geography, complexities of, 6–7
Gerwani
  affiliation with the WIDF, 32–38
  end of, 47
  growth of, 31–32
The Gold Coast (Robinson 1988), 220
Gompers, Samuel, 101, 102
González, Valentín "El Campesino", 180–81
Gorkin, Julián, 180–82
Great Leap Forward, 151
Guevara, Ernesto "Che", 6, 191
Guided Democracy, political system of, 40
Gurley, John, 152

happiness
  fabricated culture of, 78–85
  in Orange County, 218–21
  and women, 80
Hatch Act (1939), AFL support of, 110
Holies, R.C., 210
Hollywood, unions in, 104–7
Hollywood Independent Citizens Committee of the Arts, Sciences, and Professions (HICCASP), 112
Homem Novo, discourse of, 10, 187–88, 191
Hook, Sidney, 167
Horchem, Hans Josef, 134–36
House Un-American Activities Committee (HUAC), 107
  following of WIDF campaigns, 54–55
human rights, as women's rights, 65–66
Hungarian Peoples' Republic, establishment of, 86
Hungarian Workers' Party (*Magyar Dolgozók Pártja* or MDP), 86
Hungary
  cultural identities in, 84–85
  Stalinism in, 76–85
  support of the Cold War in, 77
hydrogen-bomb testing, 15

IATSE, 105, 113
imperialism, in Indonesia, 40–46
individual citizens
  and the image of female terrorists, 134–36
  surveillance practices of, 136–38
Indonesia
  communism in, 33–35
  Confrontation campaign, 43
  Round Table Agreement (1949), 34–35
  support of Dutch Women's Movement, 41
Indonesian Communist Party (*Partai Komunis* Indonesia, PKI) *see* PKI
Indonesian Women's Congress (Kowani) *see* Kowani
Indonesian Women's Movement (*Gerakan Wanita* Indonesia– Gerwani) *see* Gerwani
Information Group of Switzerland, 130–31
Institute for the Study of Contemporary Political Questions, 131–32, 135–36
International Alliance of Women (IAW), 53

International Association of Theater and Stage Employees (IATSE), 105, 113
international politics, transition in, 148–49
International Women's Year (IWY), 65–66
internationalism, and feminism, 46

Japan Communist Party, 24
Japan Socialist Party, 24
Johnson-Odim, Cheryl, 61–62

Kádár, János, 86
Karl, Rebecca, 160
Koikari, Mire, 46
Korea, WIDF campaign for peace in, 57
Kowani, affiliation with the WIDF, 33

labor communism, 85–88, 101–3
labor movement
  anti-communism in, 100–101
  establishment of, 86
Latin America
  communism in, 177
  Continental Cultural Congress (CCC), 175–79
  propaganda in, 179
Laville, Helen, 46–47
Lerner, Gerda, 55
Limited Test Ban Treaty (LTBT), 16–17
Linares, Francisco Walker, 178
Lippmann, Walter, 213
Lucky Dragon Number 5
  museum, 25–27
  restoration of, 24–25

MacCannell, Dean, 218–19
Machel, Samora, 190
Magurozuka see tuna mound
Maoism, demise of, 160–63
  see also China
Marxism, 191
masculinization of opponents, 125
maternalism, and access to global political networks, 62–65
McCarthyism, and the Lucky Dragon crew, 23
McWilliams, Carey, 215
Mensagem, 189
Merchán, Paquita, 59
Mexico, attempt to establish a Peace Movement in, 171–74
militarism, in Indonesia, 40–46

Movimento Popular de Libertação de Angola (Popular Movement for the Liberation of Angola, MPLA), 192–93
Mozambique, 190
MPLA, 192–93
Mudigdo, at the fourth WIDF Congress, 39–40
museums
 in Angola, 192–98
 peace museums, 25–26

National Union of Angolan Plastic Artists (UNAP), 191–92
Neruda, Pablo, 171–72, 175–76
Neto, Agostinho, 188–90
New Deal labor policy, 106
New Man, discourse of, 187–88, 191
Nixon, Richard, 116
nuclear energy, Japanese acceptance of, 28
nuclear weapons
 in Indonesia, 40–46
 testing, 16–17

Ōishi Matashichi, 17–18, 26–27
OMGUS (US Office of Military Government), 56
Orange County
 California State University, Fullerton, 207–9
 cultural vulnerability in, 218–21
 prophecies of, 209–13
 working class in, 214–18
Orrego Salas, Juan, 178
Orwell, George, use of the term "Cold War", 213–14
othering, practice of, 124–26

Palestine Liberation Organization (PLO), 132
Partisans of Peace Movement, 168
peace, WIDF emphasis on, 54–57
Peace Movement, 168
peace museums, 25–26
phallic women, 133
 see also female terrorists
PKI, 33–35
politics
 transition in, 148–49
 and WIDF, 57–59
Popova, Nina, 55, 59
Popular Front, 106–7

Popular Movement for the Liberation of Angola, 192–93
power, conceptualization of, 124–26
Pritt, Marie, 40
Project Camelot, in Chile, 1–2
proletarian culture, Trotsky on, 83–84
propaganda
 and elimination of the "enemy", 81–85
 in Latin America, 179
 singing as, 82–83
 and vulnerable groups, 56

Rákosi, Mátyás, 79–80, 88–91
Ransome-Kuti, Funmilayo, 61–62
Reagan, Ronald
 anti-communist stance of, 99–101
 and civil liberties, 112–17
 HUAC testimony, 99
 involvement with HICCASP, 112
 involvement with SAG, 113
 shift to the right, 117
 union background of, 105–6
Robinson, Kim Stanley, 220
Round Table Agreement (1949), 34–35

SAG (Screen Actors Guild), Reagan's involvement with, 113
Sanders, Betty, 176
A Scanner Darkly (Philip K. Dick), 219
Schell, Orville, 159
Screen Actors Guild (SAG), Reagan's involvement with, 113
Selden, Mark, 150–51
self-affirmation, practice of, 124–26
singing as propaganda, 82–83
Sleeper, Jim, 210
Smith, Samantha, letter to Andropov, 3
Smith Act, AFL support of, 110
socialism
 in Japan, 24
 and women, 87
soft terrorism, 132
Sorrell, Herbert, 111–14
Spain, fascism in, 58–59
Stalin, Joseph
 personality cult of, 90
 poster depicting, *173*
Stalinism
 in Hungary, 76–85
 and women, 87–88
Suharti, 38–39
Sumampouw-Lapian, 35–36

Switzerland, contextualizing the Cold War in, 126–29
symbolism, father-party-family, 89–90

Teixeira, Victor Manuel "Viteix", 195–201
Tenney, Jack
  and communist unions, 107–12
  as head of Fact-Finding Committee on Un-American Activities, 99
terrorism, soft, 132
terrorists
  female, 129–34
  and individual citizens, 134–36
  surveillance of, 136–38
Test Bravo, 18–20, 41–42
Theory and Practice of Angolan Plastic Art (Viteix 1983), 195–201
Tophoven, Rolf, 132–33
Trotsky, Leon, on proletarian culture, 83–84
tuna mound
  after Fukushima nuclear disaster, 27–28
  meaning of, 17–18

Umi Sardjono, 43–45
UNAP (National Union of Angolan Plastic Artists), 191–92
unions, in Hollywood, 104–7
Uruguay, attempt to establish a Peace Movement in, 174–75
US Atomic Bomb Casualty Commission (ABCC), 23–24
US Office of Military Government (OMGUS), 56

Vietnam, peace efforts of women in, 63–65, *64*
Viteix (Victor Manuel Teixeira), 195–201, *202*, 202–4
Vögeli, Robert, 131–32

We Accuse report, 57
Western New Guinea, incorporation into the Netherlands, 39

Wieringa, Saskia, 31–32
Wolfson, Alice J., 63–64
Woll, Matthew, 113–14
women
  access to global political networks, 62–65
  in China, 161–62
  and communist happiness, 80
  peace efforts in Vietnam, 63–65, *64*
  perceived as communists, 54–55
  phallic women, 133
  rights of, 65–66
  and socialist work, 87
  and Stalinism, 87–88
Women in the Land of Socialism (Popova 1949), 59
Women United for United Nations (WUUN), 57
Women's International Democratic Federation (WIDF)
  affiliation with Gerwani, 32–38
  bureau meeting in Jakarta, 31
  establishment of, 32–33
  foundational meeting (Paris 1945), 52–53
  HUAC monitoring of, 54–55
  and political campaigns, 57–59
  World Congress of Women (Copenhagen 1953), 35–38
  World Congress of Women (Vienna 1958), 39–40
  World Gathering of Women for Disarmament (Vienna 1962), 42
workers' movement *see* labor movement
working class, in Orange County, 214–18
World Congress of Intellectuals for Peace (Wroclaw 1948), 55
World Gathering of Women for Disarmament (Vienna 1962), 42
world peace *see* peace

Zhdanovism, 83